FROMMER'S

COMPREHENSIVE
TRAVEL GUIDE

Los Angeles '95

by Dan Levine

MACMILLAN • USA

ABOUT THE AUTHOR

Dan Levine, who has a degree in history from New York University, is an incessant traveler and a demanding gourmand. In addition to *Los Angeles '95,* he has written Frommer guides to California, Florida, San Francisco, Miami, and Prague. He is also the author of *London on $45 a Day,* a contributor to *Europe on $50 a Day,* and co-author of two Frommer's Walking Tour guides: *London* and *England's Favorite Cities.* When not on the road, Dan lives and writes in Santa Barbara.

MACMILLAN TRAVEL

A Prentice Hall Macmillan Company
15 Columbus Circle
New York, NY 10023

Copyright 1977, 1979, 1981, 1983, 1987, 1989, 1991, 1993, 1995 by Simon & Schuster, Inc.

ISBN 0-02-860048-7
ISSN 0899-3238

Design by Michele Laseau
Maps by Geografix Inc. and Ortelius Design

Special Sales

Bulk purchases (10+ copies) of Frommer's Travel Guides are available to corporations at special discounts. The Special Sales Department can produce custom editions to be used as premiums and/or for sales promotion to suit individual needs. Existing editions can be produced with custom cover imprints such as corporate logos. For more information write to: Special Sales, Prentice Hall, 15 Columbus Circle, New York, NY 10023.

Manufactured in the United States of America

Contents

List of Maps

What the Symbols Mean

★ **FROMMER'S FAVORITES**—hotels, restaurants, attractions, and entertainments you should not miss

$ **SUPER-SPECIAL VALUES**—really exceptional values

In Hotel & Other Listings

The following symbols refer to the standard amenities available in all rooms:

A/C   air conditioning
MINIBAR   refrigerator stocked with beverages and snacks
TEL   telephone
TV   television

The following abbreviations are used for credit or charge cards:

AE   American Express
CB   Carte Blanche
DC   Diners Club
DISC   Discover
MC   MasterCard
V   Visa

Trip Planning with this Guide

Use the following features:

Calendar of Events   To plan for or avoid

Suggested Itineraries   For seeing the city

What's Special About Checklist   A summary of the city's highlights

Easy-to-Read Maps   Walking tours, sights, hotel and restaurant locations

Fast Facts   All the essentials at a glance: currency, embassies, emergencies, taxes, tipping, and more

Other Special Frommer Features

Frommer's Smart Traveler Tips   Hints on how to secure the best value for your money

Cool for Kids   Hotels, restaurants, and attractions

Did You Know . . . ?   Offbeat, fun facts

Impressions   What others have said

Invitation to the Readers

In researching this book I have come across many fine establishments, the best of which are included here. However, I'm sure that many of you will discover other wonderful hotels, restaurants, shops, and attractions. Please don't keep them to yourself. Share your experiences, especially if you want to comment on places I have covered in this edition that may have changed for the worse. You may address your letters to:

Dan Levine
Frommer's Los Angeles '95
Macmillan Travel
15 Columbus Circle
New York, NY 10023

A Disclaimer

Readers are advised that prices fluctuate in the course of time and travel information changes under the impact of the varied and volatile factors that affect the travel industry. Neither the author nor the publisher can be held responsible for the experiences of readers while traveling. Readers are invited to write to the publisher with ideas, comments, and suggestions for future editions.

Safety Advisory

Whenever you're traveling in an unfamiliar city or country, stay alert. Be aware of your immediate surroundings. Wear a moneybelt and keep a close eye on your possessions. Be particularly careful with cameras, purses, and wallets—all favorite targets of thieves and pickpockets.

1

Introducing Los Angeles

Bustling Los Angeles is not merely a microcosm of the United States: It's a magnification of America and all that's good and bad about this country. Los Angeles is the epitome of American fulfillment, revealing both the country's murky shadows and its celebrated strengths. Nowhere in the world are dreams more likely to be realized than in Los Angeles, a city whose citizens embrace the new and different to an almost disturbing extreme.

Los Angeles has always been a fantasyland of dreams and ambition, a sunny pleasure ground of movie and TV studios and Disneyland extravaganzas, a place where inhibitions are released and imagination given full rein—an entranceway to the real-life magic of southern California. The city is, and always has been, a haven for the offbeat and eccentric who somehow coexist alongside what has been called "the most seriously dedicated conservative constituency in America."

Whether or not you agree with the direction they're headed, Angelenos (as the inhabitants are called) continue to be trend-setters, leading the nation toward a lifestyle that includes shopping malls, sprawling suburbs, jogging, holistic medicine, and roller skating. Angelenos are also one of the most fashion-conscious people (albeit, sometimes tasteless and pretentious) in the world, trailing only New Yorkers, Parisians, and the Milanese.

Much of the unofficial capital of southern California sprawls across endless miles of uneventful flat terrain, marked by monotonous housing developments and unending strip malls. Yet the city is also packed with arresting sights and tremendous variety. In both quality and quantity, L.A. has some of the best restaurants in the world, yet for many status-conscious Angelenos, food often takes a back seat to seeing and being seen. Since Los Angeles is the home of the world's most important film industry, it may be difficult for people to distinguish art from reality on the streets of Santa Monica or Hollywood. And yet this smoggy suburbia, crisscrossed by an astonishing number of freeways, is somehow intensely magnetic. A colossal Technicolor ode to pop culture, Los Angeles is a scene like no other. The variety of lifestyles, activities, and places to see can be mind-boggling. Forget your preconceptions and discover L.A. for what it is—a glitzy, grimy, glittery, and gritty study in contemporary Americana. Whether you love it or hate it, your life cannot be called complete if you've never had at least one good look at L.A.

1 Geography & History

Geography

Los Angeles occupies a relatively flat basin surrounded on the west by the Pacific Ocean and on all other sides by a phalanx of rugged mountain ranges that leap from sea level to more than 11,000 feet. While the mountains provide city dwellers with protection from the

What's Special About Los Angeles

Film and TV Studios
- Universal Studios Hollywood—more an amusement park than a backstage tour, but fun!
- Warner Brothers Studios, an intimate look into the world of television production.
- Game-show tapings—fun to watch and even more fun to participate in as a contestant.

Museums
- The J. Paul Getty Museum, reputedly the most heavily endowed museum in the world.
- The Rancho La Brea Tar Pits, a prehistoric find in the center of one of the world's most contemporary cities.

Hollywood Sights
- The Walk of Fame, where you can see your favorite stars honored on the world's most famous sidewalk.
- Mann's Chinese Theatre, fantastic for its unusual architecture but best known for the stars' hand- and footprints (and occasionally noses) pressed in concrete in the theater's forecourt.
- The "HOLLYWOOD" sign, internationally recognized symbol of the city of film.

Shopping
- Rodeo Drive, the poshest street in Beverly Hills, containing the city's most chic shops.
- Santa Monica's Third Street Promenade, fun shopping by the sea.
- Melrose Avenue, the place to go for cutting-edge youth-oriented street fashions.
- Malls, where Angelenos really shop.

Beaches
- Zuma Beach, Malibu's famous seafront stretch, one of the largest and most popular in Los Angeles.
- Santa Monica, easy to reach and jam-packed on hot summer weekends.
- Southern beaches, great for swimming and sunning.

Theme Parks
- Disneyland, the most famous of them all, the state's largest single tourist attraction.
- Knott's Berry Farm, close to Disneyland, really a farm that almost accidentally became a theme park.

sweltering heat of the Mojave Desert that lies just east, the peaks also lock in automobile fumes—smog that becomes more concentrated as it's pushed closer to the mountains.

The valleys encompassing Los Angeles are separated from the basin by the Santa Monica Mountains, the only major U.S. range that bisects a large city.

History

Dateline

- **1542** João Cabrilho enters San Diego Bay and sails up the California coast in the first documented visit by a European.
- **1579** Sir Francis Drake drops anchor in the area of San Francisco Bay and claims the land for Britain's Elizabeth I.
- **1602** Spanish explorer and merchant Sebastián Vizcaíno sails up the coast and names many areas.
- **1769–76** Spanish missions are founded along the so-called Royal Road (Camino Real) from San Diego to Sonoma.
- **1775** Juan Manuel de Ayala maps San Francisco Bay.
- **1776** The San Francisco presidio (fort) is founded.
- **1777** Monterey is made the capital of Spain's California territory.
- **1781** Los Angeles is founded.
- **1804** Spain divides its California territory into Baja (Lower) California and Alta (Upper) California; José Joaquin de Arrillaga
➤

EUROPEAN DISCOVERY & COLONIZATION Although very little remains to mark the existence of West Coast Native Americans, anthropologists estimate that as many as half a million aboriginals flourished on this naturally abundant land for thousands of years before the arrival of Europeans in the mid-16th century. Sailing from a small colony, established 10 years before, on the southern tip of the Baja (Lower) California, Portuguese explorer João Rodrigues Cabrilho (in the service of Spain) is credited with being the first European to "discover" California, in 1542. Over the next 200 years, dozens of sailors mapped the coast, including British explorer Sir Francis Drake, who in 1579 sailed his Golden Hind into what is now called Drake's Bay, north of San Francisco, and Spanish explorer Sebastián Vizcaíno, who in 1602 bestowed most of the place names that survive today.

THE FOUNDATION OF LOS ANGELES European colonial competition and Catholic missionary zeal prompted Spain to establish settlements along the Alta (Upper) California coast and claim the lands as its own. In 1769, Fr. Junípero Serra, accompanied by 300 soldiers and clergy, began forging a path from Mexico to Monterey. A small mission and presidio (fort) were established early that year at San Diego, and a few months later, in August 1769, Los Angeles came into being.

Los Angeles was "discovered" by Gaspar de Portolá and Father Crespi. What their expedition really found was a small Native American village, which they named "Pueblo del Río de Nuestra Señora la Reina de los Angeles."

By 1804, the Spanish missionaries had erected a chain of 21 missions, each a day's walk from the next along a dirt road called the Camino Real (Royal Road), stretching all the way from San Diego to Sonoma.

During that time, thousands of Native Americans were converted to Christianity and coerced into labor. Many others died from diseases brought over by the Europeans. Because not all the natives welcomed their conquerors with open arms, many missions and pueblos (small towns) suffered from repeated attacks, leading to the construction of California's now-ubiquitous fireproof red-tile roofs.

No settlement contained more than 100 inhabitants when Spain's sovereignty was compromised by an 1812 Russian outpost called Fort Ross, 60 miles north of San Francisco. But the biggest threat came from the British—who had strengthened their own claims to America with the Hudson's Bay Company trading firm—and their short-lived, last-ditch effort to win back their territories in the War of 1812.

Embattled at home as well as abroad, the Spanish finally relinquished their claim to Mexico and to Spain's California possessions in 1821. Under Mexican rule, Alta California's Spanish missionaries fell out of favor and lost much of their land to the increasingly wealthy Californios—Mexican immigrants who'd been granted vast tracts of land.

AMERICAN EXPANSION Beginning in the late 1820s, Americans from the East began to make their way to California via a three-month sail around Cape Horn. Most of them settled in the territorial capital of Monterey and in northern California.

From the 1830s on, motivated in part by the doctrine of Manifest Destiny—an almost religious belief that the United States was destined to cover the continent from coast to coast—more and more settlers headed west. Among them were daring explorers. In 1843, missionary Marcus Whitman, seeking to prove that

Dateline

becomes the first governor of Alta California.

- **1808** Connecticut sea captain William Shaler publishes his *Journal*, containing the first extensive account of California.

- **1809** Russians settle Bodega Bay.

- **1814** John Gilroy becomes California's first non-Hispanic settler.

- **1821** Spain grants independence to Mexico and, thus, California.

- **1836** Governor Juan Batista Alvarado declares California a "free and sovereign state."

- **1842** Gold is discovered in California near the San Fernando Mission, six years before the discovery at Sutter's Mill.

- **1844** The first wagon train crosses into California; U.S. Army officer John Charles Frémont discovers Lake Tahoe.

- **1846** The so-called Bear Flag Republic is proclaimed: California is drawn into the Mexican-American War; the U.S. flag is raised in Yerba Buena (San Francisco) and Los Angeles.

- **1848** James Wilson Marshall discovers gold at Coloma, on

➤

Dateline

the south fork of the American River.

- **1849** The Gold Rush is in full swing; a constitutional convention meets in Monterey; San Jose becomes the state capital.

- **1850** California, with a population of nearly 93,000, becomes the 31st state.

- **1854** Sacramento becomes the permanent state capital.

- **1871** The first ice-cream parlor opens in Los Angeles.

- **1875** The Santa Fe Railroad reaches Los Angeles.

- **1879** The University of Southern California is founded.

- **1881** The *Los Angeles Times* begins publication.

- **1892** Oil is discovered in downtown Los Angeles where 2nd Street and Glendale Boulevard presently are.

- **1893** The Bradbury Building, at 3rd Street and Broadway, is built; today it's the city's oldest commercial building.

- **1894** The *Los Angeles Times* begins a carrier-pigeon service to and from Catalina Island; the birds carry information from

➤

settlers could travel overland through the Oregon Territory's Blue Mountains, helped blaze the Oregon Trail; the first covered-wagon train made the four-month transcontinental trip in 1844. Over the next few years, several hundred Americans traveled to California over the Sierra Nevada range via Truckee Pass, just north of Lake Tahoe.

As increasing numbers of people moved to the West, the U.S. government sought to extend its control over Mexican territory north of the Rio Grande, the river that now separates the United States from Mexico. In 1846, President James Polk offered Mexico $40 million for the land that now encompasses California and New Mexico. The offer might have been accepted, but America's simultaneous annexation of Texas, to which Mexico still laid claim, resulted in a war between the two countries. Within months, the United States overcame Mexico and took possession of the entire West Coast.

In January 1847, Los Angeles was claimed for the United States by Commodore Stockton and Gen. Stephen Kearny.

GOLD & STATEHOOD In 1842, a Mexican rancher named Francisco López discovered gold in a canyon near what is now Newhall. The news spread, and several hundred men excavated the canyon, only to find that the load was shallow; the gold was gone in a few months. However, this was only a hint of things to come. In 1848, California's non–Native American population numbered about 7,000. That same year, flakes of gold were discovered by workers who were building a sawmill along the American River. Word of the discovery spread quickly. By 1850 the state's population had approached 93,000, although very few settlers found significant gold. Within 15 years interest in gold had waned, but the new residents intended to stay.

In 1850, California was admitted to the Union as the 31st state. The state constitution on which California applied for admission included several noteworthy provisions. In order to protect the miners, slavery was prohibited. To attract women from the East Coast, legal recognition was given to a married woman's own property. (California was the first state to offer such recognition.) By 1870, almost 90% of the state's Native American population had been wiped out, and most of the rest were removed to undesirable inland reservations.

Mexican and Chinese laborers were brought in to help local farmers as well as to work on the transcontinental railroad, completed in 1869. The new rail line, which could transport Easterners to California in just five days, marked a turning point in the settlement of the West. In 1875, when the Santa Fe Railroad reached Los Angeles, southern California's population of just 10,000 was divided equally between Los Angeles and San Diego.

In 1885, the Southern Pacific and the Santa Fe rail companies—fierce competitors—reduced their fares to only $1 from cities on the Mississippi River to Los Angeles. Another "rush" was on. Of course, not everybody came by rail. It is said that Charles F. Lummis (1859–1928), later to become a well-known writer, editor, and historian of the Southwest, walked from Cincinnati! Obviously, he was a man who took his own advice: He originated the slogan "See America First."

GROWTH & THE FILM INDUSTRY   Los Angeles really began to grow in the second decade of the 20th century, when the film industry moved there from the East Coast to take advantage of cheap land and a warm climate that allowed movies to be shot outdoors year-round. By 1912, 16 motion picture companies were operating out of Hollywood. *Birth of a Nation* (1915) established Hollywood in the eyes of the world and earned for its director, D. W. Griffith, the moniker "father of American cinema."

By World War I the Hollywood studio system was firmly entrenched, led by the

Dateline

the summer vacation colony to the mainland.
- **1896** Welsh newspaperman Griffith J. Griffith donates to the city 4,400 acres, now known as Griffith Park, the nation's largest urban park.
- **1900** The population of California approaches 1.5 million; San Francisco has more than 342,000 residents, Los Angeles more than 102,000.
- **1902** The first movie house, the Electric Theatre, opens on Main Street.
- **1904** The first Buddhist temple in the United States opens in Los Angeles.
- **1906** San Francisco is largely destroyed by an earthquake and a resulting fire.
- **1910** The Beverly Hills Hotel is built, luring movie industry people to Beverly Hills from Hollywood.
- **1911** Hollywood's first film studio is established.
- **1912** More than 16 motion-picture companies are operating out of Hollywood; the first U.S. gas station opens at the corner of Grand Avenue and Washington Street.

➤

young trio of Charles Chaplin, Douglas Fairbanks, Sr., and Mary Pickford. William S. Hart rode into the hearts of Saturday-afternoon moviegoers as the first prototype of the American Western hero while Theodosia Goodman, daughter of an Ohio haberdasher, vamped across the screen as Theda Bara.

In the 1920s, salaries and box office receipts multiplied fantastically. An opulent spending spree was launched as each star or producer tried to outdo the other. Newly rich stars created a mystique of luxury and glamour. Rudolph Valentino electrified women around the world in *The Sheik* (1921). Mae Murray, the eternal *Merry Widow* with "bee-stung" lips, was "self-enchanted." Clara Bow, with her red chow dogs to match her flaming hair, was the "It" girl. And Cecil B. DeMille saw to it that Gloria Swanson took a lot of on-screen baths!

On August 6, 1926, the Manhattan Opera House in New York City screened Vitaphone's *Don Juan,* with John Barrymore. Although the great actor didn't speak, there was background music. Warner Brothers released *The Jazz Singer,* with Al Jolson, in October of the following year and the Talkie Revolution was on. Garbo could speak, albeit with a Swedish accent, though her romantic leading man, John Gilbert, couldn't—at least not very well. The invasion of voice-trained Broadway stage stars began, including the likes of Tallulah Bankhead, who made a number of films but later said, "I'd rather forget about them."

Perhaps no invader was as formidable as Mae West, who wondered if she could "show [her] stuff" in a "land of palm trees, restaurants shaped like derby hats, goose-fleshed bathing beauties, and far-flung custard pies." She could and did! Her invitation to "Come up 'n' see me" was accepted around the world, and she became a phenomenal success at the box office. Or, to use her own modest summation: "More people had seen me than saw

➤

Napoleon, Lincoln, and Cleopatra. I was better known than Einstein, Shaw, or Picasso."

The 1930s marked the rise of some of Hollywood's greatest stars: Bette Davis, Joan Crawford, Humphrey Bogart, Cary Grant, Jean Harlow, Clark Gable, James Cagney, Marlene Dietrich, Gary Cooper, Shirley Temple, James Stewart, Katharine Hepburn, Spencer Tracy, and Claudette Colbert. The decade was climaxed by the release of an astounding number of screen classics: *Gone with the Wind, The Wizard of Oz, Wuthering Heights, Dark Victory, Mr. Smith Goes to Washington, Ninotchka, Stagecoach,* and *The Hunchback of Notre Dame*—to name just a few.

The movies' glamorous, idyllic portrayal of California boosted the region's popularity and population, especially during the Great Depression of the 1930s, when thousands of families packed up their belongings and headed west in search of a better life. In 1939, John Steinbeck summed up the migrant experience with *The Grapes of Wrath.*

In 1940, Dudley C. Gordon wrote: "Having survived a long, leisurely pioneering infancy, and an uncouth adolescence characterized by intensive exploitation, Los Angeles has now blossomed into one of the major cities of the nation." It was at the dawn of great change.

World War II brought heavy industry to southern California, in the form of munitions factories, shipyards, and airplane manufacturing. Freeways were built, military bases opened, and suburbs developed.

After the war, the threat of television loomed over Hollywood, but instead of being destroyed by the "tube," Los Angeles was strengthened by it, as the television industry headquartered itself in the region.

In the 1950s, California became popular with artists and intellectuals. The so-called beat generation appeared and inspired later alternative-culture groups, notably the "flower children" of the 1960s. During the 1967 "Summer of Love," as the war in Vietnam escalated student protests

Dateline

development (the five-foot-high sign originally read "HOLLYWOODLAND").

■ **1924** The first transcontinental airmail flight takes place from San Francisco to New York.

■ **1925** An earthquake hits Santa Barbara.

■ **1927** The first "talkie" is released, *The Jazz Singer* with Al Jolson; Graumann's (now Mann's) Chinese Theatre opens; the Academy of Motion Picture Arts and Sciences is founded at the Biltmore Hotel; the first sketch of the Oscar is scrawled on a linen napkin in the Crystal Ballroom.

■ **1928** Los Angeles's first airport, Mines Field, opens with only a dirt strip as a runway on the current site of LAX.

■ **1929** The Academy of Motion Pictures Arts and Sciences bestows its first Oscar.

■ **1930s** Hollywood's heyday. Great stars like Bette Davis, Joan Crawford, Humphrey Bogart, Cary Grant, Jean Harlow, Clark Gable, James Cagney, and Shirley Temple become household names.

■ **1939** John Steinbeck writes *The Grapes of Wrath* about

➤

Dateline

migrants to California; Union Station for passenger trains is built in downtown Los Angeles—now a historic landmark, the building is one of the finest examples of California mission-style architecture.

- **1942** California's Japanese-American residents are forcibly relocated to inland camps because of World War II security concerns.
- **1945** The world's largest toy manufacturer, Mattel, maker of Barbie, is founded in Hawthorne.
- **1947** The first TV station west of the Mississippi, KTLA, begins broadcasting; the Rams, a professional football team, comes to Los Angeles from Cleveland, Ohio.
- **1950** California's population swells to more than 10.5 million; San Francisco has more than 674,000 residents but is surpassed by Los Angeles, with nearly 2 million.
- **1955** Disneyland opens.
- **1956** Capitol Records Building, the nation's first circular office tower, opens for business.

➤

increased at Berkeley and elsewhere in California, as they did across the country. A year later, amid rising racial tensions, Martin Luther King, Jr., was killed, setting off riots in the Watts section of Los Angeles and in other cities; and Robert F. Kennedy was fatally shot in Los Angeles after winning the California Democratic Party presidential primary.

Indeed, as Los Angeles entered the 1970s, it appeared to some that the dream factory had become a near nightmare. One large studio reported a loss of $67 million; another announced that its 52-acre main lot was for sale. In the following months, MGM, which once boasted that it had "more stars than there are in heaven," auctioned off Clark Gable's trench coat. The days of film glory seemed to be over, but few doubted that a more stable cinema would emerge and remain as one of Los Angeles's chief attractions and employers.

Perhaps in response to an increasingly violent society, the 1970s also gave rise to several exotic religions and cults that found eager adherents in California. The spiritual "New Age" continued into the 1980s, along with a growing population, environmental pollution, and escalating social ills. California also became very rich. Real estate values soared; the computer industry, centered in "Silicon Valley," south of San Francisco, boomed; and banks and businesses prospered.

From 1991 through mid-1994, the city of Los Angeles has been featured frequently in the world media. On March 3, 1991, African-American motorist Rodney King led a group of L.A. police officers on an eight-mile car chase, refusing to pull over. Four white officers were videotaped beating King in the street after his arrest. The videotape was shown to TV audiences the world over, and soon after Laurence Powell, Stacey Koon, and two other officers were tried in state court. Their shocking April 29, 1992, acquittal sparked three days of rioting and looting in the Los Angeles area. Later, Powell and Koon were tried in federal court for violating King's civil rights and were found guilty; each was sentenced to 30 months in federal prison. Koon is currently writing a book about the incident while he serves his time: *Presumed Guilty: The Tragedy of the Rodney King Affair.*

During the rioting, a news station's reporter in a helicopter videotaped a truckdriver named Reginald Denny being pulled from the cab of his truck and beaten by several young men; he was even struck in the skull with a brick. Two of his assailants were later identified as Damian Williams and Henry Watson. Three of the rioters, including Williams and Watson, were eventually charged with attempted murder and went to trial: a fourth pled guilty and was sentenced without trial. Eighteen months after the riots, in October 1993, two of the rioters were found guilty of lesser charges and released. Damian Williams was convicted of simple mayhem and is now serving a maximum prison sentence of 10 years.

Three years after his beating by the police officers, Rodney King was awarded $3.8 million in compensatory damages.

Los Angeles received even more publicity during the first trial of Lyle and Erik Menendez for the 1989 shotgun slayings of their wealthy Beverly Hills parents, Jose and Kitty. The brothers, who at first pled innocent, eventually admitted to the killings but claimed they acted out of fear after years of physical, emotional, and sexual abuse. The trial—which garnered worldwide media attention—required two juries, lasted more than six months, and cost Los Angeles County over a million dollars. Unfortunately for the county's taxpayers, neither jury was able to reach a verdict. The Menendez brothers' second trial is scheduled for 1995. Not surprisingly since this is "Hollywoodland," the Menendez case has already been detailed in two TV movies, and a feature film version is currently being cast.

Dateline

- **1960** John F. Kennedy is named the Democratic presidential candidate at the Democratic National Convention in Los Angeles.
- **1961** Hollywood's Walk of Fame, which honors great achievements, is started by the Hollywood Chamber of Commerce.
- **1962** California overtakes New York as the nation's most populous state; Dodger Stadium opens on land purchased by owner Walter O'Malley.
- **1967** The "Summer of Love" is centered in San Francisco's Haight-Ashbury; the *Queen Mary* docks at Long Beach, its final home.
- **1968** Robert F. Kennedy is fatally shot in Los Angeles after winning California's Democratic Party presidential primary.
- **1975** Jerry Brown becomes governor.
- **1980** Since 1950, the population of California more than doubles, to nearly 24 million; San Francisco now has some 775,000 inhabitants, while Los Angeles has nearly 3 million.

➤

Dateline

- 1984 Los Angeles hosts the Summer Olympic Games.
- 1990 Designed by I. M. Pei, First Interstate Tower, the tallest building west of Chicago, opens; MetroRail's Blue Line opens with service between Long Beach and downtown Los Angeles.
- 1991 The presidential library of Richard Nixon opens in Yorba Linda, his birthplace (1913).
- 1992 Los Angeles experiences the worst race riots in modern American history: more than 40 dead, hundreds injured.
- 1993 Firearms sales reach their highest point ever; firestorms sweep through the Los Angeles area.
- 1994 An earthquake measuring 6.8 on the Richter scale shakes the city; former president Richard Nixon dies and is buried beside his wife at the Nixon Library and Birthplace; Los Angeles hosts the World Cup soccer finals and closing ceremonies.

During the final deliberations of Lyle Menendez's jury, on January 17, 1994, a 6.8-magnitude earthquake hit Los Angeles County; countless aftershocks followed. The results were death, fires, and freeway collapses. Many residents of the city of Northridge and the surrounding areas were left homeless. At the time of this writing, all L.A. area freeways have been repaired.

L.A.'s freeways were the focus of a bizarre game of follow-the-leader in June 1994 when football great O. J. Simpson—wanted for questioning in the murders of his ex-wife, Nicole Brown Simpson, and her friend Ronald Goldman—led a convoy of police cars on a long, televised chase that ended at his home, where he was arrested. Soon after, a pretrial hearing was held—which garnered even more attention than the Menendez trial, for it was televised on almost every major network—and the judge ruled that there was enough cause for Simpson to be tried. At the time of this writing, the trial had reached the jury-selection phase. And, at least one TV movie about the case is awaiting broadcast.

In the mid-1990s, southern Californians still like to think of themselves as being on the cutting edge of American society. Whatever happens in the country, they say proudly, takes place here first. But Angelenos, delving beneath their characteristic superficiality, have realized that being on the cutting edge isn't all it's cracked up to be as the nation's economic, social, and environmental problems have become their own. The fires, the rioting, the mud slides, and the earthquake and its aftershock that barraged Los Angeles in the early to mid-1990s emphasized the city's fragility and forced its citizens to take notice of their new urban reality. Out of the ashes a new consciousness is rising. Citizens of L.A.'s famous collection of neighboring suburbs are realizing that these neighborhoods are not separate entities at all—they are one large racially and economically mixed neighborhood whose inhabitants, despite their differences, are all striving toward the same good-life dream.

2   Politics & People

POLITICS   After Democrat Jerry Brown, an avowed liberal, succeeded conservative Republican Gov. Ronald Reagan in the 1970s, California gained a reputation for progressive leadership. The state enacted some of the most stringent antipollution measures in the world, actively encouraged the development of renewable forms of energy, and protected the coastline from development and despoliation. At the same time, California emerged at the forefront of the gay-rights movement, and there was a general resurgence of interest among Californians in alternative lifestyles and the exploration of foreign cultures.

Southern California's reputation as a liberal mecca, however, is largely mistaken, for the state as a whole has traditionally leaned to the right; Governor Brown's tenure almost seems an aberration. In 1990, Republican Pete Wilson was elected governor, succeeding Republican George Deukmejian, whose conservative fiscal and social policies, consonant with the swing to the right that occurred nationally during the 1980s, he promised to continue.

Wealthy Orange County and, to a lesser extent, Los Angeles (surprisingly) have always been more conservative than the rest of the state. Residents of Orange County, who have consistently voted for right-wing candidates since they firmly supported Barry Goldwater in 1964, are mocked by other Californians as living in splendid isolation behind the "Orange Curtain." San Diego, with a large military presence, is also predominantly Republican, supporting those administrations in Washington that promise to serve its economic interests. California has a chance to once again swing to the left since Jerry Brown's popular sister, Kathleen, has gained the 1994 Democratic nomination for governor. Only the November 1994 election—held after press time—will tell how long the state's conservative tendencies will endure.

PEOPLE   When most first-time visitors think of L.A., they think of Beverly Hills and Bel Air and are awed not by the beauty of these residential areas but primarily by the apparent endless wealth of their residents. What most visitors don't imagine is the cultural, social, and economic mix of Angelenos.

In general, hilltops and oceanfronts are the city's highest-priced parcels, often topped with spectacular homes. But for every rich landlord there are countless struggling tenants whose work-a-day lifestyles are Los Angeles's real bread and butter. The city's strong, conservative old-money crowd vies for power with the newer, more Jewish,

IMPRESSIONS

If [Los Angeles] is hell, why is it so popular?
—Bryce Nelson, *New York Times*

It's a nice place to live . . . if you're an orange.
—Fred Allen, Actor/comedian

more liberal West Siders. And while these two sides struggle, even newer immigrants are quickly tipping the political and cultural balance toward themselves. Some 15% of the city's 3.4 million residents are either Asian or African-American, and over one-third are of Mexican origin, making Los Angeles County the world's third-largest Hispanic city, after Mexico City and Guadalajara. The recent mass migration of Latinos has profoundly transformed the city's cultural and physical landscape. There are Mexican neighborhoods, school classes are taught in Spanish, and specialized Mexican-oriented shops abound. The Spanish-language radio station, KLAX, which programs Mexican *ranchera* music, has topped the Arbitron ratings; and in supermarkets, you'll find salsa not in the ethnic food section but with condiments such as mustard and ketchup.

Economically and culturally speaking, Los Angeles life revolves around the making and promoting of films and television shows. Industry executives, stars on both sides of the camera, and wannabes are literally everywhere, with additional wannabes pouring in daily. Entertainment-related talk is standard restaurant and party fare. Reminders that you are in the land of "players" abound in all the media, most notably on those ego-stroking billboards that tout the latest stars.

3   Famous Los Angelenos

Charles Bukowski (b. 1920)   Although more Angelenos know him for his beachside bar tabs than for his writing, Bukowski is one of the city's most important writers and has penned more than 45 books of poetry and prose. His novel *Barfly* (1983) was made into a 1987 film starring Mickey Rourke and Faye Dunaway.

Betty Friedan (b. 1921)   Author of the classic *The Feminine Mystique* (1963) and the more recent best-seller *Fountain of Age* (1993), Friedan is cofounder of the National Organization for Women. She spends half the year living in Santa Monica and teaching at USC; the other half she spends at New York University.

David Geffen (b. 1943)   The CEO of the David Geffen Company is one of Los Angeles's richest and most powerful men. Geffen, who is openly gay, always gets a good table at the latest restaurant.

David Hockney (b. 1937)   One of the world's best-known contemporary artists, English-born Hockney creates as a painter, photographer, and set designer, among other things.

Barbara Lazaroff (b. 1955)   The wife of Wolfgang Puck, Los Angeles's most famous chef, Lazaroff is an accomplished designer who has created the interiors for all of Puck's L.A. restaurants.

Arnold Schwarzenegger (b. 1947)   Known worldwide, Schwarzenegger maintains high visibility in hometown L.A., where he regularly makes appearances at his Santa Monica restaurant, Schatzi, on Main Street.

Steven Spielberg (b. 1947)   The most successful film director of all time is almost synonymous with today's Hollywood. Spielberg's credits include the *Star Wars* trilogy, *E.T. the Extra-Terrestrial,* the three Indiana Jones films, *Jurassic Park,* and the Oscar-winner *Schindler's List.*

Barbra Streisand (b. 1942)   After a decade without making a public appearance, Streisand has reemerged as one of the hottest tickets of the 1990s. In 1993, the actress/singer donated her lavish 24-acre Malibu estate to the Santa Monica Mountains Conservancy—the most important land gift in modern L.A. history.

Kurt Vonnegut (b. 1922)   The writer of bizarre novels like *Slaughterhouse Five* (1969) and *Cat's Cradle* (1963), Vonnegut lives on L.A.'s Westside.

4   Art & Architecture

ART   Prior to the 1920s, there were few artists of note in southern California. Then expatriates returned and European-trained artists moved here, creating a vibrant artistic community almost overnight. Lorser Feitelson moved west, bringing with him the knowledge of cubism and futurism. Stanton McDonald-Wright came here from Europe after gaining international fame as a cofounder of synchronism. The Hollywood film industry brought out Man Ray and Oskar Fischinger, and a unique southern Californian art sensibility was born. To this day, an emphasis on the abstract remains in the mainstream. Art in L.A. is youthful, exploratory, brash, and very conscious of the new money. There is an emphasis on new materials and on universal ideas. And although the majority of works still seem bright, colorful, and clean, recent examples are reflecting the city's darker new realities.

ARCHITECTURE   Los Angeles's buildings reflect several historical styles of architecture. The first, dating from the late 18th century, during the Mexican era, consists of Spanish-style adobe structures, often topped with red-tile roofs. Several structures, primarily missions, exemplify that style. The missions also tended to employ distinctive Native American construction methods.

The second major style, popularized about a century later, reflects a Victorian tendency in design and ornateness. Although this style is more obvious in San Francisco, Victorian homes and offices can be found along the entire California coast.

The city's most interesting and varied buildings are the art deco structures from the 1930s. Kitsch diners and buildings constructed to look like objects were popular in the 1950s, and there are still many examples around Los Angeles.

Concrete was the preferred building material in the late 1960s and the 1970s; as a consequence, a plethora of rather uniform ugly concrete structures mar almost every urban center. Glass-and-steel office buildings—a trend that took hold in the 1980s—dominate much of downtown Los Angeles, giving it a sleek, futuristic look.

5 Food & Drink

California cuisine is one of the most dynamic and important genres in regional American cooking. The style stresses local ingredients and light preparations that are both calorie- and health-conscious. "Designer" vegetables are often used, as are fresh local spices and locally produced wines.

A strong Mexican influence is apparent; avocados can be found everywhere, and salsa is served with almost every meal. Mexican restaurants are the most popular ethnic eateries; you'll never be very far from a taco or a burrito. Yet nearly every other ethnic cuisine is also represented here. Sushi is fresh and popular; Chinese food, especially in Los Angeles and San Francisco, is excellent; and superior French cuisine can be found in the state's major cities.

The growing emphasis on health food has inspired a debate about whether California's water is safe to drink. Opinions vary, according to various studies. The state's inhabitants consume more bottled water per capita than those of any other region in America, but many more locals drink water straight from the tap. Suffice it to say that if you do decide to order bottled water at a restaurant, there are usually plenty of brands, both domestic and foreign, to choose from.

Few will argue, however, with the assertion that California is wine country. You'll find that what supremely enhances a good California meal is a bottle of wine from a local growing region. Many state restaurants offer excellent selections, which usually include several good buys. Try some new wines from a vineyard you've never heard of and enjoy further exploration of a region you may have thought you knew well.

6 Recommended Books, Films & Recordings

BOOKS Almost from the beginning, novelists and poets were an essential part of the melange that settled in California. Although their personal stays were often in the nature of passing through, their works have left lasting records of the history of America's fastest-changing region. From Mark Twain, who created vivid tales of the Comstock Lode silver mines and 1860s frontier, to Joan Didion and Amy Tan, contemporary novelists who write about the California of their childhoods, there has been no lack of talent here. Writing in between we find Aldous Huxley, who lived in and wrote about California and Hollywood; and Jack Kerouac, who was one of the most influential of the "beat" writers.

Recommended nonfiction readings include *Adobe Days* by Sarah Bixy Smith (Valley, 1925; reprint, J. Zcitlin, 1931), an autobiography chronicling life during L.A.'s transition from a farm town to a modern metropolis. Otto Friedrich's *City of Nets* (Harper & Row, 1986) is a portrait of 1940s Hollywood, when media moguls first discovered their powers as international image creators. *Sex, Death, & God in L.A.,* edited by David Reid (Pantheon, 1992), is a compilation of works by novelists, journalists, and cultural critics pontificating on the myths, truths, and iconography of the city. Jack Smith's *Alive in La La Land* (Franklin Watts, 1989) is an essay on L.A. life through the eyes of a best-selling author.

Sunshine and Wealth by Bruce Henstell (Chronicle, 1984) glorifies L.A.'s heyday in the 1920s and 1930s with informative text and plenty of pictures. Michael Engh's *Frontier Faiths* (University of New Mexico Press, 1992) is a scholarly examination of the origins of organized religions and cults in Los Angeles and of the city's current unique religious mosaic. *Los Angeles at 25 MPH* by Steve Diskin and Joseph Giovanni (Van Nostrand Reinhold, 1993) argues that it's no longer hip to hate L.A., which has become a powerful symbolic expression of America's cultural disenfranchisement. *Chief: My Life in the LAPD* by Daryl Gates (HarperCollins, 1993) is the best-selling autobiography of the city's most controversial police chief.

Novels written about Los Angeles and Hollywood abound—from the literary to the trashy. A few examples include most of Jackie Collins's mega-best-sellers as well as those of her sister, Joan; most of Judith Krantz's novels; *Hollywood* by Gore Vidal (Ballantine Books, 1991); *An Inconvenient Woman* by Dominick Dunne (Crown, 1990); and *Postcards from the Edge* by Carrie Fisher (Pocket Books, 1989).

FILMS   Los Angeles's beautiful sights and year-round good weather have always made it a natural for directors searching for captivating yet relatively inexpensive film locations. Tens of thousands of movies and TV shows have been shot here—too many to mention them all. However, here are a few examples:

Neil Simon's *California Suite* (1978) is set in one suite at the Beverly Hills Hotel. L.A. City Hall serves as the *Daily Planet* newspaper office building in TV's "Lois & Clark: The New Adventures of Superman," and *Pretty Woman* (1990), starring Julia Roberts and Richard Gere, was partially filmed at the Beverly Wilshire Hotel. The Queen Anne–style cottage and adjoining "jungle" in the Los Angeles State and County Arboretum served as the backdrop for the opening scenes of the TV series "Fantasy Island." Beverly Hills's Rodeo Drive has been featured in several movies, including *Beverly Hills Cop* (1984), with Eddie Murphy, and LAX was last seen in *City Slickers* (1991). Downtown's art deco–style Union Station was transformed into a 21st-century police station for *Blade Runner* (1982). Santa Monica Pier Carousel was featured in *The Sting* (1973), starring Robert Redford and Paul Newman. TV's "M*A*S*H" was filmed in Malibu Creek State Park, as were *Planet of the Apes* (1972) and *Logan's Run* (1976). And the Westin Bonaventure's glass elevators and renovated ballroom set the stage for the climactic conclusion to *In the Line of Fire* (1993), starring Clint Eastwood and John Malkovitch.

Also, countless films have been made about Los Angeles and Hollywood. Some of the most recent include *Down and Out in Beverly Hills* (1986), with Bette Midler, Richard Dreyfuss, and Nick Nolte; *Father of the Bride* (1991), starring Steve Martin and Diane Keaton;

L.A. Story (1991), with Steve Martin and Victoria Tennant; *The Player* (1992), starring Tim Robbins, Greta Scacchi, and Whoopi Goldberg; *Poetic Justice* (1993), with Janet Jackson; *Speed* (1994), starring Keanu Reeves and Dennis Hopper; and *Pulp Fiction* (1994), with John Travolta, Samuel L. Jackson, and Uma Thurman.

Los Angeles has also been the setting for TV series, both past and present. Examples range from "Dragnet" to "L.A. Law," "Fresh Prince of Bel-Air," "Beverly Hills, 90210," "Melrose Place," "Models Inc.," and "South Central." And who could ever forget Lucy and Ricky Ricardo's hilarious trip to Hollywood with the Mertzes on "I Love Lucy"?

RECORDINGS   California has made a major contribution to the American musical scene, from the classical to the popular. Composer Arnold Schoenberg, violinist Jascha Heifetz, and conductor Zubin Mehta are just a few who attracted world attention to Los Angeles and gave the city a fittingly prominent place in classical music. Popular composers from George Gershwin and Jerome Kern to Henry Mancini have enriched America's musical heritage with the songs and scores they wrote for movies, a medium that helped spread American culture abroad and made it as likely that you'd hear those songs hummed in Paris and Buenos Aires as in New York and St. Louis.

In the past three decades, the influence of rock music has thrust California into the forefront of a different musical tradition that has outlasted its critics and been felt as far away as Moscow and Beijing. That tradition derives from the various groups that emerged in the mid-1960s and changed American music. Of those groups, the Grateful Dead, formed in 1965, is the only surviving psychedelic band. Santana, a local band known for its innovative blending of Latin rhythms and low-key jazz vocals, debuted in California. Soon after, Santana landed a deal with Los Angeles–based Columbia Records.

In the 1960s and 1970s, the Beach Boys and the Eagles perfected the "California sound," a blend of sweet harmonies and fun, if somewhat sentimental, lyrics. Of course, the Doors was one of the most famous bands to come out of Los Angeles. More recent L.A. rockers include Van Halen, Motley Crüe, Warrent, Guns 'n' Roses, and the Red Hot Chili Peppers.

2

Planning a Trip to Los Angeles

Hᴏᴡ ʏᴏᴜ ɢᴇᴛ ᴛᴏ Lᴏs Aɴɢᴇʟᴇs ᴀɴᴅ ʜᴏᴡ ʏᴏᴜ ɢᴇᴛ ᴀʀᴏᴜɴᴅ ɪᴛ ᴏʙᴠɪᴏᴜsʟʏ depend on where you're coming from, how much you want to spend, and how much time you have. It's possible to arrive in L.A. without an itinerary or reservations, but your trip will be much more rewarding if you do a bit of advance planning. This chapter will help you discover your options and plan the trip that's best suited to your needs and interests.

1 Information & Money

INFORMATION   Tourism is big in Los Angeles, and the city is rich with information on what to see and do. To receive a free packet of general information on the city, contact the **Los Angeles Convention and Visitors Bureau,** 633 W. 5th St., Suite 600, Los Angeles, CA 90071 (☎ **213/624-7300**).

You should know that almost every city and town in California has a dedicated tourist bureau or chamber of commerce that will be happy to send you information on its particular site. See "Tourist Information" under "Orientation" in Chapter 4 for a list of local tourist boards.

Foreign travelers should also check Chapter 3 for entry requirements and other pertinent information.

MONEY   Soaring real estate prices have made Los Angeles one of America's most expensive cities. U.S.-dollar traveler's checks are the safest, most negotiable way to carry currency. They are accepted by most restaurants, hotels, and shops and can be exchanged for cash at banks and check-issuing offices. American Express offices are open Monday through Friday from 9am to 5pm and Saturday from 9am until noon. See "Fast Facts: Los Angeles" in Chapter 4 for L.A. office locations.

Most banks offer automated-teller machines (ATMs) that accept cards connected to a particular network. The ubiquitous Bank America accepts Plus, Star, and Interlink cards, while First Interstate Bank is on-line with the Cirrus system. Each bank has dozens of branches all around the city. For additional locations, dial toll free **800/424-7787** for the Cirrus network or **800/843-7587** for the Plus system.

Credit and charge cards are widely accepted in Los Angeles. MasterCard and Visa are the most common, followed by American Express, Carte Blanche, Diners Club, and Discover. ATMs at the above-listed banks will make cash advances against MasterCard and Visa. American Express cardholders can write a personal check, guaranteed against the card, for up to $1,000 in cash at an American Express office.

Foreign travelers should also see Chapter 3 for monetary descriptions and currency-exchange information.

What Things Cost in Los Angeles	U.S. $
Taxi from the airport to downtown	30.00
Bus fare to any destination within the city	1.10
Double room at the Beverly Hills Hotel (very expensive)	250.00
Double room at the Radisson-Huntley Hotel (expensive)	145.00
Double room at the Royal Palace Westwood Hotel (inexpensive)	66.00
Lunch for one at Tom Bergin's Tavern (moderate)	12.00
Lunch for one at Roscoe's House of Chicken (inexpensive)	7.00
Dinner for one, without wine, at Morton's (expensive)	40.00
Dinner for one, without wine, at Antonio's (moderate)	30.00
Dinner for one, without wine, at the Source (inexpensive)	12.00
Glass of beer	3.00
Coca-Cola	1.25
Cup of coffee	1.00
Admission to the J. Paul Getty Museum	Free
Movie ticket	7.50
Theater ticket	25.00

2 When to Go

Summer is Los Angeles's primary tourist season, but moderate temperatures and year-round visitor services make it a pleasure to travel there during less busy seasons as well. The city is particularly delightful from early autumn to late spring, when skies are bluest; theater, opera, and ballet seasons are in full swing; and restaurants and stores are less crowded.

It's possible to sunbathe throughout the year, but only die-hard enthusiasts and surfers in wet suits venture into the water in winter. You can swim in spring, summer, and fall, though the Pacific is still quite chilly.

Los Angeles is usually much warmer than the Bay Area, and it gets significantly more sun. L.A.'s beaches are the golden sands that have given the entire state a worldwide reputation for tropical temperatures and the laid-back lifestyle they encourage. Even in winter, daytime thermometer readings regularly reach into the 60s and warmer. Summers can be stifling inland, but this city's beach communities are always comfortable. Don't pack an umbrella.

As you can see from the temperature chart below, Los Angeles remains relatively temperate year-round.

Los Angeles's Average Temperatures

	Jan	Feb	Mar	Apr	May	June	July	Aug	Sept	Oct	Nov	Dec
Avg. High (°F)	65	66	67	69	72	75	81	81	81	77	73	69
Avg. Low (°F)	46	48	49	52	54	57	60	60	59	55	51	49

Los Angeles Calendar of Events

January

✪ Tournament of Roses

An annual celebration of the first day of the new year.
Festivities include the spectacular parade down Colorado
Boulevard, famous for its lavish floats, music, and
extraordinary equestrian entries, followed by the Rose
Bowl Game.
Where: Pasadena. **When:** January 1. **How:** For more
details, contact the Pasadena Tournament of Roses office
at 391 S. Orange Grove Blvd., Pasadena, CA 91105
(☎ **818/449-4100**).

- **Oshogatsu,** Little Tokyo. The Japanese New Year is
  celebrated annually at the Japanese American Cultural and
  Community Center. Participate in traditional Japanese
  ceremonies and enjoy ethnic foods and crafts. For more
  information, call **213/628-2725.** First weekend in January.
- **Martin Luther King Parade,** Long Beach. This annual
  parade down Alameda and 7th Streets ends with a festival
  in Martin Luther King Park. For more information, contact
  the Council of Special Events (☎ **310/570-6816**). Third
  Monday in January.

February

- **Chinese New Year,** New Chinatown. Colorful dragon
  dancers parade through the streets of downtown's New
  Chinatown. An event not to be missed. For this year's
  schedule, contact the Chinese Chamber of Commerce,
  977 N. Broadway, Room E, Los Angeles, CA 90012
  (☎ **213/617-0396**). Early February.

March

✪ Los Angeles Marathon

It might seem counterproductive healthwise, but this
26.2-mile run through the streets of Los Angeles attracts
thousands of participants.
Where: Downtown Los Angeles. **When:** Early March.
How: Call **310/444-5544** for registration or spectator
information.

★ **American Indian Festival and Market**

Showcase and Festival of Native American arts and culture. The fun includes traditional dances, storytelling, and a display of arts and crafts as well as a chance to sample ethnic foods.

Where: Los Angeles Natural History Museum. **When:** Late March. **How:** Admission to museum includes festival tickets. For further details, call **213/744-3314.**

April

★ **Renaissance Pleasure Fair**

One of America's largest Renaissance festivals, this annual happening, set in L.A.'s relatively remote countryside, looks very much like an authentic, albeit somewhat touristy, old English village. The fair provides an entire day's activities, shows and festivities, food and crafts. Participants are encouraged to come in costume.

Where: Glen Ellen Regional Park, San Bernardino. **When:** Weekends from April through June. **How:** For ticket information, phone toll free **800/523-2473.**

★ **Toyota Grand Prix**

An exciting weekend of Indy-class auto racing and entertainment in and around downtown Long Beach. **Where:** Long Beach. **When:** Mid-April. **How:** Contact Grand Prix Association, 3000 Pacific Ave., Long Beach, CA 90806 (☎ **310/436-9953**).

May

★ **Cinco de Mayo**

A week-long celebration of one of Mexico's most jubilant holidays takes place throughout the city of Los Angeles. The fiesta's Carnival-like atmosphere is created by large crowds, live music, dances, and food.

Where: Main festivities held in El Pueblo de los Angeles State Historic Park, downtown; other events around the city. **When:** One week surrounding May 5. **How:** Phone **213/628-1274** for information.

- **Redondo Beach Wine Festival.** The largest outside wine-tasting event in southern California is held in Redondo Beach. For exact dates and this year's locations, contact the Redondo Beach Chamber of Commerce, 200 N. Pacific Coast Hwy., Redondo Beach, CA 90277 (☎ **310/376-6912**). Early May.
- **National Orange Show,** San Bernardino. This 11-day county fair includes various stadium events, celebrity entertainment, livestock shows, and carnival rides. Phone **909/888-6788** for information. Mid-May.

June

- **Playboy Jazz Festival,** usually held in the Hollywood Bowl. This event is widely recognized for the great artists it attracts. Phone **310/246-4000** for details. Mid-June.

⭐ **Annual Grand National Irish Fair and Music Festival**

Bagpipes, Gaelic music, song, and dance ring in this traditional event. You may even see a leprechaun, if you're lucky.
Where: Griffith Park. **When:** Mid-June. **How:** Phone **213/395-8322** for dates and more information.

July

⭐ **Fourth of July Celebration**

Southern California's most spectacular display of fireworks follows an evening of live entertainment.
Where: The Rose Bowl, 1001 Rose Bowl Dr., Pasadena.
When: July 4. **How:** Phone **818/577-3100** for further information.

- **Fireworks Display at the Marina,** Marina del Rey. Burton Chase Park is a favorite place to view traditional Fourth of July fireworks. Arrive in the afternoon for best parking and viewing sites. July 4.

⭐ **Hollywood Bowl Summer Festival**

Summer season at the Hollywood Bowl brings the world's best sounds of jazz, pop, and classical music to an open-air setting. The season includes an annual Fourth of July concert.
Where: 2301 N. Highland Blvd., Hollywood. **When:** July through mid-September. **How:** Phone the Bowl's box office (☎ **213/850-2000**) for information.

⭐ **International Surf Festival**

Four beachside cities collaborate in the oldest international surf festival in California. Competitions include surfing, boogie boarding, sand-castle building, and other beach-related categories.
Where: Hermosa Beach, Manhattan Beach, Redondo Beach, and Torrance. **When:** The end of July. **How:** Contact the International Surf Festival Committee (☎ **310/376-6911**) for information.

August

- **Nisei Week Japanese Festival,** Little Tokyo. This week-long celebration of Japanese culture and heritage is held in the Japanese American Cultural and Community Center Plaza. Festivities include parades, food, music, arts, and crafts. Phone **213/687-7193** for details. Mid-August.

- **African Marketplace and Cultural Fair,** Rancho Cienega Park. African arts, crafts, food, and music are featured during this cultural-awareness event. Phone **213/734-1164** for more information. Mid-August.
- **Long Beach Sea Festival.** This festival is dedicated to a variety of water-related events, including a sailboat regatta and jet ski and swimming competitions. For specific scheduling information, contact the Long Beach Department of Parks and Recreation, 2760 Studebaker Rd., Long Beach, CA 90804 (☎ **310/421-9431**). Last two weeks of August.

September

✪ Los Angeles County Fair

Horse racing, arts, agricultural displays, celebrity entertainment, and carnival rides are among the attractions of the largest county fair in the world. **Where:** Los Angeles County Fair and Exposition Center, in Pomona. **When:** Late September. **How:** Call **909/623-3111** for information.

- **Long Beach Blues Festival.** An annual outdoor festival featuring top names in blues music. Call **310/985-5566** for information. Usually in late September.

October

- **Annual Bob Hope Celebrity Golf Tournament,** Riverside. Bob Hope is the honorary chairman of this annual tournament. For ticket and other information, contact the Riverside Visitors and Convention Bureau, 3443 Orange St., Riverside, CA 92501 (☎ **909/787-7950;** fax **909/787-4940**).

November

- **Bandfest,** Hollywood. Bands participating in the Hollywood Christmas Parade compete in various categories in a battle of the marching bands. Call **213/469-8311** for details. Late November.

✪ Hollywood Christmas Parade

This spectacular star-studded parade marches through the heart of Hollywood just after Thanksgiving. **Where:** Hollywood Boulevard. **When:** End of November. **How:** For information, phone **213/469-2337**.

---

3 Insurance, Safety & Other Concerns

Insurance and safety are serious issues. Take a little time before your trip to make sure these concerns don't ruin it. Foreign travelers should see Chapter 3 for entry information and other related matters.

INSURANCE   Most travel agents sell low-cost health, loss, and trip-cancellation insurance to their vacationing clients. Compare these rates and services with those offered by local banks as well as by your personal insurance carrier.

Most American travelers are covered by their hometown health insurance policies in the event of an accident or sudden illness while away on vacation. Make sure that your Health Maintenance Organization (HMO) or insurance carrier can provide services for you in California. If there's any doubt, a health insurance policy that specifically covers your trip is advisable. Foreign travelers should check to see if they are covered by their home insurance companies and see Chapter 3 for more information.

You can also protect your travel investment with travel-related insurance to cover you against lost or damaged baggage and trip-cancellation or interruption costs. These coverages are often combined into a single comprehensive plan, sold through travel agents, credit- and charge-card companies, and automobile and other clubs.

SAFETY   Innocent tourists are rarely the victims of violent crime. Still, there are precautions you can take to protect yourself and your possessions.

When sightseeing, it's best to plan your route in advance; consult maps indoors before leaving your hotel room. Ask directions from service providers—hotel desk staff, telephone or power company employees, or police officers. Avoid asking strangers for directions and don't discuss your plans with them. If you get lost, find an open business and ask for directions there. Always be aware of your surroundings and leave an area if it appears unsafe. Remember that alcohol consumption diminishes awareness.

Use traveler's checks or credit and charge cards whenever possible. Carry only as much cash as you'll need and never display it openly. Carry your wallet in the front pocket of your pants or inside your jacket; carry pocketbooks and other bags under your arm, not by the handle. If you have a shoulder bag, don't carry it draped over a shoulder; place the strap over your head and wear it so the strap crosses your torso diagonally, with the bag held securely under your arm. While sitting, hold your handbag in your lap. In a restaurant, never sling your purse over the back of a chair. Keep your bag next to you in a public restroom instead of using door hooks. Consider using a "fanny-pack" or a concealable moneybelt to carry cash and credit and charge cards. Keep some of your cash and credit and charge cards separately, in a second pocket or wallet, and carry new purchases in old bags. Stay especially alert in crowded situations, such as in department stores, at bus stops, and on public transportation.

Don't let your car advertise that you're a visitor. Place maps, travel brochures, this guidebook, and other valuables out of sight in the glove compartment or trunk. Never leave wallets, credit or charge cards, checkbooks, or purses anywhere in the vehicle, which you should always lock—and don't forget to take the keys. Park in well-lighted, busy areas. Check the interior of your vehicle before getting in, and when parking for the night, ask yourself if you've left anything in your car that could be of any value whatsoever—then remove it.

Keep an eye on your luggage when checking in and out of your hotel. Make sure that no one hears your name and room number while at the front desk. Phone the front desk to verify the identity of room service and other hotel employees—especially if you did not call for them. Know what the hotel identification badge looks like. Deposit your valuables in the hotel safe (or in a room safe if you have one) and keep an inventory of what was deposited; never leave cash or other valuables in your room. Lock your luggage when it's left in the room, know how to double-lock your room door, and use the door viewer to identify anyone trying to gain entry to your room. Never leave your room key at an unattended front desk.

Los Angeles's homeless problem is immense—panhandlers are especially prevalent in Santa Monica and Venice as well as downtown. Most homeless people are harmless; however, some are chronic law violators who may infringe on the rights of others. I suggest a combination of respect and caution around panhandlers and other strangers.

See "Fast Facts: Los Angeles" in Chapter 4 for city-specific safety tips. Also see "Safety" under "Preparing for Your Trip" in Chapter 3.

SUNBURN   We now know that the sun is healthful only in moderation. Over a long period too much exposure to the sun's rays can be detrimental and can even cause cancer. Sunning can be fun, but you should also take it seriously and exercise precautions.

Protect yourself with a high Sun Protection Factor (SPF) lotion or screen and don't expose yourself to too much sun in one day—especially if you've been out of the sun for months. If you burn easily, a product with an SPF of at least 8 is recommended. Also, wear sunglasses—the kind that block out ultraviolet rays—and bring a hat with a wide bill or rim. You may laugh now, but when you're walking on the beach in the middle of the afternoon or driving west while the sun is setting you'll want your hat.

EARTHQUAKES   There will always be earthquakes and their aftershocks in California—most of which you'll never notice. However, in the event of an earthquake, there are a few basic precautionary measures to take whether you're inside a high-rise hotel or out driving or walking.

If you're inside a building, don't run outside; instead, move away from windows in the direction of what would be the center of the building. Get under a desk or table or stand against a wall or under a doorway. If you're in bed, get under the bed or stand in a doorway or crouch under a sturdy piece of furniture. When exiting the building, use stairwells, *not* elevators.

If you're in your car, pull over to the side of the road and stop, but wait until you're away from bridges or overpasses and telephone or power poles and lines. Stay in your car.

If you're out walking, stay outside and away from trees, power lines, and the sides of buildings. If you're in an area with tall buildings, find a doorway to stand in.

4   What to Pack

It's unwise to bring more than you can carry. There's no need to overpack and be a slave to your luggage; many smaller hotels don't have porters. Don't worry if you forget something or need an emergency item. Almost anything you could possibly want can be purchased in Los Angeles.

Warm weather translates into informal dress. Few places require jackets and ties; if you're on vacation, you'll rarely feel out of place without them.

From May through October, weather in Los Angeles warrants lightweight summer clothing, with a sweater or lightweight jacket for the occasional brisk evening or over-cool restaurant. November through April temperatures are milder and generally require spring-weight clothing and a raincoat. During winter, it's a good idea to plan for cold snaps and cool nights with clothes appropriate to more northerly climes. Of course, you should bring shorts, a bathing suit, and sunglasses. Keep your rain gear at home; there's little chance you'll need it.

If you're currently taking medication, bring along enough of each drug to last your entire stay and pack all prescriptions (in the generic, not brand-name, form) in case your medication is lost. Eyeglass and contact lens wearers should also carry their prescriptions.

5   Tips for the Disabled, Seniors & Families

FOR THE DISABLED   Most of Los Angeles's major museums and tourist attractions are fitted with wheelchair ramps to accommodate physically challenged visitors. In addition, several hotels offer special accommodations and services for wheelchair-bound and other disabled visitors. These include large bathrooms, ramps, and telecommunication devices for the deaf. The **California Travel Industry Association,** 2500 Wilshire Blvd., Suite 603, Los Angeles, CA 90057 (☎ **213/384-3178**), provides information and referrals to specially equipped sights and hotels around the city and state. California issues special license plates to physically disabled drivers

IMPRESSIONS

"People here still believe. The sun comes out every day and smacks them in the face and they march off gamely to face insurmountable odds. Los Angeles may be the most renewable city in the world."
—Tom Shales, *Washington Post*

and honors plates issued by other states. Special "handicapped" parking spots are located near the entrances to most buildings.

FOR SENIORS   In California, "senior citizen" usually means anyone 65 or older. Seniors regularly receive discounts at museums and attractions; when available, these discounts are listed in the following chapters under their appropriate headings. Ask for discounts everywhere—at hotels, movie theaters, museums, restaurants, and attractions. You may be surprised how often you'll be offered reduced rates. When making airline reservations, ask about a senior discount, but find out if there's a cheaper promotional fare before committing yourself.

Older travelers are particularly encouraged to purchase travel insurance (see "Insurance," under "Insurance, Safety, and Other Concerns," earlier in this chapter) and would be well advised to exercise frugality when packing.

FOR FAMILIES   Children add joy and a different level of experience to travel. They help you see things in a different way and can sometimes attract reticent local people like a magnet. Taking kids to California obviously means additional, more thorough planning. On airplanes, special-order children's meals as far in advance as possible. Most airlines don't carry baby food, but the flight attendants will be glad to heat up any you've brought with you. Pack essential first-aid supplies, such as Band-Aids, a thermometer, children's pain reliever, and cough drops; and always carry with you some snacks, such as raisins, crackers, and fruit, as well as water or juice.

Frommer's Los Angeles with Kids is an excellent specialized guide to the city for parents with kids in tow. Los Angeles is full of sightseeing opportunities and special activities geared toward children. In this guide, see the "Cool for Kids" listings for restaurant and hotel suggestions.

6   Getting There

Los Angeles is easy to reach, but not all transportation options are created equal. Shopping around will ensure you get there the right way at the best price.

By Plane

Almost every major scheduled airline flies into Los Angeles International Airport (LAX). Many carriers also service the half a dozen smaller gateways located around the city. If you're not planning to visit the city center, it might be wise to avoid it entirely and fly into a smaller regional airport. Airlines often offer special deals that can make it as cheap to fly into Orange County, for instance, as it is to fly into LAX. Explore this possibility before buying your ticket.

THE MAJOR AIRLINES   Some 36 international airlines, and all major American carriers, serve the Los Angeles International Airport (LAX), one of the busiest airports in the world. Domestic airlines flying in and out of LAX include Alaska Airlines (☎ toll free

800/426-0333), American Airlines (☎ toll free **800/433-7300**), Delta Air Lines (☎ toll free **800/221-1212**), Northwest Airlines (☎ toll free **800/225-252**5), Southwest Airlines (☎ toll free **800/435-9792**), Trans World Airlines (☎ toll free **800/221-2000**), United Airlines (☎ toll free **800/241-6522**), and USAir (☎ toll free **800/428-4322**).

Several smaller carriers are known for the excellent and comprehensive service they provide up and down the California coast. America West (☎ toll free **800/235-9292**), American Eagle (☎ toll free **800/433-7300**), Skywest (☎ toll free **800/453-9417**), United Express (☎ toll free **800/241-6522**), and USAir Express (☎ toll free **800/428-4322**) are some of the biggest carriers offering regular service between California cities.

REGULAR FARES   Depending on your point of origin, travel agents may not feel it worth their while to help you find a really inexpensive ticket to Los Angeles. To get the lowest price, I usually do the legwork and make the reservation myself, and then visit my travel agent for ticketing. Check the newspapers for advertisements and call a few of the major carriers before committing yourself.

The cheapest standard economy-class fare usually comes with serious restrictions and steep penalties for altering dates and itineraries. When purchasing these tickets, don't use terms like "APEX" and "excursion" or other airline jargon—just ask for the lowest fare. If you're flexible with dates and times, say so. Ask if you can get a lower fare by staying an extra day or by flying during the middle of the week (many airlines won't volunteer this type of information). At the time of this writing, the lowest round-trip fare to Los Angeles from New York was $398 and from Chicago, $298; the lowest round-trip fare to Los Angeles from San Francisco was $198. You may find even lower fares.

Business-class seats can easily cost twice the price of coach seats. When buying a full-fare ticket to Los Angeles, expect to pay about $1,600 from New York and about $2,000 from Chicago. Note, however, that competition is stiff for luxury-class passengers, and prices are sometimes more elastic in this category than they are in economy class. Call several airlines and compare prices before committing yourself.

Frommer's Smart Traveler: Airfares

1. Check the fares of all airlines that fly to your destination.
2. Always ask for the lowest fare, not "discount," "APEX," or "excursion."
3. Keep calling the airline—availability of cheap seats changes daily.
4. Seek out budget alternatives. Phone "bucket shops," charter companies, and discount travel agents.
5. Plan to travel midweek, when rates are usually lower.

If you fly first class, expect to pay about $2,500 from New York and about $2,000 from Chicago to Los Angeles. Many short hops to L.A. don't have a first-class section, but when they do, they're predictably expensive.

DISCOUNTED AIRFARES   Alternatives to the traditional travel-agent ticket have their advantages (usually price) and their drawbacks (usually lack of flexibility).

CONSOLIDATORS   By negotiating directly with airlines, consolidators (or "bucket shops") can sell tickets on major scheduled carriers at deeply discounted rates—often 20% to 30% lower. Such fares are often the least-expensive means of traveling to Los Angeles, lower in most instances than charter-flight fares. For example, in winter from New York you can buy bucket-shop tickets to Los Angeles on well-known international airlines for as little as $150 each way; prices rise to about $225 in summer. There are drawbacks, however. The tickets are restrictive, valid only for a particular date or flight, usually nontransferable, and nonrefundable except directly from the bucket shop. Also, consolidators usually don't offer travel counseling and don't book hotels or rental cars. On the plus side, bucket-shop tickets are rarely restricted by advance-purchase requirements; if space is available, you can buy your ticket just days before departure.

The lowest-priced bucket shops are usually local operations with low profiles and overheads. Look for their advertisements in the travel or classified section of your local newspaper. Ads for consolidators are typically small, usually a single column in width and a few lines deep. They contain a list of cities and, opposite, a list of corresponding prices.

While prices for flights available through bucket shops are low, at times they may be eclipsed by special offers by the airlines. As usual, compare prices before you commit.

Nationally advertised consolidators are usually not as competitive as the smaller boiler-room operations, but they have toll-free numbers and are easily accessible. Such consolidators include **Travac,** 989 Ave. of the Americas, New York, NY 10018 (☎ **212/563-3303**, or toll free **800/TRAV-800**), and **Unitravel,** 1177 N. Warson Rd. (P.O. Box 12485), St. Louis, MO 63132 (☎ **314/569-0900,** or toll free **800/325-2222**).

CHARTER FLIGHTS   Competition from the bucket shops, not to mention fiercely competitive commercial airlines, has pared the number of charters somewhat, but there are still plenty to choose from. Most charter operators advertise and sell their seats through travel agents, making these local professionals your best source of information for available flights. Before deciding to take a charter flight, check the ticket restrictions. You may be asked to purchase a tour package, pay far in advance of the flight, be amenable if the day of departure or the destination is changed, pay a service charge, fly on an airline you're not familiar with, and pay harsh penalties if you cancel—but be understanding if the charter doesn't fill up and is cancelled up to 10 days before departure. Summer charters fill up more quickly than others and are almost sure to fly, but if you decide on a charter flight, seriously consider cancellation and baggage insurance.

FLYING AS A COURIER   Since courier flights are primarily for long-distance travel, they're usually not available for short domestic flights. But if you're crossing the country, or an ocean, becoming a mule might be a good bargain for you. Companies that hire couriers use your luggage allowance for their business baggage; in return, you get a deeply discounted ticket. Flights are often offered at the last minute, and you may have to arrange a pretrip interview to make sure you're right for the job. **Now Voyager, Inc.** (☎ **212/431-1616** from 11:30am to 6pm), flies from New York and sometimes has flights to Los Angeles for as little as $199 round-trip.

By Train

Traveling by train takes a long time and usually costs as much as, or more than, flying. But if you're afraid of airplanes, or want to take a leisurely ride through America's countryside, rail may be a good option. **Amtrak** (☎ toll free **800/USA-RAIL**), the nation's most complete long-distance passenger railroad network, connects about 500 American cities with points all over California.

Trains bound for Los Angeles leave daily from New York and pass through Chicago and Denver. The journey takes about $3^1/_2$ days, and seats fill up quickly. As of this writing, the lowest round-trip fare was $339 from New York and $269 from Chicago. These heavily restricted tickets are good for 45 days and allow up to three stops along the way.

Amtrak also runs trains up and down the California coast, connecting Los Angeles with San Francisco and all points in between. A one-way ticket can often be had for as little as $50.

Ask about special family plans, tours, and other money-saving promotions the rail carrier may be offering. Call for an excellent brochure outlining routes and prices for the entire system.

By Bus

Bus travel is an inexpensive and often flexible option. **Greyhound/ Trailways** (☎ toll free **800/231-2222**) can get you here from anywhere and offers several money-saving multiday passes. Round-trip fares vary depending on your point of origin, but few, if any, ever exceed $200. The main Los Angeles bus station is downtown at 1716 E. 7th St. For additional area terminal locations and local fare and schedule information, phone **213/620-1200.**

By Car

California is well connected to the rest of the United States by several major highways. Among them are Interstate 5, which enters the state from the north; Interstate 10, which originates in Jacksonville, Florida, and terminates in Los Angeles; and U.S. 101, which follows the western seaboard from Los Angeles north to the Oregon state line.

By car is a great way to go if you want to become acquainted with the countryside; but after figuring in food, lodging, and automobile expenses, it may not be your cheapest option. Still, driving down the California coast is one of the world's ultimate journeys. Always drive within the speed limit, and keep an eye out for "speed traps," where the limit suddenly drops. Buy a good road map of the state before you start your trip and keep it handy in the glove compartment for easy reference. Before setting out on a long drive, call **415/557-3755** for a recorded announcement on California road conditions. See "Getting Around" in Chapter 4 for more information on driving.

ROAD MAPS   California's freeway signs frequently indicate direction by naming a town rather than a point on the compass. If you've never heard of Canoga Park you might be in trouble, unless you have a map. The best state road guide is the comprehensive Thomas Bros. *California Road Atlas,* a 300-plus-page book of maps with schematics of towns and cities statewide. It costs $20 but is a good investment if you plan to do a lot of exploring. Smaller, accordion-style maps are handy for the state as a whole or for individual cities and regions. These foldout maps usually cost $2 to $3 and are available at gas stations, pharmacies, supermarkets, and tourist-oriented shops everywhere.

BREAKDOWNS & ASSISTANCE   Before taking a long car trip you should seriously consider joining a major automobile association. Not only do automobile associations offer travel insurance and helpful information, but also they can perform vacation-saving roadside services, including towing. The **American Automobile Association (AAA),** 1000 AAA Dr., Heathrow, FL 32746-5063 (☎ **407/444-7000,** or toll free **800/763-6600**), is the nation's largest auto club, with more than 850 offices. Membership fees range from about $20 to $60, depending on where you join.

Other recommendable auto clubs include the **Allstate Motor Club,** 1500 Shure Dr., Arlington Heights, IL 60004 (☎ **708/253-4800**), and the **Amoco Motor Club,** P.O. Box 9046, Des Moines, IA 50369 (☎ toll free **800/334-3300**).

HITCHHIKING   Thumbing a ride is the cheapest and most unpredictable way of traveling. Unfortunately, it can also be dangerous. Small country roads are best, and cities are worst. Use common sense: Sit next to an unlocked door, keep your bags within reach, and refuse a ride if you feel uneasy. The best way to become a rider is to strike up a conversation at a gas station or truck stop. Better still, find a driver through a ride board, located at most colleges and in some local cafés.

Package Tours

Tours and packages, put together by airlines, charter companies, hotels, and tour operators, are sold to travelers either directly or through travel agents. A **tour** usually refers to an escorted group and often includes transportation, sightseeing, meals, and accommodations. The entire group travels together and shares the same preplanned activities. A **package,** on the other hand, can include any or all of the above components, but travelers are usually unescorted and free to make their own itinerary. Many travelers purchase plane tickets, hotel accommodations, and airport transfers from a travel agent without even knowing that they're buying a tour operator's package. This is fine since packages can be a good value. Because packagers buy in bulk, they can often sell their services at a discount.

To find out what tours and packages are available to you, check the ads in the travel section of your newspaper or visit your travel agent. Before signing up, however, read the fine print carefully and do some homework:

How reputable is the tour operator? Ask for references of people who have participated in tours run by the same company. Call travel agents and the local Better Business Bureau, and check with the consumer department of the U.S. Tour Operators Association, 211 E. 51st St., Suite 12B, New York, NY 10022 (☎ **212/750-7371**). Be leery of any outfit that doesn't give you details of the itinerary.

What is the size of the tour group? Decide how you feel about sharing an experience with 40 other people, or if your limit is 20. A smaller group usually means a better-quality tour.

What kinds of hotels have been booked and where are they located? Get the names of the hotels and then look them up in guidebooks or in your travel agent's hotel guide. If you sense that the hotels provide only minimal essentials, that might be a clue about everything else on the tour. If the hotels are not conveniently located, they will be less expensive; however, if you feel isolated or unsafe, you may have to spend extra money and time getting to and from various attractions and nightspots.

If meals are included, how elaborate are they? Is breakfast continental, English, or buffet? Is the menu for the group limited?

How extensive is the sightseeing? You may be able to get on and off the bus many times to explore various attractions, or you may be obliged to see them only from the bus window. If you like to explore, pick an attraction you're interested in and ask the operator precisely how much time you can expect to spend there. Find out if all admissions are included in the price of the tour.

Are the optional activities offered at an additional price? This is usually the case, so make sure that the activities that particularly interest you are included in the tour price.

What is the refund policy if you decide to cancel? Check this carefully; some tour operators are more lenient than others regarding trip cancellations.

How is the package price paid? If a charter flight is involved, make sure that you can pay into an escrow account (ask for the name of the bank) in order to ensure proper use of the funds or their return in case the operator cancels the trip.

Most of the airlines listed above offer both escorted tours and on-your-own packages. Dozens of other companies also compete for this lucrative business. Discuss your options with a travel agent and compare tour prices with those in this guide.

3

For Foreign Visitors

Aᴌᴛʜᴏᴜɢʜ Aᴍᴇʀɪᴄᴀɴ ꜰᴀᴅꜱ ᴀɴᴅ ꜰᴀꜱʜɪᴏɴꜱ ʜᴀᴠᴇ ꜱᴘʀᴇᴀᴅ ᴀᴄʀᴏꜱꜱ Eᴜʀᴏᴘᴇ and other parts of the world so much that the United States may seem like familiar territory before your arrival, there are still many peculiarities and uniquely American situations that any foreign visitor will encounter.

In this chapter I'll point out to you many of the perhaps unexpected differences from what you are used to at home, and explain some of the more confusing aspects of daily life in the United States.

1   Preparing for Your Trip

Entry Requirements ────────────────────────

DOCUMENT REQUIREMENTS   Canadian citizens may enter the United States without passports or visas; they need only proof of residence.

British subjects and citizens of New Zealand, Japan, and most western European countries traveling on valid passports may not need a visa for holiday or business travel to the United States for less than 90 days, providing they hold a round-trip or return ticket and they enter the United States on an airline or cruise line participating in the visa waiver program. (Note that citizens of these visa-exempt countries who first enter the United States may then visit Mexico, Canada, Bermuda, and/or the Caribbean islands and then reenter the United States by any mode of transportation, without needing a visa. Further information is available from any U.S. embassy or consulate.)

Citizens of countries other than those stipulated above, including citizens of Australia, must have two documents: (1) a valid passport with an expiration date at least six months later than the scheduled end of their visit to the United States; and (2) a tourist visa, available without charge from the nearest U.S. consulate.

To obtain a visa, the traveler must submit a completed application form (either in person or by mail) with a $1^1/_2$-inch-square photo and must demonstrate binding ties to a residence abroad. Usually you can obtain a visa at once or within 24 hours, but it may take longer during the summer rush from June to August. If you cannot go in person, contact the nearest U.S. embassy or consulate for directions on applying by mail. Your travel agent or airline office may also be able to provide you with visa applications and instructions. The U.S. embassy or consulate that issues your visa will determine whether you will be issued a multiple- or single-entry visa and any restrictions regarding the length of your stay.

MEDICAL REQUIREMENTS   No inoculations are needed to enter the United States unless you're coming from, or have stopped over in, areas known to be suffering from epidemics, particularly cholera or yellow fever.

If you have a disease requiring treatment with medications containing narcotics or drugs requiring a syringe, carry a valid signed prescription from your physician to allay any suspicions that you are smuggling drugs.

CUSTOMS REQUIREMENTS   Every adult visitor may bring in free of duty: one liter of wine or hard liquor; 200 cigarettes or 100 cigars (but no cigars from Cuba) or three pounds of smoking tobacco; and $100 worth of gifts. These exemptions are offered to travelers who spend at least 72 hours in the United States and who have not claimed them within the preceding six months. It's altogether forbidden to bring into the country foodstuffs (particularly cheese, fruit, cooked meats, and canned goods) and plants (vegetables, seeds, tropical plants, and so on). Foreign tourists may bring in or take out up to $10,000 in U.S. or foreign currency with no formalities; larger sums must be declared to Customs on entering or leaving.

Insurance

There is no national health system in the United States. Because the cost of medical care is extremely high, I strongly advise every traveler to secure health insurance coverage before setting out.

You may want to take out a comprehensive travel policy that covers (for a relatively low premium) sickness or injury costs (medical, surgical, and hospital); loss or theft of your baggage; trip-cancellation costs; guarantee of bail in case you are arrested; costs of accident, repatriation, or death. Such packages (for example, "Europe Assistance" in Europe) are sold by automobile clubs at attractive rates, as well as by insurance companies and travel agencies.

Money

CURRENCY & EXCHANGE   The U.S. monetary system has a decimal base: one American **dollar ($1)** = 100 **cents** (100¢).

Dollar bills commonly come in $1 ("a buck"), $5, $10, $20, $50, and $100 denominations (the last two are not welcome when paying for small purchases and are not accepted in taxis or at subway ticket booths). There are also $2 bills (seldom encountered).

There are six denominations of coins: 1¢ (one cent or "penny"), 5¢ (five cents or "a nickel"), 10¢ (ten cents or "a dime"), 25¢ (twenty-five cents or "a quarter"), 50¢ (fifty cents or "a half dollar"), and the rare $1 piece.

Note: The "foreign-exchange bureaus" so common in Europe are rare even at airports in the United States, and nonexistent outside major cities. Try to avoid having to change foreign money, or traveler's checks denominated other than in U.S. dollars, at a small-town bank, or even a branch in a big city; in fact, leave any currency other than U.S. dollars at home—it may prove more nuisance to you than it's worth.

TRAVELER'S CHECKS   Traveler's checks denominated in U.S. dollars are readily accepted at most hotels, motels, restaurants, and large stores. But the best place to change traveler's checks is at a bank. Do not bring traveler's checks denominated in other currencies.

CREDIT & CHARGE CARDS The method of payment most widely used is credit and charge cards: Visa (Barclaycard in Britain), MasterCard (EuroCard in Europe, Access in Britain, Chargex in Canada), American Express, Diners Club, Discover, and Carte Blanche. You can save yourself trouble by using "plastic money" rather than cash or traveler's checks in most hotels, motels, restaurants, and retail stores (a growing number of food and liquor stores now accept credit and charge cards). You must have a credit or charge card to rent a car. It can also be used as proof of identity (often carrying more weight than a passport) or as a "cash card," enabling you to draw money from banks and automated-teller machines (ATMs) that accept it.

Safety

GENERAL While tourist areas are generally safe, crime is on the increase everywhere, and U.S. urban areas tend to be less safe than those in Europe or Japan. Visitors should always stay alert. This is particularly true of large U.S. cities. It's wise to ask the city's or area's tourist office if you're in doubt about which neighborhoods are safe. Avoid deserted areas, especially at night. Don't go into any city park at night unless there is an event that attracts crowds. Generally speaking, you can feel safe in areas where there are many people and many open establishments.

Avoid carrying valuables with you on the street, and don't display expensive cameras or electronic equipment. Hold on to your pocketbook, and place your billfold in an inside pocket. In theaters, restaurants, and other public places, keep your possessions in sight.

Remember also that hotels are open to the public, and in a large hotel, security may not be able to screen everyone entering. Always lock your room door—don't assume that once inside your hotel you are automatically safe and no longer need be aware of your surroundings.

DRIVING Safety while driving is particularly important. Question your rental agency about personal safety, or ask for a brochure of traveler safety tips when you pick up your car. Obtain written directions, or a map with the route marked in red, from the agency showing how to get to your destination. And, if possible, arrive and depart during daylight hours.

Recently more and more crime has involved cars and drivers. If you drive off a highway into a doubtful neighborhood, leave the area as quickly as possible. If you have an accident, even on the highway, stay in your car with the doors locked until you assess the situation or until the police arrive. If you are bumped from behind on the street or are involved in a minor accident with no injuries and the situation appears to be suspicious, motion to the other driver to follow you. *Never* get out of your car in such situations. You can also keep in your car a pre-made sign which reads: PLEASE FOLLOW THIS VEHICLE TO REPORT THE ACCIDENT. Show the sign to the other driver and go directly to the nearest police precinct, well-lighted service station, or all-night store.

If you see someone on the road who indicates a need for help, do *not* stop. Take note of the location, drive on to a well-lighted area, and telephone the police by dialing 911.

Park in well-lighted, well-traveled areas if possible. Always keep your car doors locked, whether attended or unattended. Look around you before you get out of your car, and never leave any packages or valuables in sight. If someone attempts to rob you or steal your car, do *not* try to resist the thief/carjacker—report the incident to the police department immediately.

Also, make sure that you have enough gasoline in your tank to reach your intended destination, so that you're not forced to look for a service station in an unfamiliar and possibly unsafe neighborhood—especially at night.

2 Getting to & Around the U.S.

GETTING TO THE U.S.   Travelers from overseas can take advantage of the **APEX (advance-purchase excursion) fares** offered by all the major international carriers. Aside from these, attractive values are offered by Icelandair on flights from Luxembourg to New York and by Virgin Atlantic Airways from London to Los Angeles.

British travelers should check out **British Airways** (☎ 081/897-4000 in the U.K., or toll free **800/247-9297** in the U.S.), which offers direct flights from London to Los Angeles International Airport (LAX), as does **Virgin Atlantic Airways** (☎ 02/937-47747 in the U.K., or toll free **800/862-8621** in the U.S.). Canadian readers might book flights on **Air Canada** (☎ toll free **800/776-3000**), which offers direct service from Toronto, Montréal, and Calgary to Los Angeles. Many other international carriers also serve Los Angeles, including **Japan Airlines** (☎ toll free **800/525-3663** in the U.S.) and **SAS** (☎ toll free **800/221-2350** in the U.S.).

GETTING AROUND THE U.S. • By Plane   Some large American airlines (for example, American Airlines, Delta, Northwest, TWA, and United) offer travelers on their transatlantic or transpacific flights special discount tickets under the name **Visit USA**, allowing travel between any U.S. destinations at minimum rates. They're not on sale in the United States, and must, therefore, be purchased before you leave your foreign point of departure. This system is the best, easiest, and fastest way to see the United States at low cost. You should obtain information well in advance from your travel agent or the office of the airline concerned, since the conditions attached to these discount tickets can be changed without advance notice.

The visitor arriving by air, no matter what the port of entry, should cultivate patience and resignation before setting foot on U.S. soil. Getting through Immigration control may take as long as two hours on some days, especially summer weekends. Add the time it takes to clear Customs and you'll see that you should make very generous allowance for delay in planning connections between international and domestic flights—an average of two to three hours at least.

In contrast, travelers arriving by car or by rail from Canada will find border-crossing formalities streamlined to the vanishing point. And air travelers from Canada, Bermuda, and some places in the Caribbean can sometimes go through Customs and Immigration at the point of departure, which is much quicker and less painful.

• **By Train**   Long-distance trains in the United States are operated by Amtrak, the national rail passenger corporation. International visitors can buy a **USA Railpass,** good for 15 or 30 days of unlimited travel on Amtrak. The pass is available through many foreign travel agents. Prices in 1994 for a 15-day pass were $208 off-peak, $308 peak; a 30-day pass cost $309 off-peak, $389 peak. (With a foreign passport, you can also buy passes at some Amtrak offices in the United States, including locations in Boston, Chicago, Los Angeles, Miami, New York, San Francisco, and Washington, D.C.) Reservations are generally required and should be made for each part of your trip as early as possible.

However, visitors should be aware of the limitations of long-distance rail travel in the United States. With a few notable exceptions (for instance, the Northeast Corridor line between Boston and Washington, D.C.), service is rarely up to European standards: Delays are common, routes are limited and often infrequently served, and fares are rarely significantly lower than discount airfares. Thus cross-country train travel should be approached with caution.

• **By Bus**   The cheapest way to travel the United States is by bus. Greyhound, the sole nationwide bus line, offers an **Ameripass** for unlimited travel for 7 days (for $250), 15 days (for $350), and 30 days (for $450). Bus travel in the United States can be both slow and uncomfortable, so this option is not for everyone.

• **By Car**   Travel by car gives visitors the freedom to make—and alter—their itineraries to suit their own needs and interests. And it offers the possibility of visiting some of the off-the-beaten-path locations, places that cannot be reached easily by public transportation. For information on renting cars in the United States, see "Automobile Organizations" and "Automobile Rentals" in "Fast Facts: For the Foreign Traveler," later in this chapter, and "By Car" under "Getting Around" in Chapter 4.

Fast Facts: For the Foreign Traveler

Accommodations   Some of the major hotels listed in this guide maintain overseas reservation networks and can be booked either directly or through travel agents. Some hotels are also included in tour operators' package tours. Since tour companies buy rooms in bulk, they can often offer them at a discount. Discuss this option with your travel agent and compare tour prices with those in this guide.

Automobile Organizations   Auto clubs will supply maps, suggested routes, guidebooks, accident and bail-bond insurance, and emergency road service. The major auto club in the United States, with 955 offices nationwide, is the **American Automobile Association (AAA).** Members of some foreign auto clubs have reciprocal arrangements with the AAA and enjoy its services at no charge. If you belong to an auto club in your home country, inquire about AAA reciprocity before you leave. You may be able to join the AAA even if you're not a member of a reciprocal club; to inquire, call the AAA (☎ toll free **800/336-4357**). The AAA can provide you with an **International Driving Permit,** validating your foreign license.

In addition, some automobile-rental agencies now provide many of these same services. Inquire about their availability when you rent your car.

Automobile Rentals   To rent a car you will need a major credit or charge card and a valid driver's license. In addition, you usually need to be at least 25 (some companies do rent to younger people but add a daily surcharge). Be sure to return your car with the same amount of gas you started out with; rental companies charge excessive prices for gasoline. See "By Car" under "Getting Around" in Chapter 4 for the phone numbers of car-rental companies in Los Angeles.

Business Hours   **Banks** are generally open Monday through Friday from 9am to 3 or 4pm, and there's 24-hour access to the automated-teller machines (ATMs) at most banks and other outlets. Generally, **offices** are open Monday through Friday from 9am to 5pm. **Stores** are open six days a week, with many open on Sunday too; department stores usually stay open until 9pm at least one night a week.

Climate   See "When to Go" in Chapter 2.

Currency   See "Money" under "Preparing for Your Trip," earlier in this chapter.

Currency Exchange   You'll find currency-exchange services in major airports with international service. Elsewhere, they may be quite difficult to come by. In Los Angeles, a very reliable choice is **Thomas Cook Currency Services, Inc.,** which has been in business since 1841 and offers a wide range of services. It sells commission-free foreign and U.S. traveler's checks, drafts, and wire transfers; it also does check collections (including Eurochecks). The rates are competitive and the service excellent. Thomas Cook maintains an office in Los Angeles in the Hilton Hotel Center, 900 Wilshire Blvd. (☎ **213/624-4221**).

Drinking Laws   See "Liquor Laws" under "Fast Facts: Los Angeles" in Chapter 4.

Electricity   The United States uses 110–120 volts AC, 60 cycles, compared to 220–240 volts AC, 50 cycles, as in most of Europe.

In addition to a 100-volt transformer, small appliances of non-American manufacture, such as hairdryers and shavers, will require a plug adapter, with two flat, parallel pins.

Embassies/Consulates   All embassies are located in the national capital, Washington, D.C.; some consulates are located in major U.S. cities, and most countries maintain a mission to the United Nations in New York City. The embassies and consulates of the major English-speaking countries—Australia, Canada, the Republic of Ireland, New Zealand, and the United Kingdom—are listed below. If you're from another country, you can get the telephone number of your embassy by calling "Information" in Washington, D.C. (☎ **202/555-1212**).

The embassy of **Australia** is at 1601 Massachusetts Ave. NW, Washington, DC 20036 (☎ **202/797-3000**). There is an Australian consulate at 611 N. Larchmont Blvd., Los Angeles, CA 90004 (☎ **213/469-4300**). Other Australian consulates are in Honolulu, Houston, New York, and San Francisco.

The embassy of **Canada** is at 501 Pennsylvania Ave. NW, Washington, DC 20001 (☎ **202/682-1740**). There's a Canadian consulate in Los Angeles at 300 S. Grand Ave., 10th Floor, Los Angeles, CA 90071 (☎ **213/346-2700**). Other Canadian consulates are in Atlanta, Buffalo (N.Y.), Chicago, Cleveland, Dallas, Detroit, Miami, Minneapolis, New York, San Francisco, and Seattle.

The embassy of the **Republic of Ireland** is at 2234 Massachusetts Ave. NW, Washington, DC 20008 (☎ **202/462-3939**). The nearest Irish consulate is at 655 Montgomery St., Suite 930, San Francisco, CA 94111 (☎ **415/392-4214**). Other Irish consulates are in Boston, Chicago, and New York.

The embassy of **New Zealand** is at 37 Observatory Circle NW, Washington, DC 20008 (☎ **202/328-4848**). The only New Zealand consulate in the United States is at 12400 Wilshire Blvd., 11th Floor, Los Angeles, CA 90025 (☎ **310/477-8241**).

The embassy of the **United Kingdom** is at 3100 Massachusetts Ave. NW, Washington, DC 20008 (☎ **202/462-1340**). There's a British consulate in Los Angeles at 11766 Wilshire Blvd., Suite 400, Los Angeles, CA 90025 (☎ **310/477-3322**). Other British consulates are in Atlanta, Chicago, Houston, Miami, and New York.

Emergencies   Call **911** to report a fire, call the police, or get an ambulance. This is a toll-free call (no coins are required at a public telephone).

If you encounter traveler's problems, check the local telephone directory to find an office of the **Travelers Aid Society,** a nationwide, nonprofit, social-service organization geared to helping travelers in difficult straits. Their services might include reuniting families separated while traveling, providing food and/or shelter to people stranded without cash, or even emotional counseling. If you're in trouble, seek them out.

Gasoline (Petrol)   One U.S. gallon equals 3.8 liters or .85 Imperial gallons. There are usually several grades (and price levels) of gasoline available at most gas stations, and their names change from company to company. The unleaded ones with the highest octane rating are the most expensive (most rental cars take the least expensive "regular" unleaded gas); leaded gas is the least expensive, but only older cars can use this anymore, so check if you're not sure. Prices rise in winter, when gas stations are required by state law to sell only "oxygenated" gasoline, fuel that reduces exhaust emissions. And often the price is lower if you pay in cash instead of by credit or charge card. Also, many gas stations now offer lower-priced self-service gas pumps—in fact, some gas stations, particularly at night, are all self-service.

Holidays   On the following legal national holidays, banks, government offices, post offices, and many stores, restaurants, and museums are closed: January 1 (New Year's Day), the third Monday in January (Martin Luther King Day), the third Monday in February (Presidents Day, Washington's Birthday), the last Monday in May (Memorial Day), July 4 (Independence Day), the first Monday in September (Labor Day), the second Monday in October (Columbus Day), November 11 (Veterans Day/Armistice Day), the last Thursday in November (Thanksgiving Day), and December 25 (Christmas). Also, the Tuesday following the first Monday in November is Election Day, and is a legal holiday in presidential-election years (next in 1996).

Information   See "Tourist Information" under "Orientation" in Chapter 4.

Languages   Major hotels may have multilingual employees. Unless your language is very obscure, they can usually supply a translator upon request.

Legal Aid   The foreign tourist, unless positively identified as a member of the Mafia or of a drug ring, will probably never become involved with the American legal system. If you are pulled up for a minor infraction (for example, of the highway code, such as speeding), never attempt to pay the fine directly to a police officer; you may wind up arrested on the much more serious charge of attempted bribery. Pay fines by mail, or directly into the hands of the clerk of the court. If you're accused of a more serious offense, it's wise to say and do nothing before consulting a lawyer. Under U.S. law, an arrested person is allowed one telephone call to a party of his or her choice. Call your embassy or consulate.

Mail   If you want your mail to follow you on your vacation and you aren't sure of your address, your mail can be sent to you, in your name, **c/o General Delivery** (Poste Restante) at the main post office of the city or region where you expect to be. The addressee must pick it up in person and must produce proof of identity (driver's license, credit card, passport, etc.).

Domestic **postage rates** are 19¢ for a postcard and 29¢ for a letter. Check with any local post office for current international postage rates to your home country.

Generally found at intersections, mailboxes are blue with a red-and-white stripe and carry the designation U.S. MAIL. If your mail is addressed to a U.S. destination, don't forget to add the five-digit postal code, or ZIP (Zone Improvement Plan) Code, after the two-letter abbreviation of the state to which the mail is addressed (CA for California, FL for Florida, NY for New York, and so on).

Medical Emergencies   To call an ambulance, dial **911** from any phone. No coins are needed. For a list of hospitals and other emergency information, see "Fast Facts: Los Angeles" at the end of Chapter 4.

Newspapers/Magazines   National newspapers include the *New York Times, USA Today,* and the *Wall Street Journal.* National news weeklies include *Newsweek, Time,* and *U.S. News & World Report.* Most city newsstands offer a small selection of the most popular foreign periodicals and newspapers, such as *The Economist, Le Monde,* and *Der Spiegel.* For information on local publications, see "Fast Facts: Los Angeles" in Chapter 4.

Radio/Television   Audiovisual media, with four coast-to-coast networks—ABC, CBS, NBC, and Fox—joined in recent years by the Public Broadcasting System (PBS) and the cable network CNN, play a major part in American life. In big cities, televiewers have a choice of about a dozen channels (including the UHF channels), most of them transmitting 24 hours a day, without counting the pay-TV channels showing recent movies or sports events. All options are usually indicated on your hotel TV set. You'll also find a wide choice of local radio stations, each broadcasting particular kinds of talk shows and/or music—classical, country, jazz, pop, gospel—punctuated by news broadcasts and frequent commercials. For the radio and TV choices in Los Angeles, see "Fast Facts: Los Angeles" in Chapter 4.

Safety   See "Safety" under "Preparing for Your Trip," earlier in this chapter.

Taxes   In the United States there is no VAT (value-added tax) or other indirect tax at the national level. Every state, and each county and city in it, has the right to levy its own local tax on purchases (including hotel and restaurant checks, airline tickets, and so on) and services. Taxes are already included in the price of certain services, such as public transportation, cab fares, telephone calls, and gasoline. The amount of sales tax varies from about 4% to 10%, depending on the state and city, so when you're making major purchases, such as photographic equipment, clothing, or stereo components, it can be a significant part of the cost.

In Los Angeles, the combined Los Angeles County and California state sales taxes amount to 8.25%. And the local hotel-occupancy taxes add another 14% to 17%.

Telephone/Telegraph/Telex/Fax   The telephone system in the United States is run by private corporations, so rates, especially for long-distance service and operator-assisted calls, can vary widely—even on calls made from public telephones. Local calls in the United States usually cost 25¢ (they're 25¢ throughout California).

Generally, hotel surcharges on long-distance and local calls are astronomical. You're usually better off using a **public pay telephone,** which you'll find clearly marked in most public buildings and private establishments as well as on the street. Outside metropolitan areas, public telephones are more difficult to find. Stores and gas stations are your best bet.

Most **long-distance and international calls** can be dialed directly from any phone. For calls to Canada and other parts of the United States, dial 1 followed by the area code and the seven-digit number. For international calls, dial 011 followed by the country code (Australia, 61; Republic of Ireland, 353; New Zealand, 64; United Kingdom, 44), the city code, and the telephone number of the person you wish to call.

Note that all calls to area code 800 are toll free. However, calls to numbers in area codes 700 and 900 (chat lines, bulletin boards, "dating" services, etc.) can be very expensive—usually a charge of 95¢ to $3 or more per minute, and they sometimes have minimum charges that can run as high as $15 or more.

For **reversed-charge or collect calls,** and for **person-to-person calls,** dial 0 (zero, *not* the letter "O") followed by the area code and number you want; an operator will then come on the line, and you should specify that you are calling collect, or person-to-person, or both. If your operator-assisted call is international, ask for the overseas operator.

For local **directory assistance** ("information"), dial 411; for **long-distance information,** dial 1, then the appropriate area code and **555-1212.**

Like the telephone system, **telegraph** and **telex** services are provided by private corporations like ITT, MCI, and above all, Western Union, the most important. You can bring your telegram in to the nearest Western Union office (there are hundreds across the country) or dictate it over the phone (a toll-free call, **800/ 325-6000**). You can also telegraph money (using a major credit or charge card), or have it telegraphed to you, very quickly over the Western Union system. (Note, however, that this service can be very expensive—the service charge can run as high as 15% to 25% of the amount sent.)

Most hotels have **fax** machines available for guest use (be sure to ask about the charge to use it), and many hotel rooms are even wired for guests' fax machines. You'll probably also see signs for public faxes in the windows of local shops.

Telephone Directory   There are two kinds of telephone directories available to you. The general directory is the so-called *White Pages,* in which private and business subscribers are listed in alphabetical order. The inside front cover lists the emergency number for police, fire, and ambulance, and other vital numbers (like the Coast Guard, poison-control center, crime-victims hotline, and so on). The first few pages are devoted to community-service numbers, including a guide to long-distance and international calling, complete with country codes and area codes.

The second directory, printed on yellow paper (hence its name, *Yellow Pages*), lists all local services, businesses, and industries by type of activity, with an index at the back. The listings cover not only such obvious items as automobile repairs by make of car, or drugstores (pharmacies), often by geographical location, but also restaurants by type of cuisine and geographical location, bookstores by special subject and/or language, places of worship by religious denomination, and other information that the tourist might otherwise not readily find. The *Yellow Pages* also include city plans or detailed area maps, often showing postal ZIP Codes and public transportation routes.

Time   The United States is divided into four **time zones** (six, if Alaska and Hawaii are included). From east to west, these are: eastern standard time (EST), central standard time (CST), mountain standard time (MST), Pacific standard time (PST), Alaska standard time (AST), and Hawaii standard time (HST). Always keep changing time zones in mind if you're traveling (or even telephoning) long distances in the United States. For example, noon in New York City (EST) is 11am in Chicago (CST), 10am in Denver (MST), 9am in Los Angeles (PST), 8am in Anchorage (AST), and 7am in Honolulu (HST).

California is on Pacific standard time, eight hours behind Greenwich mean time. **Daylight saving time** is in effect from the last Sunday in April through the last Saturday in October (actually, the change is made at 2am on Sunday), except in Arizona, Hawaii, part of Indiana, and Puerto Rico. Daylight saving time moves the clock one hour ahead of standard time.

Tipping   This is part of the American way of life, on the principle that you must expect to pay for any service you get (many service personnel receive little direct salary and must depend on tips for their income). Here are some rules of thumb:

In **hotels,** tip bellhops $1 per piece and tip the chamber staff $1 per day. Tip the doorman or concierge only if he or she has provided you with some specific service (for example, calling a cab for you or obtaining difficult-to-get theater tickets).

In **restaurants, bars, and nightclubs,** tip the service staff 15% of the check, tip bartenders 10% to 15%, tip checkroom attendants $1 per garment, and tip valet-parking attendants $1 per vehicle. Tip the doorman only if he has provided you with some specific service (such as calling a cab for you). Tipping is not expected in cafeterias and fast-food restaurants.

Tip **cab drivers** 15% of the fare.

As for **other service personnel,** tip redcaps at airports or railroad stations $1 per piece and tip hairdressers and barbers 15% to 20%.

Tipping ushers in cinemas, movies, and theaters and gas-station attendants is not expected.

Toilets   Foreign visitors often complain that public toilets are hard to find in most U.S. cities. True, there are none on the streets, but the visitor can usually find one in a bar, restaurant, hotel, museum, department store, or service station—and it will probably be clean (although the last-mentioned sometimes leaves much to be desired). Note, however, a growing practice in some restaurants and bars of displaying a notice that "toilets are for the use of patrons only." You can ignore this sign, or better yet, avoid arguments by paying for a cup of coffee or soft drink, which will qualify you as a patron. The cleanliness of toilets at railroad stations and bus depots may be more open to question, and some public places are equipped with pay toilets, which require you to insert one or more coins into a slot on the door before it will open.

The American System of Measurements ——————

Length

1 inch (in.)	=	2.54cm					
1 foot (ft.)	=	12 in.	=	30.48cm	=	.305m	
1 yard	=	3 ft.	=	.915m			
1 mile (mi.)	=	5,280 ft.	=	1.609km			

To convert miles to kilometers, multiply the number of miles by 1.61 (for example, 50 miles × 1.61 = 80.5km). Note that this conversion can be used to convert speeds from miles per hour (m.p.h.) to kilometers per hour (km/h).

To convert kilometers to miles, multiply the number of kilometers by .62 (for example, 25km × .62 = 15.5 miles). Note that this same conversion can be used to convert speeds from kilometers per hour to miles per hour.

Capacity

1 fluid ounce (fl. oz.)			=	.03 liter		
1 pint	=	16 fl. oz.	=	.47 liter		
1 quart	=	2 pints	=	.94 liter		
1 gallon (gal.)	=	4 quarts	=	3.79 liter	=	.83 Imperial gal.

To convert U.S. gallons to liters, multiply the number of gallons by 3.79 (example, 12 gal. × 3.79 = 45.48 liters).

To convert U.S. gallons to Imperial gallons, multiply the number of U.S. gallons by .83 (example, 12 U.S. gal. × .83 = 9.96 Imperial gal.).

To convert liters to U.S. gallons, multiply the number of liters by .26 (example, 50 liters × .26 = 13 U.S. gal.).

To convert Imperial gallons to U.S. gallons, multiply the number of Imperial gallons by 1.2 (example, 8 Imperial gal. × 1.2 = 9.6 U.S. gal.).

Weight

1 ounce (oz.)			=	28.35 grams		
1 pound (lb.)	=	16 oz.	=	453.6 grams	=	.45 kilograms
1 ton	=	2,000 lb.	=	907 kilograms	=	.91 metric ton

To convert pounds to kilograms, multiply the number of pounds by .45 (example, 90 lb. × .45 = 40.5kg).

To convert kilograms to pounds, multiply the number of kilograms by 2.2 (example, 75kg × 2.2 = 165 lb.).

Area

1 acre	=	.41 hectare		
1 square mile (sq. mi.)	=	640 acres	=	2.59 hectares
	=	2.6km		

To convert acres to hectares, multiply the number of acres by .41 (example, 40 acres × .41 = 16.4ha).

To convert square miles to square kilometers, multiply the number of square miles by 2.6 (example, 80 sq. mi. × 2.6 = 208km^2).

To convert hectares to acres, multiply the number of hectares by 2.47 (example, 20ha × 2.47 = 49.4 acres).

To convert square kilometers to square miles, multiply the number of square kilometers by .39 (example, 150km^2 × .39 = 58.5 sq. mi.).

Temperature

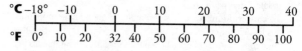

To convert degrees Fahrenheit to degrees Celsius, subtract 32 from °F, multiply by 5, then divide by 9 (example, 85°F − 32 × 5/9 = 29.4°C).

To convert degrees Celsius to degrees Fahrenheit, multiply °C by 9, divide by 5, and add 32 (example, 20°C × 9/5 + 32 = 68°F).

4

Getting to Know Los Angeles

EVEN NATIVES HAVE TROUBLE NEGOTIATING THEIR WAY AROUND THIS sprawling city. The freeways, which cross and connect L.A.'s disparate regions, are your lifeline to the sights; they will take a little time to master. This chapter will help familiarize you with the city and its various parts.

1 Orientation

Arriving

BY PLANE   There are five airports in the Los Angeles area, but the largest and best known is:

Los Angeles International Airport   Most visitors who arrive by plane fly into Los Angeles International Airport—better known as LAX—situated oceanside, southwest of downtown L.A., between Santa Monica and Manhattan Beach. One of the largest airports in the world, LAX (☎ **310/646-5252**) contains eight terminals, including the Tom Bradley International Terminal, named for a former mayor who was a frequent overseas traveler on official city business. Despite its size, the airport has a rather straightforward, easy-to-understand design. Free blue-and-green–striped shuttle buses connect the terminals, and Travelers Aid of Los Angeles operates booths in each.

To reach Santa Monica and other northern beach communities, exit the airport, turn left onto Sepulveda Boulevard, then follow the signs to Calif. 1 (the Pacific Coast Highway) north.

To reach Huntington, Newport, and other southern beach communities, turn right onto Sepulveda Boulevard, then follow the signs to Calif. 1 (the Pacific Coast Highway) south.

To reach Beverly Hills or Hollywood, exit the airport via Century Boulevard, then take I-405 north to Santa Monica Boulevard.

To reach downtown, exit the airport via Century Boulevard, then take I-405 north to I-10 east.

To reach Pasadena, exit the airport, turn right onto Sepulveda Boulevard south, then take I-105 east to I-110 north.

Transportation from LAX   All the major American car-rental firms operate off-site offices that are reached via free van or bus from outside each terminal. See "Getting Around," later in this chapter, for a list of major car-rental companies.

Taxis line up outside each terminal, and rides are metered. Expect to pay about $25 to downtown and Hollywood, $22 to Beverly Hills, $20 to Santa Monica, and $45 to Pasadena. These prices include a $2.50 service charge for rides originating at LAX.

The city's new Metro Green Line, scheduled for completion by 1995, will connect LAX with downtown L.A. Fares had not been set by press time.

Many city hotels provide free shuttles for their guests; ask about transportation when you make reservations. Super Shuttle (☎ 310/782-6600), a private ride-sharing service, offers regularly scheduled minivans from LAX to any location in the city. The set fare can range from about $10 to $50, depending on your destination. When traveling to the airport, reserve your shuttle at least one day in advance.

The city's MTA buses also go between LAX and many parts of the city. Phone MTA Airport Information (☎ toll free 800/252-7433) for the schedules and fares. Free Blue, Green, and White Airline Connections shuttle buses (☎ 310/646-2911) connect the terminals at LAX and stop in front of each ticket building. Special handicapped-accessible minibuses are also available.

Other Airports   LAX is the city's largest airport, but Los Angeles is full of smaller regional airports that are usually easier to reach and may be closer to your destination. To the north is the **Burbank-Glendale-Pasadena Airport,** 2627 N. Hollywood Way, Burbank (☎ 818/840-8840); to the south are the **Long Beach Municipal Airport,** 4100 Donald Douglas Dr., Long Beach (☎ 310/421-8293), and the **John Wayne Airport,** 19051 Airport Way N., Anaheim (☎ 714/252-5200); and to the east is the **Ontario International Airport,** Terminal Way, Ontario (☎ 909/988-2700).

BY TRAIN   Amtrak service to and from San Diego to the south and Oakland and Seattle to the north, as well as to and from points in between, operates out of Union Station at 800 N. Alameda (☎ 213/624-0171), on the north side of downtown L.A.

BY BUS   The Greyhound/Trailways bus system serves most cities in California. In Los Angeles, the main terminal is downtown at 1716 E. 7th St., half a block east of Alameda (☎ 213/629-8430), a rather seedy part of the city. Although there are other Greyhound stations around L.A., not all of them are serviced by interstate buses. If you're planning to arrive by bus, tell the operator where you want to go and see if there's a stop closer to your destination.

BY CAR   Almost all the Interstate highways that crisscross L.A. run right through the downtown area. From the east, you'll arrive on I-10, the San Bernardino Freeway. From the north or south, the most direct route is via I-5. You may wish to avoid the clogged downtown area entirely, in which case you should turn off I-5 onto I-405, which runs by LAX. Non-Interstate entries include U.S. 101, which comes into

IMPRESSIONS

Whatever its future, L.A. right now is, despite its well-publicized flaws, a vital, eclectic, almost irresistible and eminently puzzling place. . . . It is a vast and sprawling city that defies easy definition or direction, but offers immense rewards for the traveler who has a sense of the larger puzzle.
—Don George, *San Francisco Examiner*

the downtown area from Santa Barbara and the north; and Calif. 1, which follows the coast through Santa Monica.

Tourist Information

Los Angeles Convention and Visitors Bureau, 633 W. 5th St., Suite 600, Los Angeles, CA 90071 (☎ **213/624-7300**), is the city's main source for information. Write for a free visitors kit. The bureau staffs a Visitors Information Center at 685 S. Figueroa St., between Wilshire Boulevard and 7th Street, which is open Monday through Friday from 8am to 5pm and Saturday from 8:30am to 5pm.

Many Los Angeles–area communities also have their own tourist offices, including:

Visitor Information Center Hollywood, Janes House, 6541 Hollywood Blvd., Hollywood, CA 90028 (☎ **213/689-8822**), open Monday through Saturday from 9am to 5pm.

Beverly Hills Chamber of Commerce and Visitors Bureau, 239 S. Beverly Dr., Beverly Hills, CA 90212 (☎ **310/271-8174,** or toll free **800/345-2210**).

Hollywood Arts Council, P.O. Box 931056, Dept. 1991, Hollywood, CA 90093 (☎ **213/462-2355**), distributes the free magazine *Discover Hollywood.* It contains good listings of the area's many theaters, galleries, music venues, and comedy clubs.

Long Beach Convention and Visitors Council, One World Trade Center, Suite 300, Long Beach, CA 90831 (☎ **213/ 436-3645,** or toll free **800/234-3645**).

Marina del Rey Chamber of Commerce, 4629-A Admiralty Way, Marina del Rey, CA 90292 (☎ **213/821-0555**).

Pasadena Convention and Visitors Bureau, 171 S. Los Robles Ave., Pasadena, CA 91101 (☎ **818/795-9311**; fax 818/795- 9656).

Santa Monica Convention and Visitors Bureau, 2219 Main St., Santa Monica, CA 90405 (☎ **310/393-7593**). The Santa Monica Visitors Center is located near the Santa Monica Pier, at 1400 Ocean Ave.

City Layout

Los Angeles is an incongruous patchwork of communities sewn into an ever-expanding quilt. Sprawled between sea and mountains, the city encompasses both seaside resorts and treeless desert foothills. With notable exceptions, the better homes are in the hills—built on shelves of granite in shrub-covered mountains.

"Sky-high" Mulholland Drive rolls along the crest of the Santa Monica mountain chain through part of Beverly Hills and Hollywood. Popular with sightseeing tourists and teenage locals, the drive offers excellent views of the city to the west and the San Fernando Valley to the north. The valley, located between the Hollywood Hills and the Mojave Desert mountains, was once covered with orange groves but is now both residential and commercial.

Downtown Los Angeles lies about 12 miles east of the Pacific Ocean on a direct line with the coastal town of Santa Monica. This is the city's primary business district, but by no means the only one.

Most of the commercial areas of Los Angeles have remained in the flatlands, including Wilshire Boulevard ("Miracle Mile"), which runs from the downtown area to the sea. The highest point in the city is Mount Hollywood. Sunset and Hollywood Boulevards—the main thoroughfares—run along the foot of the mountains.

Because of earthquake concerns, skyscrapers weren't permitted in the city of Los Angeles until recent times—which partially explains why the city is so spread out, encompassing more than 450 square miles.

MAIN ARTERIES & STREETS The city's main arteries are freeways that crisscross L.A. in a complicated maze. U.S. 101 runs across L.A. from the San Fernando Valley to the center of downtown. I-5 bisects the city on its way from San Francisco to San Diego. I-10 connects the downtown area with Santa Monica and nearby beach areas. And I-405 skirts the downtown area completely, connecting the San Fernando Valley with LAX and the city's southern beach areas. Los Angeles's newest freeway, Century Freeway (I-105), extends from LAX east to the San Gabriel River Freeway (I-605), through the cities of Hawthorne and Lynwood.

Hollywood, located northwest of downtown, is best reached by the Hollywood Freeway (U.S. 101). Beverly Hills, which adjoins Hollywood on the southwest, is most accessible by taking the Hollywood Freeway from the Civic Center to Santa Monica Boulevard.

Wilshire Boulevard, L.A.'s main drag, connects the downtown area with Beverly Hills, then continues on through Westwood en route to Santa Monica. As Wilshire Boulevard enters Beverly Hills, it intersects La Cienega Boulevard. The portion of La Cienega that stretches north from Wilshire Boulevard to Santa Monica Boulevard is known as Restaurant Row.

Hollywood's Sunset Boulevard, between Laurel Canyon Boulevard and La Brea Avenue, is the famed Sunset Strip. Just north of the strip lies the equally famous Hollywood Boulevard.

Farther north still, via the Hollywood Freeway, is the San Fernando Valley; here you'll find Universal City. A right turn on the Ventura Freeway takes you to downtown Burbank.

Venice, the yacht-filled harbors of Marina del Rey, and the Los Angeles International Airport (LAX) are located on Calif. 1, south along the shore from Santa Monica.

FINDING AN ADDRESS Use a map—there's no other way. It's important to know in what area of the city the address you're looking for is located. When you know, for instance, that the hotel is in Santa Monica, finding it is much easier. For that reason, all Los Angeles addresses in this guide either include the city area or are listed under a helpful heading.

STREET MAPS Because Los Angeles is so spread out, a good map of the area is essential. Foldout accordion-style maps are available at gas stations, hotels, bookshops, and tourist-oriented shops around the city.

Los Angeles Freeways & Orientation

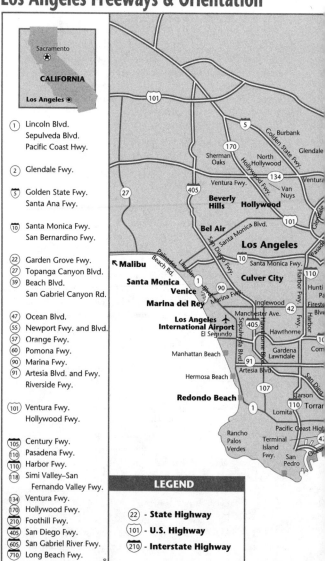

1. Lincoln Blvd.
   Sepulveda Blvd.
   Pacific Coast Hwy.

2. Glendale Fwy.

5. Golden State Fwy.
   Santa Ana Fwy.

10. Santa Monica Fwy.
    San Bernardino Fwy.

22. Garden Grove Fwy.
27. Topanga Canyon Blvd.
39. Beach Blvd.
    San Gabriel Canyon Rd.

47. Ocean Blvd.
55. Newport Fwy. and Blvd.
57. Orange Fwy.
60. Pomona Fwy.
90. Marina Fwy.
91. Artesia Blvd. and Fwy.
    Riverside Fwy.

101. Ventura Fwy.
     Hollywood Fwy.

105. Century Fwy.
110. Pasadena Fwy.
110. Harbor Fwy.
118. Simi Valley–San
     Fernando Valley Fwy.
134. Ventura Fwy.
170. Hollywood Fwy.
210. Foothill Fwy.
405. San Diego Fwy.
605. San Gabriel River Fwy.
710. Long Beach Fwy.

LEGEND

22 - **State Highway**

101 - **U.S. Highway**

210 - **Interstate Highway**

NEIGHBORHOODS IN BRIEF

Hollywood   The legendary city where actresses once posed with leashed leopards is certainly on everyone's must-see list. Unfortunately, the glamour—what's left of it—is badly tarnished, and Hollywood Boulevard has been accurately labeled the "Times Square of

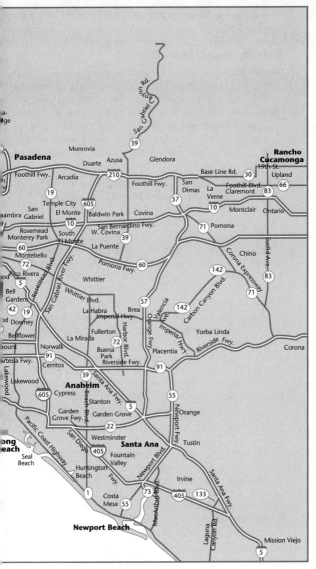

the West." But Hollywood seems unaware of its own decline. For one thing, the HOLLYWOOD sign is still on the hill, and the prices keep going up.

The legend of Hollywood as the movie capital of the world still persists, though many of its former studios have moved to less-expensive and more spacious venues. The corner of Hollywood and Vine is legendary—its fame larger than it deserves. Architecturally dull, it was known for the stars who crossed the intersection—all the big names in Hollywood.

Beverly Hills   The aura of Beverly Hills is unique. Beneath its veneer of wealth, it's a curious blend of small-town neighborliness and cosmopolitan worldliness. Many of southern California's most prestigious hotels, restaurants, high-fashion boutiques, and department stores are located here. Don't miss that remarkable group of European-based super-upscale stores along Rodeo Drive. A shopping guide is available from the Beverly Hills Chamber of Commerce and Visitors Bureau (see "Tourist Information," above).

Downtown Los Angeles   This ever-expanding sprawl of a city did have a point of origin: in and around the Old Plaza and Olvera Street. The first buildings included some (now demolished) elegant residences and the (still-standing) deluxe-class Biltmore Hotel. Because of concern about earthquakes, city-planning authorities originally prohibited the construction of buildings over 150 feet in height. This limitation led many companies to move to Wilshire Boulevard and outlying areas, leaving the original downtown to fall into relative disrepair. In 1957, new construction technology permitted tall buildings to be constructed safely. Construction of the shimmering $35-million Music Center in the 1960s marked the beginning of a long-overdue renaissance for downtown Los Angeles, which later included new office buildings and several major new hotels. One of the most magnificent newer buildings in the downtown area is the Museum of Contemporary Art (MOCA), designed by Japanese architect Arata Isozaki. MOCA is the only Los Angeles institution that is devoted exclusively to art from 1940 to the present.

Chinatown & Little Tokyo   Neither is on the scale of its San Francisco equivalent, and neither is worth going out of your way to see. Still, both offer a group of ethnic shops and restaurants that you might enjoy exploring. Chinatown, bounded by North Broadway, North Hill Street, Bernard Street, and Sunset Boulevard, centers on a Chinese mall called Mandarin Plaza at 970 N. Broadway.

Little Tokyo is located close to City Hall, bordered by Alameda and Los Angeles Streets and 1st and 3rd Streets. It is the site of the luxury-class Japanese hotel, the New Otani, as well as many Japanese shops and restaurants.

Century City   Nestled between Beverly Hills and Westwood, this compact and busy area bustles with businesses, shops, cinemas, and theaters. It's a good, central place to locate.

Malibu   Located 25 miles from downtown Los Angeles, Malibu occupies a long stretch of northern L.A. shoreline from Topanga Canyon to the Ventura County line. Once a privately owned ranch—purchased in 1857 for 10¢ an acre—Malibu is now a popular seaside resort and substantially more expensive. During the 1920s the

Hollywood

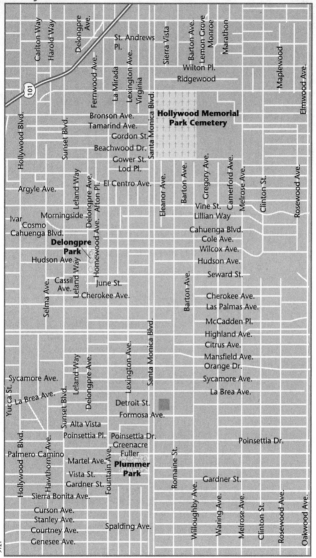

emerging movie colony flocked here, and Malibu became famous for wild parties and extravagant lifestyles. Although many famous people still live here, they tend to keep a low profile.

At its widest point, the Malibu strip is only three miles across; at its narrowest, just one mile. Malibu's wide, sandy beaches are among the best in the county for bathing, surfing, and sunning.

Wilshire Boulevard   In many ways, Wilshire Boulevard is Los Angeles's primary thoroughfare—the city's "Fifth Avenue" or "Champs-Elysées." Commencing in downtown Los Angeles, near Grand Street, Wilshire runs all the way to the beach in Santa Monica. Along the way it's the address for an impressive string of hotels, contemporary apartment houses, department stores, office buildings, and plush restaurants. In the 1930s, some optimistic developers dubbed one stretch of Wilshire—between Highland and Fairfax—"Miracle Mile." Only recently, however, is their ambitious label becoming a reality as new stores and glass-and-steel office buildings locate here.

Wilshire Boulevard passes by MacArthur and Lafayette Parks, as well as the Los Angeles County Museum and La Brea Tar Pits in Hancock Park. The boulevard also runs through a portion of the Beverly Hills shopping section.

Marina del Rey   Located oceanside, just south of Venice, Marina del Rey is best known for its small-craft harbor, which may be the largest of its kind in the world. You can watch the boats negotiate their way through a maze of piers, while strolling along an excellent Restaurant Row, packed with eateries for all palates and pocketbooks.

Santa Monica   Los Angeles's premier beach community is one of the most dynamic, fun, and pretty places in the entire city. Filled with art deco buildings and fronting a sizable swath of beach, the town is known for its long ocean pier and cutting-edge, artistic lifestyle. The new Third Street Promenade, lined with great shops and restaurants, is one of the most successful revitalization projects in the United States. Main Street, which runs south to Venice Beach, is also crammed with creative shops and eateries.

Redondo Beach & San Pedro   Established in the 1880s by railway tycoon Henry E. Huntington, Redondo Beach experienced a great land boom as it became the largest shipping port between San Diego and San Francisco. Located south of Marina del Rey and the Los Angeles International Airport, the area has since settled into a modest oceanside resort. Still largely commercial, Redondo fronts King Harbor, which now anchors a small fishing fleet, and about 2,000 pleasure craft.

Now L.A.'s busiest commercial port, San Pedro handles an estimated two million tons of cargo annually. There's not much for tourists here, but it's worth going out of your way to drive along the San Pedro coast, past seemingly never-ending, huge container ships and docks.

Long Beach   L.A.'s biggest beach town is actually the sixth-largest city in California. True to its name, it does, in fact, have a very long beach—$5^{1}/_{2}$ miles of sand. It's also well equipped with tennis, golf, sailing, fishing, and boating facilities.

Pasadena   The grande dame of the Greater Los Angeles area, Pasadena is a residential city 11 miles northwest of the downtown district, hugging the foothills of the Sierra Madre mountain range in the San Gabriel Valley. It features street after street of large estates, surrounded by semitropical gardens—a haven for "old money."

The city is known chiefly for its Rose Bowl and its annual Tournament of Roses Parade. Since its beginnings in 1890—with "flower-bedecked buggies and surreys"—the parade has included such "grand marshals" as Bob Hope and Mary Pickford, even Richard Nixon and Shirley Temple. Downtown Pasadena has recently seen a tremendous renaissance, attracting young, upscale professionals, top restaurants, and terrific nightlife.

Old Pasadena is a 14-block turn-of-the-century commercial district that has been transformed into one of the region's liveliest nightlife areas, with specialty boutiques, movie theaters, pool halls, and more than 60 restaurants.

San Fernando Valley   The media popularized the Valley by focusing on the "Valley Girl" stereotype—a Galleria (mall)-hopping teen whose favorite word is "ohmygod." The Valley snuggles between the Santa Monica and the San Gabriel mountain ranges, just west of Hollywood. It is mostly residential and commercial, and off the beaten tourist track. Cities in the Valley include Studio City, Sherman Oaks, Van Nuys, Tarzana, Reseda, and Encino.

2   Getting Around

By Public Transportation

I've heard rumors about visitors to Los Angeles who have toured the city entirely by public transportation—and they might even be true. It's hard to believe that anyone can comprehensively tour "Carland" without an auto of his or her own, but if you're in the city for only a short time, are on a very tight budget, or don't expect to be moving around a lot, public transport might be for you. The city's trains and buses are operated by the **Los Angeles County Metropolitan Transit Authority (MTA),** 425 S. Main St., Los Angeles, CA 90013 (☎ **213/626-4455**). Stop in at, write, or call the MTA for maps, schedules, and detailed trip information. The office publishes a handy pamphlet outlining about two dozen self-guided MTA tours, including visits to Universal Studios, Beverly Hills, and Disneyland. A second, more convenient MTA office is located in the ARCO Towers, 515 S. Flower St.

BY BUS   Spread-out sights, sluggish service, and frequent transfers make extensive touring by bus impractical. For short hops and occasional jaunts, however, buses could prove both economical and environmentally correct. Be sure to take a good book along to while away ride time (*War and Peace,* perhaps?).

The **basic bus fare** is $1.10 for all local lines, with transfers costing 25¢. Express buses, which travel along the freeways, and buses on intercounty routes charge higher fares. Phone for information.

The **Downtown Area Short Hop (DASH) shuttle system** operates buses throughout downtown and the west side of L.A. Service runs approximately every 5 to 20 minutes, depending on the time of day, and costs just 25¢. Phone the MTA for schedules and route information.

BY RAIL   In June 1990, the first line of a planned 300-mile network of commuter rail lines opened. The Metro Blue Line, an aboveground rail system, connects downtown with Long Beach. Trains operate daily from 6am to 9pm, with a $1.10 fare.

L.A.'s first subway, the Metro Red Line, which opened in 1993, currently runs just 4.4 miles and makes just five stops in the downtown area. The fare is 25¢. The Red Line will be extended to Hollywood and the San Fernando Valley by 1999.

Construction of the Metro Green Line is scheduled for completion by 1995. The line will connect Norwalk in eastern Los Angeles County to LAX. The Green Line will connect with the Blue Line downtown.

By Taxi

Distances are long in L.A., and cab fares are high. Even a short trip can cost $10 or more. Taxis charge $1.90 at the flagdrop, plus $1.60 per mile. A service charge is added to fares originating at LAX.

Except in the heart of downtown, passing cabs will usually not pull over when hailed. Cab stands are located at airports, at Union Station, and at major hotels. To assure a ride, order a taxi in advance from **Checker Cab** (☎ 213/221-2355), **L.A. Taxi** (☎ 213/627-7000), or **United Independent Taxi** (☎ 213/483-7604).

By Car

Need I tell you that Los Angeles is a car city? The elaborate network of freeways that connects this incredible urban sprawl is often jammed, especially during rush hours, when parking lots of traffic can seemingly slog along for hours. The golden rule of Los Angeles is always to allow more time to get to your destination than you reasonably think it will take. In case you're wondering, all the freeways damaged by the 1994 earthquake have been repaired.

RENTALS   Los Angeles is one of the cheapest places in America to rent a car. Major national car-rental companies usually offer their cheapest economy vehicles for about $30 per day and $100 per week with unlimited mileage. The best-known firms, with locations throughout the city, include **Alamo** (☎ toll free **800/327-9633**), **Avis** (☎ toll free **800/331-1212**), **Budget** (☎ toll free **800/527-0700**), **Dollar** (☎ toll free **800/421-6868**), **General** (☎ toll free **800/327-7607**), **Hertz** (☎ toll free **800/654-3131**), **National** (☎ toll free **800/328-4567**), and **Thrifty** (☎ toll free **800/367-2277**).

Most rental firms pad their profits by selling Loss/Damage Waiver (LDW), which usually costs an extra $9 per day. Before agreeing to this, however, check with your insurance carrier and credit- and charge-card companies. Many people don't realize that they are already covered by either one or both. If you're not already protected, the LDW is a wise investment.

For renters, the minimum age is usually 19 to 25. Some agencies have also set maximum ages. If you're concerned that these limits may affect you, ask about rental requirements at the time of booking to avoid problems later.

Finally, think about splurging on a convertible. Few things in life can match the feeling of flying along warm California freeways with the sun smiling on your shoulders and the wind whipping through your hair.

PARKING   Parking throughout the city is usually ample. In most places you'll be able to find metered street parking (carry plenty of quarters). Space gets scarce downtown, and in West Hollywood, where you'll probably have to pay in excess of $10 for a spot in an indoor garage. Most of the hotels listed in this book offer off-street parking, usually for an additional charge. This can get pricey—up to $20 per day. Check the listings and ask at the hotel before committing yourself.

DRIVING RULES   You may turn right at a red light (unless otherwise indicated), after yielding to traffic and pedestrians and making a complete stop. Pedestrians have the right-of-way at intersections and crosswalks. Pay attention to signs and arrows on the streets and roadways or you may find that you're in a lane that requires exiting or turning when you wanted to go straight. What's more, the city's profusion of one-way streets can create a few small difficulties; most road maps of the city, however, indicate in which direction the traffic flows.

THE FREEWAYS   Los Angeles has the most extensive freeway system in the world. In addition to a number, each freeway also has a name, or series of names, as it passes through various communities. See the "Los Angeles Freeways and Orientation" map (pp. 54–55) for a listing of major highways and freeways, along with their locally known names.

By Bicycle

If you care about your life, you won't try to bicycle in the city as a means of getting around. Traffic is heavy, and often you just can't get there from here with a bike. Cycles are terrific for recreation, however, especially along the car-free beach bike path in Venice and Santa Monica. See "Sports and Recreation" in Chapter 7 for complete information.

Fast Facts: Los Angeles

American Express   There are several American Express Travel Service offices, including 327 N. Beverly Dr. in Beverly Hills, and 901 W. 7th St. in downtown Los Angeles. To report lost or stolen cards, call toll free **800/528-4800**. To report lost or stolen traveler's checks, call toll free **800/221-7282.**

Area Code   All phone numbers in this guide are prefaced with area codes. You'll need to use them when calling from one calling area to another.

There are three area codes in Los Angeles. Most numbers, including Hollywood and downtown L.A., are within the 213 code. Phone numbers in the city's beach communities, including the Los Angeles International Airport (LAX), Malibu, and Santa Monica, begin with a 310 area code. Many inland suburbs, including Pasadena and towns of the San Fernando Valley, are within the 818 calling area.

Babysitters   If you're staying at one of the larger hotels, the concierge can usually recommend a reliable babysitter. If not, contact the Baby Sitters Guild, P.O. Box 3418, South Pasadena, CA 91031 (☎ **818/441-4293**). This company, in business since 1948, provides mature, bonded sitters, on call 24 hours.

Business Hours   Stores are usually open Monday through Saturday from 10am to 6pm; closed on Sunday.

Car Rentals   See "Getting Around" earlier in this chapter.

Climate   See "When to Go" in Chapter 2.

Currency Exchange   Foreign-currency exchange services are provided by the Bank of America at 525 S. Flower St., Level B (☎ **213/228-4622**). Thomas Cook Currency Services, at 677 S. Figueroa, and in the Hilton Hotel Center, 900 Wilshire Blvd. (☎ **213/624-4221**), also offer foreign-currency exchange services.

Dentists   Hotels usually have a list of dentists in case you need one. For other referrals, you can call the Los Angeles Dental Society (☎ toll free **800/422-8338**).

Doctors   Here again, hotels usually have a list of doctors on call. For referrals, you can contact the Los Angeles Medical Association (☎ **213/483-6122**), or for a free, confidential physician referral, call toll free **800/922-0000**.

Drugstores   Walgreens Pharmacies are all over town. Ask at your hotel or check the local phone directory for a location near you.

Embassies/Consulates   See "Fast Facts: For the Foreign Traveler" in Chapter 3.

Emergencies   For police, fire, highway patrol, or in case of life-threatening medical emergencies, dial **911.**

Eyeglasses   Lenscrafters makes glasses in about an hour. Offices include 301 Wilshire Blvd. in Santa Monica (☎ **310/394-6692**); and 4518 Van Nuys Blvd., Sherman Oaks (☎ **818/501-6474**).

Hairdressers/Barbers   B.O.B.S, 230 S. Robertson Blvd., Beverly Hills (☎ **310/657-4232**), offers high-quality haircuts, a high-design upscale atmosphere, and reasonable prices. Ronnie

Romoff at Romoff, 1615¹/₂ Montana Ave., Santa Monica (☎ 310/394-2709), located in an alley, has just one chair and one mirror and offers no colors or perms, just professional cuts. Patrick Swayze, Michael Keaton, and Raquel Welch get clipped here. The cost is $250.

Holidays   See "Fast Facts: For the Foreign Traveler" in Chapter 3.

Hospitals   In an emergency, dial **911** from any phone. The Santa Monica Hospital Medical Center, 1250 16th St., Santa Monica (☎ 310/319-4000), is just one of many hospitals in the city. Ask at your hotel or check the front pages of a telephone directory for the hospital closest to you.

Information   See "Tourist Information" under "Orientation," earlier in this chapter.

Laundry/Dry Cleaning   Any major hotel can take care of these services for you, but allow two days for the job.

Library   Gutted by fire in 1986, the Los Angeles Central Library, 630 W. 5th St. (☎ 213/228-7000), reopened in 1993 to become the third largest in America. There's a park atop the library's 1¹/₂-acre parking garage.

Liquor Laws   Liquor and grocery stores can sell packaged alcoholic beverages between 6am and 2am. Most restaurants, nightclubs, and bars are licensed to serve alcoholic beverages during the same hours. The legal age for purchase and consumption is 21, and proof of age is required. In California you can purchase packaged liquor with your credit or charge card; however, most stores usually have a minimum dollar amount for charging.

Newspapers/Magazines   The *Los Angeles Times* is distributed throughout the country. Its Sunday "Calendar" section is an excellent and interesting guide to the world of entertainment in and around L.A., and includes listings of what's doing and where to do it. The free weekly events magazine *L.A. Weekly* is packed with news of events and a calendar of happenings around town. It's available from sidewalk newsracks and in many stores and restaurants around the city. Melrose News, at the corner of Melrose and Martel Avenues, is one of the city's best outdoor newsstands.

Photographic Needs   Photofinishing labs can be found in almost every shopping mall and on major streets around the city. Fromex, 406 Broadway, Santa Monica (☎ 310/395-5177), is one of southern California's largest developers.

Police   See "Emergencies," above. For nonemergency police matters, phone **213/485-2121** or, in Beverly Hills, **213/550-4951**.

Post Office   Post offices are located all over the city. Call **213/586-1467** to find the one closest to you.

Radio Stations   There are literally dozens of radio stations in L.A. FM classical music stations include KCSN (88.5), KCPB (91.1),

KUSC (91.5), and KKGO (105.1). Country music stations include KFOX (93.5), KIKF (94.3), and KFRG (95.1). Rock music stations include KUCI (88.9), KLOS (95.5), KLSX (97.1), and KROQ (106.7). The top AM news and information station is KNX (1070).

Religious Services Los Angeles has hundreds of churches and synagogues and at least 100 denominations, formal and informal. Should you be seeking a house of worship, your hotel desk person or bell captain can usually direct you to the nearest church of most any denomination.

Restrooms Stores rarely let customers use the restrooms, and many restaurants offer their facilities to customers only. But most malls have bathrooms, as do the ubiquitous fast-food restaurants. Many public beaches and large parks provide toilets, though in some places you have to pay or tip an attendant. If you have the time to find one, go into a large hotel. Most have well-stocked, clean restrooms in their lobbies.

Safety Innocent tourists rarely become victims of violent crime. Still, few locals would recommend walking alone late at night. South Central L.A., an inland area where tourists rarely venture, is the city's most infamous area. See Chapters 2 and 3 for additional safety tips.

Taxes The combined Los Angeles County and California state sales taxes amount to 8.25%; hotel taxes add another 14% to 17%.

Taxis See "Getting Around," earlier in this chapter.

Television Stations All the major networks and several independent stations are represented. They are KCBS, Channel 2; KNBC, Channel 4; KTLA, Channel 5; KABC, Channel 7; KCAL, Channel 9; KTTV (Fox), Channel 11; and KCOP, Channel 13.

Transit Information See "Getting Around," earlier in this chapter.

Useful Telephone Numbers Call for the correct time at **213/853-1212**.

Weather Call Los Angeles Weather Information (☎ **213/554-1212**) to find out that it will once again be 74°F. and sunny tomorrow.

3 Networks & Resources

FOR STUDENTS Students will find that their valid high school or college I.D. often entitles them to discounts at museums and other attractions, as well as at many bars during "college nights." When student prices are available, I have noted them in this book under the appropriate listing.

For additional information, contact the student affairs offices at the best-known universities in the Los Angeles area: The **University** of Southern California (USC) (☎ 213/740-5693) is a private university located on the corner of Exposition Drive and Figueroa Street downtown. California State University, Los Angeles (CSULA), 5151 State University Drive (☎ 213/343-3000), is largely a commuter school. The University of California, Los Angeles (UCLA), 405 Hilgard Ave. (☎ 310/825-7086), is located in Westwood, where there are many shops, coffee houses, restaurants, and bars all catering to students.

FOR GAY MEN & LESBIANS Like everything else in Los Angeles, the gay and lesbian community is spread throughout the city; you'll have to drive to get to bars, businesses, and other congregating places. The city's many gay-oriented publications are the best places to find out what's happening when you're there. Popular titles, available at most good newsstands, include *The Advocate,* a biweekly national magazine; *Frontiers,* a southern California–based biweekly serving the local community; and *Nightlife,* which offers good listings of entertainment places complete with maps.

A Different Light, 8853 Santa Monica Blvd., West Hollywood (☎ 310/854-6601), is Los Angeles's best gay bookshop; in fact, it's one of the largest of its kind on the West Coast.

See Chapter 10 for listings of clubs and bars that cater primarily to gays and lesbians.

FOR WOMEN Several Los Angeles women's bookstores are the best places in the city to get up-to-date information on feminist issues and happenings. Page One Bookstore, 966 N. Lake Ave., Pasadena (☎ 818/798-8694), is one of the best, selling feminist music, books by and for women, and tickets to women's events. Sisterhood Bookstore, 1351 Westwood Blvd. (☎ 310/477-7300), provides similar services in West Los Angeles.

FOR SENIORS Seniors aged 62 and older often receive discounts at attractions, museums, movies, and some restaurants. It can't hurt to ask if there is a senior price. You'd be surprised how often your proof of age will save you money during your travels in L.A.

FOR THE PHYSICALLY CHALLENGED The Los Angeles County Commission on Disabilities, 383 Hall of Administration, 500 W. Temple St., Los Angeles, CA 90012 (☎ 213/974-1053, or TDD 213/974-1707), publishes a free brochure listing services and facilities offered by the city's private- and public-sector agencies. Call or write for a copy.

FOR ETHNICALLY INTERESTED TRAVELERS The Los Angeles Convention and Visitors Bureau, Dept. CK, 633 W. 5th St., Suite 600, Los Angeles, CA 90071 (☎ 213/624-7300), distributes "Cultural Kaleidoscope Directories," booklets that list ethnically oriented attractions, shops, restaurants, and nightspots. The publications, at $2 per copy, are available in three editions—Asian and Pacific Islander, African-American, and Latino.

5

Los Angeles
Accommodations

Iɴ Lᴏs Aɴɢᴇʟᴇs, ʟᴏᴄᴀᴛɪᴏɴ ɪs ᴇᴠᴇʀʏᴛʜɪɴɢ. Wʜᴇɴ sᴇᴀʀᴄʜɪɴɢ ғᴏʀ ᴀ ʜᴏᴛᴇʟ here, think about the areas where you plan to spend most of your time and locate nearby. In sprawling Los Angeles no place is convenient to everything; wherever you stay, count on doing a lot of driving to somewhere else.

Generally, the most elegant accommodations are in Beverly Hills and Bel Air. For hard-core tourists, Hollywood is probably the most central place to stay. Businesspeople are more likely to prefer a downtown location. Santa Monica and Marina del Rey are great areas right on the beach; they are coolest in summer and trendiest year-round. Finally, families with kids might want to head straight to Anaheim or Buena Park in order to be close to the theme parks.

You'll notice that there are a disproportionate number of deluxe hostelries listed here—there are simply more of them in star-studded L.A. than in other cities. Budget inns in the city are few and far between. Nevertheless, they do exist, and I've described them below. Nearly all my selections quote daily rates, though the budget-conscious will find weekly prices lower at some hotels.

The prices listed below do not include state and city hotel taxes, which run from a whopping 14% to 17%. Be aware that most hotels make additional charges for parking (with in-and-out privileges, except where noted) and levy heavy surcharges for telephone use. Many have their own on-site health facilities. When they don't, they often have an arrangement with a nearby club, allowing you to use their facilities on a per-day basis. Charges are usually $8 to $15. Inquire about these extras before committing yourself.

Finally, even in the budget categories, all the following listings meet my pretty exacting standards of comfort and cleanliness.

There are so many hotels in Los Angeles—in every price range—that few regularly fill to capacity. Even during the height of the tourist season, you can usually drive right into the city and find decent accommodations fairly quickly. But be careful. If you really want a specific hotel, must have an ocean view, or want to be in an area where accommodations are somewhat scarce, you should book your room in advance.

Hotel-operated toll-free telephone numbers can also help you with your search. These "800" numbers will save you time and money when inquiring about rates and availability. Toll-free numbers (if offered) are listed below for each hotel. Some of the larger chains with hostelries in the Los Angeles area include Best Western (☎ 800/528-1234), Days Inn (☎ 800/325-2525), Holiday Inn (☎ 800/465-4329), Motel 6 (☎ 800/437-7486), Quality Inn (☎ 800/228-5151), Ramada Inn (☎ 800/272-6232), and Travelodge (☎ 800/255-3050).

To help you decide what accommodations are best for you, the hotels listed below are categorized first by area, then by price, according to the following guide: "Very Expensive," doubles for more than $160; "Expensive," $120 to $159; "Moderate," $80 to $119; "Inexpensive," $40 to $80; and "Budget," below $40. These categories reflect the price of an average double room during high season. Read it carefully. Many hotels also offer rooms at rates above and below the assigned price range. Unless otherwise specified, all rooms come with private bath.

The city's tourist season is loosely defined; it runs from about April through September. In general, hotel rates are rather inelastic; they don't vary much throughout the year. However, the recent economic sluggishness has led to small rate reductions throughout the city, and bargains and special packages are available. Ask about weekend discounts, corporate rates, and family plans.

1 Downtown Los Angeles

Very Expensive

Biltmore, 506 S. Grand Ave., Los Angeles, CA 90071.
☎ **213/624-1011,** or toll free 800/245-8673. Fax 213/612-1545. 700 rms, 40 suites. A/C MINIBAR TV TEL **Directions:** From U.S. 101, take the Grand Avenue exit; the hotel is located between 5th and 6th Streets.

Rates: $185–$275 single; $215–$275 double; from $325 suite. AE, CB, DC, MC, V. **Parking:** $18.

Built in 1923, this gracious and elegant hotel was the site of the Academy Awards ceremonies during the 1930s and 1940s, including the year *Gone with the Wind* swept them all. The always-beautiful Biltmore now looks better than ever following a $40-million facelift completed in 1987. Contemporary additions complement traditional styles, state-of-the-art door locks, and other mechanical systems.

Lavishly appointed rooms are spacious and attractively decorated in pastel tones. Modern marble bathrooms, color TVs, and in-room minibars are offset by traditional French furniture.

Frommer's Smart Traveler: Hotels

1. A hotel room is a perishable commodity; if it's not rented, there is no revenue. Always ask if a hotel has a lower rate, and make it clear that you're shopping around.

2. For the best rates, seek out business-oriented hotels on week ends and in the summer; and tourist-oriented bed-and-breakfasts during the off-season.

3. Ask about summer discounts, corporate rates, and special packages. Most hotel reservations offices won't tell you about promotional rates unless you ask.

4. Always inquire about parking and telephone charges. In Los Angeles, it could add $20 per night for your car and $1 per local call.

Dining/Entertainment: The grand Rendezvous Court serves afternoon tea and evening cocktails. Its ornate cathedral-like vaulted ceiling was hand-painted by Italian artist Giovanni Smeraldi. Bernard's, the hotel's top dining room, features fluted columns and hand-painted beamed ceilings. The cuisine combines classical French and regional American dishes. Smeraldi's Ristorante is open daily for breakfast, lunch, and dinner. The full-service dining room features homemade pastas and California cuisine with an Italian flair. The Grand Avenue Bar offers a cold lunch buffet, and showcases top-name jazz entertainment in the evening.

Services: 24-hour room service, concierge, evening turndown, overnight shoeshine.

Facilities: Health club (including Roman spa pool, steam room, sauna, Jacuzzi, Nautilus equipment, and free weights), business center.

Hyatt Regency Los Angeles, 711 S. Hope St., Los Angeles, CA 90017. ☎ **213/683-1234,** or toll free **800/233-1234.**
Fax 213/612-3179. 484 rms, 40 suites. A/C TV TEL
Directions: From Calif. 110, exit at 91 Street, turn left on Hope Street, and the hotel is on the corner of 7th and Hope Streets.

Rates: $129–$209 single; $174–$234 double; from $225 suite. AE, CB, DC, DISC, MC, V. **Parking:** $13.50.

The 24-story Hyatt Regency is a dazzlingly ultramodern fixture in Broadway Plaza, a 21st-century-style complex of shops, restaurants, offices, and galleries in the middle of downtown L.A. Topped by bright skylights, the two-story ground-floor lobby entrance has a garden plaza, lounges, a sidewalk café, and several boutiques. Wide escalators glide down to the lobby/reception area and lower gardens. Giant wall graphics and exposed brick surround potted plants, trees, old-fashioned gaslight streetlamps, and overstuffed furniture.

The hotel's guest rooms are of the same high comfort and unquestionable taste. Both innovative and attractive, the accommodations boast enormous windows that provide surprisingly nice views for a downtown hotel. Deep pile carpeting, oversize beds, and small sofas are all futuristic in design and utilize the same bold textures and russet-gold color scheme that's prevalent throughout the hotel.

Dining/Entertainment: Both the informal, lobby-level Brasserie and the more opulent Pavan restaurant are open for lunch and dinner Monday through Saturday. There is also the Lobby Bar.

Services: Room service, concierge, evening turndown.

Facilities: Fitness center, business center.

Los Angeles Hilton and Towers, 930 Wilshire Blvd., Los Angeles, CA 90017. ☎ **213/629-4321,** or toll free **800/445-8667.**
Fax 213/612-3987. 900 rms, 32 suites. A/C MINIBAR TV TEL
Directions: From Calif. 110 north, exit onto Wilshire Boulevard; the hotel is located at the corner of Figueroa Street.

Rates: $147–$177 single; $167–$197 double; from $375 suite. AE, CB, DC, MC, V. **Parking:** $16.50.

This hotel is centrally located, near many downtown attractions, and it offers easy access to major freeway entrances. The hotel's modern exterior is matched by equally modern rooms outfitted with comfortable furnishings colored in soft shades. Like other Hiltons, this is a business-oriented hotel, offering a good, if unremarkable, standard of service. Furnishings are contemporary and clean; such amenities as in-house movies, a writing desk, and double-panel glass windows to minimize outside noise are also included. No-smoking rooms are available, as are those specially equipped for disabled guests. The best rooms overlook the oval swimming pool, where there are poolside tables for drinking and dining.

The premium Towers rooms—on the 15th and 16th floors—have separate check-in facilities and a dedicated staff. Premium rates include a two-line telephone, morning newspaper delivery, continental breakfast, and a daily cocktail hour with complimentary hors d'oeuvres.

Dining/Entertainment: There are four hotel restaurants. The Gazebo Coffee Shop serves breakfast and burgers daily from 6am to 11pm; the City Grill, open for lunch only, specializes in California cuisine; and Minami of Tokyo serves Japanese breakfasts, lunches, and dinners. Cardini, a northern Italian restaurant, is the hotel's top eatery and offers good pastas, as well as a good selection of fish and veal dishes.

Services: Room service.

Facilities: Fitness center, pool, car rental, tour desk, beauty salon.

★ **New Otani Hotel and Garden,** 120 S. Los Angeles St., Los Angeles, CA 90012. ☎ **213/629-1200,** or toll free **800/421-8795, 800/273-2294** in California. Fax 213/622-0980. 434 rms, 15 suites. A/C MINIBAR TV TEL **Directions:** From U.S. 101, take the Los Angeles Street exit south to the corner of 1st Street.

Rates: $145–$205 single; $170–$230 double; from $340 Japanese-style suite. AE, CB, DC, MC, V. **Parking:** $11.

This 21-story triangular tower is the city's only Japanese-style hotel; its classical 16,000-square-foot tea garden is for the exclusive use of guests. Most of the luxurious rooms are Western in style and are furnished with refrigerators, oversize beds, bathroom telephones and radios, and individual doorbells. For a special treat, choose a Japanese-style suite, with tatami-mat bedrooms, deep whirlpool baths, and balconies overlooking the hotel garden.

Dining/Entertainment: The Canary Garden is an informal coffee shop serving breakfast, lunch, and dinner (fresh-baked breads and pastries are a specialty). Commodore Perry's, named for the infamous naval officer who forced Japan to open trade with the West, features American and continental specialties in an intimate setting. A Thousand Cranes is the evocative name of the Otani's Japanese restaurant, which serves traditional breakfasts, lunches, and dinners, including sushi.

Services: 24-hour room service, concierge, evening turndown, same-day valet cleaning.

Facilities: Japanese-style health club (with saunas, baths, and shiatsu massages), shopping arcade with more than 30 shops, car-rental desk, airport limousine service. Golf and tennis are available in conjunction with a nearby country club.

Sheraton Grande, 333 S. Figueroa St., Los Angeles, CA 90012.
☎ **213/617-1133**, or toll free **800/325-3535.** Fax 213/613-0291.
469 rms, 69 suites. A/C MINIBAR TV TEL **Directions:** From Calif.
110 (Pasadena Freeway), exit onto Wilshire Boulevard and turn left onto Figueroa Street; the hotel is located between 3rd and 4th Streets.
Rates: $165–$210 single; $200–$235 double; from $275 suite. AE, CB, DC, DISC, MC, V. **Parking:** $17.

One of downtown's newest hotels, the Sheraton Grande is a splendid smoky-mirrored-glass structure located right in the heart of the hustle. The large open lobby and lounge are decorated with skylights and plants. A pianist entertains in the lounge daily from noon to 10:30pm.

Pastel-colored guest rooms are well lit and outfitted with the usual furnishings, including a writing desk, minibar, color TV, and firm mattresses. Bathrooms are equally functional, featuring good-quality fittings and hotel-quality Italian marble.

Dining/Entertainment: The Back Porch, an informal dining room overlooking the pool, serves three meals a day. The gourmet room, Ravel, features California cuisine nightly.

Services: 24-hour room service, concierge, evening turndown, overnight shoeshine.

Facilities: Four movie theaters, heated outdoor pool and sun deck, access to an off-premises health club.

Westin Bonaventure, 404 S. Figueroa St., Los Angeles, CA 90071.
☎ **213/624-1000**, or toll free **800/228-3000.** Fax 213/612-4800.
1,500 rms, 94 suites. A/C MINIBAR TV TEL **Directions:** From Calif. 110 (Pasadena Freeway), exit onto Wilshire Boulevard and turn left onto Figueroa Street; the hotel is located between 4th and 5th Streets.
Rates: $150–$195 single; $175–$215 double; from $335 suite. AE, CB, DC, MC, V. **Parking:** $18.

One of California's most innovative hotels, the space-age Westin Bonaventure is known for its five gleaming cylindrical towers, which constitute one of downtown's most distinctive landmarks. Designed by architect John Portman (who also designed San Francisco's Hyatt Regency), the Westin features a beautiful six-story skylight lobby that houses a large lake, trees, splashing fountains, and gardens. Twelve glass-enclosed elevators appear to rise from the reflecting pools.

The best city views are available from the highest guest rooms in this 35-story hotel. Like the lobby, accommodations are elegantly modernistic, complete with floor-to-ceiling windows and every amenity you'd expect at a top big-city hotel. It's even nice to know that despite the hotel's large size, no bedroom is more than six doors from an elevator.

Dining/Entertainment: The Sidewalk Cafe, a California bistro, and the adjacent Lobby Court, with tables under large fringed umbrellas, are the focus of the hotel's nightly entertainment, which varies from jazz combos to cocktail-hour music, and dancing. The Flower Street Bar, a mixture of marble, brass, and mahogany, is a popular spot for cocktails.

The Top of Five rooftop restaurant features panoramic views and gourmet continental cuisine. A revolving cocktail lounge, the Bona Vista, is located just below, on the 34th floor. Beaudry's, on the lobby level, features haute cuisine in a stunning contemporary setting.

Services: 24-hour room service, concierge, evening turndown, overnight shoeshine.

Facilities: Outdoor pool and sun deck, tennis courts, health club, five levels of shops and boutiques (which comprise the Shopping Gallery above the lobby), car-rental desk.

Inexpensive

$ The Kawada Hotel, 200 S. Hill St., Los Angeles, CA 90012. ☎ **213/621-4455,** or toll free **800/752-9232.** Fax 213/687-4455. 116 rms, 1 suite. A/C TV TEL **Directions:** From Calif. 110, exit at 4th Street, turn left on Broadway, left on 2nd Street, and left again on Hill Street; the hotel is on the corner of Hill and 2nd Streets.

Rates: $62–$75 single; $74–$80 double; $145 suite. AE, DISC, MC, V. **Parking:** $6.60.

This pretty, well-kept, and tightly managed hotel is a pleasant oasis in the otherwise gritty heart of downtown L.A. Behind the three-story, clean red-brick exterior can be found almost 10 dozen pristine rooms, all with handy kitchenettes and simple rose-colored furnishings. Although the rooms are not large, they're extremely functional, providing both VCRs with complimentary movie rentals and two phones. No-smoking rooms are available.

The hotel's popular lobby-level Epicentre restaurant features an eclectic international menu, and is open for breakfast, lunch, and dinner.

Hotel Stillwell, 838 S. Grand Ave., Los Angeles, CA 90017. ☎ **213/627-1151,** or toll free **800/553-4774.** Fax 213/622-8940. 250 rms. A/C TV TEL **Directions:** From U.S. 101, exit at Grand Avenue; the hotel is located between 8th and 9th Streets.

Rates: $35–$45 single; $45–$60 double. AE, DC, MC, V. **Parking:** $5.

Conveniently situated in the downtown area, the hotel is close to the Civic Center's Ahmanson Theater and Dorothy Chandler Pavilion. It's also close to the Museum of Contemporary Art, Little Tokyo, Olvera Street, Union Station, and a variety of exceptional restaurants.

The decently decorated rooms include no-smoking accommodations and larger rooms for guests traveling with children. The simple yet comfortable facilities are decorated in soft blue and gray tones.

It's not a fancy place, but the Stillwell is relatively clean and a good choice for modestly priced accommodations in an otherwise expensive neighborhood.

There are two restaurants on the premises: Gills Cuisine of India, serving competent northern Indian dishes; and Hank's American Grill, offering simple American meals. There's also a business center and tour desk.

2   Hollywood

Very Expensive

⭐ **Le Bel Age Hotel de Grande Classe,** 1020 N. San Vicente Blvd., West Hollywood, CA 90069. ☎ **310/854-1111,** or toll free **800/434-4443.** Fax 310/854-0926. 188 suites. A/C MINIBAR TV TEL **Directions:** From I-405, exit onto Santa Monica Boulevard and continue east about 4$^{1}/_{2}$ miles; turn left onto San Vicente Boulevard and the hotel will be on your right.

Rates: $195–$335 single or double; $500 suite. AE, CB, DC, MC, V. **Parking:** $14.

One of the darlings of the hip record and film industry crowd, this luxurious all-suite hotel is as opulent as it is pretentious. The hotel's most notable attribute is its vast collection of quality contemporary oil paintings and collages, which are liberally spread throughout the lobby, hallways, and guest rooms.

Dark wood, large retro sofas and chairs, and balcony patio furniture complete the art-filled suites. Extras in every suite include pay-for-view movies, hairdryers, terry-cloth robes, multiline telephones, and milled soaps, lotions, and shampoos. Guests are welcomed with mineral water and a fruit basket upon arrival. Rooms facing the neighboring Hollywood foothills are nice, but accommodations on the other side have an even better view of the city and the valley.

Dining/Entertainment: The Diaghilev Restaurant serves Franco-Russian dinners Tuesday through Saturday from 6:30pm. The Brasserie, which is less formal, serves California cuisine in dining rooms with great views of the city. The Brasserie bar regularly features top-notch jazz performers, and is one of the prettiest drinking rooms in the neighborhood.

Services: 24-hour room service, concierge, complimentary shoeshine, business services.

Facilities: Rooftop pool and Jacuzzi, fitness room, hair salon, gift shop, art gallery, florist.

Sunset Marquis Hotel and Villas, 1200 N. Alta Loma Rd., West Hollywood, CA 90069. ☎ **310/657-1333,** or toll free **800/858-9758.** Fax 310/652-5300. 9 rms, 96 suites, 12 villas. TV TEL **Directions:** From U.S. 101, exit onto Sunset Boulevard west, then turn left onto North Alta Loma Road, one block past La Cienega Boulevard.

Accommodations in
Beverly Hills, Hollywood & Downtown

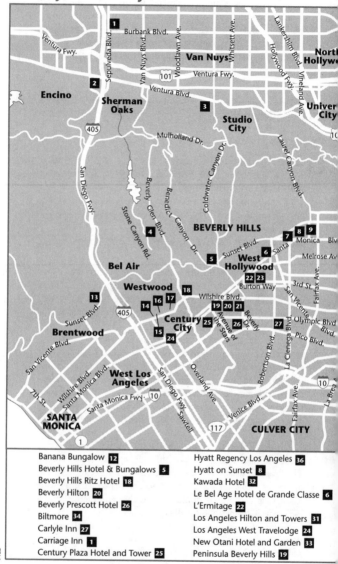

Banana Bungalow **12**	Hyatt Regency Los Angeles **36**
Beverly Hills Hotel & Bungalows **5**	Hyatt on Sunset **8**
Beverly Hills Ritz Hotel **18**	Kawada Hotel **32**
Beverly Hilton **20**	Le Bel Age Hotel de Grande Classe **6**
Beverly Prescott Hotel **26**	L'Ermitage **22**
Biltmore **34**	Los Angeles Hilton and Towers **31**
Carlyle Inn **27**	Los Angeles West Travelodge **24**
Carriage Inn **1**	New Otani Hotel and Garden **33**
Century Plaza Hotel and Tower **25**	Peninsula Beverly Hills **19**

Rates: $215–$295 single or double; from $430 two-bedroom suite; from $450 villa. AE, DC, MC, V. **Parking:** Free.

Two things make the Sunset Marquis special: Its villas and its clientele. This is the ultimate music-industry hostelry, regularly hosting the biggest names in rock. Musicians and their hangers-on stay here while recording in the city. Sometimes they even record in the hotel's

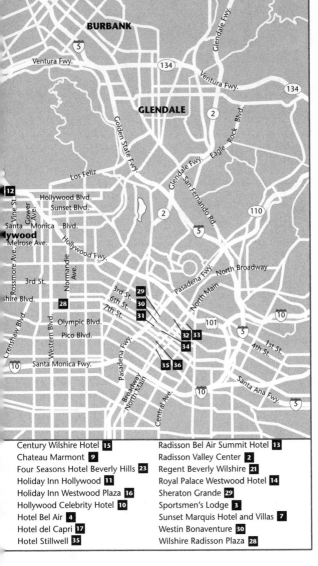

basement studios, then retire to the lobby bar, where their session can be piped-in directly.

The hotel's standard rooms are outfitted in traditional motel style—neither the bedrooms nor the baths are particularly special. But each comes with an adjoining sitting area, outfitted with a VCR and a good-size refrigerator. The villas represent a totally different level of quality: These free-standing cottages overlooking 3 acres of rolling grounds are top of the line, featuring wooden floors; sunken living rooms; opulent baths; canopied beds; and even grand pianos and fireplaces, with private saunas, steam rooms, or Jacuzzis.

Dining/Entertainment: Notes, a small Mediterranean restaurant with California influences, serves either indoors or poolside. The Whiskey, the hotel's lobby bar, is one of the most exclusive rooms in Hollywood. Rock 'n' rollers like Mick Jagger, Axel Rose, and Robert Plant turn the bar into a celebrity-fest Wednesday through Saturday nights. Unless you're staying at the hotel, you'll probably never get in.

Services: 24-hour full-menu room service, concierge, business services, overnight laundry.

Facilities: Two pools, health facilities, sauna, Jacuzzi.

Expensive

⭐ **Chateau Marmont,** 8221 Sunset Blvd., West Hollywood, CA 90046. ☎ **213/656-1010,** or toll free **800/242-8328.** Fax 213/655-5311. 63 rms, 53 suites. A/C TV TEL **Directions:** From U.S. 101, exit onto Highland Avenue and turn right onto Sunset Boulevard; the hotel is located between La Cienega and Crescent Heights Boulevards, at Marmont Lane.

Rates: $160 single or double; from $210 suite; from $495 bungalow. AE, CB, DC, MC, V.

There isn't enough space here to list all the famous people who have stayed at this chateau-style apartment hotel situated on a cliff just above Sunset Strip. Humphrey Bogart, Jeanne Moreau, Boris Karloff, Al Pacino, James Taylor, Richard Gere, Bianca Jagger, John Lennon and Yoko Ono, Sophia Loren, Sidney Poitier, and Whoopi Goldberg are just a few famous former guests. Carol Channing met her husband here, Greta Garbo used to check in under the name Harriet Brown, and even Howard Hughes once maintained a suite here.

Now a historical monument, the hotel was built in 1927. It mimics the architectural style of the French Normandy region and is surrounded by private gardens with views of the city and the Hollywood hills. Chateau Marmont is famous for its privacy and personal attention, not to mention its magnificently stocked wine cellar.

Guests often gather in the great baronial living room furnished with local antiques. On warm days, you might lounge around the oval swimming pool amid semitropical trees and shrubbery. Guest rooms are beautifully furnished in a tasteful English style. Suites have fully equipped kitchens, and most pets are welcome.

Services: Room service, concierge, twice-daily maid service.

Facilities: Pool, fitness room.

Hyatt on Sunset, 8401 Sunset Blvd., West Hollywood, CA 90069. ☎ **213/656-1234,** or toll free **800/233-1234.** Fax 213/650-7024. 262 rms. A/C TV TEL **Directions:** From U.S. 101, exit onto Highland Avenue and turn right onto Sunset Boulevard; the hotel is located two blocks east of La Cienega Boulevard.

Rates: $119–$135 single; $144–$160 double; $350–$550 suite. Special weekend rates available. AE, CB, DC, DISC, MC, V. **Parking:** $7 self-parking, $10 valet.

This lively place is well located: close to Restaurant Row on La Cienega Boulevard and to Sunset Strip nightlife. Spacious bedrooms on 13 floors have views of the Los Angeles skyline and the Hollywood hills; most have private balconies. Rooms have modern furnishings and dressing areas, plus all the conveniences you'd expect from a Hyatt, including in-room movies on color TVs and large, modern bathrooms.

Dining/Entertainment: The Silver Screen Restaurant pays homage to the old days of Hollywood. Giant stills from old movies surround ancient movie cameras and lights. Meals are served daily from 6:30 to 11am and 5 to 11pm. The Sports Bar and Deli serves sandwiches and pastas daily. In addition to a full bar the deli has a large-screen TV with five monitors and a pool table.

Services: Room service, concierge.

Facilities: Rooftop pool, sun deck, business center, gift shop.

Moderate

Holiday Inn, 1755 N. Highland Ave., Hollywood, CA 90028. ☎ **213/462-7181,** or toll free **800/465-4329.** Fax 213/466-9072. 470 rms, 22 suites. A/C TV TEL **Directions:** From U.S. 101, take the Franklin Avenue exit and head west; at Highland Avenue, turn left and the hotel is located between Franklin and Hollywood Boulevards.

Rates: $100–$145 single or double; from $135 suite. Additional person $10 extra. Children 18 and under stay free in parents' room. AE, DC, DISC, MC, V. **Parking:** $5.50.

This 22-story hostelry in the heart of Old Hollywood offers perfectly acceptable rooms that are both pleasant and comfortable. Each room is equipped with a clock radio and a digital safe. There are three laundry rooms and on every floor ice and soda machines. Suites here are a particularly good buy, since they include a small kitchenette that can help you save on restaurant meals. There's a pool and sun deck on the hotel's second floor.

A revolving circular rooftop restaurant, called Windows on Hollywood, features great Hollywood views while dancing and dining. The Show Biz Café, an unusually plush coffee shop, serves breakfast, lunch, and dinner. The Front Row Lounge, an intimate cocktail lounge, is open daily until 2am.

Inexpensive

Hollywood Celebrity Hotel, 1775 Orchid Ave., Hollywood, CA 90028. ☎ **213/850-6464,** or toll free **800/222-7017, 800/222-7090** in California. Fax 213/850-7667. 38 rms. A/C TV TEL **Directions:** From U.S. 101, take the Highland Avenue exit, turn right onto Hollywood Boulevard, then take the first right onto Orchid Avenue.

Rates (including continental breakfast): $55 single; $60–$65 double. Additional person $8 extra. AE, CB, DC, DISC, MC, V. **Parking:** Free.

One of the best budget buys in Hollywood is this small but centrally located hotel, just half a block behind Mann's Chinese Theatre. Spacious and comfortable units are decorated in an original art deco style. Breakfast is brought to your room along with the morning newspaper. Each room has cable TV and a radio. Small pets are allowed but require a $50 deposit.

Budget

Banana Bungalow, 2775 Cahuenga Blvd., West Hollywood, CA 90068. ☎ **213/851-1129,** or toll free **800/4-HOSTEL.** Fax 213/851-2022. 200 beds, 25 doubles. **Directions:** From U.S. 101, take the Cahuenga Boulevard exit and drive north to the hostel.

Rates: $40 double; $15 per person in multibed room. MC, V. **Parking:** Free.

Price notwithstanding, if you're under 35, Banana Bungalow is probably the most fun place to stay in all of Los Angeles. Nestled in a little Hollywood Hills valley, a short drive from the Walk of Fame and Universal Studios, the Bungalow has double and multishare rooms, kitchen facilities, a restaurant, a lounge, an outdoor pool, a movie theater, and an arcade/games room. International guests always seem to be looking for a good time, and the atmosphere is always upbeat. The hostel offers free airport pickup and regular excursions to the beach, Disneyland, and other Los Angeles–area destinations.

3   Beverly Hills & Century City

Very Expensive

⭐ **Beverly Hills Hotel & Bungalows,** 9641 Sunset Blvd., Beverly Hills, CA 90210. ☎ **310/276-2251,** or toll free **800/283-8885.** Fax 310/271-0319. 268 rms, 21 bungalows and garden suites. A/C TV TEL **Directions:** From I-405, exit at Sunset Boulevard and drive east; the hotel is located on the corner of Sunset Boulevard and Rodeo Drive.

Rates: $185–$295 single; $230–$320 double; from $395 suite; from $545 bungalow. AE, DC, MC, V. **Parking:** $15.

This is the real stomping ground of millionaires and maharajahs, jet-setters and movie stars. There are hundreds of anecdotes about this famous hotel, most of which took place in the hotel's Polo Lounge, one of the world's most glamorous bars. For years Howard Hughes maintained a complex of bungalows, suites, and rooms here, using some of the facilities for an elaborate electronic-communications security system, and a separate room to house his personal food-taster. Years ago Katharine Hepburn did a flawless dive into the pool—fully clad in her tennis outfit, shoes and all. Dean

Martin and Frank Sinatra once got into a big fistfight with other Polo Lounge habitués. And in 1969 John Lennon and Yoko Ono checked into the most secluded bungalow under assumed names, then stationed so many armed guards around their little hideaway that discovery was inevitable. So it goes. The stories are endless and relate to everyone from Charlie Chaplin to Madame Chiang Kai-shek.

What attracts them all? For one thing, each other. And, of course, you can't beat the service—not just the catering to such eccentricities as a preference for bear steak, but little things like being greeted by your name every time you pick up the phone. It doesn't hurt that the Beverly Hills Hotel is a beauty; its green and pink stucco buildings are set on 12 carefully landscaped and lushly planted acres. There are winding paths lined with giant palm trees throughout, and the privacy of each veranda is protected by flowering and leafy foliage.

Each gorgeous accommodation is custom-designed with tropical overtones and equipped with every amenity from hairdryers to in-room VCRs.

Dining/Entertainment: The world-famous Polo Lounge has been the rendezvous headquarters of international society for more than 40 years. The Loggia and Patio (which adjoin the Polo Lounge) serve breakfast and lunch in a delightful garden setting.

Services: 24-hour room service, concierge, evening turndown, overnight laundry, shoeshine.

Facilities: Olympic-size pool, cabanas, two tennis courts, fitness room, Cinema Room for private screenings.

Beverly Hilton, 9876 Wilshire Blvd., Beverly Hills, CA 90210. ☎ **310/274-7777,** or toll free **800/445-8667.** Fax 310/285-1313. 581 rms, 90 suites. A/C MINIBAR TV TEL **Directions:** From I-405 north, exit onto Santa Monica Boulevard and go east three miles to the hotel at Wilshire Boulevard.

Rates: $200–$240 single; $225–$265 double; from $300 suite. Additional person $25 extra. Children and teens stay free in parents' room. AE, CB, DC, DISC, MC, V. **Parking:** $15.

Easily one of the poshest in the Hilton chain, this luxuriously decorated hotel is like a mini-city, complete with a small shopping mall and several restaurants, making it unnecessary to leave the premises.

Individually decorated rooms are full of amenities, including refrigerators and in-room, first-run movies. Most rooms have balconies that overlook an Olympic-size pool and the surrounding hillsides. The more expensive rooms are on higher floors.

Dining/Entertainment: L'Escoffier, the rooftop restaurant, combines gourmet French cuisine with a panoramic view of the city. It's open for dinner Tuesday through Saturday. The award-winning Trader Vic's sports a nautical theme and serves South Seas and continental dishes along with exotic drinks.

Mr. H, another elegant continental-style eatery is known for its Sunday champagne brunch and daily lunch and dinner buffets. The Cafe Beverly and the lively Lobby Bar round out the offerings.

Services: 24-hour room service, concierge, evening turndown, overnight shoeshine.

Facilities: Two heated pools, health club, business center, shops (including Princess Ermine Jewels, Cecily L. boutique, and a gift and sundry shop).

Century Plaza Hotel and Tower, Ave. of the Stars, Century City, CA 90067. ☎ 310/277-2000, or toll free 800/228-3000. Fax 310/551-3355. 996 rms, 76 suites. A/C TV TEL Directions: From Santa Monica Boulevard, exit south onto the Avenue of the Stars; the hotel is two blocks ahead on your left.

Rates: Hotel, $130–$165 single; $130–$190 double; from $250 suite. Tower, $170–$200 single; $170–$220 double; from $900 suite. AE, CB, DC, MC, V. **Parking:** $10 self-parking, $16 valet.

The imposing Century Plaza Hotel and Tower complex is comprised of two separate and distinctive properties on 10 tropical plant–covered acres. Occupying a commanding position near Beverly Hills and right across the street from the ABC Entertainment Center and the 1,850-seat Schubert Theater, the Westin-managed hotel was built on what was once a Twentieth-Century-Fox back lot.

The 20-story, 750-room hotel is enormous—it appears to be roughly the size of New York's Grand Central Terminal—complete with vaulted cathedral ceilings, two-story windows, and sunken lounge areas. It has the feel of a bustling city of tomorrow. Rooms follow a garden motif with marble-topped oak furnishings and beautiful teal-blue or forest-green carpeting. Each has a balcony and is equipped with every amenity, including a color TV discreetly hidden in an oak armoire; three phones (bedside, tableside, and bath); a refrigerator; an AM/FM radio; a clock; a big closet; and a tub/shower bath with marble sink, hairdryers, oversize towels, and scales. Special hotel extras range from a dedicated kitchen elevator in which food is kept warm on its way to your room, to the homey practice of leaving a mint and a good-night note from the management on each guest's pillow when the beds are turned down for the night.

The 30-story, $85-million Tower at Century Plaza (where former President Reagan once stayed) has 322 exceptionally spacious rooms—that's only 14 rooms per floor. All have private balconies; a wet bar and refrigerator; three conveniently located phones; and an all-marble bath with separate soak tub and shower, double vanity and washbasins, and a heat lamp. Writing desks have travertine marble tops, and there's a live tree or green plant in each room. All Tower guests receive a complimentary newspaper each morning, as well as such deluxe bath amenities as robes, slippers, and oversize bath towels. Tower suites are all fitted with marble Jacuzzis.

The Tower and Hotel are linked by a marble corridor hung with more than $4 million worth of art. The property underwent a $16.5-million renovation in 1990.

Dining/Entertainment: The Lobby Court cocktail lounge features nightly entertainment and is surrounded by two-story windows that overlook the hotel's pools and garden. La Chaumière restaurant blends contemporary California ingredients and classic French techniques to produce an innovative cuisine in a setting reminiscent of a fine European club. The Terrace is an excellent choice for Mediterranean and classic California dining. Filled with greenery and located on the lobby level, it serves breakfast, lunch, and dinner daily, as well as a champagne brunch on Sunday. The Cafe Plaza, a provincial-style coffee shop with a simple bakery, deli, and charcuterie, is open from 6am to 1am.

Services: 24-hour room service, concierge, evening turndown, business center, multilingual staff, same-day laundry, complimentary car service to and from Beverly Hills.

Facilities: Two large outdoor heated pools, three Jacuzzis, a children's pool, 10 shops, airline desk, car-rental office, ticket agency, tour desk, free access to an off-premises health club.

Four Seasons Hotel Beverly Hills, 300 S. Doheny Dr., Los Angeles, CA 90048. ☎ **310/273-2222.** Fax 310/859-3824. 179 rms, 106 suites. A/C MINIBAR TV TEL **Directions:** From Santa Monica Boulevard, exit onto Wilshire Boulevard east, then turn north onto Doheny Drive; the hotel is on your right, at the corner of Burton Way.

Rates: $280–$330 single; $310–$360 double; from $430 suite. AE, DC, MC, V. **Parking:** Free self-parking, $8 valet.

As the world's superintendent of traditionalist wealth, the ultraconservative 16-story Four Seasons can always be counted on for im-peccable service and standards. On the plus side, this means intense attention to detail, butlers on 24-hour call, and high-quality furnishings and food. On the minus side, it means muted beiges and browns, dull designs chosen for their inability to offend, and doting saccharine service.

The hotel is expensive and attractive to both the old and the new kind of rich. The dated decor includes firm king-size beds and three two-line telephones. French doors in each room lead to a private balcony. European art hangs throughout the hotel, and marble baths are fitted with telephones, hairdryers, robes, and miniature TVs. They contain only a single sink, however, and rooms are devoid of stereos or VCRs—accoutrements that are increasingly common in more cutting edge hotels.

Dining/Entertainment: The Gardens Restaurant serves three California-inspired meals daily. In addition to light meals, Windows is open daily for cocktails and afternoon tea on Saturday from 3 to 4pm. The less formal Cafe, open all day, offers afternoon tea during the week from 3 to 4:30pm.

Services: 24-hour room service, concierge, overnight laundry, complimentary shoeshine, twice-daily maid service.

Facilities: Pool, Jacuzzi, workout facilities, gift shop, florist, car-rental desk.

★ **L'Ermitage,** 9291 Burton Way, Beverly Hills, CA 90210.
☎ **213/278-3344,** or toll free **800/424-4443.** Fax 213/278-8247.
112 suites. A/C MINIBAR TV TEL **Directions:** From Santa Monica
Boulevard, exit onto Burton Way; the hotel is located 10 blocks
ahead, at the corner of Maple Drive.

Rates: $285–$325 one-bedroom executive suite; $385–$475
one-bedroom town-house suite; $455–$625 two-bedroom town-house
suite; $1,000 three-bedroom town-house suite. AE, CB, DC, MC, V.
Parking: $14.

L'Ermitage is one of the finest hotels in the world. In addition to a
kitchenette, each of the small suites includes a sunken living room,
wet bar, dressing area, and powder room. Town-house suites are
slightly larger and have fully equipped kitchens. Accommodations
here are furnished like rooms in a fine home. The rooms and hallways are hung with oil paintings, and every unit has a fireplace.

Strawberries and brown sugar are delivered to each suite at 4pm,
and complimentary caviar is served each afternoon in the elegant bar
on the top floor.

Dining/Entertainment: The Club restaurant, which is hung with
original paintings by Renoir, Braque, and de la Peña, caters exclu-
sively to hotel guests.

Services: 24-hour room service, concierge, overnight shoeshine,
limousine service, morning newspaper.

Facilities: Rooftop garden, mineral spa, heated pool, private
solarium.

The Peninsula Beverly Hills, 9882 Santa Monica Blvd., Beverly
Hills, CA 90212. ☎ **310/551-2888,** or toll free **800/462-7899.**
Fax 310/788-2319. 162 rms, 48 suites. A/C MINIBAR TV TEL
Directions: From I-405, exit onto Santa Monica Boulevard east; the
hotel is located about two miles ahead, at the corner of Wilshire
Boulevard.

Frommer's Cool for Kids: Hotels

Century Plaza Hotel and Tower   (see p. 80) Although it's not
inexpensive, older children will love exploring this labyrinthine
hotel, which features two large outdoor heated swimming pools,
three Jacuzzis, and a children's pool. Kids are given free amenity
packs filled with games, crayons, coloring books, and an inflat-
able beach ball.

Loews Santa Monica Beach Hotel   (see p. 94) One of the few
beachfront hotels in Los Angeles, it offers a complete children's
program during summer. For $25 per day, kids are treated to tours,
classes, and activities monitored by a trained staff.

Hotel Stillwell   (see p. 72) Ask for one of their larger guest rooms
and the kids will have plenty of room for romping. It's an inexpensive hotel in an otherwise pricey neighborhood.

Rates: $280–$425 single or double; from $500 suite. AE, CB, DC, DISC, MC, V. **Parking:** $17.

Los Angeles loves successful newcomers, and this monied recent arrival quickly found wide acceptance with Beverly Hills's fresh-face seekers. The Peninsula is a very good hotel that strives to be more personalized than most top-of-the-line business-oriented properties. Fronted by a flower-hedged circular motorcourt, the squat French Renaissance–style structure houses a small but elegant lobby as well as most of the hotel's rooms and suites.

Like the hotel itself, guest rooms are decorated in a residential style and feature French doors, marble baths, two-line voicemail telephones, and ample closet space. Suites, many located in five surrounding two-story villas, are particularly nice and feature fireplaces, spas, and terraces.

Additional attractions include a heated rooftop lap pool and a spa that includes body treatments, saunas, and steam rooms.

Dining/Entertainment: The Belvedere Restaurant serves heavy continental-style meals all day. Afternoon tea and cocktails are served daily in the lobby-level Living Room. Light lunches are served seasonally in the Roof Garden. The Club Bar serves cocktails in a, well, clublike setting.

Services: 24-hour room service, 24-hour concierge, business center, overnight dry cleaning, courtesy Rolls-Royce service in the area.

Facilities: Lap pool, weight and exercise rooms, steam room, sauna, whirlpool, sundry shop.

★ **Regent Beverly Wilshire,** 9500 Wilshire Blvd., Beverly Hills, CA 90210. ☎ **310/275-5200,** or toll free **800/421-4354.** Fax 310/274-2851. 300 rms, 144 suites. A/C TV TEL
Directions: From Santa Monica Boulevard, exit onto Wilshire Boulevard and continue east eight blocks to the hotel.

Rates: $255–$315 standard single or double; $335–$405 deluxe single or double; from $425 suite. Additional person $30 extra. Children under 15 stay free in parents' room. AE, CB, DC, DISC, MC, V. **Parking:** $15.

This grand Beverly Hills hotel has long attracted international royalty, media celebrities, stage personalities, presidents, and the usual smattering of rich and famous. Parts of *Pretty Woman,* with Richard Gere and Julia Roberts, were filmed here. The spacious lobby contains French Empire (Directoire) furnishings, French and Italian marble flooring, restored bronze and crystal chandeliers, handwrought sconces, and two paintings by Verhoven.

Upon arrival, visitors are greeted by a guest-relations officer who personally escorts you to your room; luggage is recorded by computer and arrives by a separate elevator. There is steward service on every floor (a concept that began with the Regent's Hong Kong hostelry), as well as 24-hour concierge service.

El Camino Real, a private cobblestone and gas lamp street, separates the Beverly and Wilshire wings of the hotel. On average, guest rooms here are larger than those in comparable hotels. Wilshire Wing rooms are largest, but many on the Beverly side are prettier, with balconies overlooking the pool area. Every room is beautifully appointed with a mix of period furniture, three telephones, three cable color TVs, and special double-glazed windows that ensure absolute quiet.

The baths, lined with marble, feature a large vanity, excellent lighting, deep soaking tubs, and a separate glass-enclosed shower that's large enough for three or more. Amenities include fresh flowers in each room, plush deep-pile white bathrobes, scales, hairdryers, and specially packaged toiletries.

Dining/Entertainment: The Café, an elegant, updated version of the old-fashioned soda fountain, serves lox and eggs, cheese blintzes, sandwiches, salads, and changing daily main courses. It's open from 6am to midnight. The Lobby Lounge is an elegant European-style salon for tea (served from 3 to 5pm), light menus, late-night dinner fare, and cocktails—a place "to be seen." There's live entertainment in the evening. The Dining Room, outfitted in lush woods and soft fabrics, offers a lengthy list of elegant American lunch and dinner fare. Reservations are recommended.

Services: 24-hour room service, concierge, evening turndown, overnight shoeshine.

Facilities: Health club, pool, hot tubs, massage, business center, shops (including Escada and Buccellati).

Expensive

Beverly Prescott Hotel, 1224 S. Beverwil Dr. (P.O. Box 3065), Beverly Hills, CA 90212. ☎ **310/277-2800,** or toll free **800/421-3212.** Fax 310/203-9537. 128 rms, 12 suites. A/C TV TEL **Directions:** From I-405, exit east onto Pico Boulevard, continue about two miles, then turn left onto Beverwil Drive.

Rates: $145–$195 single or double; from $250 suite. AE, DC, DISC, MC, V. **Parking:** $12.

After a multimillion-dollar renovation that rendered the former Beverly Hillcrest Hotel unrecognizable, the Beverly Prescott opened its doors in 1993 and garnered raves from all quarters. Managed by the Kimpton Group, owners of about a dozen high-quality "boutique" hotels in San Francisco, the Prescott is knowledgeably run and joyfully decorated, with comfortable, colorful, funky furnishings carefully chosen by a confident designer. The Prescott's distinctiveness begins in the lobby, where an alluring sitting area is made particularly inviting with mixed-print plush furnishings surrounding a working fireplace.

Rooms are decorated in salmon and cream stripes or black and tan checks, each accentuated with bright bedspreads and pillows. An emphasis on details means oversize TV screens, remote phones with up to three lines, and dimmer switches on most lights. Suites are fitted with down comforters, and most come with VCRs. Every room has a private balcony with good city views. All in all, the Beverly Prescott represents one of the best deals in town.

Dining/Entertainment: Röx, the lobby-level restaurant owned by celebrity chef Hans Röckenwagner, serves top-quality meals either indoors or out (see Chapter 6 for complete information).

Services: 24-hour room service, concierge, nightly turndown with a chocolate placed on your pillow, free morning newspaper, complimentary shuttle service to nearby business centers and shopping, overnight laundry/shoeshine, massage and manicure service.

Facilities: Pool, business services, health club.

Moderate

Hotel del Capri, 10587 Wilshire Blvd., Los Angeles, CA 90024. ☎ 310/474-3511, or toll free 800/444-6835. Fax 310/470-9999. 36 rms, 45 suites. A/C TV TEL **Directions:** From I-405 north, exit onto Wilshire Boulevard, turn right, and continue on Wilshire for about 1¼ miles; the hotel is on the left at the corner of Westholme Avenue and Wilshire Boulevard.

Rates (including continental breakfast): $85–$105 single or double; from $110 suite. Additional person $10 extra. AE, CB, DC, MC, V. **Parking:** Free.

Although it sits squarely in the middle of L.A., this hotel's muted aqua-and-pink exterior seems to come right from "Miami Vice." The del Capri is actually two buildings: one a two-story motel surrounding a kidney-shaped swimming pool, the other a four-story hotel overlooking the courtyard and the boulevard.

Although each room is a little different, most are outfitted with pretty pastels and contemporary black accents. Many look out onto the courtyard through lace curtains that cover floor-to-ceiling windows. All the beds here are electrically adjustable—a nice, if unconventional, touch. The more expensive rooms are slightly larger, and have whirlpool baths and an extra phone in the bathroom. No-smoking rooms are available.

In addition to continental breakfast, the hotel provides free shuttle service to nearby shopping and sights in Westwood, Beverly Hills, and Century City.

4 Bel Air

Very Expensive

⭐ **Hotel Bel Air,** 701 Stone Canyon Rd., Bel Air, CA 90077. ☎ 310/472-1211, or toll free 800/648-4097. Fax 310/476-5890. 52 rms, 39 suites. A/C MINIBAR TV TEL **Directions:** From I-405, exit onto Sunset Boulevard east; after two miles, turn left onto Stone Canyon Road.

Rates: $245–$395 single; $275–$435 double; from $495 suite. AE, CB, DC, MC, V. **Parking:** $12.50.

Yet another top hotel in one of the world's fanciest neighborhoods, the Spanish-style Hotel Bel Air regularly wins praise from guests for its attentive service and ultra-deluxe guest rooms. Set on exquisite tropical grounds and surrounded by the Santa Monica hills, the Bel Air is entered via a long awning-covered pathway, actually an arched stone bridge over a swan-filled pond. A large oval swimming pool is set amid the lush gardens and surrounded by a flagstone terrace. Inside, you'll find richly traditional public rooms furnished with fine antiques, and a fire that's kept burning in the entrance lounge.

The individually decorated rooms and garden suites, all with large picture windows, are equally stunning; many have patios or terraces, and some have wood-burning fireplaces. Each room has two telephones, and VCRs are delivered to your room on request.

Dining/Entertainment: Even if you're not staying here, it's worth showing up for a drink at the Bar or dinner in the Restaurant. Terrace seating overlooks a small lake. The Bar, a cozy drinkery adjacent to the Restaurant, has a wood-burning fireplace and nightly entertainment.

Services: 24-hour room service, concierge, evening turndown.

Facilities: Pool, access to off-premises health club.

Expensive

Radisson Bel Air Summit Hotel, 11461 Sunset Blvd., Los Angeles, CA 90049. ☎ **310/476-6571,** or toll free **800/333-3333.** Fax 310/471-6310. 161 rms, 6 suites. A/C MINIBAR TV TEL **Directions:** From I-405, exit onto Sunset Boulevard west; the hotel is immediately ahead on your right.

Rates: $109–$139 single; $119–$149 double; from $179 suite. Additional person $15 extra. AE, CB, DC, DISC, MC, V. **Parking:** $5.

Set in an eight-acre garden estate, the Radisson Bel Air Summit is just minutes away from Beverly Hills, Westwood Village and UCLA, and Century City; it's eight miles north of LAX.

Spacious rooms and suites all feature large balconies and have subtle color schemes and understated decor. All rooms have hairdryers, refrigerators, coffee makers, electronic security keys, radios, and two telephones. There's a heated swimming pool and a single unlit tennis court on the premises.

Dining/Entertainment: Echo, the hotel dining room, serves breakfast, lunch, dinner, and a fabulous Sunday brunch. The Oasis bar serves cocktails nightly and complimentary hors d'oeuvres Monday through Saturday from 5 to 7pm.

Services: Room service, concierge, shuttle service.

Facilities: Pool, fitness room, tennis court, gift shop, beauty salon with spa treatments, car-rental and tour desks.

5   Wilshire

Wilshire is a very long street that connects Beverly Hills with downtown L.A. The two listings below are on opposite ends of the street.

Expensive

Wilshire Radisson Plaza, 3515 Wilshire Blvd., Los Angeles, CA 90010. ☎ 213/381-7411, or toll free **800/333-3333.**

Fax 213/386-7379. 396 rms, 5 suites. A/C TV TEL
Directions: From U.S. 101, take the Melrose/Normandie exit
and turn south onto Normandie Avenue; the hotel is located
about two miles ahead, at the corner of Wilshire Boulevard.

Rates: $110–$140 single; $120–$160 double; from $250 suite. AE, DC,
DISC, MC, V. **Parking:** $8 self-parking, $10 valet.

Located close to downtown, this 12-story luxury hotel is popular with
businesspeople for its push-button comfort and convenient location.
Rooms are attractively furnished in a modern style; each has a
glass-brick wall and functional furniture. One- and two-bedroom
suites have two bathrooms and an additional living room.

Dining/Entertainment: Tulip's Restaurant is open for breakfast,
lunch, and dinner, serving basic American fare such as prime rib and
grilled swordfish. Sake-E Restaurant serves authentic Japanese
cuisine.

Services: Room service, concierge, business center.

Facilities: Heated outdoor pool, fitness center, barbershop,
car-rental and tour desks.

Moderate

Ritz Hotel, Beverly Hills, 10300 Wilshire Blvd., Los Angeles, CA
90024. ☎ **310/275-5575,** or toll free **800/800-1234.**
Fax 310/278-3325. 116 suites. A/C MINIBAR TV TEL
Directions: From I-405 south, exit onto Wilshire Boulevard east;
the hotel is located just before Beverly Hills, at Comstock Street.

Rates: $175–$275 standard suite; $275–$350 one-bedroom kitchen
suite; $395–$600 two-bedroom kitchen suite. Monthly rates available.
AE, CB, DC, DISC, MC, V. **Parking:** $8.

Dedicated to the comfortable, homelike suite business, this quiet,
peaceful hotel offers a standard of intimacy and privacy not usually
available at larger hotels. Understandably, the Ritz, located just outside Beverly Hills, attracts many celebrity guests.

The large rooms are decorated in either a traditional hotel style
or a colorful California modern flair. The units, which surround a
central courtyard pool and garden area, have private balconies or
patios. There are telephones and TVs in both bedrooms and bathrooms. The kitchen suites are particularly large, ranging from 1,000
to 2,000 square feet. These well-equipped accommodations have a
living room, a dining area, and completely equipped kitchens with
china service.

Dining/Entertainment: Le Petit Cafe, a continental restaurant,
serves breakfast, lunch, and dinner, and it offers a full-service
bar.

Services: Room service, concierge, overnight laundry.

Facilities: Pool, Jacuzzi, access to off-premises health
club.

6 Westwood & West Los Angeles

Wedged between Santa Monica and glamorous Beverly Hills, the
UCLA-student-dominated community of Westwood has more than

400 shops, about 100 restaurants, and 15 first-run movie theaters. West Los Angeles, as a glance at your L.A. map will show you, is just slightly south of Westwood, and within easy reach of Beverly Hills, Century City, and Santa Monica.

Expensive

Holiday Inn Westwood Plaza, 10740 Wilshire Blvd., Los Angeles, CA 90024. ☎ **310/475-8711,** or toll free **800/472-8556, 800/235-7973** in California. Fax 310/475-5220. 295 rms, 8 suites. A/C MINIBAR TV TEL **Directions:** From I-405, take the Westwood exit and follow Wilshire Boulevard east one mile to the hotel, at the corner of Selby Avenue.

Rates: $120–$130 single; $130–$140 double; from $225 suite. Children 18 or under stay free in parents' room. AE, CB, DC, DISC, MC, V. **Parking:** Free.

Attractively furnished twin-bedded rooms are decorated according to an English Tudor theme, which includes hunting prints on most walls. Special touches include marble sinks in the bathrooms and complimentary morning newspapers delivered to your door. The hotel also provides complimentary shuttle service to anyplace within a 2$^{1}/_{2}$-mile radius.

Dining/Entertainment: The hotel restaurant, Cafe Le Dome, is best known for its cocktail lounge, which is popular with basketball and football players, many of whom stay at the hotel.

Services: Concierge, laundry service.

Facilities: Pool, sun deck, sauna, Jacuzzi, exercise room, car-rental and tour desks, gift shop.

Moderate

Carlyle Inn, 119 S. Robertson Blvd., Los Angeles, CA 90035. ☎ **310/275-4445,** or toll free **800/322-7595.** Fax 310/859-0496. 32 rms, 10 suites. A/C MINIBAR TV TEL **Directions:** From Santa Monica Boulevard, turn east onto Wilshire Boulevard, then south onto Robertson; the hotel is about eight blocks ahead on your right.

Rates: $95–$140 single or double; $160 suite. AE, DC, DISC, MC, V. **Parking:** Free.

Hidden in a modest location just south of Beverly Hills, on an otherwise uneventful stretch of Robertson Boulevard, the Carlyle Inn is one of the best-priced quality finds in Los Angeles. This cleverly designed hotel sports thoroughly contemporary rooms, complete with recessed lighting, deco wall sconces and lamps, clean pine furnishings, and well-framed Roman architectural monoprints. Facilities include a coffee and tea maker (and a bottle of Evian to fill it with), a clock radio, and a TV with VCR. The hotel's only drawback is the lack of view; and curtains must remain drawn to maintain privacy.

Suites are slightly larger and contain full-length mirrors and well-outfitted baths with telephones, lighted magnified mirrors, hairdryers, and plenty of counter space for toiletries.

The small size of the hotel directly translates into great personal service.

Inexpensive

Century Wilshire Hotel, 10776 Wilshire Blvd., Los Angeles, CA 90024. ☎ **310/474-4506,** or toll free **800/421-7223.** Fax 310/474-2535. 100 rms, 58 suites. TV TEL

Directions: From I-405 north, exit onto Wilshire Boulevard, turn right, and continue on Wilshire Boulevard for about one mile; the hotel is on the right between Malcolm and Selby Avenues.

Rates (including continental breakfast): $65–$75 single; $65–$85 double; $80–$95 junior suite; $125–$150 one-bedroom suite. AE, CB, DC, MC, V. **Parking:** Free.

This large white hotel in downtown Westwood is conveniently located near UCLA and Beverly Hills. The otherwise sparsely decorated rooms are enlivened with floral wallpaper and certain special touches. Some rooms feature French doors that open onto balconies, and many other rooms come complete with kitchenettes. No-smoking rooms are available. The hotel surrounds a quiet courtyard and has an Olympic-size pool out back. Breakfast is served each morning in the breakfast room or out in the courtyard.

Los Angeles West Travelodge, 10740 Santa Monica Blvd., Los Angeles, CA 90025. ☎ **310/474-4576,** or toll free **800/631-0100.** Fax 310/470-3117. 36 rms. A/C TV TEL **Directions:** From I-405, exit onto Santa Monica Boulevard; the hotel is two miles ahead, at Overland Avenue.

Rates: $60–$90 single; $66–$96 double. Additional person $6 extra. AE, CB, DC, MC, V. **Parking:** Free.

This clean and friendly establishment offers good value for the area. The pleasant, modern rooms are equipped with clocks, in-room coffee makers, and refrigerators. There are no restaurant or health facilities in the hotel, but there is an enclosed private heated swimming pool with a sun deck, plus plenty of parking.

Royal Palace Westwood Hotel, 1052 Tiverton Ave., Los Angeles, CA 90024. ☎ **310/208-6677,** or toll free **800/631-0100.** Fax 310/824-3732. 36 rms, 6 suites. A/C TV TEL

Directions: From I-405, take the Westwood exit and follow Wilshire Boulevard east for half a mile; turn left onto Glendon Avenue and bear right onto Tiverton Avenue to the hotel.

Rates: $60 single; $66–$76 double; from $96 suite. Additional person $8 extra. AE, CB, DC, DISC, MC, V. **Parking:** Free.

Located between Beverly Hills, Century City, Santa Monica, West Los Angeles, and Bel Air, the Royal Palace is convenient to Hollywood, the beach, the airport, and most important, the San Diego Freeway. There are dozens of shops and restaurants within easy walking distance of the hotel.

This is not a fancy place by any stretch of the imagination, but each comfortable, redecorated guest room has a bed, desk, dresser, and color TV. Some accommodations have stoves, refrigerators, and stainless-steel countertops, while others have microwave ovens. There are marble vanities in the bathrooms. Facilities include a free exercise room, a lounge, and a tour desk for area activity information and reservations.

7   San Fernando Valley

Moderate

Carriage Inn, 5525 Sepulveda Blvd., Sherman Oaks, CA 91411. ☎ **818/787-2300,** or toll free **800/854-2608.** Fax 818/782-9373. 183 rms, 2 suites. A/C TV TEL **Directions:** From I-405 north, take the Burbank Boulevard exit and turn right onto Sepulveda Boulevard; the hotel will be ahead on your right.

Rates: $100 single or double; from $150 suite. AE, CB, DC, DISC, MC, V. **Parking:** Free.

The Carriage Inn is on "motel row," near the San Diego Freeway (I-405) at Burbank Boulevard. It's a super structure, with a seemingly endless maze of accommodations. In the middle is a small swimming pool, a Jacuzzi, a coffee shop and dining room, and a cocktail bar, which features nightly entertainment. The rooms are not new, but large, each with a small sitting area.

Radisson Valley Center, 15433 Ventura Blvd., Sherman Oaks, CA 91403. ☎ **818/981-5400.** Fax 818/981-3175. 215 rms, 3 suites. A/C TV TEL **Directions:** From either U.S. 101 or I-405 north, exit at Sherman Oaks and continue on Ventura Boulevard to the hotel.

Rates: $115 single or double Sun–Thurs, $90 single or double Fri–Sat; from $225 suite. Special discount packages available. AE, CB, DC, MC, V. **Parking:** $5.

Well located in the heart of the valley, the Radisson Valley Center sits at the crossroads of two major freeways—the San Diego (I-405) and Ventura (U.S. 101). Universal Studios, NBC, Magic Mountain, Griffith Park, Hollywood, and Beverly Hills are all nearby. The spacious rooms are attractively decorated with only slightly out-of-date baths and furnishings, and each has a private balcony.

    Hotel facilities include a heated rooftop pool, Jacuzzi, and sun deck. The ground-floor Orion Café and Lounge serves breakfast, lunch, and dinner and is open late for cocktails.

Sportsmen's Lodge, 12825 Ventura Blvd., Los Angeles, CA 91604. ☎ **818/769-4700,** or toll free **800/821-8511, 800/821-1625** in California. Fax 213/877-3898. 193 rms, 13 suites. A/C TV TEL **Directions:** From U.S. 101 north, take the Coldwater Canyon exit and turn left; after one mile, turn left onto Ventura Boulevard and the hotel will be about a quarter of a mile ahead on your left.

Rates: $101–$111 single; $111–$140 double; poolside executive studio, $165 single; $175 double. Additional person $10 extra. AE, CB, DC, DISC, MC, V. **Parking:** Free.

Movie, TV, and recording industry people all know about the Sportsmen's Lodge. Out in the valley, it's so near many of the studios that actors sometimes stay here during a stretch of shooting.

While here, you'd hardly know you're in the middle of a big city. Located just west of Universal City, the Sportsmen's Lodge is surrounded by redwood trees, waterfalls, rock gardens, lush tropical greenery, and rustic wooden footbridges that cross freshwater ponds. In fact, the hotel's name derives from the fact that guests used to fish for trout right on the premises.

Rooms are large and comfortable, but not luxurious in any way. They have AM/FM radios, many have balconies, and refrigerators are available. The poolside executive studios are the most appealing accommodations.

The hotel's attractive restaurant features a glass-enclosed dining room overlooking a tropical lagoon-style pond and small waterfall. You might begin a meal here with an order of baked clams topped with bacon bits and pimento, then order a main dish of veal piccata or duckling à l'orange with wild rice, priced from $15 to $28. Cakes and rolls are baked fresh daily. An adjacent coffee shop serves simpler breakfasts, lunches, and dinners.

Facilities include a heated Olympic-size pool with a Jacuzzi and large sun deck. A well-equipped exercise room has Lifecycles, rowing machines, and weights. There are also a variety of shops and service desks in the hotel, and both bowling and golf are available nearby. Complimentary afternoon tea is served in the lobby at 4pm.

8   Pasadena

Expensive

The Pasadena Hilton, 150 S. Los Robles Ave., Pasadena, CA 91101. ☎ **818/577-1000,** or toll free **800/445-8667.** Fax 818/584-3148. 291 rms, 15 suites. A/C MINIBAR TV TEL **Directions:** From 1-210, take the Lake Avenue South exit and turn right on Cordova Street; the hotel is straight ahead, on the corner of Cordova Street and Los Robles Avenue.

Rates: $120–$150 single; $135–$165 double; from $250 suite. AE, CB, DC, MC, V. **Parking:** $8.

This 13-story hostelry is 15 minutes from downtown Los Angeles, and only 1 1/2 blocks south of Colorado Boulevard, which is famous as the route of the annual Rose Parade. The rooms have been redecorated in soft earth tones. Some have beds with elaborate high headboards, and all have refrigerators and in-room movies. The higher rates command accommodations with king-size beds and balconies.

The hotel does a lot of convention business. It's also affiliated with the nearby, exclusive L.A. Canada/Flintridge Country Club, which allows hotel guests to use its facilities.

Dining/Entertainment: The Trevos restaurant, serving a California cuisine, offers breakfast, lunch, and dinner. There's an all-you-can-eat, fresh buffet daily. The Lobby Bar is a favorite rendezvous during happy hour.

Services: Room service, concierge, evening turndown, overnight laundry, shuttle service.

Facilities: Outdoor pool, exercise room (with Universal equipment, StairMasters, Lifecycles, and free weights), business center.

★ **The Ritz-Carlton Huntington Hotel,** 1401 S. Oak Knoll Ave., Pasadena, CA 91109. ☎ **818/568-3900,** or toll free **800/241-3333.** Fax 818/568-3700. 383 rms, 21 suites. A/C MINIBAR TV TEL **Directions:** From LAX, take I-105 east to Calif. 110 north (Pasadena Freeway) until the freeway ends at the corner of Arroyo Parkway and Glenarm; turn right onto Glenarm, right again onto El Molino, then left onto Elliott, and right onto Oak Knoll Avenue.

Rates: $160–$275 single or double; from $350 suite. AE, DC, MC, V. **Parking:** $12.

Originally built in 1906, the landmark Huntington Hotel quickly became the place to be seen, as celebrated writers, entertainers, political leaders, royalty, and business leaders discovered the elegance of this special place. The hotel managed to survive the 1929 stock market crash, the Great Depression, and World War II, but it could not survive the major earthquake that struck in 1985. After a painstaking 2^1/$_2$-year restoration, the Huntington reopened in 1991 under the Ritz-Carlton banner. The fantastically beautiful hotel is set on 23 meticulously landscaped acres nestled in the shadows of the San Gabriel Mountains and overlooking the San Gabriel Valley.

Throughout the hotel, careful attention has been given to re-create the genteel, timeless ambience of the original resort. Overstuffed sofas and club chairs upholstered in natural fabrics sit on Oriental carpets and are surrounded by fine 18th- and 19th-century oil paintings.

The hotel consists of a main building and six suite-filled cottages. Each room is oversized and elegantly appointed with marble baths, sitting areas, desks, large closets, and two telephones. There are remote-controlled color TVs, thick terry bathrobes, and in-room minibars.

Dining/Entertainment: The Grill offers a comfortable clublike setting for grilled meats, chops, and fresh fish. The 100-seat Georgian Room is the hotel's premier restaurant, serving continental cuisine prepared by renowned French chef Bernard Bordaris. The Café serves breakfast, lunch, and dinner, either inside or outdoors. The menu offers American standards, as well as light spa cuisine. A champagne brunch is served on Sunday. The Bar serves appetizers and cocktails into the night. The Lobby Lounge offers continental breakfast, cocktails, and traditional afternoon tea with—a pleasant touch—classical music accompaniment.

Services: 24-hour room service, concierge, evening turndown, babysitting.

Facilities: Olympic-size pool, outdoor whirlpool, fitness center, three tennis courts, pro shop, gift shop, Japanese gardens, car rental, mountain bike rental.

Inexpensive

Saga Motor Hotel, 1633 E. Colorado Blvd., Pasadena, CA 91106. ☎ 818/795-0431. 69 rms. A/C TV TEL **Directions:** From I-210, exit onto Fair Oaks Avenue south and turn left on Colorado Boulevard, the second major street; the hotel is about a mile ahead, between Allan Avenue and Sierra Bonita.

Rates (including continental breakfast): $55 single; $57 double; $59 single or double with king-size bed and refrigerator; $75 suite. AE, CB, DC, MC, V. **Parking:** Free.

The Saga Motor Hotel is about a mile from the Huntington Library and reasonably close to Pasadena City College, Cal Tech, and the Jet Propulsion Lab. It's also within easy distance of the Rose Bowl. But the bottom line is that the Saga has, by far, some of the most attractive rooms in its price range, as well as an inviting, sunlit, and spotlessly clean reception area.

Comfortable accommodations, which include cable TVs, are nicely decorated with brass beds, blue-and-white-checkered spreads, and blue-and-white tile baths with both showers and tubs. Guest rooms are split between two buildings: The first is a single-story structure wrapped around a pool; the other is a small three-story building between the pool and a quiet street at the rear of the building.

---

9   Malibu

Moderate

★ **Casa Malibu,** 22752 Pacific Coast Hwy., Malibu, CA 90265. ☎ 310/456-2219, or toll free 800/831-0858. Fax 310/456-5418. 21 rms. TV TEL **Directions:** From Santa Monica, take Calif. 1 north to Malibu; the hotel is located directly on Calif. 1 about a quarter of a mile before the Malibu Pier.

Rates: $90–$110 single or double with garden view, $130 single or double with ocean view, $145–$155 single or double oceanfront. Room with kitchen $10 extra. Additional person $10 extra. AE, MC, V. **Parking:** Free.

Inexpensive accommodations in Malibu are hard to obtain. Your best bet is the Casa Malibu, a ranch-style motel built around a palm-studded inner courtyard with well-tended flowerbeds and cuppa d'oro vines growing up the balcony. The squat hostelry sits directly on the ocean, in front of a large swath of private, sandy beach. The rooms are cheerful and attractively furnished—some with private balconies. Each is equipped with oversize beds, bathrobes, a coffee maker, and refrigerator. Oceanfront rooms are particularly lovely, since they have private decks hanging over the sandy beach.

10   Santa Monica & Venice

Not only does choosing Santa Monica or adjacent Venice mean being near the beach, it means getting away from the smog and staying in one of the most attractive, dynamic neighborhoods in L.A.

Very Expensive

⭐ **Loews Santa Monica Beach Hotel,** 1700 Ocean Ave., Santa Monica, CA 90401. ☎ **310/458-6700,** or toll free **800/223-0888.** Fax 310/458-6761. 349 rms, 22 suites. A/C MINIBAR TV TEL
Directions: From the Santa Monica Freeway (I-10), exit west onto 4th Street, turn left onto Colorado Boulevard, and then left onto Ocean Avenue.

Rates: $195–$245 single; $215–$265 double; from $305 suite. Additional person $20 extra. Children under 18 stay free in parents' room. AE, CB, DC, MC, V. **Parking:** $13 self-parking, $15 valet.

Loews is one of the few beachfront hotels in all of Los Angeles. Located just two blocks from the Santa Monica Pier, this relatively new lavish hotel is easily the best in the area.

In addition to all the amenities you'd expect from a top hotel, each room is equipped with three TVs, three telephones (with two phone lines), plush terry bathrobes, hairdryers, and VCRs on request.

Dining/Entertainment: There are two restaurants and a poolside snack service. A pianist entertains in the lounge most afternoons, and during the evening, when the bar gets busy. Comedians perform on Sunday nights; admission is $6.

Services: 24-hour room service, concierge, twice-daily maid service, overnight shoeshine, babysitting, summer children's program.

Facilities: Pool, Jacuzzi, fitness center, business center, bike and roller-skate rental.

Miramar Sheraton Hotel, 101 Wilshire Blvd., Santa Monica, CA 90401. ☎ **310/576-7777,** or toll free **800/325-3535.** Fax 310/458-7912. 301 rms, 61 suites. A/C MINIBAR TV TEL
Directions: From the Santa Monica Freeway (I-10), exit west onto 4th Street and, after five blocks, turn left onto Wilshire Boulevard; the hotel is four blocks ahead on your left, between Ocean Avenue and 2nd Street.

Rates: $195–$225 single or double; from $275 suite. Additional person $20 extra. AE, CB, DC, MC, V. **Parking:** $11.

Miramar means "ocean view" and that's just what this hotel offers from its cliff-top perch overlooking Santa Monica Beach. The hotel was originally built in the 1920s, and that era's elegance is clearly in evidence throughout the public areas. In the courtyard is a century-old fig tree that casts its shadow over the garden and adjacent swimming pool.

Guest rooms are split between older low buildings and the newer tower. Each is comfortable and luxurious for a beach hotel. Amenities include a king-size bed or two double beds, in-room safe, and digital clock radio. Bathrooms are plush, outfitted with extra phones, honor bars, special soaps and shampoos, and oversize towels.

Dining/Entertainment: The Miramar Grille, a California-style bistro, is open for lunch and dinner. The Cafe serves continuously from breakfast to dinner.

Services: 24-hour room service, concierge, evening turndown, same-day laundry and valet service, complimentary newspaper.

Facilities: Heated pool, health center, gift shop, beauty salon, women's boutique, car- and bike-rental desks.

Shutters on the Beach, 1 Pico Blvd., Santa Monica, CA 90405. ☎ **310/458-0030,** or toll free **800/334-9000.** Fax 310/458-4589. 186 rms, 12 suites. MINIBAR TV TEL **Directions:** From I-10, exit onto 4th Street and turn left; after one long block, turn right onto Pico Boulevard and continue all the way to the ocean, to the hotel.

Rates: $230–$350 single or double; from $550 suite. AE, DC, DISC, MC, V. **Parking:** $15.

The only L.A. luxury hotel actually on the beach, light and bright Shutters enjoys one of the city's most enviable locations, a block from the Santa Monica Pier. Opened in 1993, the hotel is ingeniously designed to optimize its space. Gray-shingled Shutters is divided into two connecting parts; squat beachfront cottagelike structures are separated from the taller building behind by the hotel's pool. And although the beach-cottage rooms are plainly more desirable than those in the tower, when it comes to rates, the hotel doesn't distinguish between them.

The hotel is justifiably proud of its extensive contemporary art collection, which is liberally and almost casually hung throughout. Ocean views and the sound of crashing waves are the most outstanding qualities of the guest rooms. Some accommodations have fireplaces, most have Jacuzzi tubs, and all have sliding wooden shutters on floor-to-ceiling windows that open. Large TVs are connected to VCRs, and showers come with waterproof radios and biodegradable bath supplies.

Dining/Entertainment: One Pico, the hotel's premier restaurant, enjoys panoramic views of Santa Monica beach. The more casual Pedals, located directly on the beach path, serves three meals daily and has a wood-burning grill. The adjacent Handle Bar is an upbeat drinkery with good happy hour specials.

Services: 24-hour room service, concierge, overnight laundry, evening turndown, massage.

Facilities: Pool, Jacuzzi, health facilities, sauna, beach equipment and bicycle rentals.

Expensive

Pacific Shore Hotel, 1819 Ocean Ave. (at Pico Blvd.), Santa Monica, CA 90401. ☎ **310/451-8711,** or toll free **800/622-8711.** Fax 310/394-6657. 168 rms. A/C TV TEL **Directions:** From the Santa Monica Freeway (I-10) south, exit at 4th Street and turn right and, after two blocks, turn right onto Pico Boulevard; the hotel is straight ahead, at the corner of Ocean Avenue.

Rates: $125–$135 single or double. AE, MC, V. **Parking:** Free.

An eight-story hotel, just a half block from the beach, the Pacific Shore lives up to its name, offering excellent views from the higher-priced rooms. Every guest room looks out onto the ocean or pool through an entire wall of tinted glass; you can see out but nobody can see in. Accommodations are attractively decorated in cheerful colors. Each has a small dressing area, rattan and walnut furnishings, and an AM/FM radio. There are ice and soft-drink machines on every floor. A cocktail lounge offers nightly entertainment.

   Facilities: Shops, car-rental and tour desks, guest laundry, outdoor heated pool, whirlpool, Jacuzzi, saunas for men and women.

Radisson-Huntley Hotel, 1111 2nd St., Santa Monica, CA 90403. ☎ **310/394-5454,** or toll free **800/333-3333.** Fax 310/458-9776. 213 rms, 6 suites. A/C TV TEL **Directions:** From the Santa Monica Freeway (I-10), exit west onto 4th Street; after five blocks, turn left onto Wilshire Boulevard, then right onto 2nd Street to the hotel.

Rates: $120–$145 single; $135–$160 double; from $150 suite. Ask about the "Supersaver Rates" promotion. AE, CB, DC, DISC, MC, V. **Parking:** $5.50.

One of the tallest buildings in Santa Monica, the Radisson-Huntley offers nondescript rooms just two blocks from the beach. Accommodations are basic yet comfortable; attractive, with ocean or mountain views; and equipped with AM/FM radios, color TVs, and other modern amenities. Toppers, the rooftop Mexican restaurant, has a great view, serves good margaritas, and offers free live entertainment nightly. The lobby-level Garden Cafe is a classy coffee shop serving American standards.

Moderate

$ **Holiday Inn Bay View Plaza,** 530 Pico Blvd. (at 6th St., west of Lincoln), Santa Monica, CA 90405. ☎ **310/399-9344,** or toll free **800/465-4329.** Fax 310/399-2504. 309 rms, 11 suites. A/C MINIBAR TV TEL **Directions:** From the Santa Monica Freeway (I-10), exit onto 4th Street and turn left onto Lincoln Boulevard south; after six blocks, turn right onto Pico Boulevard to the hotel.

Rates: $103–$133 single or double; from $250 suite. AE, CB, DC, MC, V. **Parking:** Free.

Although not particularly cheap, this Holiday Inn represents some of the best value on the beach, with good-sized, well-outfitted rooms. Accommodations on the highest floors of this 10-story hotel offer nice views of either the ocean or the city. There's a heated, outdoor pool and adjacent spa pool, as well as a small exercise room for guests' use. The hotel's Bay View Café is open daily for breakfast, lunch, and dinner. Guests are provided with free shuttle service to and from Los Angeles International Airport.

Accommodations in
Southern Los Angeles County

Holiday Inn Bay View Plaza **6**
Hotel *Queen Mary* **15**
Loew's Santa Monica Beach Hotel **3**
Los Angeles Airport Marriott **13**
Marina del Rey Hotel **11**
Marina del Rey Marriott **10**
Marina International **9**
Miramar Sheraton Hotel **2**

Pacific Shore Hotel **5**
Portofino Inn **14**
Radisson-Huntley Hotel **1**
Santa Monica International AYH Hostel **4**
Sheraton Los Angeles Airport Hotel **12**
Shutters on the Beach **7**
Travelodge **16**
Venice Beach House **8**

★ **Venice Beach House,** 15 30th Ave., Venice, CA 90291.
☎ **310/823-1966.** Fax 310/823-1842. 9 rms, 5 suites. TV TEL
Directions: From Calif. 1, turn west onto Washington Boulevard,
then right onto Pacific Avenue; 30th Avenue is a small walkway on
the left; there's a parking lot behind the house.

Rates (including continental breakfast): Mon–Thurs, $80–$130 single or double without bath, $110 single or double with bath. Fri–Sun, $90–$150 single or double without bath, $120 single or double with bath. From $130 suite. Additional person $10 extra. AE, MC, V. **Parking:** Free.

Built in 1911 by Warren Wilson, this former family home is now one of the area's finest bed-and-breakfasts. While admiring the Victorian building's hardwood floors, bay windows, lattice porch, and large Oriental rugs, it's easy to forget the hustle and bustle of the beach that's just steps away.

Each of the inn's nine rooms is different, outfitted with white rattan dressers and nightstands, or antique wood furnishings. Some are punctuated with country prints or shelves packed with worn hardcover books. Every room has an alarm clock and access to a fan, and one particularly romantic room has an ocean view and a fireplace. The inn provides bicycles for guests and can make picnic baskets for day excursions.

Continental breakfasts that include cereal, breads, juice, and coffee are served each morning in the comfortable downstairs sitting room. Afternoon tea or cool lemonade is also served with fresh-baked cookies every day.

Be aware that the Venice Beach House can get noisy, and despite this simple B&B's relative homeyness, it's not for everyone. No smoking is permitted in the house.

Budget

Santa Monica International AYH Hostel, 1436 2nd St.

(P.O. Box 575), Santa Monica, CA 90401. ☎ **310/393-9913.** Fax 310/393-1769. 38 rms. **Directions:** From the Santa Monica Freeway (I-10), exit on 4th Street and make a right turn; turn left on Colorado and then right on 2nd Street.

Rates: $14 per person with an IYHF card, $17 per person without. $3 surcharge for twin rooms. MC, V. **Parking:** 50¢ per hour.

Opened in April 1990, the Santa Monica hostel is just two blocks from the beach and Santa Monica Pier, and about one mile from Venice Beach. It's within walking distance of shops and restaurants and about two blocks from regional bus lines, including a direct bus to Los Angeles International Airport (about seven miles).

This is one of the largest specifically built hostels in this country and can accommodate up to 200 guests, including groups and families on a space-available basis. Accommodations are dormitory style, with shared bedrooms and bathrooms. The hostel has guest kitchen facilities, a travel library, and a travel center. It's pretty nice too, designed in muted earth tones and centered around an open courtyard. Six twin rooms are reserved for couples, and four family rooms cater to families.

There are a TV lounge, laundry room, games room, information desk, vending machines, a dining room, library, and secure lockers.

You must provide sheets; you are asked to be quiet after 11pm; and you are not permitted to smoke or drink alcohol.

Reservations are highly recommended, especially from May to October. Write at least two weeks in advance and include your dates of stay; the number of males and females in your party; your name, address, and telephone number; and the first night's deposit. To reserve by phone, call between 1 and 5pm Monday through Saturday.

IYHF membership is required during peak times. Individual membership in the American Youth Hostel organization costs $25 per year and entitles you to discounted rates in any AYH-affiliated hostel. You can buy a membership at the hostel. Guests are limited to three-night stays; however, this can be extended to five nights with the approval of the manager.

11   Marina del Rey

Sandwiched between Santa Monica and the Los Angeles International Airport, Marina del Rey is a popular waterfront resort, just two minutes from major freeways that connect with most L.A. attractions. More than 6,000 pleasure boats dock here, making its marina the world's largest small-craft harbor.

Expensive

Marina del Rey Hotel, 13534 Bali Way, Marina del Rey, CA 90292. ☎ **310/301-1000,** or toll free **800/882-4000, 800/862-7462** in California. Fax 310/301-8167. 154 rms, 6 suites. A/C TV TEL
Directions: From I-405, exit onto Calif. 90, which ends at Lincoln Boulevard; turn left onto Lincoln Boulevard, then right onto Bali Way to the hotel.

Rates: $120–$185 single; $140–$205 double; from $350 suite. AE, CB, DC, MC, V. **Parking:** Free.

Located at the tip of a pier jutting into the harbor, this hotel specializes in rooms that look out over one of the world's largest yacht-filled harbors. The only hotel located on a harbor pier, the Marina del Rey is almost completely surrounded by water. First-class guest rooms are decorated in a soothing blue-and-tan color scheme and are fitted with all the expected amenities. Most rooms have balconies or patios. If yours doesn't, go down to the heated waterside swimming pool where great views can be enjoyed from the beautifully landscaped sun deck area.

Dining/Entertainment: The Dockside Cafe, a coffee shop, is open daily for breakfast and lunch. The Crystal Seahorse serves continental dinners from 6 to 11pm daily. The restaurant overlooks the marina, and its mirrored tables, walls, and ceilings reflect the view.

Services: Room service, concierge, evening turndown, complimentary airport limousine.

Facilities: Heated pool, putting green, car-rental desk, nearby tennis, golf, and beach.

Marina del Rey Marriott, 13480 Maxella Ave., Marina del Rey, CA 90292. ☎ **310/822-8555,** or toll free **800/228-9290.** Fax 310/823-2996. 283 rms, 3 suites. A/C MINIBAR TV TEL
Directions: From I-405, exit onto Calif. 90, which ends at Lincoln Boulevard; turn right onto Lincoln Boulevard, and right again onto Maxella Avenue.

Rates: $90–$135 single; $130–$160 double; from $275 suite. AE, CB, DC, DISC, MC, V. **Parking:** Free.

This delightful resortlike hotel offers excellently appointed rooms with AM/FM clock radios, first-run movies, and bright tropical-style rooms accented with splashy floral-design spreads and drapes. Tile baths, pretty furnishings, and good service make this an excellent place to stay. Many rooms have patios or balconies.

The hotel is conveniently located next to the Villa Marina Center, a small mall with about 30 shops.

Dining/Entertainment: Maxfield's Restaurant and Lounge serves American-continental dishes in cheery surroundings. The outdoor pool bar is in a landscaped courtyard complete with a rock waterfall, pond, and bridge over a stream.

Services: Room service, concierge, evening turndown, complimentary airport transportation.

Facilities: Pool, whirlpool, car and bicycle rental.

Marina International, 4200 Admiralty Way, Marina del Rey, CA 90292. ☎ **310/301-2000,** or toll free **800/882-4000, 800/862-7462** in California. Fax 310/301-6687. 135 rms, 24 suites, 25 bungalows. A/C TV TEL **Directions:** From I-405, exit onto Calif. 90, which ends at Lincoln Boulevard; turn left onto Lincoln Boulevard, right onto Bali Way, and then right onto Admiralty Way to the hotel.

Rates: $110–$150 single; $125–$298 double; from $130 suite; from $150 bungalow. AE, CB, DC, MC, V. **Parking:** Free.

Located at the top end of the harbor, the Marina International's lovely rooms are both bright and contemporary; many offer unobstructed water views. Suites have an additional sitting room and an extra phone in the bathroom. The hotel's bungalows are located off a private courtyard. An especially good value, the spacious bungalows offer truly private accommodations. They're fitted with luxuriously appointed sitting areas, bedrooms, and bathrooms. Larger than suites, some bungalows have raised ceilings, while others are split-level duplexes. Most rooms are decorated in a warm, casual, contemporary California style, with soft pastels and comfortable textured fabrics.

Dining/Entertainment: The Crystal Fountain features continental cooking served indoors or out. It's open daily for breakfast and lunch.

Services: Room service, concierge, complimentary airport shuttle.

Facilities: Heated pool, whirlpool, tour desk, business center; nearby golf and tennis.

12   Near the Airport

Expensive

Los Angeles Airport Marriott, Century Blvd. and Airport Blvd., Los Angeles, CA 90045. ☎ **310/641-5700,** or toll free **800/228-9290.** Fax 310/337-5358. 1,020 rms, 19 suites. A/C TV TEL **Directions:** From I-405, take Century Boulevard west toward the airport; the hotel is on your right, at Airport Boulevard.

Rates: $99 single; $164 double; from $375 suite. AE, CB, DC, DISC, MC, V. **Parking:** $9.

Built in 1973 and last renovated in 1987, this business hotel is not on the cutting edge, but it's a good choice near the airport. There are cheerfully decorated bedrooms with AM/FM-stereo radios and alarm clocks. The hotel is designed for travelers on the fly; you can use ironing boards, irons, and hairdryers if needed. There's also a guest laundry room on the premises.

Dining/Entertainment: The Lobby Bistro serves buffet breakfasts, lunches, and dinners. The Capriccio Room offers continental specialties in a Mediterranean ambience. The Fairfield Inn coffee shop serves American food and is open all day. Cocktails and entertainment are offered in Champions lounge.

Services: Room service, concierge, complimentary airport limousine service.

Facilities: Giant pool, swim-up bar, garden sun deck, whirlpool, business center, car-rental and tour desks.

Sheraton Los Angeles Airport Hotel, 6101 W. Century Blvd., Los Angeles, CA 90045. ☎ **310/642-1111,** or toll free **800/325-3535.** Fax 310/410-1267. 807 rms, 91 suites. A/C MINIBAR TV TEL **Directions:** From I-405, take Century Boulevard west toward the airport; the hotel is on your right, near Sepulveda Boulevard.

Rates: $115–$155 single; $135–$175 double; from $300 suite. AE, CB, DC, DISC, MC, V. **Parking:** $9.

The airport area has been developing in the last few years and this Sheraton is one of the newer additions. Rooms have a quintessential California look, with rattan chairs and live plants; color-coordinated drapes and bedspreads are dark green and burgundy. All rooms are equipped with digital alarm clocks; TVs with free sports, news, and movie channels; and AM/FM radios. Bathrooms are carpeted and are fitted with shower heads over bathtubs.

Dining/Entertainment: The Plaza Brasserie, an airy, contemporary café, is open from 6am to 11pm. At Landry's, which is open for lunch and dinner, the focus is on steak, chops, and seafood, including a sushi bar. The Plaza Lounge serves cocktails nightly.

Services: 24-hour room service, concierge, evening turndown, business center, same-day laundry, complimentary airport shuttle, complimentary morning newspaper.

Facilities: Heated outdoor pool, spa, shops, boutiques, unisex hair salon, exercise room with Universal equipment, car-rental desk, tour desk.

13 Redondo Beach & Long Beach

Expensive

Portofino Hotel and Yacht Club, 260 Portofino Way, Redondo Beach, CA 90277-2092. ☎ **213/379-8481,** or toll free **800/468-4292.** Fax 213/372-7329. 170 rms, 3 suites. A/C MINI-BAR TV TEL **Directions:** From Calif. 1 south, turn west onto Beryl Street; continue straight on Beryl Street as it turns into Portofino Way and follow the signs to the hotel.

Rates: $133–$150 single or double with marina view, $170–$180 single or double with ocean view; $160–$170 king room with marina view, $190–$200 king room with ocean view; $245 double with ocean view and private Jacuzzi; $275 one-bedroom suite. Children under 12 stay free in parents' room. Weekend and other packages available. AE, CB, DC, MC, V. **Parking:** $5.

Resting on its own little peninsula between the Pacific Ocean and the Redondo Beach Marina, this large salmon-colored inn offers dated yet elegant seclusion in this busy seaside community.

An imposing fireplace and spectacular two-story oceanfront windows make the hotel's large lobby a natural gathering place.

While the standard single or double rooms are a little small, the slightly more expensive king rooms are well worth the extra money. No matter which you choose, all have lattice balconies, a refrigerator, and a view of either the ocean or the marina. The large bathrooms come with complimentary robes, plush towels, and the usual package of shampoos and soaps.

Dining/Entertainment: The Marina Cafe, which serves breakfast and lunch, has outdoor seating. The Marina Grill is open for dinner only, and serves fresh seafood and steaks, as well as salads and sandwiches.

Services: Room service, complimentary coffee and tea service in the lobby.

Facilities: Exercise room, pool, spa, bicycle rental.

Moderate

Hotel *Queen Mary*, 1126 Queen's Hwy., Long Beach, CA 90802-6390. ☎ **310/435-3511** or **310/432-6964,** or toll free **800/437-2934.** Fax 310/437-4531. 348 rms, 17 suites. A/C TV TEL **Directions:** From I-405 west, take I-710 south to the end and follow the signs to the ship.

Rates: $65–$160 single or double; from $350 suite. Additional person $15 extra. AE, DC, MC, V. **Parking:** $5.

The *Queen Mary* is considered the most luxurious ocean liner ever to sail the Atlantic. The last survivor of the era of the great superliners, the ship is now permanently docked in Long Beach. In addition to being a popular tourist attraction, the ship functions as a working hotel.

While the rooms are the largest ever built aboard a ship, they're not exceptional compared to those on terra firma. And though the charm and elegance of the art deco era is recalled in each stateroom's decor, modern amenities like TVs and carpeting seem ready for replacement. Only outside rooms have portholes. The *Queen Mary* is thoroughly recommendable for its upbeat originality and truly spectacular public areas. A historical treasure from a bygone era, the ship's beautifully carved interior is a festival for the eye and fun to explore. If you're planning to be in Long Beach during the week, the *Queen Mary's* low room rates are hard to beat.

Dining/Entertainment: Sir Winston's offers a terrific view of the coastline through the large windows of its formal dining room. The Chelsea restaurant specializes in seafood dinners. The Promenade serves all day. Sunday Champagne brunch is served in the ship's Grand Salon. Cocktails are served each evening in the art deco Observation Bar.

Services: Room service, concierge, overnight laundry.

Facilities: Shops.

Inexpensive

$ **Travelodge,** 80 Atlantic Ave., Long Beach, CA 90802. ☎ **310/435-2471.** Fax 310/437-1995. 63 rms. A/C TV TEL **Directions:** From the Long Beach Freeway (I-710) south, exit at 6th Street and turn right onto Atlantic Avenue; the hotel is on your left, on the corner of 1st Street and Atlantic Avenue.

Rates: $49 single; $54–$59 double. AE, DC, DISC, MC, V. **Parking:** Free.

Literally surrounded by budget hotels, this chain motel is consistently one of the cleanest and cheapest; it represents one of the best values in the area. Nothing fancy here, but the location is good, right in downtown Long Beach, adjacent to an all-night coffee shop.

6

Los Angeles Dining

As RECENTLY AS 10 YEARS AGO, IT WAS HARD TO GET A GREAT MEAL IN LOS Angeles. Today, however, the city boasts some of the most interesting and inventive eateries in the world and consistently rates among the top culinary venues anywhere. Supported by a diverse range of ethnic choices, year-round outdoor seating, and California-inspired imaginative interiors, the many eateries in the city are also blessed with creative and skilled chefs.

In the past decade or so Angelenos have become more knowledgeable about their food. They eat well and love to discuss restaurants and their respective chefs. Dining out is an important part of the entertainment industry; it's where you see and are seen, meet important contacts, and, ultimately, make significant deals.

New restaurants and chefs are regular topics of conversation in Los Angeles. Deciding where to eat can spark a lengthy debate about the positive and negative aspects of various restaurants. In general, Angelenos are well versed about their city's restaurants and the city's continually changing chefs.

Like so many other aspects of externally oriented L.A., dining places are a major part of the local status scene—to the see-and-be-seen crowd, it matters not only which restaurant you patronize but also the table where you are seated. Although it hardly matters to the average tourist, almost every "important" restaurant has its "A" tables and its socially less-important sections, often known as "Siberia." Some film industry watchers even infer who's "in" and who's "out" according to where they are seated in some of the more famous restaurants.

There are lots of places to eat for less than $5. The problem is that you can "starve" in the time it takes to get from one place to another. On the other hand, you can also spend as much as $75 for a meal, per person, without wine or even valet parking. Los Angeles has restaurants for everyone—from American to Lithuanian to Vietnamese.

To help you choose where to eat, the restaurants listed below are categorized first by area, then by price, according to the following guide: "Expensive," over $35 per person; "Moderate," $20 to $35 per person; and "Inexpensive," under $20 per person. These categories reflect the price of most dinner menu items, including appetizer, main course, coffee, dessert, tax, and tip. Keep in mind that many of the restaurants listed as "expensive" are moderately priced at lunch. Also, many of the hotel restaurants listed here and mentioned in Chapter 5 should be considered. Reservations are usually advised at most Los Angeles–area restaurants.

In 1993, Los Angeles passed an ordinance banning smoking from its more than 7,000 restaurants. Opponents of this local legislation have taken the battle to the state legislature, where it continues to smolder.

1 Downtown Los Angeles

Expensive

Horikawa, 111 S. San Pedro St. ☎ 213/680-9355.

Cuisine: JAPANESE. **Reservations:** Recommended at dinner. **Directions:** From U.S. 101, exit onto Alameda Street south; after two blocks, turn right on 1st Street, then left on San Pedro Street.

Prices: Appetizers $5–$9; main courses $18–$30; lunch $10–$15; complete dinner $25–$75; Ryotei dinner $75–$110. AE, CB, DC, MC, V.

Open: Lunch Mon–Fri 11:30am–2pm; dinner Mon–Fri 6–10pm; Sat 5–10pm.

This tranquil restaurant is an excellent choice for good Japanese cooking. At the entrance there's a small fountain similar to those found in traditional Japanese gardens. Reproductions of works by Japanese artist Shiko Munakata hang in the separate Teppan Grill Room. It's worth coming here just to see them.

You can begin your dinner at Horikawa with a sushi sampler or seafood teriyaki. A complete dinner might include shrimp tempura, sashimi appetizer, dobin-mushi (a seafood-and-vegetable soup served in a minipot), kani (crab) salad, filet mignon tobanyaki (served on a sizzling minicooker), rice, tea, and ice cream or sherbet. You can also order à la carte. In the Teppan Grill Room you might opt for filet mignon and lobster tail served with fresh vegetables.

Pacific Dining Car, 1310 W. 6th St. ☎ 213/483-6000.

Cuisine: AMERICAN. **Reservations:** Recommended. **Directions:** From U.S. 101, exit onto Alvarado Street south and take the third left onto 6th Street; the restaurant is one block ahead on your right.

Prices: Appetizers $7–$15; main courses $23–$45; lunch $15–$30; breakfast $11–$25. AE, MC, V.

Open: Daily 24 hours (breakfast 11pm–11am; lunch 11am–4pm; dinner anytime).

Located just a few short blocks from the center of downtown Los Angeles, this restaurant has been authentically decorated to evoke the golden age of rail travel. Walls are paneled in warm mahogany with brass luggage racks (complete with luggage) overhead. Old menus and prints from early railroading days line the walls, and brass wall lamps with parchment shades light some tables.

Steaks are prime, aged on the premises, and cooked over a mesquite-charcoal fire. At dinner, top sirloin, a New York steak, fresh seafood, veal, and lamb are all available. For starters, try the excellent calamari; weight watchers, however, might prefer the beefsteak-tomato and onion salad. Menu items are basically the same at lunch. On a recent visit I enjoyed a perfectly charcoal-broiled boneless breast of chicken, with choice of potato or tomato. There's an outstanding wine list too. Desserts are simple fare, such as apple pie. There's also a breakfast menu featuring egg dishes, salads, and steaks.

Frommer's Smart Traveler: Restaurants

1. Go ethnic. The city has some great, inexpensive ethnic dining establishments.

2. Eat your main meal at lunch when prices are lower; you can sample gourmet hot spots for a fraction of the price charged at dinner.

3. Watch the liquor; it can add greatly to the cost of any meal.

4. Look for fixed-price menus, two-for-one specials, and coupons in local newspapers and magazines.

A second restaurant is located in Santa Monica, at 2700 Wilshire Blvd., one block east of 26th Street (☎ 310/453-4000).

Moderate

Cha Cha Cha, 656 N. Virgil Ave., Silver Lake. ☎ 213/664-7723.

Cuisine: CARIBBEAN. **Reservations:** Recommended, required Fri–Sat nights. **Directions:** From U.S. 101, exit onto Vermont Avenue north and turn right onto Melrose Avenue; the restaurant is at the corner of Melrose and Virgil Avenues.

Prices: Appetizers $3–$6; main courses $8–$15; breakfast or lunch $5–$9. AE, DC, DISC, MC, V.

Open: Sun–Thurs 7am–10pm, Fri–Sat 7am–11pm.

Cha Cha Cha serves the West Coast's best Caribbean food. Period. The very spicy black-pepper jumbo shrimp gets top marks, as does the paella, a veritable festival of flavors. Other Jamaican/Haitian/Cuban/Puerto Rican–inspired recommendations include garlic pizza; shrimp cakes; jerk pork; and corn tortillas wrapped around black beans, chicken, and vegetables. Only beer and wine are served.

Hardcore Caribbean food eaters might visit for breakfast, when the fare ranges from plantain, yucca, onion, and herb omelets to scrambled eggs and fresh tomatillos served on hot grilled tortillas.

Cha Cha Cha's location, on the fringes of seedy downtown, authenticate the restaurant's offbeat charm. Dining rooms, located inside a small Créole-like house and in a completely enclosed courtyard, are romantic island settings, made funky with Caribbean music, wild tiling, and a hodgepodge of colorful clutter.

Grand Star, 943 Sun Mun Way. ☎ 213/626-2285.

Cuisine: CHINESE. **Reservations:** Recommended. **Directions:** From U.S. 101, exit to North Broadway and continue north about seven blocks to Sun Mun Way, between College and Bernard Streets.

Prices: Appetizers $3–$7; main courses $8–$16; fixed-price meals from $20. AE, CB, DC, MC, V.

Open: Mon–Thurs and Sat 5–10pm, Fri 11:30am–10pm, Sun 2–10pm.

Owned and operated by the Quon family since 1967, the Grand Star offers an unusual selection of top-notch Chinese dishes. There are four complete meals, including a gourmet selection of spicy shrimp in a lettuce shell, wonton soup, spicy chicken wings, Mongolian beef with mushrooms, lobster Cantonese, barbecued pork with snow peas, fried rice, tea, and dessert. If there are four or five people in your party, Mama Quon's chicken salad is added, along with larger portions of everything else. A la carte items are also available, ranging from rum-flamed dumplings to lobster sautéed in ginger and green onion. Steamed fish, priced according to size, is a house specialty, as are the cashew chicken, Mongolian beef, and Chinese string beans.

The building began life as a penny arcade. On the street level the Grand Star looks more Italian than Chinese; it's dimly lit, with black-leather booths and big bunches of dried flowers here and there. I prefer to sit upstairs, where tables are covered with red cloths and the family's fine collection of Chinese embroideries adorns the walls. Entertainment—usually a female vocalist with piano accompaniment—is featured at cocktail time and most evenings.

Little Joe's, 900 N. Broadway. ☎ 213/489-4900.

Cuisine: ITALIAN. **Reservations:** Recommended. **Directions:** From U.S. 101, exit to North Broadway and continue north about five blocks to the restaurant, at the corner of College Street.

Prices: Appetizers $5–$8; main courses $10–$19; lunch $6–$14. AE, CB, DC, DISC, MC, V.

Open: Mon–Fri 11am–9pm, Sat 3–9pm.

Little Joe's, a vestige of this once-Italian neighborhood, now finds itself in touristy New Chinatown. Opened as a grocery in 1927, Joe's has grown steadily over the years; it now encompasses several bars and six dining rooms. It's a wonderfully cozy restaurant with sawdust on the floors, hand-painted oil murals of Rome and Venice, soft lighting, and seating in roomy leather booths.

A meal here ought to begin with a plate of the special hot hors d'oeuvres—fried cheese, zucchini, and homemade ravioli. A complete six-course meal will consist of soup, antipasto, salad, pasta, vegetable or potato, bread and butter, and dessert; main dishes include veal scaloppine, scallops, or halibut steak. You can also get a full pasta dinner or order à la carte. Less expensive lunches include dishes like eggplant parmigiana, sausage and peppers, and rigatoni. Without doubt, Little Joe's is the best Occidental restaurant in Chinatown.

Otto Rothschild's Bar and Grill, on the ground floor of the
Dorothy Chandler Pavilion, 135 N. Grand Ave. ☎ 213/972-7322.

Cuisine: CONTINENTAL. **Reservations:** Recommended. **Directions:** From U.S. 101, exit onto Grand Avenue and go one block to the Music Center.

Prices: Appetizers $6–$9; main courses $14–$25; after-theater dinner $12–$19; lunch $8–$13. AE, CB, DC, MC, V.

Open: Mon 11am–6pm, Tues–Fri 11am–midnight, Sat–Sun 11:30am–midnight.

This restaurant celebrates the unparalleled visual history of the motion picture industry and its stars. Photographs of stage and screen celebrities taken by Otto Rothschild over a period of 40 years adorn the walls of this handsome eatery.

There's nothing commonplace about lunch. I tend to focus on the appetizers and light dishes, such as the jalapeño–tuna salad with jicama, green onion, and black-bean salsa or the prime rib chili served with corn chips. Heavier dishes includes sautéed scallops with rosemary marinara over linguine and Santa Fe chicken served with black-bean salsa and grilled scallions.

The list of dinner main courses includes excellent choices of prime meats and pastas. Herb-roasted prime rib is served with whipped-horseradish sauce; the mixed grill contains a breast of chicken, sausage, and lamb chop. An after-theater menu, served from 9pm to midnight, ranges from light main dishes (smoked ham–and–Cheddar omelet, Rothschild burger, salad) to the more substantive (pasta and a Black Angus Steak).

Tokyo Kaikan, 225 S. San Pedro St. ☎ 213/489-1333.

Cuisine: JAPANESE. **Reservations:** Recommended. **Directions:** From U.S. 101, exit onto Alameda Street south and, after two blocks, turn right on 1st Street, then left onto San Pedro Street; the restaurant is located between 2nd and 3rd Streets.

Prices: Appetizers $4–$8; main courses $10–$17; complete lunch $8–$30; complete dinner $16–$40. AE, DISC, MC, V.

Open: Lunch Mon–Fri 11:30am–2pm; dinner Mon–Fri 6–10:30pm, Sat 5–10pm.

Tokyo Kaikan is among the most popular Japanese restaurants in Los Angeles. It's designed to look like a traditional Japanese country inn, with colored globe lights overhead, barnwood, and bamboo- and rattan-covered walls adorned with straw baskets and other provincial artifacts.

A la carte dinner main dishes, served with soup and rice, include beef sukiyaki, shrimp and vegetable tempura, and chicken and beef teriyaki. Several combination plates let you try a number of native dishes without ordering everything on the menu. Green tea, sake, and beer are served at both lunch and dinner, as is ginger ice cream.

Inexpensive

Cassell's Hamburgers, 3266 W. 6th St., in New Chinatown.
☎ 213/480-8668.

Cuisine: AMERICAN. **Reservations:** Not accepted. **Directions:** From the Pasadena Freeway (Calif. 110), exit at 6th Street and head west; the restaurant is just ahead on your right.

Prices: Hamburgers $4–$7. No credit cards.

Open: Lunch only, Mon–Sat 10:30am–4pm.

Yellow Formica tables with bridge chairs and linoleum floors prove that the owner prefers to put profits into the hamburger, not the "ambience." And it's agreed, Cassell's flips one of the best burgers in town. For more than 30 years this dive has been importing its own steer beef, almost daily, from Colorado. You can order your burger medium, rare, well done, or "blue" (simply whisked over the fire).

Help yourself to fixings that include lettuce, homemade mayonnaise, Roquefort dressing, freshly sliced tomatoes, onions, and pickles. You can also have all the peaches, pineapple slices, cottage cheese, and delicious homemade potato salad you want.

Clifton's Brookdale Cafeteria, 648 S. Broadway.
☎ 213/627-1673.

Cuisine: AMERICAN. **Reservations:** Not accepted. **Directions:** From the Pasadena Freeway (Calif. 110), exit at 6th Street and head east; turn right onto Spring Street, another right onto 7th Street, and then right again onto Broadway.

Prices: Appetizers $1–$3; main courses $3–$7. No credit cards.
Open: Daily 7am–7pm.

This is one of a chain of economy cafeterias that has kept the less prosperous of Los Angeles nourished for more than five decades. Clifford Clinton—not Clifton—founded the business on what, today, would seem to be a unique principle: "We pray our humble service be measured not by gold, but by the Golden Rule." During the Depression he kept thousands from starving by honoring an extraordinary policy: "No guest need go hungry. Pay what you wish, dine free unless delighted."

Those shopping or sightseeing downtown can enjoy a huge, economical meal that might consist of split-pea soup, hand-carved roast turkey with dressing, baked squash with brown sugar, and Bavarian cream pie—an excellent meal for under $10. There are more than 100 à la carte items at modest prices. However, since there's a charge for everything, including bread and butter, you must limit your choices to keep your meal inexpensive. It's all fresh, delicious, and homemade too; even the baking is done on the premises. Fresh bakery items are sold at the front counter.

A second Clifton's is located nearby, at 515 W. 7th St., at Olive Street (☎ 213/485-1726). It's open Monday through Saturday from 7am to 3:30pm.

Langer's, 704 S. Alvarado St. ☎ 213/483-8050.

Cuisine: JEWISH. **Reservations:** Not accepted. **Directions:** From the Pasadena Freeway (Calif. 110), exit west onto Olympic Boulevard and, after 10 blocks, turn right (north) on Alvarado Street; the restaurant is three blocks ahead, on the corner of 7th Street.

Prices: Appetizers $4–$10; main courses $6–$14. MC, V.
Open: Daily 6:30am–9pm.

Dating from 1947, Langer's is a big, roomy place with counter seating and brown tufted-leather booths. The walls are lined with portraits of the Langer family and grandchildren, and the corner location (two windowed walls) is light and airy.

The food is kosher *style* rather than kosher, which means you can mix milk and meat and order the likes of pastrami and Swiss cheese on rye. The main dishes include stuffed kishka with soup or salad, vegetable, and potatoes; meat blintzes with gravy; and an interesting sandwich combination of cream cheese and cashews.

The Original Pantry Cafe, 877 S. Figueroa St. ☎ 213/972-9279.

> **Cuisine:** AMERICAN. **Reservations:** Not accepted. **Directions:** From Calif. 110 (Pasadena Freeway), exit onto Wilshire Boulevard and turn left onto Figueroa Street; the restaurant is located at 9th Street.
> **Prices:** Appetizers $2–$4; main courses $6–$11. No credit cards.
> **Open:** Daily 24 hours.

This place has been open 24 hours a day for more than 60 years; they don't even have a key to the front door. Its well-worn decor consists of shiny cream-colored walls with old patined oil paintings and hanging globe lamps overhead; big stainless-steel water pitchers and bowls of celery, carrots, and radishes are placed on every Formica table. Besides the bowl of raw veggies, you also get a whopping-big portion of homemade creamy coleslaw and all the homemade sourdough bread and butter you want—a meal in itself—before you've even ordered. Owned by L.A. Mayor Richard Riordan, the Pantry is especially popular with politicos who come here for weekday lunches.

When you order, you'll be amazed at the bountiful portions. A Pantry breakfast might consist of a huge stack of hotcakes, big slabs of sweet cured ham, home fries, and cup after cup of freshly made coffee. A huge T-bone steak, home-fried pork chops, baked chicken, and macaroni and cheese are served later in the day. The Pantry is an original—don't miss it.

Philippe the Original, 1001 N. Alameda St. ☎ 213/628-3781.

> **Cuisine:** AMERICAN. **Reservations:** Not accepted. **Directions:** From U.S. 101, exit onto Alameda Street and go north to the intersection of North Main, Alameda, and Ord Streets.
> **Prices:** Appetizers $1–$3; main courses $3–$7. No credit cards.
> **Open:** Breakfast daily 6–10:30am; lunch/dinner daily 10:30am–10pm.

Good old-fashioned value and quality are what this establishment is all about—people come here for the good beef, pork, ham, turkey, or lamb French-dip sandwiches served on the lightest, crunchiest French rolls. Philippe's has been around since 1908, and there's nothing stylish about the place. Stand in line while your French-dip sandwich is being assembled, then carry it to one of several long wooden tables. Other menu items include homemade beef stew, chili, two different soups daily, and pickled pigs' feet. A variety of desserts include New York–style cheesecake, cream and fruit pies, puddings, and custards.

A hearty breakfast is served until 10:30am daily, including Philippe's special cinnamon-dipped French toast. All the egg dishes can be topped with their zesty homemade salsa. Beer and wine are available, and there's free parking in the rear and in a lot across the street.

Vickman's, in the produce market, 1228 E. 8th St. ☎ 213/622-3852.

> **Cuisine:** AMERICAN. **Reservations:** Recommended. **Directions:** From U.S. 101, exit at Alameda Street and turn right onto 8th Street; the produce market is located at Central Avenue.

Dining in
Beverly Hills, Hollywood & Downtown

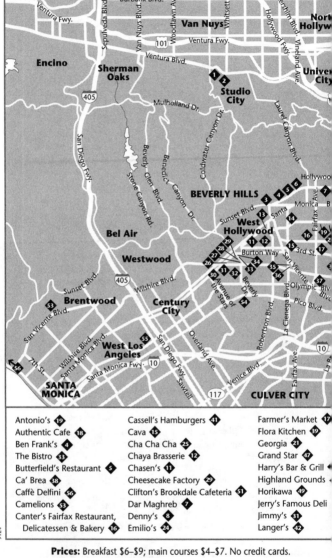

Antonio's ⟨19⟩
Authentic Cafe ⟨18⟩
Ben Frank's ⟨4⟩
The Bistro ⟨33⟩
Butterfield's Restaurant ⟨5⟩
Ca' Brea ⟨38⟩
Caffè Delfini ⟨56⟩
Camelions ⟨53⟩
Canter's Fairfax Restaurant,
   Delicatessen & Bakery ⟨16⟩

Cassell's Hamburgers ⟨41⟩
Cava ⟨15⟩
Cha Cha Cha ⟨25⟩
Chaya Brasserie ⟨12⟩
Chasen's ⟨11⟩
Cheesecake Factory ⟨29⟩
Clifton's Brookdale Cafeteria ⟨51⟩
Dar Maghreb ⟨7⟩
Denny's ⟨8⟩
Emilio's ⟨24⟩

Farmer's Market ⟨17⟩
Flora Kitchen ⟨39⟩
Georgia ⟨21⟩
Grand Star ⟨47⟩
Harry's Bar & Grill ◀
Highland Grounds ◀
Horikawa ⟨49⟩
Jerry's Famous Deli
Jimmy's ⟨31⟩
Langer's ⟨42⟩

Prices: Breakfast $6–$9; main courses $4–$7. No credit cards.
Open: Mon–Sat 3am–3pm.

Established in 1930, this is one of the oldest restaurants in downtown Los Angeles. During Depression days Vickman's sold a beef-tip sandwich for 10¢, less than today's tax on the same item. Still, prices are low by current standards. Practically unchanged, however, are the

unusual hours and the decor (or lack thereof)—creamy walls, linoleum floors, fluorescent lighting, big Formica tables, and wooden booths. Vickman's managers are always on the scene making sure the service and food are up to snuff. It is, and their clientele is so loyal it almost amounts to a cult.

Patrons come for hearty breakfasts, perhaps a Spanish omelet, fresh-baked Danish pastries, or the market omelet with fresh mushrooms and shallots. Fresh-squeezed orange juice is also available. At lunch there are chalkboard specials like cold poached salmon with caper sauce, stuffed pork chops, and boiled chicken. On the other hand, you could order a bagel with cream cheese and lox, a chopped-liver sandwich, or a bowl of chili and beans. Leave room for a big hunk of home-baked fresh-fruit pie (possibly strawberry or peach) with gobs of real whipped cream. It's all cafeteria style; there is no table service. Dinner is not available.

2   Hollywood

Expensive

Dar Maghreb, 7651 Sunset Blvd. ☎ 213/876-7651.

Cuisine: MOROCCAN. **Reservations:** Recommended. **Directions:** From U.S. 101, exit onto Sunset Boulevard and turn right; the restaurant is straight ahead, between Fairfax and La Brea Avenues, at the corner of Stanley Avenue.
Prices: Fixed-price dinners $18–$29. CB, DC, MC, V.
Open: Dinner only, daily 6–11pm.

When you pass through these immense carved brass doors, you enter an exotic Arab world. Step into a Koranic patio, at the center of which is an exquisite fountain under an open skylight. The floor is marble and the carved wood-and-plaster walls are decorated with handmade tiles in geometric designs. A kaftaned hostess greets you and leads you to either the Rabat Room or the Berber Room. The former features rich Rabat carpets, marquetry tables, and silk cushions with spun-gold-thread designs. The Berber Room is more rustic, with warm earth tones, mountain rugs, and brass furniture from Marrakech. In both rooms diners sit on low sofas against the wall and on goatskin poufs (cushions). Berber and Andalusian music are played in the background, and there's belly dancing nightly.

The fixed-price meal is a multicourse feast, including a choice of chicken, lamb, turkey, beef, squab, quail, or shrimp, eaten with your hands and hunks of bread, and shared, from the same dish, with other members of your party. There are eight possible dinners, most of which come with Moroccan salads of cold raw and cooked vegetables; and b'stilla, an appetizer of shredded chicken, eggs, almonds, and spices wrapped in a flaky pastry shell and topped with powdered sugar and cinnamon. Other dishes include a tajine of chicken cooked with pickled lemons, onions, and fresh coriander; and couscous, with lamb and vegetables—squash, carrots, tomatoes, garbanzo beans, turnips, onions, and raisins.

Moderate

⭐ **Ca' Brea,** 346 S. La Brea Ave. ☎ 213/938-2863.
Cuisine: ITALIAN. **Reservations:** Recommended. **Directions:** From U.S. 101 south, take the Normandie Avenue exit and turn right (south),

then turn right again, onto Beverly Boulevard, and then left onto La Brea Avenue; the restaurant will be two blocks ahead on your left, between 3rd and 4th Streets. From the Santa Monica Freeway, take the La Brea Avenue exit and head north; the restaurant is located about $2^1/_2$ miles ahead on your right.

Prices: Appetizers $5–$10; main courses $9–$21; lunch $7–$20. AE, CB, DC, MC, V.

Open: Lunch Mon–Sat 11:30am–2:30pm; dinner Mon–Thurs 5:30–10:30pm, Fri–Sat 5:30pm–midnight.

Even with reservations you can expect a wait here, since Ca' Brea is one of the most celebrated new restaurants in Los Angeles.

The restaurant's refreshingly bright dining room is hung with over-sized contemporary oil paintings and backed by an open prep-kitchen where you can watch your sautéed seafood cakes being made. The booths are the most coveted seats, but with only 20 tables, surrounded by colorfully upholstered, heavy wooden chairs, be thankful you are sitting anywhere.

Chef Antonio Tommasi watches over a gifted kitchen that turns out consistently excellent dishes that are as pretty as they are tasty. New Italian dishes like roasted pork sausage with braised Napa cabbage, homemade ravioli stuffed with butter squash, and duck served with a light honey/balsamic-vinegar sauce are typical of the restaurant's offerings. The menu is the same for both lunch and dinner.

Emilio's, 6602 Melrose Ave. ☎ 213/935-4922.

Cuisine: ITALIAN. **Reservations:** Recommended. **Directions:** From U.S. 101, exit onto Highland Avenue and continue straight to the corner of Melrose Avenue and the restaurant.

Prices: Appetizers $5–$10; main courses $10–$24; Sun buffet $22. AE, CB, DC, MC, V.

Open: Lunch Thurs–Fri 11:30am–2:30pm; dinner daily 5pm–midnight; Sun buffet 5–9pm.

This award-winning restaurant attracts a celebrity clientele with its authentic Italian cooking. The downstairs dining room surrounds a colorfully lit "Fountain de Trevi." The decor is ornate Italian, with marble columns from floor to lofty ceiling, brick archways, stained-glass windows, gilt-framed oil paintings, and fresh flowers on every table.

Order lavishly and savor every bite. You might begin with the antipasti of mussels with spicy tomato sauce and garlic, or the scallops with oil and garlic. For your second course, the brodetto adriadico (it's like cioppino) is heartily recommended, as are any of the several veal main dishes. Homemade pastas are also excellent, including linguine with shrimp and lobster, and rondelli stuffed with ricotta, mortadella, and spinach. Homemade noodles with sun-dried tomatoes, baby corn, carrots, and peas are less caloric, but good. Depending on the day, you may also find roast suckling pig or osso buco on the menu.

Georgia, 7250 Melrose Ave. ☎ **213/933-8420.**

> **Cuisine:** SOUTHERN. **Reservations:** Recommended. **Directions:** From Santa Monica Boulevard, exit south onto Fairfax Avenue and turn left onto Melrose Avenue; the restaurant is about 10 blocks ahead at the corner of Alta Vista.
>
> **Prices:** Appetizers $6–$9; main courses $13–$19; lunch $6–$15. AE, MC, V.
>
> **Open:** Lunch Mon–Fri noon–3pm; dinner Mon–Sat 6:30–11pm, Sun 5:30–11pm.

Soul food and power ties commingle at this calorie-unconscious ode to southern cooking in the heart of Melrose's funky shopping district. Owned by a group of investors that include actors Denzel Washington and Eddie Murphy, the restaurant is especially popular with Hollywood's African-American arts crowd—at least those who can afford to pay for L.A.'s highest-priced pork chops, fried chicken, and grits. Other offerings include turtle soup, fried oysters, blue-crab cakes, meatloaf, smoked baby back ribs, grilled gulf shrimp, candied yams, and cornmeal mush. Some dishes, like catfish, are more delicately fried than is traditional. Others are smothered in onion gravy, and most are sided with corn pudding, string beans, or coleslaw.

The dining room itself is built to resemble a fine southern house, complete with mahogany floors, Spanish moss, and wrought-iron gates. Palm tree artwork and a bourbon bar continue the theme.

★ **Musso & Frank Grill,** 6667 Hollywood Blvd. ☎ 213/467-7788.

> **Cuisine:** AMERICAN. **Reservations:** Recommended. **Directions:** From U.S. 101, exit onto Cahuenga Boulevard and continue to the restaurant at the corner of Hollywood Boulevard.
>
> **Prices:** Appetizers $5–$9; main courses $10–$32. AE, CB, DC, MC, V.
>
> **Open:** Tues–Sat 11am–11pm.

By the restaurant's own estimation, this is Hollywood's oldest extant eatery, established in 1919. People have kept coming back for the comfortable ambience, superb service, and consistently excellent food for more than half a century; it's also where Faulkner and Hemingway hung out during their screenwriting days. The Musso & Frank Grill is a favorite of Jonathan Winters, Merv Griffin, Ben Gazarra, and Ralph Edwards—to name just a few.

The setting is richly traditional—oak beamed ceilings, red-leather booths and banquettes, mahogany room dividers (complete with coathooks)—enhanced by soft lighting from wall sconces and chandeliers with tiny shades.

The menu is extensive; everything from soups to salads to seafood is served à la carte. Try the delicious seafood salads such as the chiffonade or shrimp Louie, perhaps with some Camembert that comes with crusty bread and butter. Diners desiring heartier fare might consider the veal scaloppine marsala, roast spring lamb with mint jelly, or broiled lobster. Sandwiches and omelets are also available. The back of the menu lists an equally extensive liquor and wine selection.

Ristorante Chianti & Chianti Cucina, 7383 Melrose Ave.
☎ 213/653-8333.
Cuisine: ITALIAN. **Reservations:** Recommended. **Directions:** From U.S. 101, exit onto Highland Avenue, turn right onto Melrose Avenue, and continue straight for about 10 blocks to the restaurant, at the corner of Martel Avenue, between Fairfax and La Brea Avenues.
Prices: Appetizers $6–$8; main courses $13–$20. AE, CB, DC, MC, V.
Open: Ristorante Chianti, dinner only, daily 5:30–11:30pm. Chianti Cucina, Mon–Sat noon–11:30pm, Sun 5pm–midnight.

Begun in 1938 by the famous New York restaurateur Romeo Salta, this charming northern Italian restaurant has a long history in Hollywood: The cast party for *Gone with the Wind* was held here. The restaurant has won several prestigious awards, including accolades for its excellent wine list. Although it operates as a single entity, Ristorante Chianti & Chianti Cucina offers two completely different dining experiences and menus.

Ristorante Chianti is traditional Italian in looks—quiet, intimate, complete with red-velvet seating and sepia-tone murals. Hot and cold appetizers range from fresh handmade mozzarella and prosciutto to lamb carpaccio with asparagus and marinated grilled eggplant filled with goat cheese, arugula, and sun-dried tomatoes. As for main dishes, the homemade pasta is both exceptional and deliciously untraditional. Try black tortellini filled with fresh salmon, or giant ravioli filled with spinach, ricotta, and quail eggs topped with shaved black truffle. Other dishes include fresh fish and prawns, poultry, and a fine selection of meat dishes.

Chianti Cucina is bright, bustling, attractive, and loud; it makes you feel as if you're dining right in the kitchen. Although the menu changes frequently, it typically features exceptional antipasti, pastas, and a pleasing main-dish selection that's somewhat more limited than Ristorante Chianti's. Good first-course selections include smoked duck with pearls of mozzarella and steamed spinach, and carpaccio with alfalfa sprouts and Parmesan cheese. Of the pasta dishes, you might try the lobster- and shrimp-filled tortellini or the simpler pasta dumplings with roasted pepper sauce, basil, and Parmesan.

Shanghai Winter Garden, 5651 Wilshire Blvd. ☎ 213/934-0505.
Cuisine: CHINESE. **Reservations:** Accepted only for parties of four or more. **Directions:** From U.S. 101, exit onto Highland Avenue and turn right onto Sunset Boulevard; after about a mile, turn left onto Fairfax Avenue, and after another mile turn right onto Wilshire Boulevard. The restaurant is about 10 blocks ahead at the corner of Hauser Boulevard.
Prices: Appetizers $4–$11; main courses $10–$25; lunch $6–$10. AE, DC, MC, V.
Open: Lunch Mon–Sat 11:30am–3pm; dinner daily 4–10:30pm.

This is one of my favorite L.A. Chinese restaurants. An archway depicting a phoenix and dragon, set in an intricately carved teak wall, separates the dining areas; Chinese paintings and wood carvings adorn the walls; and large tasseled Chinese lamps hang overhead.

The menu features more than 150 main dishes, including diced fried chicken sautéed with spinach, shrimp with bamboo shoots and green peas in a delicious sauce with crisp sizzling rice, crispy duckling made with five spicy ingredients, and crushed white meat chicken sautéed with diced ham, pine nuts, and green peas. As you can see, this is no ordinary take-out joint.

Tom Bergin's Tavern, 840 S. Fairfax Ave. ☎ 213/936-7151.

> **Cuisine:** IRISH. **Reservations:** Not required. **Directions:** From U.S. 101, exit onto Highland Avenue, turn right onto Sunset Boulevard, and, after about a mile, turn left onto Fairfax Avenue; the restaurant is located about a mile ahead, at Barrows Drive, between Wilshire and Olympic Boulevards.
>
> **Prices:** Appetizers $5–$7; main courses $13–$20; bar lunch $4–$10. AE, DC, DISC, MC, V.
>
> **Open:** Lunch Mon–Fri 11am–4pm; dinner daily 4–11pm. (Bar, 11am–2am.)

Tom Bergin's is L.A.'s Irish community's unofficial headquarters. Since 1936 this has also been a gathering place for sportswriters, athletes, and fans. Actors Bing Crosby and Pat O'Brien were early friends of the house. Bergin's was the first city restaurant to charter buses to pro football games—they still do, and they hold 230 seats to the games reserved five years in advance.

Mesquite-fired New York steak with onion rings, garlic-cheese toast, salad, and potatoes is the specialty of the house. More traditional Irish fare like Dublin-style corned beef and cabbage with a steamed potato, or chicken Erin, simmered in cream-and-cider sauce, with bacon, leeks, mushrooms, and rice pilaf, are also served, along with burgers and salads. For dessert you can choose from fresh-fruit pies or Bailey's Irish Cream cheesecake, and wash it down with an Irish coffee.

Inexpensive

Authentic Cafe, 7605 Beverly Blvd. ☎ 213/939-4626.

> **Cuisine:** SOUTHWESTERN. **Reservations:** Not accepted. **Directions:** From Santa Monica Boulevard, turn south onto Fairfax, then right onto Beverly Boulevard; the restaurant is about six blocks ahead at Curson Avenue.
>
> **Prices:** Appetizers $2–$9; main courses $8am–$13; lunch $5–$9. MC, V.
>
> **Open:** Mon–Thurs 11:30am–10pm, Fri 11:30am–11pm, Sat 10am–11pm, Sun 10am–10pm.

True to its name, this excellent restaurant serves authentic southwestern food in a casual café atmosphere, a winning combination that has made it one of my friend Billy Rose's favorite restaurants. A trendy dining room that's terrific for people-watching, very good food, and large portions translates into long waits almost every night of the week.

Chef Roger Hayot cooks up southwestern American meals that sometimes have Asian influences—like Brie, papaya, and chili quesadillas. Blue-corn chiles rellenos, potstickers, and pizza bread round out the appetizers. A long list of main courses includes chicken casserole made with cornbread crust; fettuccine tossed with chicken, fresh corn, and red peppers in chile-cream sauce; and meatloaf with caramelized onions. Lunches are lighter and may include cheeseless pizza with tomato sauce, red onion, garlic, zucchini, eggplant, and basil; grilled sausage sandwiches; or Thai chicken salad.

Flora Kitchen, 460 S. La Brea Ave. ☎ 213/931-9900.

Cuisine: AMERICAN. **Reservations:** Not accepted. **Directions:** From Santa Monica Boulevard, exit east onto Wilshire Boulevard, drive about four miles, then turn left onto La Brea Avenue; the restaurant is one block ahead, at 6th Street.
Prices: Appetizers $2–$6; main courses $5–$10. AE, MC, V.
Open: Sun–Thurs 8am–10pm, Fri–Sat 8am–11pm.

Imagine an upscale hip-happening bright funky cafeteria and you've imagined Flora Kitchen. Known for its tuna and chicken salads served on most-exalted La Brea Bakery breads, the restaurant is equally comfortable dishing out more eclectic meals like cayenne-spiced potato soup, poached salmon with dill sauce, and seared ahi with roast vegetables.

Flora is popular with doyens of nearby art galleries by day, and on warm summer nights, with music lovers who take the restaurant's dinners, boxed, to the Hollywood Bowl.

Noura Cafe, 8479 Melrose Ave. ☎ 213/651-4581.

Cuisine: MIDDLE EASTERN. **Reservations:** Accepted only for large parties. **Directions:** From Santa Monica Boulevard, exit east onto Melrose Avenue; the restaurant is near the corner of La Cienega Boulevard.
Prices: Salads and pitas $4–$7; plates $5–$11. MC, V.
Open: Sun–Thurs 11am–11pm, Fri–Sat 11am–midnight.

The best find on Melrose, the Noura Cafe is packed with beautiful underweight women who love the restaurant's healthful, largely vegetarian Middle Eastern cuisine. Seating is either inside or out, beside a warm firepit. Most meals are served with pita bread for stuffing with broiled lamb, beef, chicken, or one of a number of salads. Traditional Mediterranean salads include baba ghanoush (grilled eggplant with tahini and lemon), Turkish (tomatoes, green onions, and spices), and tabbouleh (cracked wheat, parsley, and tomatoes). The thinnest women order just a glass of fresh carrot juice and a home-baked muffin.

Pink's Hot Dogs, on the northwest corner of La Brea and Melrose Aves. ☎ 213/931-4223.

Cuisine: AMERICAN. **Directions:** From the Santa Monica Freeway (I-10), exit north onto La Brea Avenue; the stand is about four miles ahead at Melrose Avenue.
Prices: Hot dogs $2.
Open: Sun–Thurs 9:30am–2am, Fri–Sat 9:30am–3am.

Pink's is not your usual guidebook recommendation, but then again this hot-dog stand, near the heart of old Hollywood, is not your usual doggery. Even health-conscious Angelenos sometimes forgo their principles to stand in line at this corner stand. The chili dogs are famous, and thousands are served daily. There are a few tables scattered around the corner, but most people stand while they down their dogs. Pray the bulldozers stay away from this little nugget of a place.

Roscoe's House of Chicken 'n' Waffles, 1514 N. Gower St. ☎ **213/466-7453.**

Cuisine: AMERICAN. **Reservations:** Not accepted. **Directions:** From U.S. 101, exit onto Highland Avenue and turn left onto Sunset Boulevard; the restaurant is straight ahead, at Gower Street.

Prices: Main courses $4–$11. No credit cards.

Open: Sun–Thurs 9am–midnight, Fri–Sat 9am–4am.

Proximity to the CBS Studios alone would probably guarantee a celebrity clientele. Roscoe's devotees have included Jane Fonda, Stevie Wonder, Flip Wilson, Eddie Murphy, Alex Haley, and the Eagles. The setting is very simple, with slanted cedar and white stucco walls, changing art exhibits, track lighting overhead, lots of plants, and good music in the background.

Only chicken and waffle dishes are served, though that includes eggs and chicken livers. A chicken-and-cheese omelet with french fries accompanied by an order of homemade biscuits makes for a unique and delicious breakfast. One specialty is a quarter chicken smothered in gravy and onions, served with waffles or grits and biscuits. You can also get chicken salad and chicken sandwiches. Homemade cornbread, sweet-potato pie, homemade potato salad, greens, and corn on the cob are all available as side orders, and wine and beer are sold.

A second Roscoe's is located at 4907 W. Washington Blvd., at La Brea Avenue (☎ **213/936-3730**).

3   West Hollywood

Expensive

Chasen's, 9039 Beverly Blvd. ☎ **310/271-2168.**

Cuisine: AMERICAN. **Reservations:** Recommended. **Directions:** From Santa Monica Boulevard, exit onto Beverly Boulevard and continue straight for four blocks to the restaurant at Doheny Drive.

Prices: Appetizers $9–$19; main courses $22–$37; lunch $5–$18. AE, DISC, MC, V.

Open: Lunch Tues–Fri 11:30am–2pm; dinner Tues–Sun 6pm–1am.

The original Chasen's, a chili parlor, was financed by *New Yorker* editor Harold Ross, and early patrons at this "Algonquin West" included Jimmy Durante and James Cagney. James Thurber once spent hours drawing murals on the men's room wall; unfortunately, they were immediately removed by an overly industrious janitor. Chasen's is a real restaurant, with professional waiters serving great American food. Even after all these years, it's thoroughly recommendable.

The main dining room of this enduring favorite is wood-paneled and softly lit, with beamed ceilings, brass reading lamps, and plush tufted red-leather booths. The menu has come a long way since chili (Elizabeth Taylor's favorite; she's even ordered it shipped to her), but the continental fare still retains its American simplicity. Specialties include the exceptional hobo steak (not listed on the menu), veal bone chop, and rack of lamb. You can top off your meal with the house special: banana or strawberry shortcake.

Morton's, 8764 Melrose Ave. ☎ 310/276-5205.

> **Cuisine:** CALIFORNIAN. **Reservations:** Recommended. **Directions:** From Santa Monica Boulevard, exit east onto Melrose Avenue; the restaurant is about one block ahead on your right.
>
> **Prices:** Appetizers $7–$14; main courses $17–$29; lunch $7–$15. AE, MC, V.
>
> **Open:** Mon–Fri noon–11:30pm, Sat 6–11:30pm.

In 1994, Hard Rock Cafe founder Peter Morton moved his successful self-named restaurant to a new, bigger location across the street. Surviving the odds, Morton's reopened to raves—especially from the entertainment community that has long been this restaurant's bread and butter. Morton's has long been an important part of the Hollywood "scene." In its new location, the restaurant has become the site of one of the most important post-Oscar celebrations. On Monday night throughout the year, entertainment's high and mighty consider these the most highly coveted tables in the city.

The restaurant's single, wood-ceilinged, lofty dining room is big enough to see everybody, yet dark enough to keep it feeling personal. Tables are spaced far enough apart to assure privacy, and servers are attentive without being obtrusive.

Meals at Morton's are straightforward and good. It's easy to understand every word on the unintimidating menu, and meals arrive without a lot of visual froufrou. An emphasis on simplicity, quality, and freshness translates into appetizers like Maryland fresh soft-shell crabs, tuna sashimi, and lobster-stuffed sweet-corn pancakes. Typical main courses on the seasonal menu include lime-grilled free-range chicken, grilled swordfish, roast pork tenderloin, and New York steak.

Frommer's Cool for Kids: Restaurants

Aunt Kizzy's Back Porch   (see p. 142) This restaurant was practically invented for children. It serves fried chicken and has a down home fun atmosphere.

Carlos and Pepe's   (see p. 136) This place is bright and festive, and the kids will be entertained by the ocean views and the fish-filled aquarium to one side of the dining room. Besides, what kid can resist a good taco, burrito, or chips and salsa?

The Warehouse   (see p. 140) Kids won't have any trouble finding something they like from this extensive international menu. The atmosphere is quite leisurely, and the thousands of moored boats will hold the kids' interest.

Desserts, like hot-fudge sundaes and warm fruit tarts, are equally forthright in taste and description.

⭐ **Spago,** 8795 Sunset Blvd. ☎ **310/652-4025.**

Cuisine: CALIFORNIAN. **Reservations:** Required, three to four weeks in advance. **Directions:** From U.S. 101, exit onto Highland Avenue and turn right onto Sunset Boulevard; the restaurant is about three miles ahead, at Horn Avenue.

Prices: Appetizers $10–$15; main courses $18–$28. DC, DISC, MC, V.

Open: Dinner only, daily 6–11:30pm.

Celebrity chef Wolfgang Puck has a flair for publicity and has made Spago one of the best-known restaurants in America. This noisy L.A. restaurant is popular with celebrities, wannabes, and tourists throughout the year. Designed by Barbara Lazaroff, the restaurant is elegantly decorated in clean, light shades punctuated with armfuls of flowers. A huge picture window and an open kitchen give diners an alternative view when they get tired of looking at each other.

Puck invented California-style gourmet pizza, baked in a wood-burning oven and topped with exotic ingredients like duck sausage, shiitake mushrooms, leeks, artichokes, and even lox and sour cream. Pastas like black-pepper fettuccine with Louisiana shrimp, roasted garlic, and basil ratatouille; or angel-hair spaghetti with goat cheese and broccoli are also available, as are more substantial dishes like roast Sonoma lamb with braised shallots and herb butter, and grilled chicken with garlic and parsley. Despite all the hype, Spago is really terrific.

Moderate

Antonio's, 7472 Melrose Ave. ☎ **213/655-0480.**

Cuisine: MEXICAN. **Reservations:** Not required. **Directions:** From U.S. 101, exit onto Highland Avenue and turn right onto Melrose Avenue; the restaurant is located about a mile ahead, between Fairfax and La Brea Avenues.

Prices: Appetizers $5–$7; main courses $11–$15. AE, MC, V.

Open: Lunch Tues–Fri 11am–3pm; dinner Tues–Fri 5–10:30pm.

There's "gringo food"—fiery tamales, with lots of cheese, sour cream, and refried beans—and then there's the subtle, delicate, and delicious Mexican cooking of Antonio's. For 25 years this gourmet Mexican restaurant has been serving top-notch food without the bright reds, yellows, and greens of the usual taco joint. The true cuisine of Mexico City is delicious, well seasoned, high in protein, low in cholesterol, and lean on calories. A variety of fresh seafood and meats with exotic vegetables are featured, and most of the main dishes are steamed rather than fried.

The menu changes daily, but fresh fish is available at all times. Chicken is served in a variety of ways—Guadalajara style, in tamales stuffed with assorted fresh vegetables; or stewed in a delicate green sauce of tomatillos, green peppers, and exotic spices. Meat-stuffed cabbage and spareribs with chile-and-herb sauce are both recommended.

A second Antonio's is located in Santa Monica, at 1323 Montana Ave., at 14th Street (☎ 213/395-2815).

Butterfield's Restaurant, 8426 Sunset Blvd. ☎ 213/656-3055.

Cuisine: CONTINENTAL. **Reservations:** Recommended. **Directions:** From Santa Monica Boulevard, turn north onto Fairfax Avenue, then turn left onto Sunset Boulevard; the restaurant is about 10 blocks ahead on your left, at the corner of Olive Drive.

Prices: Appetizers $4–$8; main courses $9–$18; lunch $9–$12; Sat–Sun brunch $8–$10. AE, DC, MC, V.

Open: Lunch Mon–Fri 11:30am–3pm; dinner Sun–Thurs 6–10pm, Fri–Sat 6–11pm; brunch Sat–Sun 10:30am–3pm.

Tucked beneath the Sunset Strip on the former John Barrymore estate, Butterfield's is a woody oasis in the heart of the city. Dining al fresco here is like eating in the middle of a leafy forest. A small pond enlivened with mature koi helps make this one of the most comfortable outdoor patios in L.A. The inside dining room, coveted only when the temperature drops, is located in a guest cottage that once housed Errol Flynn.

Dinners might begin with sea-scallop ceviche or tangy mushroom bisque. Of pastas, the best is topped with sun-dried tomatoes and red bell peppers, and an excellent meaty chicken breast is stuffed with Cheddar cheese and apricots before being baked with an apricot-brandy glaze.

At lunch, Cobb salads, fresh fruits, and sandwiches are the preferred meals. Patio brunches on warm weekend mornings include filling dishes like smoked salmon Benedict; spicy scrambled eggs with prosciutto, bacon, venison sausage, and jalapeño; and Aztec eggs—poached and served with cheese and black-bean sauce on a blue-corn tortilla.

Inexpensive

 The Source, 8301 W. Sunset Blvd. ☎ 213/656-6388.

Cuisine: CALIFORNIA HEALTH FOOD. **Reservations:** Not accepted. **Directions:** From U.S. 101, exit onto Highland Avenue and turn right onto Sunset Boulevard; the restaurant is located about two miles ahead at Sweetzer Avenue, between La Cienega Boulevard and Fairfax Avenue.

Prices: Appetizers $3–$5; main courses $5–$11. AE, CB, DC, MC, V.

Open: Mon–Fri 8am–midnight, Sat–Sun 9am–midnight.

This is where Woody Allen met Diane Keaton for a typical L.A. lunch in *Annie Hall*—part of his New York–centric statement about southern California. Inside it's cozy, with curtained windows, tables set with fresh flowers, and a plant-filled stone fireplace in one corner. Those who want fresh air with their health food shouldn't be in L.A., but outdoor dining on their covered patio is available.

Cheese-walnut loaf, served with homemade soup or salad, and a basket of whole-wheat rolls and butter comprises a typical meal. Salads and sandwiches are also available. Most menu items are vegetarian, but chicken and fish are also served. Portions are huge. Drinks include yogurt shakes, beer, and wine. The homemade date-nut cheesecake is so good it's hard to believe it's healthy.

4 Beverly Hills & Century City

Expensive

The Bistro, 246 N. Canon Dr., Beverly Hills. ☎ 213/273-5633.

> **Cuisine:** CONTINENTAL. **Reservations:** Required. **Directions:** From Santa Monica Boulevard, exit onto Canon Drive; the restaurant is two blocks ahead at Dayton Way.
>
> **Prices:** Appetizers $8–$13; main courses $15–$27. AE, CB, DC, MC, V.
> **Open:** Dinner only, Mon–Fri 6–10:30pm, Sat 6–11pm.

Conceived more than two decades ago by film director Billy Wilder and Romanoff's maître d'Kurt Niklas, the Bistro is both elegant and charming. The restaurant is decorated in authentic Parisian Belle Epoque, with mirrored walls, hand-painted panels with classical motifs, tables set with gleaming silver, soft pink lighting, and fresh roses on every table.

Both the service and the cuisine are top-notch. The mussel soup is outstanding, and the rich lobster bisque and cream of watercress soups are excellent. Two appetizers you won't want to overlook are the salmon and the pheasant pâté. You might choose a cold main dish of duck or quail salad, or one such as linguine with raddichio, asparagus, and scallops. The rack of lamb is also recommended. All the pasta is homemade and fresh. For dessert, I recommend the sumptuous chocolate soufflé. Jackets are required at dinner, when there is live piano music.

Chaya Brasserie, 8741 Alden Dr., Los Angeles ☎ 310/859-8833.

> **Cuisine:** CALIFORNIAN. **Reservations:** Recommended. **Directions:** From Santa Monica Boulevard, exit south onto Robertson, then turn right onto Alden Drive to the restaurant.
>
> **Prices:** Appetizers $7–$15; main courses $11–$24; lunch $9–$16. AE, CB, DC, MC, V.
> **Open:** Lunch Mon–Fri 11am–2:30pm; dinner Mon–Thurs 6–10:30pm, Fri–Sat 6–11pm, Sun 6–10pm.

Opened by a family of Japanese restaurateurs, Chaya has long been one of Los Angeles's best restaurants. Popular with film agents during lunch, the restaurant regularly packs in stars and stargazers who love great food served in a noisy but homey atmosphere. On warm afternoons and evenings, the best tables are on the outside terrace, overlooking the busy street.

A continental bistro with Asian flair, the restaurant is best known for its grilled items, like seared soy-marinated Hawaiian tuna and Long Island duckling. Hot and cold starters include seaweed salad with ginger-soy rice vinaigrette, escargots with chopped mushrooms, and sautéed foie gras over hearts of daikon. Similarly styled main courses include lobster ravioli with pesto-cream sauce, plus a host of lunchtime salads and sandwiches.

Jimmy's, 201 Moreno Dr., Beverly Hills. ☎ **310/552-2394.**

Cuisine: CONTINENTAL. **Reservations:** Recommended. **Directions:** From Santa Monica Boulevard, exit east onto Wilshire Boulevard and immediately turn right onto Lasky Drive; the restaurant is three blocks ahead at Moreno Drive.

Prices: Appetizers $8–$20; main courses $23–$30; lunch $13–$18. AE, CB, DC, MC, V.

Open: Lunch Mon–Fri 11:30am–3pm; dinner Mon–Sat 5pm–1am.

Jimmy Murphy—the long-time maître d' at L.A.'s elite Bistro—struck out on his own several years ago, with backing from Johnny Carson and Bob Newhart. Jimmy's reputation has attracted a top staff, and he has created one of the prettiest and most comfortable restaurants in town. Baccarat crystal chandeliers hang from recessed ceilings, which have been painted to look like the sky. Tables are set with Limoges china, crystal glasses, and fresh flowers. One wall of windows overlooks the terrace with its small garden, fountain, shade trees, and tables under white canvas umbrellas. From the chinoiserie statues at the entrance to the considered placement of mirrors, plants, and floral arrangements, Jimmy's is perfectly lovely in every detail, including the posh bar/lounge where a pianist entertains nightly.

You could begin lunch or dinner with an hors d'oeuvre of assorted shellfish or pheasant pâté with truffles. Dinner main dishes include filet mignon with foie gras and truffles wrapped in a fluffy pastry shell, and peppered salmon with cabernet sauce. At lunch you might opt for seafood salad, cold salmon in aspic, white fish with limes, or steak tartare with fresh asparagus.

Lawry's The Prime Rib, 55 N. La Cienega Blvd., Beverly Hills. ☎ 310/652-2827.

Cuisine: AMERICAN. **Reservations:** Recommended. **Directions:** From Santa Monica Boulevard, exit onto Wilshire Boulevard and continue straight for about two miles, then turn left onto North La Cienega Boulevard; the restaurant is just half a block ahead.

Prices: Appetizers $5–$9; main courses $19–$26. AE, CB, DC, DISC, MC, V.

Open: Dinner only, Mon–Thurs 5–11pm, Fri–Sat 5pm–midnight, Sun 3–10pm.

A family enterprise begun in 1938, Lawry's enjoys an excellent Restaurant Row location, near Beverly Hills's eastern edge. The restaurant was created by Lawrence Frank and his brother-in-law, Walter Van de Kamp. Frank set out to offer "the greatest meal in America," serving just one main dish—the hearty prime rib he had enjoyed every Sunday for dinner as a boy (his father was in the meat business). Then the beef was showcased atop three gleaming silver carts, each costing as much as a Cadillac, and carved tableside by knowledgeable experts. Lawry's is also the home of the now-famous seasoned salt invented as the perfect seasoning for prime rib.

Lawry's clubroom atmosphere begins in the homey cocktail lounge, where drinks are served from a pewter-topped wood-paneled bar. The dining room is equally opulent, decorated with original oil paintings (including one of the late Duke of Windsor at age 7), Persian-carpeted oak floors, and high-backed chairs at tables draped with orange-sherbet cloths.

In addition to the restaurant's main dish—a choice of four cuts of Lawry's award-winning prime ribs of beef—there is a seafood dish. With both you get Yorkshire pudding, salad, mashed potatoes, and creamed horseradish. You can also order such side dishes as creamed spinach, corn, or buttered peas, and a good wine list is available.

Matsuhisa, 129 N. La Cienega Blvd., Beverly Hills. ☎ **310/659-9639.**

Cuisine: JAPANESE/PERUVIAN. **Reservations:** Required. **Directions:** From Santa Monica Boulevard, exit onto Wilshire Boulevard east, and turn left onto La Cienega Boulevard to the restaurant.

Prices: Appetizers $6–$14; main courses $14–$22; lunch $7–$13. AE, DC, MC, V.

Open: Lunch Mon–Fri 11:45am–2:45pm; dinner daily 5:45–10:15pm.

Japanese chef/owner Nobuyuki Matsuhisa arrived in Los Angeles via Peru and opened what may be the most creative restaurant in the entire city. A true master of fish cookery, Matsuhisa creates fantastic and unusual dishes by combining Japanese flavors with South American spices and salsas. Broiled sea bass with black truffles, sautéed squid with garlic and soy, and Dungeness crab tossed with chiles and cream are good examples of the masterfully prepared delicacies you can expect here. Sushi dishes are equally eclectic, innovative, and interesting.

Both tight and bright, the restaurant's cafeterialike dining room suffers from bad lighting and precious lack of privacy. There's lots of action behind the sushi bar, and a frenetic service staff keeps the restaurant humming at a fiery pace. But Matsuhisa remains popular with hardcore foodies who continually return for the savory surprises that come with every bite.

R.J.'s The Rib Joint, 252 N. Beverly Dr., Beverly Hills. ☎ **310/274-7427.**

Cuisine: AMERICAN. **Reservations:** Not required. **Directions:** From Santa Monica Boulevard, exit onto Beverly Drive; the restaurant is between Dayton Way and Wilshire Boulevard.

Prices: Appetizers $5–$12; main courses $9–$14 at lunch, $12–$24 at dinner. AE, DC, MC, V.

Open: Sun–Thurs 11:30am–10pm, Fri–Sat 11:30am–11pm.

No dainty endive salads and kiwi tarts here. R.J.'s gargantuan meals include steaks; oakwood-grilled beef, pork, and ribs; clams; chili; hickory-smoked chicken; crispy duck; and lobster. All dinners begin with help-yourself servings from the most sumptuous 75-foot salad bar you're ever likely to encounter. Forty or so offerings are included in the price of your main course along with sourdough rolls and butter. Doggy bags are available.

Heralded by a green-and-white-striped awning, R.J.'s casual and comfortable interior means sawdust on the floors, lots of plants, and exposed-brick and raw-pine walls cluttered with historic photos of Beverly Hills and of yesterday's stars. A pianist usually entertains with nostalgic American tunes.

The well-stocked bar features more than 500 brands. Only premium liquors and fresh-squeezed juices are used. The restaurant also carries more than 50 varieties of beer from all over the world.

Trader Vic's, at the Beverly Hilton Hotel, 9878 Wilshire Blvd., Beverly Hills. ☎ 213/274-7777.

Cuisine: POLYNESIAN. **Reservations:** Not required. **Directions:** From I-405 north, exit onto Santa Monica Boulevard and go east for three miles to the hotel at Wilshire Boulevard.

Prices: Appetizers $7–$12; main courses $16–$30. AE, DC, DISC, MC, V.

Open: Dinner only, daily 5pm–1am.

The interesting nautical interior of Trader Vic's features model ships and tropical shells. The restaurant has long been famous for its tropical rum drinks garnished with cute little umbrellas.

An eclectic South Pacific menu includes a host of puu puus (hors d'oeuvres) including absolutely delicious crisp calamari, padang prawns saté, and skewered shrimp brushed with saté-chile butter. Two excellent main dishes are barbecued squab and the Indonesian lamb roast, completely trimmed and marinated and served with a peach chutney. The chateaubriand for two is an excellent cut of matured beef. Desserts include mud pie and Aloha ice cream—vanilla ice cream in mango sauce topped with banana chips.

Moderate

Harry's Bar & Grill, 2020 Ave. of the Stars, Century City. ☎ 310/277-2333.

Cuisine: ITALIAN. **Reservations:** Required. **Directions:** From Santa Monica Boulevard, exit south onto the Avenue of the Stars.

Prices: Appetizers $5–$8; main courses $9–$20; lunch $10–$18. AE, CB, DC, MC, V.

Open: Lunch Mon–Sat 11:30am–5pm; dinner daily 5–11:30pm.

Located on the Plaza Level of the ABC Entertainment Center, Harry's is almost identical to its namesake in Florence, which is itself a spinoff of the Harry's in Venice, made famous by Ernest Hemingway in his novel *Across the River and into the Trees.* The bar is European, with high walnut counters and tall wooden stools. Former owners Larry Mindel and Jerry Magnin hand-picked the paintings, tapestries, and furnishings on various trips to Italy. Artist Lazero Donati (who created an oil painting for the Florence Harry's) was commissioned to do a similar painting for this establishment.

The northern Italian menu, which changes every six months or so, features such dishes as salmon lasagne with fresh fennel, veal scaloppine sautéed with butter and lemon, and beef tenderloin grilled with mustard, wine, and basil. You'll realize when you taste them that the pastas are homemade.

La Scala & Boutique Restaurant, 410 N. Canon Dr., Beverly Hills. ☎ 310/275-0579 or 550-8288.

Cuisine: ITALIAN. **Reservations:** Accepted at lunch only for groups of six or more; required at dinner. **Directions:** From Santa Monica Boulevard, exit onto Canon Drive; the restaurant is half a block ahead, before Brighton Way.

Prices: Appetizers $6–$12; main courses $13–$25; lunch $7–$15. AE, CB, DC, MC, V.

Open: Mon–Sat 11:30am–10:30pm.

Now an institution, Jean Leon's Scala is a busy restaurant catering primarily to customers in The Business. Easily identified by the name "La Scala" on the white bowed awnings, the restaurant's relatively small interior features faux orange trees, red-leather booths, amber mirrors, soft spotlighting, and fresh flowers. To the rear, directly above a small bar, are a number of those Gerald Price caricatures of famous Hollywood faces.

Lunch might begin with bean soup with olive oil (fagioli alla toscana con olio santo), followed by Leon's popular chopped salad. Excellent, more substantial main courses include cannelloni Gigi and grilled shrimp marinara. There are sandwiches on the menu, as well as a selection of cold plates.

At dinner, try the marinated salmon with white truffles and then move on to a pasta dish like spaghetti alla checca, with chopped tomatoes, virgin olive oil, garlic, and basil. Beautifully prepared main courses include the grilled shrimp or langostines with white wine, duck sausage with Cannelli beans, and spring chicken with rosemary and white wine. Tiramisù and cappuccino are always available.

Nate & Al's, 414 N. Beverly Dr., Beverly Hills. ☎ 310/274-0101.

Cuisine: JEWISH. **Reservations:** Not accepted. **Directions:** From Santa Monica Boulevard, exit onto Beverly Drive; the restaurant is half a block ahead at Brighton Way.

Prices: Appetizers $5–$11; main courses $8–$13. AE, DISC, MC, V.

Open: Daily 7:30am–9pm.

Nate & Al's has been slapping pastrami on fresh-baked rye since 1945, not to mention chopped liver and schmaltz (chicken fat), kosher franks, and hot corned beef. Seating is in comfortable booths and lighting is pleasantly low. A big counter up front handles take-out orders that include everything from halvah to Brie.

This place is kosher style rather than strictly kosher; the book-size menu encompasses both meat and dairy items. Sandwiches come in only one size—huge—and are overstuffed with meats, cheeses, and traditional favorites. Other offerings include chicken soup with matzoh balls, potato pancakes, and cheese, cherry, or blueberry blintzes with sour cream and applesauce. Wine and beer are available.

Röx, in the Beverly Prescott Hotel, 1224 S. Beverwil Dr., Beverly Hills. ☎ 310/772-2999.

Cuisine: CALIFORNIAN. **Reservations:** Recommended. **Directions:** From I-405, exit east onto Pico Boulevard, continue about two miles, then turn left onto Beverwil Drive.
Prices: Appetizers $5–$8; main courses $16–$20; lunch $10–$14. AE, DISC, MC, V.
Open: Mon–Thurs 7am–10pm, Fri 7am–11pm, Sat 8am–11pm, Sun 8am–9pm.

Until now, Hans Röckenwagner, one of America's greatest chefs, only had one uncomfortable Los Angeles dining room in which to show off his skills. The recent opening of Röx, a more personalized restaurant with a relaxed teak-and-denim interior, now means an all-around dining experience that's as comfortable as it is flavorful.

Ginger-duck dumplings and tuna sashimi are two appetizing examples of Röckenwagner's Asian-influenced California cuisine. The latter is served with a spicy gazpacho vinaigrette. Beautifully presented main courses might include peppered pork chops with oregano pesto, grilled scallops with vegetable couscous, or rice-crusted sea bass and sesame asparagus drizzled with soya-sake sauce.

Röx Loggia, an open-air piano bar adjacent to the restaurant, is open nightly for light meals and drinks.

Inexpensive

Cava, in the Beverly Plaza Hotel, 8384 W. 3rd St. ☎ **213/658-8898.**

Cuisine: SPANISH. **Reservations:** Not required. **Directions:** From Santa Monica Boulevard, exit south onto La Cienega Boulevard, then turn left onto 3rd Street; the restaurant is one block ahead at Orlando Avenue.
Prices: Appetizers $3–$7; main courses $8–$17; breakfast $3–$9; lunch $4–$14. AE, CB, DC, DISC, MC, V.
Open: Daily 6:30am–midnight.

There are no Mexican meals at this all-Spanish winner in the Beverly Plaza Hotel. Revelers in the mood for fun are attracted to Cava's great mambo atmosphere, made festive with flamboyant, colorful decorations, long shared tables, and loud, lively music that's live on weekends. People get drunk here, then dance off dinner.

Although main courses like beef-stuffed green peppers, pork with sautéed apples, crispy red snapper with garlic, and sherry-glazed orange chicken are truly recommendable, the large assortment of tapas offers the most comprehensive party for the palate. Top picks include grilled shrimp in garlic sauce, mussels steamed in sweet sherry, lamb riblets in red wine, and eggplant rolled in cheese and chorizo. Paellas are available with or without meat. If you have room for dessert, try the ruby-colored pears poached in port, the rice pudding, or the flan.

Cheesecake Factory, 364 N. Beverly Dr., Beverly Hills.
☎ **310/278-7270.**

Cuisine: AMERICAN. **Reservations:** Not accepted. **Directions:** From Santa Monica Boulevard, exit onto Beverly Drive; the restaurant is half a block ahead at Brighton Way.

Prices: Main courses $6–$17; cheesecake $4–$7. AE, CB, DC, DISC, MC, V.
Open: Mon–Thurs 11am–11pm, Fri–Sat 11am–12:30am, Sun 10am–11pm.

Serving great food and superb desserts, the Cheesecake Factory, off Brighton Way, is a dilemma of sorts. My advice: Go there very hungry, when you're not counting calories.

More than 40 varieties of cheesecake are available, including the incredible white-chocolate raspberry truffle, fresh strawberry, chocolate-chip cookie dough, and Kahlúa-almond fudge. Other desserts include chocolate-fudge cake, carrot cake, strawberry shortcake, tiramisù, and much, much more.

The Cheesecake Factory is also a reasonably priced restaurant with a substantial list of delicious dishes. Meals range from barbecue-style chicken to spicy specialties like cashew chicken, Cajun jambalaya, Louisiana-style blackened fish, and steak. Vegetarian dishes are also available, as are more than 15 pasta dishes, wonderful hot sandwiches, great omelets, salads, and burgers.

Other Cheesecake Factory locations include 4142 Via Marina, in Marina del Rey (☎ 310/306-3344); 605 N. Harbor Dr., in Redondo Beach (☎ 310/376-0466); and 6324 Canoga Ave., in Woodland Hills (☎ 818/883-9900).

5   West Los Angeles

Moderate

$ Mishima, 11301 Olympic Blvd. ☎ 310/473-5297.
Cuisine: JAPANESE. **Reservations:** Not accepted. **Directions:** From I-405, take the Tennessee Avenue exit, head south (toward the beach), and make an immediate right onto Sawtell Boulevard; the restaurant is in the shopping center on the corner of Sawtell and Olympic Boulevards.
Prices: Appetizers $1–$7; noodles $4–$7; combinations $5–$9. MC, V.
Open: Tues–Sun 11:30am–9pm.

Hidden on the second floor of an unobtrusive strip mall, this small Japanese eatery is well worth finding. A carbon copy of an excellent noodle shop in downtown Tokyo, Mishima is Asian-contemporary, complete with matte black tables and chairs, white walls decorated with Japanese-style prints, and plastic food displays that let you see what you're ordering.

A loyal clientele fills the small bright dining room with noodle slurps and chopstick clacks. Udon (thick wheat noodles) or soba (narrow buckwheat linguine) are the main choices here. Both are served either hot or cold in a variety of soups and sauces. Sushi, chicken dishes, and a variety of tempuras are also available. Highly recommended.

6 San Fernando Valley

Expensive

Pinot Bistro, 12969 Ventura Blvd., Studio City. ☎ 818/990-0500.

Cuisine: FRENCH. **Reservations:** Recommended. **Directions:** From U.S. 101, exit south onto Coldwater Canyon Avenue, then turn right onto Ventura Boulevard to the restaurant.

Prices: Appetizers $7–$12; main courses $16–$22; lunch $5–$14. AE, DC, DISC, MC, V.

Open: Lunch Mon–Fri 11:30am–2:30pm; dinner Mon–Thurs 6–10pm, Fri 6–10:30pm, Sat 5:30–10:30pm, Sun 5:30–9:30pm.

When Los Angeles's older, knowledgeable Valley crowd doesn't want to make the drive into town to Patina, they pack into Pinot Bistro, restaurateur Joachim Splichal's other hugely successful restaurant. The bistro's dark woods, etched glass, and cream-colored walls say "authentic French" almost as loudly as the rich, straightforward cooking.

Of the appetizers, the bistro's warm potato tart with smoked whitefish, baby lobster tails with creamy polenta, and duck-liver mousse with grilled country bread are studies in culinary perfection. Generously portioned main dishes continue the theme with baby lobster risotto; braised oxtail with parsley gnocchi; and puff pastry stuffed with bay scallops, Manila clams, and roast duck. Daily specials, always as delicious as they are interesting, might include roast suckling pig with braised cabbage, Pacific bouillabaisse, or beef strüdel. Many regulars prefer Pinot Bistro at lunch, when a less expensive menu is served to a more easy-going crowd.

Moderate

Jerry's Famous Deli, 12655 Ventura Blvd., Studio City. ☎ 818/980-4245.

Cuisine: DELICATESSEN. **Directions:** From U.S. 101, exit onto Coldwater Canyon Boulevard south and continue to the restaurant at Ventura Boulevard.

Prices: Appetizers $5–$13; main courses $9–$14; breakfast $2–$11; sandwiches and salads $4–$12. AE, MC, V.

Open: Daily 24 hours.

Just east of Coldwater Canyon Avenue there's a simple yet sizable deli where all the young "happening" people go to relieve late-night "munchies." The place probably has one of the largest menus in America—a tome that spans cultures and continents from Central America to China to New York. From salads to sandwiches to steak and seafood platters, everything, including breakfasts, is served all day. Jerry's is not the best deli in the world, but it's consistently good, and an integral part of Los Angeles's cultural landscape. It also has a full bar.

7   Pasadena

Moderate

⭐ **Mi Piace**, 25 E. Colorado Blvd., Pasadena. ☎ 818/795-3131.
Cuisine: ITALIAN. **Reservations:** Not required. **Directions:** From I-210 east, take the Fair Oaks Avenue exit and turn right; turn left onto Colorado Boulevard and the restaurant will be immediately on your left.
Prices: Appetizers $2–$5; main courses $6–$12; pasta $2–$8; lunch $4–$8. AE, DC, MC, V.
Open: Sun–Thurs 11am–11:30pm, Fri–Sat 11am–1am.

High ceilings, large windows, light wood floors, and contemporary colors all contribute to the bright, open airiness of this friendly Italian eatery. The main room has about 20 square tables, all topped with white cloths and balsamic vinegar, and surrounded by blond-wood chairs.

Pronounced "Me *Pee*-ah-che," the restaurant serves an extensive menu that includes dozens of pastas, as well as veal, chicken, and seafood dishes. Creative, individual-size pizzas are a particular specialty, as is gnocchi (potato dumplings), and linguine with New Zealand green lip mussels.

Many knowledgeable diners just visit Mi Piace for dessert. Their tremendous selection of elegant, homemade creations includes hazelnut cake layered with cappuccino mousse and covered with cappuccino bean cream; a variety of chocolates; traditional tiramisù; and spaghetinni Castagne—a chestnut pasta and white-chocolate-cream–filled meringue, topped with vanilla sauce.

Miyako, in the Livingstone Hotel, 139 S. Los Robles Ave., Pasadena. ☎ 818/795-7005.
Cuisine: JAPANESE. **Reservations:** Not required. **Directions:** From I-210, exit onto Walnut Street east and turn right (south) onto Los Robles Avenue; the restaurant is half a mile on your right, across from the Pasadena Hilton hotel, between Green and Cordova Streets.
Prices: Appetizers $5–$8; main courses $10–$23; lunch $6–$13. AE, MC, V.
Open: Lunch Mon–Fri 11:30am–2pm; dinner Mon–Sat 5:30–9:30pm, Sun 4–9pm.

The Miyako is on the same street as the Hilton, but it's been around much longer—since 1959. People come here for fine Japanese cuisine in an attractive setting. You can choose to sit either on the floor (in the Japanese tradition) in the tatami room or at Western-style tables, which overlook a small Japanese garden.

If you're not used to eating raw fish, begin with a sashimi appetizer, a small portion of tuna slices. A full Imperial dinner offers a combination of shrimp tempura, chicken teriyaki, and sukiyaki.

Pasadena Baking Company, 29 E. Colorado Blvd., Old Pasadena. ☎ 818/796-9966.
Cuisine: CONTINENTAL. **Reservations:** Not accepted. **Directions:** From I-210 east, take the Fair Oaks Avenue exit and turn right; turn left

onto Colorado Boulevard and the restaurant will be immediately on your left.
Prices: Baked goods 50¢–$3; breakfast $3–$6; lunch $2–$8. AE, MC, V.
Open: Mon–Thurs 7am–11pm, Fri 7am–midnight, Sat 8am–midnight, Sun 8am–11pm.

Located next door to Mi Piace (see above), this little bakery with large windows overlooking the boulevard holds just a handful of small tables, which spill out onto the sidewalk during nice weather.

You can practically "see the smell" of their particularly large selection of fresh pastries, tarts, truffles, cakes, and candies, all proudly displayed behind large glass cases. The bakery also makes and sells an assortment of fresh breads, including Bohemian pumpernickel, potato and dill, and even strawberry.

Breakfast foods include homemade croissants and muffins, as well as omelets, a cereal bar, and fruit stand. Fresh-cut sandwiches are lunch favorites, as are fruit and Cobb salads, and "vegestronni," a pie prepared with fresh seasonal vegetables.

A variety of espresso drinks, hot or iced, are always available.

Inexpensive

Old Town Bakery & Restaurant, 166 W. Colorado Blvd., Pasadena. ☎ 818/792-7943.
Cuisine: CONTINENTAL. **Reservations:** Not accepted. **Directions:** From I-210 south, take the Pasadena Street exit and turn left, then turn right onto Colorado Boulevard; the restaurant will be on your right, between Pasadena and Miller Streets.
Prices: Appetizers $2–$5; lunch/dinner $5–$11; breakfast $3–$7. DISC, MC, V.
Open: Sun–Thurs 7:30am–10pm, Fri–Sat 7:30am–midnight.

Set back from the street, inside a quaint courtyard, this cheery bakery is an especially popular place to read the morning paper with a cappuccino and a croissant. The tall, glass display counters are packed with cakes, muffins, scones, and other confections—all baked expressly for this shop.

Beyond bakery items, meals include eggs, potatoes, pasta, salads, sandwiches, and pan pizza, topped with chicken sausage, mushrooms, onions, and mozzarella.

8 Malibu & Topanga Canyon

Expensive

Granita, 23725 W. Malibu Rd., Malibu. ☎ 310/456-0488.
Cuisine: CALIFORNIAN. **Reservations:** Recommended.
Prices: Appetizers $8–$21; main courses $21–$26. CB, DC, DISC, MC, V.
Open: Lunch Mon–Wed 11:30am–2:30pm; dinner daily 6–10:30pm; brunch Sat–Sun 11am–2:30pm.

Granita is the latest outpost of Wolfgang Puck, one of the most successful entrepreneurial chefs in California. Together with West Hollywood's Spago and Santa Monica's Chinois on Main, Puck's Malibu restaurant consciously combines hip food and contemporary surroundings. Granita's happy interior is swirling in color. Even the service staff are outfitted in vests or ties that explode in design and color.

Puck serves many of his own house specialties here, including a lamb-sausage pizza and grilled Atlantic salmon in eggplant broth. Several new dishes have been introduced, such as a seafood risotto with shrimp, scallops, and lobster and roast Chinese duck with apricot brown butter.

La Scala Malibu, 3874 Cross Creek Rd., off Pacific Coast Hwy., Malibu. ☎ **310/456-1979.**

> **Cuisine:** ITALIAN. **Reservations:** Recommended.
> **Prices:** Appetizers $6–$10; main courses $17–$28; lunch about half price. AE, CB, DC, MC, V.
> **Open:** Lunch Mon–Fri 11:30am–3pm; dinner Mon–Sat 5:30–10pm, Sun 4–10:30pm.

This restaurant is the venture of Jean Leon, who made a name for himself with several ultra-chic Beverly Hills restaurants. But this eatery differs from the others; La Scala is known for its relaxed atmosphere and friendly, leisurely dining. Architectural highlights include an Italian marble entry, terra-cotta tile floors, and etched-glass area dividers. There's an impressive wood-paneled 1,800-bottle wine room and an exhibition kitchen. Solarium windows overlook the wilds of Malibu Creek with a view of the Pacific.

Lunch at La Scala might begin with a fresh turkey salad, smoked salmon with onions and capers, or a hot dish such as veal and peppers, swordfish, or the daily fresh pasta. For dessert, try the homemade ice cream with fresh raspberries. Dinner begins with antipasti such as mozzarella marinara, seafood salad, carpaccio, or a Caesar salad and continues with such main courses as baked sea bass, veal with pepperoni, or the nightly fresh pasta.

Moderate

Alice's, 23000 Pacific Coast Hwy., Malibu. ☎ **310/456-6646.**

> **Cuisine:** CALIFORNIAN. **Reservations:** Recommended. **Directions:** From Santa Monica, take Calif. 1 north to Malibu; the restaurant is located directly on Calif. 1 about a quarter of a mile before the Malibu Pier.
> **Prices:** Appetizers $6–$11; main courses $6–$16 at lunch, $8–$19 at dinner. AE, MC, V.
> **Open:** Mon–Fri 11:30am–10:30pm, Sat–Sun 11am–11pm.

Alice's has more than a 20-year history as one of the liveliest restaurants in Malibu. Facing the Malibu Pier, the dining area is glassed in on three sides; rear tables are on a raised platform so that everyone can view the ocean. It's light and airy, and the menu is mostly seafood—as always, beautifully fresh.

Among the tempting luncheon main courses are yellowtail tuna with spinach, lemon, and tarragon butter; and grilled chicken breast marinated in garlic, soy, and spices, served with a tomato-cilantro relish. But don't overlook the pasta choices, especially the spaghetti with hot Créole sausage, zucchini, and a sweet red-pepper sauce. Alice's also has a good selection of salads, warm and cold. Consider also the Malibu sausage burger with sautéed onions and peppers, and mustard dressing.

For dinner, you might begin with the smoked Norwegian salmon served with caviar cream. Of the salads, my choice is the hot roasted-goat-cheese salad with mixed greens, fresh herbs, walnuts, and a sherry vinaigrette. Great main dishes include grilled swordfish with herb butter and the stir-fried scallops with black-bean sauce and sweet peppers over pan-fried angel-hair pasta.

Inn of the Seventh Ray, 128 Old Topanga Canyon Rd., Topanga Canyon. ☎ 310/455-1311.

Cuisine: CALIFORNIA HEALTH FOOD. **Reservations:** Required at dinner. **Directions:** From Santa Monica, take Calif. 1 north to Malibu, then turn right onto Calif. 27 (Topanga Canyon Boulevard), which, after about two miles, turns into Topanga Canyon Road.

Prices: Appetizers $6–$10; main courses $14–$28; lunch/brunch $7–$13. MC, V.

Open: Lunch Mon–Fri 11:30am–3pm, Sat 10:30am–3pm; dinner daily 6–10pm; brunch Sun 9:30am–3pm.

Located about four miles from Pacific Coast Calif. 1, this unusual and lovely creekside inn offers tranquil dining under the shade of an ancient canyon. About half the seating is outdoors, at tables that overlook the creek and endless untamed foliage. Inside, tables are neatly arranged beneath a sloped shingle-and-stucco roof; a glass wall provides mountain views.

Although it's not vegetarian, the Inn of the Seventh Ray is the most orthodox, and the most beautiful, of L.A.'s natural-food restaurants. It was opened about 20 years ago by Ralph and Lucille Yaney as a place to practice and share their ideas about the relationship of food and energy. Main dishes are listed on the menu in order of their "esoteric vibrational value"; the lightest and least dense—hence, more purifying—items get top billing. Everything is prepared from scratch on the premises. Since top priority is given to serving chemical- and preservative-free foods, even the fish are caught in deep water far offshore and served the same day.

Lunch options include sandwiches (such as avocado, cheese, and sprouts), salads, omelets, quiche, and waffles. The dinner menu offers 10 main dishes, all served with soup or salad, complimentary hors d'oeuvres, steamed vegetables, baked potato or herbed brown rice, and stone-ground homemade bread. The lightest item is called Five Secret Rays: lightly steamed vegetables served with lemon-tahini and caraway cheese sauces; the densest—vibrationally speaking—is a 10-ounce New York steak cut from naturally fed beef. A glass of fruit wine is suggested as an apéritif, and delicious desserts are also available. Even if you're not especially enthusiastic about natural foods, all the dishes are excellent and the setting is enjoyable.

Sand Castle, 28128 W. Pacific Coast Hwy., Malibu.
☎ 213/457-2503.

Cuisine: AMERICAN. **Reservations:** Not required **Directions:** From Santa Monica, take Calif. 1 north to Malibu; the restaurant is located on Calif. 1 at Paradise Cove.
Prices: Appetizers $5–$9; main courses $12–$35. AE, MC, V.
Open: Breakfast daily 6am–noon; lunch daily 11:30am–4pm; dinner Mon–Thurs 5–10pm, Fri–Sat 5–11pm, Sun 4–10pm.

Leisurely breakfasts and lunches are the best meals to eat in this gray New England–style shingled house, complete with weather vane and widow's walk. The restaurant is located right on the beach and has a wall of windows overlooking the ocean. The rustic interior sports a nautical theme, with ship-light chandeliers, rigging decor, and the like. A giant fireplace separates the dining room from the lounge, which sees a lot of action on weekend nights.

Hearty egg breakfasts give way to lunches that can be anything from a Monte Cristo sandwich to scallops sautéed in white wine. Dinners are often meat-and-potato affairs, and include steak, fish, chicken, and the like.

Inexpensive

Carlos and Pepe's, 22706 Pacific Coast Hwy., Malibu.
☎ 310/456-3105.

Cuisine: MEXICAN. **Reservations:** Not accepted. **Directions:** From Santa Monica, take Calif. 1 north to Malibu; the restaurant is located on Calif. 1 about a quarter of a mile before the Malibu Pier.
Prices: Appetizers $3–$6; main courses $8–$12. AE, CB, MC, V.
Open: Sun–Thurs 11:30am–11pm, Fri–Sat 11:30am–midnight.

Carlos and Pepe's is a delightful weathered-wood seacoast structure. Inside you'll find a few touches from south of the border, including, at the bar, papier-mâché banana trees with tropical birds. The interior is designed so that each table has an ocean view. An immense aquarium filled with tropical fish separates the bar and dining areas. The best place to sit is on the plant-filled, glass-enclosed deck that directly overlooks the ocean.

The restaurant should be best known for its 16-ounce margaritas, made with freshly squeezed juices. But the sizable menu, which includes the usual enchiladas, chimichangas (a burrito fried crisp), and tacos, isn't too bad either. The fajitas are the restaurant's top ticket: grilled steak or chicken, served sizzling with peppers, onions, and tomatoes. Roll and fill your own tortillas with guacamole, salsa, lettuce, and beans. Hamburgers, omelets, and steaks are also available.

9   Santa Monica & Venice

Expensive

⭐ **Bikini,** 1413 5th St., Santa Monica. ☎ **310/395-8611.**

Cuisine: INTERNATIONAL. **Reservations:** Required. **Directions:** From the Santa Monica Freeway west, take the 4th Street exit and turn right, turn right again onto Colorado Avenue, then left onto 5th Street; the restaurant is on your right, between Broadway and Santa Monica Boulevard.

Prices: Appetizers $6–$30; main courses $16–$26; lunch $6–$15. AE, MC, V.

Open: Lunch Mon–Fri 11:30am–2:30pm; dinner Mon–Thurs 6–10pm, Fri–Sun 6–10:30pm; brunch Sun 11:30am–2pm.

If you needed just one morsel of proof that Los Angeles remains on the culinary edge, Bikini would provide it. Enter through huge glass doors, with handles that resemble breaking waves, into a small reception area, where a fire-engine-red hostess desk contrasts against curvaceous black-and-gray simulated stone.

A dramatic free-standing green wood stairway separates the reception area from the restaurant's ultra-colorful, multi-million-dollar dining room. Bikini's 15 main dining room tables are dwarfed by huge, two-story, floor-to-ceiling windows and surrounded by curved walls and primary colors. The less-coveted upstairs dining room is backed by a large mural of an ocean nymph, created by artist Muramasa Kudo and commissioned especially for this restaurant.

Chef/owner John Sedlar's flair for style doesn't stop in the kitchen, where he combines French techniques with flavors and spices from Japan, China, Thailand, Greece, and the American Southwest. You won't find Bikini's salmon mousse–filled corn husk tamale at any Mexican taco stand. But, along with a duck sandwich, cooked medium-rare, with wild mushrooms and orange-mint mayonnaise on potato bread, it's typical of the lunch dishes. Dinners include vanilla poached Pacific prawns and grilled saddle of lamb with green Indian curry sauce.

Camelions, 246 26th St., Santa Monica. ☎ **310/395-0746.**

Cuisine: CALIFORNIAN/FRENCH. **Reservations:** Not required. **Directions:** From Santa Monica, take Ocean Avenue west, turn right onto San Vicente Boulevard, then left onto 26th Street to the restaurant.

Prices: Appetizers $6–$14; main courses $14–$22; lunch $7–$13. AE, CB, DC, MC, V.

Open: Lunch Tues–Sun 11:30am–2:30pm; dinner Tues–Sun 6–9:30pm.

Romantic throughout, Camelions is a little French cottage offering fireside dining in several small rooms or outside on a hideaway patio. Guests enter via iron gates that are garnished with creeping ivy.

Meals are on the expensive side but for special occasions are well worth it. Winning appetizers, both hot and cold, include Norwegian salmon tartare prepared with lemon, soy sauce, capers, and dill; red-lentil cakes with smoked salmon; and braised celery hearts tossed with capers, egg, and beet-juice vinaigrette.

Creative main courses prepared by the capable kitchen include sautéed rabbit served in a clay pot, rice paper–wrapped salmon, and roast veal chops. A large selection of salads are available at lunch, including spinach with warm new potatoes, bacon, and mustard vinaigrette. Sandwiches like grilled shrimp, avocado, and bacon are also served, along with creamed-spinach omelets and grilled lamb chops.

★ **Chinois on Main,** 2709 Main St., Santa Monica.
☎ **310/392-9025.**

Cuisine: CALIFORNIAN/CHINESE. **Reservations:** Required. **Directions:** From the Santa Monica Freeway, take the 4th Street exit and turn left, then turn right onto Pico Boulevard and, after two blocks, turn left onto Main Street; the restaurant is on your left.
Prices: Appetizers $9–$21; main courses $21–$29. AE, DC, MC, V.
Open: Lunch Wed–Fri 11:30am–2pm; dinner daily 6–10:30pm.

Created by Wolfgang Puck, this is one of the trendiest spots in Santa Monica for moneyed diners. Decorated in a colorful Asian-tech, the stunning restaurant is as much an extravaganza for the eye as it is for the palate. It's loud and lively and perpetually packed.

"Chinois" means Chinese in French, and that's sort of what you get: a delicious combination of Asian, French, and California cooking. The seasonal menu might offer stir-fried garlic chicken, whole sizzling catfish, or charcoal-grilled Szechuan beef, thinly sliced, with hot chile oil and cilantro sauce.

Michael's, 1147 3rd St., Santa Monica. ☎ **310/451-0843.**

Cuisine: CONTINENTAL. **Reservations:** Required. **Directions:** From the Santa Monica Freeway west, exit at 4th Street and turn right; turn left on Wilshire Boulevard, then right onto 3rd Street, and the restaurant is on the right.
Prices: Appetizers $6–$14; main courses $18–$27; lunch $13–$23. AE, CB, DC, DISC, MC, V.
Open: Lunch Tues–Fri noon–2pm; dinner Tues–Sat 6:30–9:30pm.

Hidden behind an intimidating white facade, Michael's opens up into a friendly, airy interior that cascades back to a light indoor patio. Original art and a working fountain give the dining room an upscale bistro feel—a sensation confirmed by simple and elegant meals.

For starters, mix and match a variety of pastas with a plethora of toppings; try fettuccine with salmon, or spaghetti with scallops or lobster. Salads are composed of Hawaiian tuna, capers, and grilled onions; or papaya, avocado, and Maine lobster. Top main-course choices include grilled duck with Grand Marnier and oranges, and pork tenderloin with cream sauce and apples.

West Beach Cafe, 60 N. Venice Blvd., Venice. ☎ **213/823-5396.**
Cuisine: CALIFORNIAN. **Reservations:** Recommended. **Directions:**

From the Santa Monica Freeway, take the 4th Street exit and turn left; turn right onto Pico Boulevard and, after two blocks, turn left onto Neilson, which becomes Pacific Avenue; after about a mile, turn right onto Venice Boulevard; the restaurant is near the corner, half a block from the beach.

Prices: Appetizers $6–$8; main courses $8–$22; weekend brunch $8–$18; late-night pizzas $13–$17. AE, CB, DC, MC, V.
Open: Dinner Sun–Thurs 6–10pm, Fri–Sat 6-10:45pm; brunch Sat–Sun 10am–2:45pm; late-night snacks daily 11:30pm–1am.

This trendy, boxy eatery is minimally decorated with white cinderblock walls, track lighting, and simple wood chairs and white-clothed tables. The walls of the café serve as a gallery for an ever-changing variety of works by local artists, and the room features unobstructed views for easy table-hopping.

Lunch means fancy hamburgers, Caesar salads, pastas, and seafood main dishes. Dinners are more elaborate: Favorites on the changing weekly menu are Chilean sea bass lasagne, and oxtails with mashed potatoes and roasted vegetables. A special brunch served on weekends includes eggs Benedict, Belgian waffles, and huevos rancheros. There's a fine wine list, and good late-night pizzas, made with whatever's left in the kitchen, are also available.

Moderate

Caffè Delfini, 147 W. Channel Rd., Santa Monica.
☎ 310/459-8823.
   Cuisine: ITALIAN. **Reservations:** Required. **Directions:** From Santa Monica, take Calif. 1 north and turn right onto Channel Road to the restaurant.
   Prices: Appetizers $5–$16; main courses $9–$20. MC, V.
   Open: Dinner only, daily 6–10pm.

When you enter Caffè Delfini, you just know you're with a hip crowd, though it's hard to see individual faces through the candelit dining room's shadows. Exceedingly romantic, this neighborhood Italian trattoria is the perfect date place, provided you can get a reservation. Cozy, intimate, and charming, the atmosphere is complemented by unobtrusive servers and solid, straightforward Italian cooking.

Mixed designer-green salads, fresh mozzarella and basil, and ripe tomatoes are typical of the restaurant's traditional starters. Excellent pastas are full of Italian integrity, topped with tangy tomato-based sauces that can include garlic, anchovies, or clams. The all–à la carte menu includes veal and chicken standards, as well as a small selection of very recommendable seafood dishes that always includes fresh fish.

Inexpensive

Sidewalk Cafe, 8 Horizon Ave., at Oceanfront, Venice.
   ☎ 310/399-5547.
   Cuisine: AMERICAN. **Reservations:** Not accepted.
   Prices: Appetizers $3–$5; main courses $6–$13. MC, V.
   Open: Sun–Thurs 8am–11pm, Fri–Sat 8am–midnight.

Venice is the home and hangout of L.A.'s most eclectic creative community, and few places in Venice offer you a better view of the local action than Sidewalk Cafe. The constantly bustling restaurant is ensconced in one of the city's few remaining original early 20th-century buildings. The best seats are out front, around overcrowded open-air tables, all with a perfect view of the skaters, bikers, joggers, skateboarders, breakdancers, and sidewalk performers who provide nonstop free entertainment. If you have to sit inside, try the small bar in the back.

The extensive menu features overstuffed sandwiches and healthy portions of other American favorites such as omelets, salads, and burgers.

10 Marina del Rey, Redondo Beach & Long Beach

Expensive

Dominic's, 555 E. Ocean Blvd., Long Beach. ☎ 310/437-0626.

Cuisine: CONTINENTAL. **Reservations:** Not required. **Directions:** From I-710 south, take the Broadway exit and turn right onto Lime Avenue; the restaurant will be on your left, at the corner of Ocean Boulevard and Lime Avenue.

Prices: Appetizers $3–$10; main courses $15–$35; lunch $5–$15. AE, DC, DISC, MC, V.

Open: Lunch daily 11:30am–3pm; dinner daily 5:30–10pm. (Bar, daily until midnight.)

This restaurant's East Coast steakhouse looks are accentuated by a dark-wood bar, pressed-tin ceiling, and black-and-white marble chessboard floor. Except for the grand piano, around which the dining areas are arranged, the restaurant looks somewhat like an upscale TGI Fridays.

The restaurant's foot-long menu changes weekly, but usually includes chicken and steaks grilled over mesquite, citrus, apple, and cherry woods, and a variety of sandwiches and seafood melts. Dinner means grilled meats and poultry, as well as a good selection of seasonal seafood. Look for soft-shell crab, Maine lobster, seared scallops, and tuna. A spectacular wine list encompasses hundreds of selections from California and Europe.

The Warehouse, 4499 Admiralty Way, Marina del Rey. ☎ 213/823-5451.

Cuisine: INTERNATIONAL. **Reservations:** Not accepted. **Directions:** From I-405, exit onto Calif. 90, which ends at Lincoln Boulevard; turn left onto Lincoln Boulevard, right on Bali Way, and then right onto Admiralty Way to the restaurant.

Prices: Appetizers $4–$10; main courses $14–$23; lunch $8–$15. AE, MC, V.

Open: Lunch Mon–Fri 11:30am–3pm; dinner Mon–Thurs 4–10pm, Fri–Sat 4–11pm, Sun 5–10pm; brunch Sat 11am–3pm, Sun 10am–3pm.

Dining in
Southern Los Angeles County

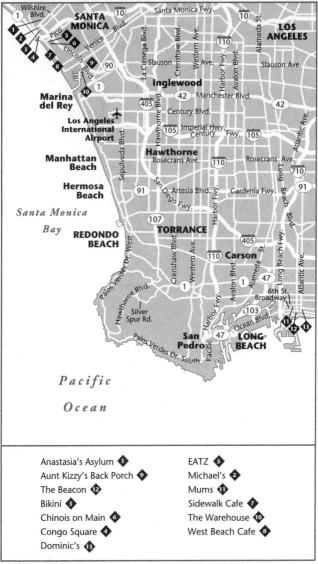

Anastasia's Asylum ◆1

Aunt Kizzy's Back Porch ◆9

The Beacon ◆12

Bikini ◆3

Chinois on Main ◆6

Congo Square ◆4

Dominic's ◆13

EATZ ◆5

Michael's ◆2

Mums ◆11

Sidewalk Cafe ◆7

The Warehouse ◆10

West Beach Cafe ◆8

Admittedly, the leisurely ambience and terrific views are better than the food, but this is still a good place to eat. The owner, photographer Burt Hixson, traveled 23,000 tax-free miles, ostensibly to find the perfect decor for his dream restaurant. The result is a two-level dockside eatery with cask-and-barrel seating, burlap coffee bag wall hangings, and a hodgepodge of nettings, ropes, peacock chairs, and the like. Hixson's photos line the walls, but the best views are in the other direction, toward the marina. During warm weather, the best tables are outside.

The cuisine is influenced by as many nations as the beer menu, and includes chicken Dijon, Malaysian shrimp, and steak teriyaki. There's also a raw bar serving oysters, and snacks like garlic bread, nachos, and quesadillas.

Moderate

Aunt Kizzy's Back Porch, in the Villa Marina Shopping Center, 4325 Glencove Ave., Marina del Rey. ☎ 213/578-1005.

> **Cuisine:** AMERICAN. **Reservations:** Not accepted. **Directions:** From I-405, exit onto Calif. 90, which ends at Lincoln Boulevard; turn right onto Lincoln Boulevard and right again onto Maxella Avenue, and the Villa Marina Shopping Center is just ahead, on the corner of Glencove Avenue.
>
> **Prices:** Appetizers $3–$6; main courses $8–$13; Sun brunch $12. No credit cards.
>
> **Open:** Lunch Mon–Sat 11am–4pm; dinner Sun–Thurs 4–11pm, Fri–Sat 4pm–midnight; brunch Sun 11am–3pm.

Authentic southern home-cooked meals are prepared from time-honed recipes by a chef from Cleveland, Mississippi.

Menu options include fried chicken, chicken Créole, jambalaya, catfish with hush puppies, and some of the best smothered pork chops you've ever tasted. Almost everything comes with two vegetables, mashed potatoes or rice and gravy, and corn muffins. Whitebread desserts include peach cobbler and sweet-potato pie.

Sunday brunches are really special. Served buffet style, dishes include meat and cheese omelets, grilled potatoes, smothered pork chops, barbecued beef ribs, fried chicken, and a choice of five vegetables.

Nothing is easy to find in the shopping center, though. Aunt Kizzy's is located to the right of Vons supermarket, across a small driveway.

Mums, 144 Pine Ave., Long Beach. ☎ 310/437-7700.

> **Cuisine:** ITALIAN. **Reservations:** Not required. **Directions:** From I-710 south, take the Broadway exit and turn right onto Pine Avenue; the restaurant will be on your left, between Broadway and 1st Street.
>
> **Prices:** Appetizers $7–$9; main courses $9–$22; lunch $7–$19. AE, CB, DC, DISC, MC, V.
>
> **Open:** Mon–Thurs 11am–10pm, Fri 11:30am–midnight, Sat 5pm–midnight, Sun 5–9pm.

Mums has jumped on the haute California bandwagon, serving contemporary Italian foods in bright wood-and-glass surroundings. The restaurant is comfortable, fun, unpretentious, and good.

Salads are good lunch choices, and include goat cheese, tomatoes, pinenuts, and a sun-dried–tomato vinaigrette; or grilled vegetables with a lime-ginger vinaigrette. An assortment of pizzas, pastas, and calzones are served for dinner, as are blackened shrimp and barbecued chicken topped with creamy pesto, peppers, and sun-dried tomatoes.

The upstairs roof garden opens on weekend nights for dining and dancing. Bring a sweater.

11 Specialty Dining

Dining Complexes

EATZ, in Santa Monica Place, Colorado Ave. at 2nd St., Santa Monica. ☎ 310/394-5451.

EATZ, the Santa Monica Place mall's ground-floor food pavilion, sells a world's array of fast foods from vendors like Charlie Kabob, Croissant de Paris, David Smith's Deli, Island Grille, Khyber Express, and Wok Inn. Röckenroll (☎ 310/587-1115), owned by celebrity chef Hans Röckenwagner, specializes in upscale sandwiches like fresh mozzarella with basil, sun-dried tomatoes, and arugula on roasted onion bread.

Farmer's Market, Fairfax and Third Aves. ☎ 213/933-9211.

Located near West Hollywood, the fun Farmer's Market is one of America's best prepared-food malls. In addition to endless isles of food stalls, the covered outdoor market is jam-packed with local produce and international goodies like pickled Georgia freestone peaches, Norwegian cod roe, beef-blood pudding, and Japanese pin-head gunpowder—a type of green tea.

The market dates from 1934, when 18 *Grapes of Wrath*–era farmers began selling fresh produce here, right from the backs of their trucks. Who knows when the first Jane Darwell predecessor decided to fry a chicken, bake some raisin bread, and whip up an old-fashioned potato salad the way the folks back home in Oklahoma like it. Eventually, tables were set up under olive trees where customers could consume the prepared food.

Today, dining is still al fresco at one of the many outdoor tables. The variety of foods is staggering. Your selections might include fresh fruit juices; barbecued beef, chicken, ribs, or Texas chili; tacos, tamales, enchiladas; waffles; hundreds of cheeses; smoked fish; blintzes; hot roasted chestnuts; fruit salads, vegetable salads, seafood salads; roast meats; seafood dishes; pizza; fish and chips; burgers; stuffed cabbage; falafel; or Italian fare, from eggplant parmigiana to lasagne.

The market is open Monday through Saturday from 9am to 6:30pm and on Sunday from 10am to 5pm.

Brunch

Aunt Kizzy's Back Porch, in the Villa Marina Shopping Center, 4325 Glencove Ave., Marina del Rey. ☎ 213/578-1005.

Cuisine: AMERICAN. **Reservations:** Not accepted. **Directions:** From I-405, exit onto Calif. 90, which ends at Lincoln Boulevard; turn right

onto Lincoln Boulevard, right again onto Maxella Avenue, and the Villa Marina Shopping Center is just ahead, on the corner of Glencove Avenue.
Prices: Sun brunch $12. No credit cards.
Open: Brunch Sun 11am–3pm.

Authentic southern home-cooked meals are prepared from time-honed recipes by a chef from Cleveland, Mississippi. Sunday brunches are really special. Served buffet style, dishes include meat and cheese omelets, grilled potatoes, smothered pork chops, barbecued beef ribs, fried chicken, and a choice of five vegetables.

The Beacon, in the Hyatt Regency, 200 S. Pine Ave., Long Beach. ☎ 310/491-1234.
   Cuisine: CALIFORNIAN. **Reservations:** Recommended. **Directions:** From the Long Beach Freeway (I-710) south, take the Shoreline Drive exit and turn left onto Pine Avenue.
   Prices: Sun brunch $22.50, half-price for children 4–12.
   Open: Brunch Sun 10am–2:30pm.

They serve other meals here, but Sunday brunch is what makes the Beacon special. Themed around a large glass lighthouse, the long, narrow dining room offers terrific views of the Long Beach Marina as well as the large ponds and walkways of the Hyatt Regency Hotel.

The buffet is an all-you-can-eat affair, and the offerings seem endless. There's an omelet bar, a ham and roast beef carving station, Belgian waffles, eggs Benedict, breakfast meats, and a huge selection of salads and seafood, including smoked salmon and peel-and-eat shrimp. Champagne and fresh juices are also bottomless. Did I mention the dessert station, which has at least seven different cakes and pies to choose from, as well as pastries and fresh fruit with hot chocolate fondue for dipping?

West Beach Cafe, 60 N. Venice Blvd., Venice. ☎213/823-5396.
   Cuisine: CALIFORNIAN. **Reservations:** Recommended. **Directions:** From the Santa Monica Freeway, take the 4th Street exit and turn left; turn right onto Pico Boulevard and, after two blocks, turn left onto Neilson, which becomes Pacific Avenue; after about a mile, turn right onto Venice Boulevard and the restaurant is near the corner, half a block from the beach.
   Prices: Weekend brunch $8–$18. AE, CB, DC, MC, V.
   Open: Brunch Sat–Sun 10am–2:45pm.

This trendy, boxy eatery is an excellent choice for any meal, but brunches are really special. Served only on weekends, the brunch menu includes eggs Benedict, Belgian waffles, and huevos rancheros.

Cafés

Anastasia's Asylum, 1028 Wilshire Blvd., Santa Monica. ☎ 310/394-7113.
   Cuisine: CAFE. **Directions:** From the Santa Monica Freeway west, take the 4th Street exit and turn right; turn right again onto Wilshire Boulevard and the café is near the corner of 11th Street.

Prices: Coffee and cakes $1–$4. CB, DC, MC, V.
Open: Sun–Thurs 7am–2am, Fri–Sat 7am–3am.

Anastasia's upscale beatnik ambience is created by an eclectic hip crowd that comes for good coffee and conversation. There's a terrific upstairs stage that's often accommodating musicians and poets.

Congo Square, 1238 3rd St., Santa Monica. ☎ **310/395-5606.**

Cuisine: CAFE. **Directions:** From the Santa Monica Freeway west, take the 4th Street exit and turn right; turn left onto Broadway and park in the Santa Monica Place garage.
Prices: Coffee and cakes $1–$4. No credit cards.
Open: Sun–Thurs 8am–1am, Fri–Sat 8am–2am.

Located on Santa Monica's pedestrians-only Third Street Promenade, this contemporary unfinished-brick café gets high marks for its outside tables—great for people-watching. Good brewed coffee is served along with well-made espresso drinks.

Espresso Bar, 34 S. Raymond St., Pasadena. ☎ **818/356-9095.**

Cuisine: CAFE. **Directions:** From I-210 east, take the Fair Oaks Avenue exit and turn right; turn left onto Colorado Boulevard, then right onto Raymond Street to the café.
Prices: Coffee and cakes $1–$4. No credit cards.
Open: Mon–Tues noon–1am, Wed–Thurs and Sun 9am–1am, Fri–Sat 9am–2am.

This simply named coffeehouse has been around so long, it almost seems as though Pasadena grew up around it. Hidden down a hard-to-find alleyway, the café is popular with punker poets who come here to read and emote in front of one of the area's most unusual audiences.

Highland Grounds, 742 N. Highland Ave., Hollywood.
☎ **213/466-1507.**

Cuisine: CAFE. **Reservations:** Not accepted. **Directions:** From U.S. 101, exit onto Highland Avenue; the café is located half a block north of Melrose Avenue.
Prices: Coffee and cakes $1–$4. MC, V.
Open: Mon–Sat 9am–midnight, Sun 10am–midnight.

In addition to excellent coffee drinks and occasional poetry readings, Highland Grounds is best known for its good line-up of local bands that play to a young crowd almost every night of the week.

Late-Night Eating

Ben Frank's, 8585 Sunset Blvd., West Hollywood. ☎ **310/652-8808.**

Cuisine: AMERICAN. **Reservations:** Not accepted. **Directions:** From Santa Monica Boulevard, turn north onto La Cienega Boulevard, then right onto Sunset Boulevard; the restaurant is two blocks ahead.
Prices: Appetizers $4–$7; main courses $7–$13; lunch $5–$7; breakfast $4–$8. AE, MC, V.
Open: Daily 24 hours.

Although it's open all day and night, the most colorful time to go to this Sunset Strip joint is late at night, when it's jammed with long-haired rockers and their attendant pierced punk-babes.

The food is never as colorful as the crowd. Ben Frank's serves typical coffee-shop fare: breakfasts of French toast and eggs Benedict; lunches of hamburgers, salads, and sandwiches; and dinners of meatloaf, pot roast, pastas, and fish and chips. Shakes and malts are also sold, as well as beer and wine.

Canter's Fairfax Restaurant, Delicatessen & Bakery, 419 N. Fairfax Ave., downtown. ☎ **213/651-2030.**

Cuisine: JEWISH. **Reservations:** Not accepted.
Prices: Appetizers $3–$7; main courses $6–$12. MC, V.
Open: Daily 24 hours.

Popular with rock stars and other celebs, Canter's has also been a hit with late-nighters since it opened 65 years ago. In addition to a full range of sandwiches, diners can get matzoh-ball soup, knishes, and other Jewish specialties. There's live music in the restaurant's Kibitz Room every Tuesday (for details, see Chapter 10).

Denny's, 7373 W. Sunset Blvd., West Hollywood. ☎ **213/876-6660.**

Cuisine: AMERICAN. **Reservations:** Not accepted.
Prices: Appetizers $2–$4; main courses $4–$7. AE, MC, V.
Open: Daily 24 hours.

When people say "Let's go to Rock and Roll Denny's," they don't mean just any restaurant in this nationwide chain; they're referring to the one at the corner of Sunset and Vista. On weekends between 2am and 4am a half-hour wait should be expected. You can get the same food at a dozen other Denny's citywide, but the crowd makes this one the best.

Larry Parker's 24-Hour Diner, 206 S. Beverly Dr., Beverly Hills. ☎ **310/274-5655.**

Cuisine: AMERICAN. **Reservations:** Not accepted.
Prices: Appetizers $3–$6; main courses $4–$8. AE, MC, V.
Open: Daily 24 hours.

On the weekend, don't be surprised to find a 45-minute wait at 4am. This is the most popular of the after-bar eateries; it blasts high-decibel hip-hop, sports a spinning disco ball, and attracts a flashy crowd. Patrons line up behind a doorman-watched velvet rope.

Restaurants by Cuisine

American

Key to Abbreviations: *E* = Expensive; *M* = Moderately priced; *I* = Inexpensive

Health Food

Inn of the Seventh Ray, Topanga
Canyon (*M*), p. 135

The Source, West Hollywood (*I*),
p. 123

International

Bikini, Santa Monica (*E*), p. 137

The Warehouse, Marina del Rey
(*E*), p. 140

Irish

Tom Bergin's Tavern, Hollywood
(*M*), p. 118

Italian

Ca' Brea, Hollywood (*M*), p. 114

Caffè Delfini, Santa Monica (*M*),
p. 139

Emilio's, Hollywood (*M*), p. 115

Harry's Bar & Grill, Century City
(*M*), p. 127

La Scala & Boutique Restaurant,
Beverly Hills (*M*), p. 128

La Scala Malibu, Malibu (*E*),
p. 134

Little Joe's, downtown (*M*), p. 108

Mi Piace, Pasadena (*M*), p. 132

Mums, Long Beach (*M*), p. 142

Ristorante Chianti & Chianti
Cucina, Hollywood (*M*), p. 117

Japanese

Horikawa, downtown (*E*), p. 106

Matsuhisa, Beverly Hills (*E*),
p. 126

Mishima, West Los Angeles (*M*),
p. 130

Miyako, Pasadena (*M*), p. 132

Tokyo Kaikan, downtown (*M*),
p. 109

Jewish

Canter's Fairfax Restaurant,
Delicatessen, and Bakery,
downtown (*I*), p. 146

Langer's, downtown (*I*), p. 110

Nate & Al's, Beverly Hills (*M*),
p. 128

Mexican

Antonio's, West Hollywood (*M*),
p. 122

Carlos and Pepe's, Malibu (*I*),
p. 136

Middle Eastern

Noura Cafe, Hollywood (*I*), p. 119

Moroccan

Dar Maghreb, Hollywood (*E*),
p. 114

Peruvian

Matsuhisa, Beverly Hills (*E*),
p. 126

Polynesian

Trader Vic's, Beverly Hills (*E*),
p. 127

Southern

Aunt Kizzy's Back Porch, Marina
del Rey (*M*), p. 142

Georgia, Hollywood (*M*), p. 116

Southwestern

Authentic Cafe, Hollywood (*I*),
p. 118

Spanish

Cava, Los Angeles (*I*), p. 128

7

What to See & Do in Los Angeles

THERE'S PLENTY TO DO IN L.A.—THE ONLY PROBLEM IS THAT YOU HAVE TO drive everywhere to do it. Traffic makes it impossible to see everything in a day; order your priorities and don't plan on seeing everything in a short time or you'll end up not seeing much of anything. Be sure to get a good map; any accordion foldout, sold in gas stations and drugstores all around town, will do. If you can, pick up a copy of the Sunday *Los Angeles Times* and check the "Calendar" for a good list of the week's events.

Suggested Itineraries

If You Have One Day

After spending the morning in Hollywood, visiting the Walk of Fame and Mann's Chinese Theatre, cruise along Sunset Boulevard or stop in at the Rancho La Brea Tar Pits. Spend the afternoon in Beverly Hills. Window-shop along Rodeo Drive and drive by famous homes.

If You Have Two Days

Spend the first day as above, then tour a television or film studio, or go shopping along Melrose Avenue and visit the world-famous Farmer's Market. In the evening, go to a baseball or football game, see a play, or visit the Griffith Observatory.

If You Have Three Days

Spend your third day exploring the city's beach communities, especially Santa Monica, Venice, and Malibu. Don't miss the scene along the Venice Beach Walk.

Did You Know . . . ?

- Los Angeles County encompasses 85 incorporated cities, of which Vernon (population 90) is the smallest and Los Angeles (population 3.4 million) is the largest.
- Los Angeles hosts more than 62 million visitors annually.
- The L.A. Harbor lighthouse was the first in the United States to be converted to solar power.
- Bert Grimm's, the nation's oldest tattoo parlor, is located in Long Beach; according to local legend, gangsters Bonnie Parker and Pretty Boy Floyd were needled here.
- The City of Long Beach has the largest Cambodian population outside Cambodia—approximately 40,000 Cambodians live here.
- Television and motion pictures comprise the third-largest industry in Los Angeles, behind aerospace and tourism.

If You Have Five Days

Visit a theme park—Universal Studios, Disneyland, or Knott's Berry Farm—or try out as a contestant on a TV game show. Perhaps join a studio audience and watch your favorite show being taped. Museum-lovers should visit the J. Paul Getty Museum or explore Forest Lawn Cemetery.

1 The Top Attractions

Griffith Observatory, 2800 E. Observatory Rd., Los Angeles.
☎ 213/664-1191.

Almost 50 million people have visited Griffith Observatory since its doors opened in 1935. Located on the south slope of Mt. Hollywood, the observatory is still one of L.A.'s best evening attractions. Visitors are invited to look through the observatory's 12-inch telescope, one of the largest in California for use by the public. On a clear night, you can see the moon, planets, and other celestial objects. Phone **213/663-8171** for the Sky Report—a recorded message on current planet positions and celestial events.

Admission: Free.

Open: Viewing times, winter, Tues–Sun 7–9:45pm; summer, daily dark–9:45pm. **Directions:** From U.S. 101, take the Vermont Avenue exit north to its end in Griffith Park.

Hollywood Sign, Hollywood.

The 50-foot-high white sheet-metal letters of the world-famous HOLLYWOOD sign have long been a symbol of the movie industry city. But it wasn't always that way. Erected in 1923, the sign was originally intended as an advertisement for an area real estate development, and the full text read "HOLLYWOODLAND" until 1949. Unfortunately, laws prohibit visitors from climbing up to the base, but that's okay since the best view is from down below in Hollywood.

⭐ **Walk of Fame,** Hollywood Blvd. and Vine St., Hollywood.

Nearly 2,000 stars are honored on the world's most famous sidewalk. Bronze medallions set into the center of each star pay tribute to famous television, film, radio, theater, and record personalities, from nickelodeon days to the present. Some of the most popular include Marilyn Monroe, 6744 Hollywood Blvd.; James Dean, 1719 Vine St.; John Lennon, 1750 Vine St.; and Elvis Presley, 6777 Hollywood Blvd. Each month another celebrity is awarded a star on the Walk of Fame, and the public is invited to attend. For dates and times, contact the Hollywood Chamber of Commerce, 6255 Sunset Blvd., Suite 911, Hollywood, CA 90028 (☎ 213/469-8311).

Directions: From U.S. 101, exit onto Highland Boulevard and turn left onto Hollywood Boulevard.

⭐ **J. Paul Getty Museum,** 17985 Pacific Coast Hwy., Malibu.
☎ 310/458-2003.

Waggishly dubbed "Pompeii-by-the-Pacific," the J. Paul Getty Museum is a spectacular reconstruction of the Roman Villa dei Papiri, which was buried in volcanic mud when Mount Vesuvius erupted in A.D. 79, destroying Pompeii and Herculaneum. Completed in 1974, this 10-acre museum is believed to have the largest endowment of any museum worldwide.

The magnificent Italian-style museum is, fittingly, particularly strong in Greek and Roman antiquities. One of the most notable pieces in the collection is a 4th-century B.C. Greek sculpture, *The Victorious Athlete* (known as the Getty bronze), possibly crafted by Lysippus, court sculptor to Alexander the Great.

A second strength is pre-20th-century European paintings and decorative arts, major examples of which include 17th- and 18th- century French furniture, tapestries, silver, and porcelain. The painting galleries accommodate an extensive Italian Renaissance collection, including Titan's *Venus and Adonis,* Pontormo's *Portrait of Cosimo I de'Medici,* and Andrea Mantegna's *Adororation of the Magi;* a Flemish baroque collection; and important paintings by such French artists as Georges de la Tour, Nicolas Poussin, Jacques-Louis David, and Jean-François Millet.

In 1990 the museum announced that it had acquired *Irises,* painted in 1889 by Vincent van Gogh. It's the Getty's most famous 19th-century painting and is among the most important works of art in the western United States. *Irises* can be seen in the museum's second-floor galleries together with a growing collection of important 19th-century works, such as Pierre-Auguste Renoir's *La Promenade,* Edouard Manet's *Rue Mosnier with Flags,* Edvard Munch's *Starry Night,* and James Ensor's *Christ's Entry into Brussels in 1889.* Among other recent acquisitions is J. M. W. Turner's *Van Trom, Going About to Please His Masters, Ships at Sea, Getting a Good Wetting.*

If that's not enough, the museum displays medieval and Renaissance illuminated manuscripts, sculpture, and drawings, as well as 19th- and 20th-century European and American photographs.

Two incredible educational interactive videodiscs allow visitors to guide themselves through the rich and complex worlds of Greek vases and illuminated manuscripts with the touch of a finger. This new technology enables you to study these subjects in depth, depending on your level of interest, and have the otherwise forbidden luxury of leafing through a medieval manuscript or handling an ancient Greek vase. Game boxes for families and a browsing room with books for young and old are some of the services available to visitors. Spanish-language materials and tours are also available.

Moderately priced snacks, salads, and sandwiches are sold in the Garden Tea Room, a cafeteria-style eatery. Picnics are not permitted on the premises.

Docent orientation lectures are given at the ocean end of the main garden every 15 minutes from 9:30am to 3:15pm. Details on educational tours are available from the Information Desk.

Important: Parking is free, but visitors are required to phone for a parking reservation 7 to 10 days in advance. Due to an agreement with local homeowners, walk-in visitors are not permitted. Carless visitors may enter the grounds by bicycle, motorcycle, taxi, or RTD bus no. 434 (phone the museum for information and request a museum pass from the driver).

In 1992, construction of a new, bigger Getty museum complex began on a 700-acre hilltop site in western Los Angeles. Scheduled to open in 1997, the $730-million museum will allow for 1.5 million visitors annually.

Admission: Free.

Open: Tues–Sun 10am–5pm (last entrance at 4:30pm). **Directions:** From Santa Monica, take Calif. 1 (Pacific Coast Highway) north about five miles to the museum entrance.

⭐ **Mann's Chinese Theatre**, 6925 Hollywood Blvd., Hollywood. ☎ 213/461-3331.

One of Hollywood's greatest landmarks, Grauman's Chinese Theatre was opened in 1927 by impresario Sid Grauman. Opulent both inside and out, the theater combines authentic and simulated Chinese decor. Original Chinese heaven doves top the facade, and two of the theater's columns actually come from a Ming Dynasty temple. Despite its architectural flamboyance, the theater is most famous for its entry court, in which movie stars' signatures and hand- and footprints are set in concrete. Sid Grauman, who was credited with originating the idea of the spectacular movie "première," was an excellent promoter. To this day countless visitors continue to match their hands and feet with those of Elizabeth Taylor, Paul Newman, Ginger Rogers, Humphrey Bogart, Frank Sinatra, and others. It's not always hands and feet, though; Betty Grable made an impression with her shapely leg; Gene Autry with the hoofprints of Champion, his horse; and Jimmy Durante and Bob Hope used (what else?) their noses. The theater's name was changed to Mann's in the 1970s.

Admission: Tickets, $7.50.

Open: Call for showtimes. **Directions:** From U.S. 101, exit onto Highland Boulevard and turn right onto Hollywood Boulevard. The theater is located three blocks ahead on your right.

Rancho La Brea Tar Pits/George C. Page Museum, Hancock Park, 5801 Wilshire Blvd., Los Angeles. ☎ 213/857-6311.

Even today a bubbling, odorous, murky swamp of congealed oil still oozes to the earth's surface in the middle of L.A. It's not pollution; it's the La Brea Tar Pits, an incredible, primal attraction right on the Miracle Mile in the Wilshire district. The pits date back some 40,000 years, when they formed a deceptively attractive drinking area for mammals, birds, amphibians, and insects, many of which are now extinct. Thousands of prehistoric animals crawled into the sticky sludge and stayed forever. Although the existence of the pits was known as early as the 18th century, it wasn't until 1906 that scientists began a systematic removal and classification of the fossils. Disengorged specimens have included ground sloths, huge vultures, mastodons (early elephants), camels, and prehistoric relatives of many of today's rodents, bears, lizards, and birds, as well as plants and freshwater shells.

There are currently six pits here, in which asphalt seeps to the surface to form sticky pools. Tar Pit tours are offered on Saturday

Los Angeles Area Attractions

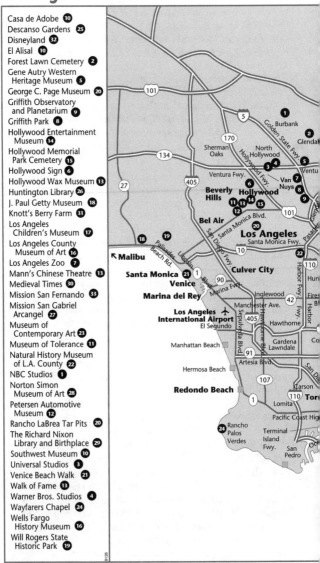

and Sunday at 1pm, starting from the Observation Pit at the west end of Hancock Park.

More than two dozen specimens have been mounted and are exhibited in the George C. Page Museum of La Brea Discoveries, at the eastern end of Hancock Park. Skeletons of trapped birds and animals are also on display. A 15-minute film documents the Tar Pit

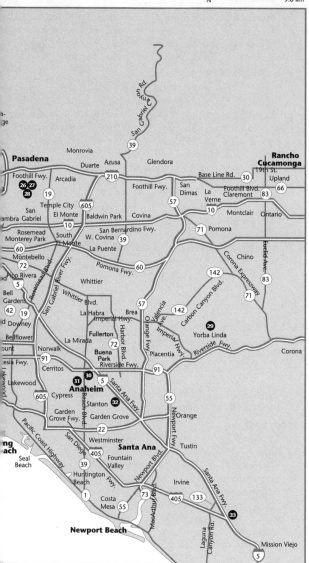

discoveries. In the adjacent Paleontology Laboratory, you can watch scientists as they clean, identify, and catalog new fossils.

Admission: $5 adults, $2.50 seniors (62 and older) and students with I.D., $2 children 5–12, free for kids 4 and under; free for everyone the second Tues of every month.

Open: Museum, Tues–Sun 10am–5pm; Paleontology Laboratory, Wed–Sun 10am–5pm; Observation Pit, Sat–Sun 10am–5pm.

Directions: From the Santa Monica Freeway (1-10), exit onto La Brea Avenue north, continue for three miles, and then turn left onto Wilshire Boulevard. The museum and tar pits are about 10 blocks ahead, between Fairfax and La Brea Avenues.

Venice Beach Walk, Venice oceanfront.

Nestled against the ocean, between Santa Monica and Marina del Rey, the city of Venice is one of the trendiest sections of Los Angeles, and a unique tourist destination. The character of Venice has undergone a remarkable change since the turn of the century, when it was founded with the idea that it would resemble its namesake in Italy. The streets, graced with canals, were connected by quaint one-lane bridges; and authentic imported gondolas plied the inland waterways. The area became fashionable when self-enchanted silent-screen star Mae Murray (*The Merry Widow*) built a pistachio-colored, Venetian-style palazzo here, near the St. Mark's hotel, an Italian-style rococo hostelry.

But then oil was discovered. Block after block of residences gave way to the profitable derricks, and the canals became slimy sewers. As a beach resort (not to mention a harbinger of Disneyland) Venice died a miserable death. The area began to revive in the '50s, when Venice attracted southern California's beatniks. And in the '60s, Venice became the hippies' primary place for turning on and dropping out.

Today, Venice is quickly becoming a chic seaside community; developers are renovating and gentrification is in full swing. Soaring real estate is bringing in scores of new restaurants and boutiques. Venice's beach walk is one of the city's greatest cultural treasures; a "Coney Island west" circus of skaters, hipsters, and posers of all ages and shapes. You go there just to stroll and watch the carnival of humanity that's attracted to this ever so L.A. meeting ground.

Queen Mary, Pier J, Long Beach. ☎ 310/435-3511.

The *Queen Mary,* permanently docked here since its 14,500-mile journey around South America in 1967, is quite an imposing sight. The black hull and white superstructure is a fifth of a mile long; its three vermilion stacks shoot up 150 feet into the air. Visitors can explore the ship's engine rooms, bridge, turbines, and machinery, as well as re-creations of all classes of accommodations. In addition to an extensive display on World War II, in which the ship took part as a troop carrier, there are a sound-and-light show that reenacts a near-collision at sea and a fine exhibit devoted to model-ship building. On board are about 25 specialty shops and a chapel for "at sea" weddings. See Chapter 5 for information about staying at the *Queen Mary* Hotel.

Admission: Free; tours, $5 adults, $3 children. Parking is $5.

Open: Daily 10am–6pm (last entry at 5:30pm). **Directions:** Take the Long Beach Freeway (I-710) to its terminus at the Marina.

Universal Studios Hollywood, Hollywood Frwy., Lankershim Blvd. exit, Universal City. ☎ 818/508-9600.

The largest and busiest movie studio in the world, Universal began offering tours to the public in 1964. Now a full-fledged amusement park, the "studio" attracts more than five million visitors a year who want to experience the rides and get a behind-the-scenes look at the movies.

Visitors board a tram for the one-hour guided tour of the studio's 420 acres. You'll pass stars' dressing rooms and countless departments involved in film production. Backlot sets are the most interesting; they include Six Point, Texas, a western town that has been used since the days of Tom Mix; and a typical New York City street. A stop at Stage 32 focuses on special effects.

The tram encounters several disasters along the way, including an attack by the deadly 24-foot *Jaws* shark, a laser battle with Cylon robots, an alpine avalanche, a bridge collapse, a flash flood, an earthquake, and more.

After the ride, visitors can wander around the Entertainment Center, where several times each day skilled stuntpeople fall off buildings, dodge knife blows, and ride trick horses. In addition, you can perform as a "guest star" in the *Star Trek Adventure,* then watch yourself perform with spliced-in pictures of Leonard Nimoy and William Shatner. Terrific special-effects shows based on the movies *An American Tail* and *Back to the Future* showcase spectacular moviemaking techniques. On Universal's newest ride, *E.T. Adventure,* visitors take a ride on simulated bicycles and relive key parts of the film. Almost any day you can be part of a live audience for the taping of a television show.

Admission: $29 adults, $23 seniors (65 and older) and children 3–11, free for kids under 3. Parking is $5.

Open: Summer, daily 7am–11pm, the rest of the year, daily 9am–7pm. **Directions:** From U.S. 101 (Hollywood Freeway), take the Lankershim Boulevard exit to the park entrance.

Warner Brothers Studios, Olive Ave., at Hollywood Way, Burbank. ☎ 818/954-1744.

Home to Warner Brothers and Lorimar Television, the Warner Brothers Studios offer the most comprehensive and the least Disneyesque of studio tours. They call it the VIP tour, because it's created for no more than 12 people per group.

The tours are flexible, since they look in on whatever is being filmed at the time. Whether it's an orchestra scoring a film or a TV program being taped or edited, you'll get a glimpse of how it's done. Whenever possible, guests visit working sets to watch actors filming actual productions. Possible stops may include the wardrobe department or the mills where sets are made.

Because you're seeing people at work—people who mustn't be disturbed—children under 10 are not admitted. It's recommended that you make a reservation at least one week in advance.

Admission: $27 per person.

Open: Tours given Mon–Fri at 9, 10, and 11am and 1, 2, and 3pm.

Television Tapings

Television producers need enthusiastic audiences for their game and talk shows. It can be fun, too. To gain admission to a taping, you must be willing to be seen on camera, and there is often a minimum age. **T.V. Ticket Hotline** (☎ 818/840-4444) will arrange for you to be part of a live audience for a television taping. They help assemble audiences for many popular game and talk shows, and their service is free. You can reserve tickets over the phone. **Audience Associates** (☎ 213/467-4697) and **Audiences Unlimited** (☎ 818/506-0043) offer similar services.

The three major television networks and Universal Studios always need audiences for their show tapings. Contact them to see what's going to be on when you're in town:

ABC-TV, 4151 Prospect Ave., Hollywood, CA 90027.
☎ **213/520-1ABC.**

You can watch the tapings of such shows as "Dave's World," "Full House," "Saved by the Bell," and "Family Matters" at the ABC studios. All tickets are free, and there are age limits for each show. Call **818/506-0067** for recorded information about which shows are being taped while you're in Los Angeles.
Open: Ticket office, Mon–Fri 9am–5pm.

CBS-TV, 7800 Beverly Blvd., Los Angeles, CA 90036.
☎ **213/852-2458.**

Tickets are available to such game shows as "The Price Is Right," "Wheel of Fortune," and "Family Feud." The age limits to the tapings vary. Call ahead for specific times and dates.
Open: Ticket office, Mon–Fri 9am–5pm, Sat–Sun 10am–5pm.

NBC Studios, 3000 W. Alameda Ave., Burbank, CA 91523.
☎ **818/840-3537** or **840-3538.**

For tickets to any of the shows taped at NBC Studios (including the "Tonight Show"), write to the address above. You'll receive a "guest letter," which can be exchanged for free tickets on your arrival in Los Angeles. It does not guarantee entrance to a specific taping. Tickets are distributed on a first-come, first-served basis. Tickets for the "Tonight Show" are available on the day of the show only; tickets for other shows may be picked up in advance. Minimum age limits vary from 8 to 18; it's 16 for the "Tonight Show."
Open: Ticket office, Mon–Fri 8am–5pm.

Universal Studios, 100 Universal City Plaza, Universal City, CA 91608. ☎ **818/777-3750.**

To see a television show being taped at Universal Studios without going to the theme park, write or call the ticket office. Be sure to

IMPRESSIONS

"I was always sort of mystified by the New York snobbery toward L.A. . . . [It's] very often on the cutting edge of new ideas."
—Tina Brown, Editor, *The New Yorker*

give them your preferred dates; they will supply you with a taping schedule. Tickets are free.

Open: Ticket office, Daily 8:30am–4pm.

TELEVISION GAME SHOWS

Have you ever dreamed of being a contestant on a television game show? Producers are choosy, but if you have the "looks" they're searching for, you may be selected. Since most contestants are from California, coordinators are especially pleased to see out-of-towners. If they like you, they'll do everything within reason to accommodate you. The average audition lasts about an hour, and usually consists of a written test. Callbacks are held anywhere from a few hours to a few days later.

With proper planning, you can audition for three or four shows in a single week and still have plenty of time to tour the city. Shows looking for contestants advertise daily on the front page of the *Los Angeles Times* classified section. You can also contact production companies directly to see if they're currently auditioning. Below is a short list of major companies, together with the game shows they produce:

Mark Goodson Productions, 5757 Wilshire Blvd., Suite 206, Los Angeles, CA 90036 (☎ 213/965-6500): "The Price Is Right" and "Family Feud."

Merv Griffin Enterprises, 1541 N. Vine St., Hollywood, CA 90028 (☎ 310/859-0188): "Wheel of Fortune" and "Jeopardy!"

2 More Attractions

Architectural Highlights

Although you won't find entire L.A. neighborhoods that are architecturally noteworthy, pockets of distinctively designed structures abound. There was a time when the city's landscape was dotted with buildings that assumed the shape of other things—including giant dogs, shoes, owls, frankfurters, and a famous brown derby. While most of these roadside businesses have vanished, several of their contemporary heirs have replaced them. Below is a brief look at the city's most exciting architectural outposts.

Capitol Records Building, 1750 Vine St., Hollywood.

This 12-story tower on Hollywood's Vine Street may be the world's only circular office building. Designed to resemble a stack of records, the structure is topped with a giant turntablelike stylus.

Chiat/Day/Mojo Headquarters, 340 Main St., Venice.

What would otherwise be an unspectacular contemporary office building is made fantastic by a three-story pair of binoculars that frames the entrance to this advertising agency. The sculpture is modeled after a design created by Claes Oldenburg and Coosje van Bruggen.

The Burger That Ate L.A., 7624 Melrose Ave., Los Angeles.

Located on one of the city's most fashionable shopping streets, between La Brea and Fairfax Avenues, this casual restaurant with outdoor seating is designed to look like a giant seeded bun that's munching away at City Hall.

The Narrowest House, 708 Gladys Ave., Long Beach.

Known as "The Skinny House," this narrow English Tudor–style home built in 1932 is the result of a bet by builder Nelson Rummond that he could not build a habitable residence on a lot that measured only 10 feet wide by 50 feet deep. The three-story, 860-square-foot structure is now featured in "Ripley's Believe It or Not" as the nation's narrowest home.

Walt Disney Corporate Offices, 500 S. Buena Vista St., Burbank.

Located at the corner of Alameda Avenue and Buena Vista Street in Burbank, this neoclassical building inspired by ancient Greece is made ultramodern by tall columns that are carved to the likenesses of the Seven Dwarfs.

Cemeteries & Churches

Hollywood Memorial Park Cemetery, 6000 Santa Monica Blvd., Hollywood. ☎ 213/469-1181.

This centrally located cemetery is a popular, if morbid, sightseeing excursion. Dedicated movie buffs can visit the graves of Rudolph Valentino, Peter Lorre, Douglas Fairbanks, Sr., Norma Talmadge, Tyrone Power, Cecil B. DeMille, Marion Davies, and others. Almost every day a mysterious lady in black pays homage at Valentino's crypt.

Admission: Free.

Open: Daily 8am–5pm. **Directions:** From U.S. 101, exit onto Sunset Boulevard west. After five blocks, turn left onto Gower Street, then turn left at the cemetery to the entrance on Santa Monica Boulevard.

Forest Lawn Cemetery, 1712 S. Glendale Ave., Glendale. ☎ 213/254-3131.

There are five Forest Lawns in L.A., but this is the one you've heard about. Comic Lenny Bruce called this place "Disneyland for the dead," but to founder Dr. Hubert Eaton, Forest Lawn was the cemetery of his dreams—a symbol of the joys of eternal life. It's quite a place. Thousands of southern Californians are entombed in the Great Mausoleum, including Jean Harlow, Clark Gable, Carole Lombard, and W. C. Fields. The Mausoleum's Memorial Court of Honor features a stunning stained-glass re-creation of da Vinci's *The Last Supper,* created by Rosa Caselli Moretti, the last member of a Perugia, Italy, family known for their secret process of making stained glass. There are special crypts in the Court that money cannot buy—they're reserved for men and women whose service to humanity has been outstanding. Those already so entombed include Gutzon Borglum, creator of Mount Rushmore, and composer Rudolph Friml.

Frommer's Favorite Los Angeles Experiences

A Visit to a Film or TV Studio   Nothing is more common to L.A. than a backstage tour of a film or television production facility. It's a lot of fun to see how your favorite TV show or a movie is actually made.

Dining at a Top Restaurant   Splurge for an expensive dinner in a trendy restaurant. L.A. is one of America's great restaurant cities. Don't just go for the food—do as the locals do and make it an evening to see and be seen.

A Day at the Beaches   Stroll along the Venice Beach Walk, cruise the Santa Monica Pier, and sunbathe in Malibu.

A Shopping Tour of the City   You might want to just window-shop along Rodeo Drive, but then seriously consider the stores on Melrose Avenue and in trendy Santa Monica. Don't miss an excursion to the Beverly Center, the city's most famous shopping mall.

A Day at a Theme Park   Whether it's Disneyland, Knott's Berry Farm, or Universal Studios Hollywood, these attractions can be fun for the entire family.

The cemetery's biggest draws are two paintings: *The Crucifixion* (called "deeply inspiring" by Pope John Paul II) and *The Resurrection* (the pope had no comment). The artworks are part of a narrated show, presented daily every hour from 10am to 4pm, in a special theater specifically built for this purpose.

There are a number of cemetery churches, including the Wee Kirk o' the Heather, modeled after the 14th-century Scottish church where Annie Laurie worshipped; and the Church of the Recessional, a memorial to the sentiments expressed by Rudyard Kipling. More than 30,000 marriages have been performed here, including that of Ronald Reagan and Jane Wyman.

Other attractions at the Forest Lawn Museum include 14th-century European cathedral stained glass from the William Randolph Hearst collection, and reproductions of famous artworks, including Ghiberti's *Paradise Doors* and Michelangelo's *Sotterraneo* and *David*. Pick up a map at the Information Booth at the entrance to the cemetery.

Admission: Free.

Open: Daily 8am–5pm. **Directions:** From U.S. 101, exit onto Barham Boulevard, which turns into Forest Lawn Drive; the cemetery entrance is straight ahead.

Wayfarers Chapel, 5755 Palos Verdes Dr. S., Rancho Palos Verdes. ☎ **310/377-1650.**

Built on a cliff with a broad, steep face, the Wayfarers Chapel sits serenely in a quiet spot above the lashing waves of the Pacific. Built by Lloyd Wright, son of the celebrated architect Frank Lloyd Wright, the church is constructed of glass, redwood, and native stone, and surrounded by pretty gardens.

The "glass church" is a memorial to Emanuel Swedenborg, the 18th-century Swedish philosopher and theologian who claimed to have conversed with spirits and heavenly hosts in his visions.

Rare plants, some of which are native to the Holy Land, surround the building. Phone in advance to arrange a free escorted tour.

Admission: Free.

Open: Daily 9am–5pm.

Historical Sights

Casa de Adobe, 4605 N. Figueroa St., Highland Park. ☎ 213/225-8653.

Casa de Adobe is a re-creation of an early 19th-century Mexican California rancho. Latino art and artifacts are on exhibit from the Southwest Museum's permanent collection, together with Spanish Colonial-period furnishings.

Admission: Free; donations accepted.

Open: Tues–Sat 11am–5pm, Sun 11am–1pm.

El Alisal, 200 E. Ave. 43, Highland Park. ☎ 213/222-0546.

Charles F. Lummis, founder of the Southwest Museum, built this rugged two-story "castle" himself, using rocks from a nearby arroyo and telephone poles purchased from the Santa Fe Railroad. His home became a cultural center for many famous people in the literary, theatrical, political, and art worlds. Himself an author, editor (he coined the slogan "See America First"), archeologist, and librarian, Lummis was equally at home with Will Rogers, Teddy Roosevelt, singer Mary Garden, Madame Schumann-Heink, and writers such as Blasco Ibañez.

One of the particularly interesting aspects of El Alisal is its attractive water-conserving garden. The primary plants are those that thrive in a Mediterranean climate. The experimental section, the yarrow meadow, is a substitute for a water-consuming lawn.

Admission: Free.

Open: Daily noon–4pm.

Missions

On July 16, 1769, a Franciscan padre, Junípero Serra established the first in a string of missions that were to stretch along El Camino Real (the Royal Road) from San Diego to Sonoma. Eventually, the total number of missions reached 21, each one spaced a day's walk from the next. These controversial buildings were the first European structures on the West Coast; they represented the beginning of the end for the region's Native Americans. Today, California's missions are the oldest structures in the state. Most are still owned by the church, and can be visited for a small fee.

Mission San Fernando, 15151 San Fernando Mission Blvd., Mission Hills. ☎ 818/361-0186.

Near the junction of the Golden State/Santa Ana (I-5) Freeway and the San Diego Freeway (I-405) in Mission Hills, the Mission San Fernando, established in 1797, occupies seven acres of beautiful grounds. With an arcade of 21 classic arches and adobe walls four feet thick, it was a familiar stop for wayfarers along El Camino Real. The museum and the adjoining cemetery (where half a dozen padres and hundreds of Shoshone converts are buried) are also of interest.

Admission: $4 adults, $3 seniors and children under 13.

Open: Daily 9am–5pm. **Directions:** From I-5, exit at San Fernando Mission Boulevard east and drive five blocks to the mission.

Mission San Gabriel Arcangel, 537 W. Mission Dr., San Gabriel. ☎ 818/282-5191.

San Gabriel's completely self-contained compound encompasses an aqueduct, a cemetery, a winery, a tannery, a mission church, and a famous set of bells. Construction on the church—distinguished by its buttresses—was begun in 1790. Glittering, hand-carved polychrome statues surround the altar, while a copper font in the rear has the dubious distinction of being the first one used to baptize a California Native American in 1771.

The most notable contents of the mission's museum are Native American paintings depicting the Stations of the Cross. They're painted on sailcloth, with colors made from crushing the petals of desert flowers.

The mission itself was constructed with walls that are about five feet thick—erected to withstand the ravages of time. But even they were no match for two earthquakes in 1987, which necessitated massive renovations before it reopened in 1993.

Admission: $3 adults, $1 children 6–12 years, free for kids under 6.

Open: Daily 9:30am–4:30pm. **Closed:** Easter, half day on Good Friday, Thanksgiving, Christmas.

Museums & Galleries

Museum of Contemporary Art, 250 S. Grand Ave., Los Angeles. ☎ 213/621-2766.

A permanent collection of international scope specializes in painting, sculpture, and environmental works by well-known and emerging artists. Temporary exhibits change frequently and have included retrospectives from Roy Lichtenstein; a photograph "Seascape" series by Hiroshi Sugimoto; and an exploration of the relationship between film and art that included art objects, film excerpts, and installations.

Admission: $6 adults, $4 seniors and students, free for children under 12.

Open: Tues–Wed and Fri–Sun 11am–5pm, Thurs 11am–8pm.

Huntington Library, Art Collections, and Botanical Gardens, 1151 Oxford Rd., San Marino. ☎ 818/405-2100 or 405-2141.

The 207-acre estate of pioneer industrialist Henry E. Huntington (1850–1927)—complete with gardens and mansion—has been converted into an educational and cultural center for scholars, art devotees, and the general public. Mr. Huntington's thirst for original manuscripts, rare books, great paintings, and skillfully planned gardens led to the formation of what many consider to be one of the greatest attractions in southern California.

Huntington's house is now an art gallery, containing an extraordinary collection of paintings, tapestries, furniture, and other decorative arts. Works are mainly of English and French origin and date from the 18th century. The most celebrated painting here is Gainsborough's *The Blue Boy. Pinkie,* by Sir Thomas Lawrence, is a famous portrait of the youthful aunt of Elizabeth Barrett Browning. Equally well known are Sir Joshua Reynolds's *Sarah Siddons as the Tragic Muse,* Rembrandt's *Lady with the Plume,* and Romney's *Lady Hamilton in a Straw Hat.* You'll also find a collection of Beauvais and Gobelin tapestries.

The adjacent Virginia Steele Scott Gallery for American Art contains an eclectic variety of paintings spanning more than 200 years. Some of the better-known works are Gilbert Stuart's portrait of George Washington, John Singleton Copley's *Sarah Jackson,* George Caleb Bingham's *In a Quandary,* Mary Cassatt's *Breakfast in Bed,* and Frederic Church's *Chimborazo.*

The Library Exhibition Hall displays a rotating selection of great treasures drawn from its remarkable collection of English and American first editions, letters, and manuscripts. They include a copy of the Gutenberg Bible printed in Mainz in the 1450s, a 1410 copy of Chaucer's *Canterbury Tales,* a First Folio of Shakespeare, and Benjamin Franklin's handwritten manuscript for his *Autobiography.* It's worth a trip just to see the Botanical Gardens, which are studded with rare shrubs, trees, and 17th-century statuary from Padua. Strolling paths wend their way through a variety of flora, including the Desert Garden, with extensive cacti in all shapes; the Camellia Garden, with 1,500 varieties; and the Japanese Garden, with dwarf maples, reflection pools, Zen Garden, and bonsai court.

The Huntington Library is located about 12 miles from downtown Los Angeles.

Admission: Free; $5 donation suggested.

Open: Tues–Fri 1–4:30pm, Sat–Sun 10:30am–4:30pm. **Closed:** Major holidays.

Norton Simon Museum of Art, 411 Colorado Blvd., Pasadena. ☎ 818/449-6840.

One of the most important museums in California, the Norton Simon Museum of Art features old masters from the Italian, Dutch, Spanish, Flemish, and French schools; impressionist paintings; Franco-Flemish tapestries; and 20th-century painting and sculpture. Highlights of the collection include works by Raphael, Rubens, Rembrandt, Rousseau, Courbet, Matisse, Picasso, Corot, Monet, and van Gogh. A superb collection of Southeast Asian and Indian sculpture is also displayed.

The museum itself sits among broad plazas, sculpture gardens, a reflection pool, and semitropical plantings.

Admission: $4 adults, $2 students and seniors, free for children under 12.

Open: Thurs–Sun noon–6pm; bookshop, Thurs–Sun noon–5:30pm.

Museum of Tolerance, 9786 W. Pico Blvd., Los Angeles.
☎ **310/553-8403.**

Located in the Simon Wiesenthal Center, this extraordinary new museum features interactive exhibits that illustrate the history of racism and prejudice. One of the largest installations in this high-tech gallery focuses on the events of the Holocaust. The contemporary layout of the building itself, as well as its fast-paced contents, are designed to engage both serious investigators and the MTV crowd.

Admission: $7.50 adults, $5.50 seniors, $3.50 students, $2.50 children 3–12, children under 3 free. Advance purchase recommended.

Open: Mon–Wed 10am–5pm, Thurs 10am–8pm, Fri 10am–3pm (to 1pm Nov–Mar), Sun 11am–6:30pm.

The Southwest Museum, 234 Museum Dr., Highland Park.
☎ **213/221-2164,** or **213/221-2163** for a recording.

At the top of a steep hill overlooking Arroyo Seco, the Southwest Museum is Los Angeles's oldest art museum. Founded in 1907 by amateur historian and Native American expert Charles F. Lummis, the privately funded museum contains one of the finest collections of Native American art and artifacts in the United States.

Inside the two-story structure, the whole world of the original Americans opens onto a panoramic exhibition, complete with a Cheyenne summer tepee, rare paintings, weapons, moccasins, and other artifacts of Plains life. A separate two-level hall presents the culture of the native people of southeastern Alaska, Canada's west coast, and the northern United States. A major exhibition interprets 10,000 years of history of the people of the American Southwest, featuring art and artifacts of the native peoples of Arizona, New Mexico, Colorado, and Utah. The California Hall offers insights into the lifestyles of the first Californians. The Caroline Boeing Poole Memorial Wing exhibits a changing display of more than 400 examples of native North American basketry from the museum's 11,000-plus collection.

An exceptionally interesting calendar of events includes a Native American Film Festival; lectures on the sacred art of the Huichols; Mexican songs, dance, and costumes; and Native American masks—to name just a few.

Admission: $5 adults, $3 seniors (over 55) and students, $2 children 7–18, free for kids under 7.

Open: Tues–Sun 11am–5pm. **Directions:** From the Pasadena Freeway (Calif. 110), exit onto Avenue 43; turn right onto Figueroa and follow the signs zigzagging up the hill to the museum at Museum Drive.

Natural History Museum of Los Angeles County, Exposition Park, 900 Exposition Blvd., Los Angeles. ☎ **213/744-3466.**

The largest natural-history museum in the West houses seemingly endless exhibits of fossils, minerals, birds, mammals, and the like. It's a warehouse of history, chronicling the earth and its environment from 600 million years ago to the present day. Other permanent displays include the world's rarest shark, a walk-through vault containing priceless gems, a Children's Discovery Center, Insect Zoo, and state-of-the-art Bird Hall. Dioramas depict animals in their natural habitats, and other exhibits detail human cultures, including one on American history from 1660 to 1914.

Free docent-led tours are offered daily at 1pm.

Admission: $8 adults; $5.50 children 12–17, seniors, and students with I.D.; $2 children 5–12; free for kids under 5; free for everyone the first Tues of every month.

Open: Tues–Sun 10am–5pm, and some Mons and holidays. **Directions:** From the Pasadena Freeway (Calif. 110), exit onto Exposition Boulevard east; the museum is located three blocks ahead, one block west of Hoover Street.

Los Angeles County Museum of Art, 5905 Wilshire Blvd., Los Angeles. ☎ **213/857-6111,** or **857-6000** for a recording.

A complex of five modern buildings around a spacious central plaza, the Los Angeles County Museum of Art in Hancock Park is probably one of the finest art museums in the United States.

The Ahmanson Building, with a central atrium, contains the permanent collection, which encompasses everything from prehistoric to 19th-century art. The museum's holdings include Chinese and Korean pieces; pre-Columbian Mexican art; American and European painting, sculpture, and decorative arts; ancient and Islamic art; a unique glass collection from Roman times to the 19th century; and the renowned Gilbert collection of mosaics and monumental silver. The museum also has one of the nation's largest holdings of costumes and textiles, and an important Indian and Southeast Asian art collection.

Major special loan exhibitions, as well as galleries for prints, drawings, and photographs, are in the adjacent Hammer Building.

The Robert O. Anderson Building features 20th-century painting and sculpture, as well as special exhibits. The Leo S. Bing Center has a 600-seat theater and a 116-seat auditorium where lectures, films, and concerts are held.

The Pavilion for Japanese Art was opened in 1988. It was designed by the late Bruce Goff specifically to accommodate Japanese art, though certain elements of the museum resemble New York's Frank Lloyd Wright–designed Guggenheim Museum—the curved rising ramp, the central treatment of light, the structure of the displays. An extraordinary touch was Goff's use of Kalwall (a translucent material) for the exterior walls; besides blocking out ultraviolet light, these walls, like shoji screens, permit the soft, delicate entry of natural light. The museum now houses the internationally renowned Shin'enkan collection of Edo Period (1615–1865) Japanese painting, rivaled only by the holdings of the former emperor of Japan. It also displays Japanese sculpture, ceramics, lacquerware, screens, scrolls, and prints.

Two sculpture gardens contain a dozen large-scale outdoor sculptures, as well as works by 19th-century French master Auguste Rodin and German artist George Kolbe.

Free guided tours covering the highlights of the permanent collections are given daily on a regular basis.

Admission: $6 adults, $4 students and seniors (62 and over); $1 children 6–17, free for kids under 6; free for everyone for regular exhibitions the second Wed of every month.

Open: Wed–Thurs 10am–5pm, Fri 10am–9pm, Sat–Sun 11am–6pm. **Directions:** From the Hollywood Freeway (U.S. 101), take the Santa Monica Boulevard exit west to Fairfax Avenue, then turn left onto Wilshire Boulevard to the museum.

The Gene Autry Western Heritage Museum, 4700 Western Heritage Way, Los Angeles. ☎ 213/667-2000.

A life-size bronze sculpture of Gene Autry (once called "the singing cowboy") and his horse, Champion, greet visitors to this museum of American nostalgia.

Opened in 1988, this remarkable repository is undoubtedly one of the most comprehensive historical museums in the world. More than 16,000 artifacts and art pieces, including 100 of Gene Autry's personal treasures, illustrate the everyday lives and occupations of the early pioneers who helped settle the West. There are antique firearms, common tools, saddles (some intricately tooled), clothing, stagecoaches, and many hands-on exhibits. As the tour progresses, visitors enter the West of romance and imagination, as seen by artists, authors, filmmakers, and in TV and radio productions. Show business is illustrated with items from Buffalo Bill's Wild West Show, movie clips from the silent days, contemporary films, and memorabilia from TV-western series.

The museum shop is worth a visit in itself. Gifts include cowboy hats, western posters, books, shirts, bolo ties, and silver and turquoise jewelry.

The Golden Spur Cafe serves breakfast and lunch from 8am to 4:30pm every day the museum is open.

Admission: $7 adults, $5 seniors (60 and over) and students 13–18, $3 children 2–12, free for kids under 2.

Open: Tues–Sun 10am–5pm. **Directions:** From I-5, exit at Zoo Drive and follow the signs to Griffith Park; the museum is located opposite the zoo.

Hollywood Entertainment Museum, 6433 Hollywood Blvd., Hollywood. ☎ 213/956-5469.

Scheduled to open in late 1995, this museum is devoted to Hollywood's achievements in motion pictures, television, radio, and sound recording. It is located in the historic Hollywood Pacific Theater, a 1928 structure that was once the largest theater in Los Angeles. The museum has conserved much of the original theater, including about 90% of the original plaster ornamentation, and the planetariumlike ceiling.

The Entertainment Museum's displays include collections from the silent-film era and exhibits relating to the advent of sound recording, television, special effects, animation, and computer graphics. Historical and interactive displays detail the development of the entertainment industry, while other hands-on exhibits detail other aspects of the arts, utilizing the latest technologies.

Admission and hours were not set at press time; phone for information.

The Petersen Automotive Museum, 6060 Wilshire Blvd., Los Angeles. ☎ **213/744-3524.**

It's certainly fitting that there be a good car museum in Los Angeles, so this recently opened ode to the automobile was long overdue. Located at the corner of Fairfax Avenue, this museum celebrates the history of motor vehicles and their influence on American life. Named for its founder, Robert Petersen, the publisher responsible for *Hot Rod* and *Motor Trend* magazines, the four-story museum displays over 200 automobiles. Cars on the first floor are depicted chronologically, in period settings. The three other floors are devoted to show race cars, early motorcycles, and famous movie cars.

Admission: $7 adults, $5 seniors and students, $3 children 5–12, free for kids under 5.

Open: Sat–Thurs 10am–6pm, Fri 10am–9pm.

Parks & Gardens

Descanso Gardens, 1418 Descanso Dr., La Cañada.
☎ **818/952-4402,** or **952-4400** for a recording.

E. Manchester Boddy began planting camellias in 1941 as a hobby. Today the Rancho del Descanso (Ranch of Rest) contains thousands of camellias, with more than 600 varieties and more than 100,000 plants—making it the world's largest camellia garden. The County of Los Angeles purchased the gardens in 1953, and today they're managed by the Descanso Gardens Guild.

In addition to the camellias, there's a five-acre International Rosarium that includes some 7,500 varieties. Paths and streams wind through a towering oak forest and a native plant collection. Each season features different plants: daffodils, azaleas, tulips, and lilacs in the spring; chrysanthemums in the fall; and so on. Monthly art exhibits are also held in the garden's hospitality house.

A Japanese-style teahouse is located in the camellia forest. Land-scaped with money donated by the Japanese-American community, it features pools, waterfalls, azaleas, and camellias. The teahouse serves tea and cookies on Saturday and Sunday from 11am to 4pm. Free docent-guided walking tours are offered every Sunday at 1pm; guided tram tours, which cost $1.50, run Tuesday through Friday at 1, 2, and 3pm, and on Saturday and Sunday at 11am, 1pm, 2pm, and 3pm. Picnicking is allowed in specified areas.

Admission: $5 adults, $3 students and seniors (over 62), $1 children 5–12, free for kids under 5. Parking is free.

Open: Daily 9am–4:30pm. **Directions:** From downtown L.A., take Calif 2 north and exit onto Verdugo Boulevard. Turn right; after one mile turn right again onto Descanso Drive.

★ **Griffith Park**, Los Angeles. ☎ 213/665-5188.

Encompassing more than 4,000 acres of trees and hills, verdant Griffith Park claims to be the largest municipal park in the United States. Home of the Los Angeles Zoo and the Griffith Observatory, the park's facilities include golf courses, a bird sanctuary, tennis courts, a huge swimming pool, picnic areas, an old-fashioned merry-go-round, and large expanses of wilderness.

The park is located just northeast of Hollywood. Enter via Western Avenue for the beautiful Ferndell and children's playground. Vermont Avenue is the best entrance for the observatory, bird sanctuary, and Mount Hollywood.

Will Rogers State Historic Park, 14253 Sunset Blvd., Pacific Palisades. ☎ 310/454-8212.

The 31-room ranch house and grounds of the "cracker-barrel philosopher" was willed to the state of California in 1944. The estate is now supervised as a historic site by the Department of Parks and Recreation. Visitors may explore the grounds, seeing the former Rogers stables, even watching polo games, usually on Saturday afternoon and Sunday mornings, weather permitting. The house is filled with the original comfortable furnishings, including a porch swing in the living room and many Native American rugs and baskets.

Will Rogers began in show business as a trick roper in traveling rodeos, an act he later brought to the Ziegfeld Follies in New York. Eventually he settled in Hollywood, buying his own ranch and making films, which led one movie critic to write: "Will Rogers upheld the homely virtues against the tide of sophistication and sex." He was killed in an air crash with his friend, Wiley Post, in Alaska in mid-August 1935.

The park is open from 8am to 7pm during the summer, till 6pm the rest of the year. Tours of the house are given Monday through Friday from 10:30am and continue every hour thereafter, on the half-hour, until 4:30pm. On Saturday and Sunday the house is open continually from 10am to 5pm; closed New Year's, Thanksgiving, and Christmas Days. There's a $5-per-vehicle fee for entry, including all passengers. The fee includes a guided tour of the Will Rogers home, an audio tour, and a film on Will Rogers shown in the Visitor Center. There are picnic tables, although no food is sold, and a small gift shop in the center.

Incidentally, Charles Lindbergh and his wife, Anne Morrow Lindbergh, hid out here in the 1930s during part of the kidnap craze that followed the kidnap and murder of their first son.

3 Cool for Kids

Griffith Planetarium and Hall of Science, 2800 E. Observatory Rd., Los Angeles. ☎ **213/664-1181**, or **213/664-1191** for a recording.

Griffith's "great Zeiss projector" flashes five different shows a year across a 75-foot dome. Excursions into interplanetary space might range from a search for extraterrestrial life to a quest into the causes of earthquakes, moonquakes, and starquakes. The shows last about an hour, but showtimes vary; call for information.

The Hall of Science, with many fascinating exhibits on galaxies, meteorites, and other cosmic subjects, includes a solar telescope that's trained on the sun; a Foucault Pendulum, which demonstrates the earth's rotation; six-foot earth and moon globes; meteorites; a Cosmic Ray Cloud chamber; and more.

Admission: Hall of Science, free; planetarium, $4 adults, $3 seniors (65 and older), $2 children 5–12; those under 5 are admitted to the children's programs only Sat–Sun at 1:30pm.

Open: Summer, daily 12:30–10pm; the rest of the year, Tues–Fri 2–10pm, Sat–Sun 12:30–10pm. **Directions:** From U.S. 101, take the Vermont Avenue exit north to its end in Griffith Park.

The Hollywood Wax Museum, 6767 Hollywood Blvd., Hollywood. ☎ **213/462-8860.**

Cast in the Madame Tussaud mold, the Hollywood Wax Museum features dozens of life-like figures of famous movie stars and events. The "museum" is not great, but it is entertaining. A "Chamber of Horrors" exhibit includes the coffin used in *The Raven*, as well as a scene from Vincent Price's old hit, *The House of Wax*. The "Movie Awards Theatre" exhibit is a short film highlighting Academy Award presentations from the last four decades.

Admission: $9 adults, $7.50 seniors, $7 children 6–12, free for kids under 6.

Open: Sun–Thurs 10am–midnight, Fri–Sat 10am–2am.

The Los Angeles Zoo, 5333 Zoo Dr., in Griffith Park, Los Angeles. ☎ **213/666-4090.**

Only in southern California would a zoo advertise its "cast of thousands." Here the stars include more than 2,000 mammals, birds, and reptiles walking, flying, and slithering over 113 acres. Habitats are divided by continent: North America, South America, Africa, Eurasia, and Australia. Active in wildlife conservation, the zoo is also home to an intense research facility, and it houses about 50 endangered species. There's also an aviary with a walk-in flight cage, a reptile house, an aquatic section, and Adventure Island.

Adventure Island, the revamped children's zoo, is an unusual addition that looks nothing like a zoo. Four distinct habitats blend into one another in a space of about 2½ acres, where mountains, meadows, deserts, and shorelines are re-created. Especially popular with children, Adventure Island houses an aviary, tidepool, and animal nursery.

Admission: $8.25 adults, $5.25 seniors, $3.25 children 2–12, free for kids under 2.

Open: Daily 10am–5pm. **Directions:** From I-5, exit at Zoo Drive and follow the signs to the zoo in Griffith Park.

Los Angeles Children's Museum, 310 N. Main St., Los Angeles. ☎ **213/687-8800.**

This delightful museum is a place where children learn by doing. Everyday experiences are demystified in an interactive, playlike atmosphere; children are encouraged to imagine, invent, create, pretend, and work together. In the Art Studio they can make everything from Mylar rockets to finger puppets. There's a City Street where kids can sit on a policeman's motorcycle and play at driving a bus or at being a firefighter. Young visitors can become "stars" in the recording or TV studio, learn about health in a doctor's and dentist's office and about X-rays in an emergency room, see their shadows frozen on walls in the Shadow Box, and play with giant foam-filled Velcro-edged building blocks in Sticky City.

In addition to the regular exhibits, there are all kinds of special activities and workshops, from cultural celebrations to T-shirt decorating and making musical instruments. There is a 99-seat theater for children where live performances or special productions are scheduled every weekend. Call the museum for upcoming events.

Admission: $5; free for kids under 2.

Open: Summer, Mon–Fri 11:30am–5pm, Sat–Sun 10am–5pm; the rest of the year, Wed–Thurs 2–4pm, Sat–Sun 10am–5pm. **Directions:** The museum is located just north of downtown. From U.S. 101 south, exit onto Los Angeles Street, turn right and the museum will be on the right-hand side. Northbound 101 traffic should exit at Alameda, proceed straight past Alameda, and turn left on Los Angeles Street.

Wells Fargo History Museum, 333 S. Grand Ave., downtown. ☎ **213/253-7166.**

Owned by the bank of the same name, this museum highlights the history of Wells Fargo and its impact on California and the American West. It's a delightful place. Among the exhibits are an authentic 19th-century Concord stagecoach; a coach under construction (where you can sit inside and listen to taped excerpts from the diary of a young Englishman who made the arduous trip to California by coach); tools used by coachmakers; the Challenge nugget, a two-pound gold lump of 76% purity found in 1975; mining entrepreneur and Wells Fargo agent Sam Dorsey's gold collection; and a fascinating selection of mining and Wells Fargo artifacts.

Admission: Free.

Open: Mon–Fri 9am–5pm. **Closed:** Bank holidays.

---

4   Organized Tours

BUS TOURS   Offering the largest selection of organized city tours, **Gray Line Tours,** 6541 Hollywood Blvd., Hollywood (☎ **213/856-5900**), runs several daily itineraries throughout the city. Via air-conditioned motorcoaches, visitors are taken to Sunset Strip, the movie studios, the Farmer's Market, Hollywood, and homes of the stars. Other tours visit Disneyland, Knott's Berry Farm, and Catalina Island. Phone for itineraries, times, and prices.

Marlene Gordon's Next Stage tour company takes early risers (or late-nighters) on the **Insomniacs' Tour of L.A. (☎ 213/939-2699)**, a 3am tour of the predawn city that usually includes trips to the *Los Angeles Times,* to flower, produce, and fish markets, and to the top of a skyscraper to view the sunrise. The fact-filled tour lasts about 6½ hours and includes breakfast. Tours depart twice monthly and cost $47 per person. Phone for information and reservations.

HELICOPTER TOURS   Touring the city by helicopter is a truly memorable experience. Day or night tours given by **Heli L.A., Inc.,** 3200 Airport Ave., Santa Monica (☎ 213/553-4354), buzz the studios of Paramount, Universal, Burbank, and Disney; hover over the mega-estates of the stars in Beverly Hills and Bel Air; then wind up over Hollywood's Mann's Chinese Theatre, Sunset Strip, and the HOLLYWOOD sign. The cost of a helicopter "flightseeing" tour, including lunch or dinner, ranges from $99 to $149, depending on the itinerary.

5   Sports & Recreation

Spectator Sports

BASEBALL   Los Angeles has two major-league baseball teams. The **Los Angeles Dodgers** (☎ 213/224-1500) play at Dodger Stadium, 1000 Elysian Park, near Sunset Boulevard. The **California Angels** (☎ 714/634-2000) call Anaheim Stadium home at 2000 S. State College Blvd., near Katella Avenue in Anaheim. The regular season runs from about mid-April to early October.

BASKETBALL   The two Los Angeles National Basketball Association franchises are the **L.A. Lakers** (☎ 310/419-3100), who play in Great Western Forum, 3900 W. Manchester Blvd., at Prairie Avenue, in Inglewood; and the **L.A. Clippers** (☎ 213/748-8000), who hold court in the L.A. Sports Arena, 3939 S. Figueroa Ave. The regular season runs from November to April.

FOOTBALL   The two Los Angeles–area NFL football teams are the **L.A. Raiders** (☎ 310/322-5901), playing at the L.A. Memorial Coliseum, 3911 S. Figueroa Ave.; and the **L.A. Rams** (☎ 714/937-6767), playing in 70,000-seat Anaheim Stadium, 2000 S. State College Blvd., near Katella Avenue in Anaheim. The regular season runs from August to December.

HORSE RACING   Frequented by Hollywood personalities, the scenic **Hollywood Park Racetrack,** 1050 S. Prairie Ave., in Inglewood (☎ 310/419-1500), with its lakes and flowers, features thoroughbred racing from early April through July as well as in November and December. The $1-million Hollywood Gold Cup is also run here. Well-placed monitors project views of the back stretch as well as stop-action replays of photo finishes. Races are usually held Wednesday through Sunday. Post times are 1pm in summer (at 7:30 pm on Friday) and 12:30pm in the fall. General admission is $6, $9 to the clubhouse.

One of the most beautiful tracks in the country, **Santa Anita Racetrack,** 285 W. Huntington Dr., in Arcadia (**☎ 818/ 574-7223**), offers thoroughbred racing from October through mid-November and December through late April. On weekdays during the racing season the public is invited to watch morning workouts from 7:30 to 9:30am. Post time is 12:30 or 1pm. Admission is $3.

ICE HOCKEY   The NHL **L.A. Kings** (**☎ 310/673-6003**) play at the Great Western Forum at 3900 W. Manchester Blvd., at Prairie Avenue, in Inglewood. The regular season runs from September to April.

Recreation

BEACHES   Los Angeles County's 72-mile coastline sports over 40 miles of beaches, most of which are operated by the Department of Beaches & Harbors, 13837 Fiji Way, Marina del Rey (**☎ 310/305-9503**). County-run beaches usually charge for parking ($2 to $4), and lifeguards are on duty year-round during daylight hours. Pets, alcohol, and bonfires are prohibited. Following is a selective list of some of the county's best beaches, listed from north to south:

North County Line   Fittingly located between Los Angeles and Ventura Counties, this pristine beach, with no facilities or official parking, is a popular surf spot.

Leo Carillo   Located near the point at which Mullholland Drive meets the Pacific Coast Highway, this beach is part of an adjacent inland state park, where camping is permitted. It's good for tide-pool watching at low tide and for cookouts—fire pits are allowed.

El Pescador, La Piedra & El Matador   These relatively rugged and isolated beaches front a four-mile stretch of the Pacific Coast Highway between Broad Beach and Decker Canyon Roads. It's very picturesque and perfect for picnicking.

Zuma & Point Dume   Jam-packed on warm weekends, these two adjacent Malibu beaches offer wide stretches of sand, and plenty of parking and services. These are L.A.'s most popular beaches. Families go to Zuma while younger people head toward Point Dume.

Paradise Cove   This private beach in the 28000 block of the Pacific Coast Highway charges $15 to park and $5 per person if you walk in. Changing rooms and showers are included in the price. The

IMPRESSIONS

"What is striking about Los Angeles . . . is how well it works. The famous freeways work, the supermarkets work . . . the beaches work."
—Joan Didion, American novelist

beach is often full by noon on weekends.

Surfrider   One of the city's most popular surfing spots, this beach is located between the Malibu Pier and the lagoon. Few "locals only" wave wars are ever fought here.

Santa Monica   The beaches on either side of the Santa Monica Pier are popular for their sands and easy accessibility. There are big parking lots, eateries, and lots of well-maintained bathrooms. The paved beach path runs along here, allowing you to walk, bike, or skate to Venice and points south.

Venice   The paved boardwalk gets most of the attention here, but the broad beach is alluring all on its own. Expensive parking lots abound on the small streets surrounding Windward Court.

Marina del Rey   Located right in the middle of del Rey, this family-oriented beach is popular with families, offering shaded picnic tables and rather calm waters. Parking is just off Admiralty Way, at Via Marina.

Manhattan Beach   Locals sun south of the pier and park in lots on 26th Street or at the end of 45th Street. This is an excellent swimming beach.

Hermosa Beach   One of my favorite beaches in L.A., Hermosa is popular with the younger volleyball crowd, and offers wide sands and a paved boardwalk called The Strand. There's plenty of street parking.

Redondo Beach   Beach access here is south of King Harbor, at 200 Portofino Way. The Redondo Municipal Pier, located just north, is a family-oriented fun-filled "mall by the sea."

Torrance Beach   South of Redondo, the beaches are bigger and less crowded, but offer excellent facilities, including food and toilets. Local snorkelers swear by Malaga Cove, located just south of the beach.

Long Beach   Running the entire length of the city along Ocean Boulevard, this calm, breakwater-protected beach is long indeed, and close to the good restaurants and shops that line Second Avenue. This is one of the city's best sunning beaches.

Seal Beach   Both charming and quiet, smallish Seal Beach is a terrific place to steal away from the city. A "Tot-Lot" contains diversionary play structures for the kiddies. Parking is available both at the pier and on 1st Street.

BICYCLING   The best place to bike (or skate) is on the 22-mile-long auto-free beach path that runs along Santa Monica and Venice beaches. You can rent 10-speeds from **Sea Mist Rental,** 1619 Ocean Front, Santa Monica (☎ **310/395-7076**).

BILLIARDS   Perhaps the oldest pool hall in the city, the 24-hour **Hollywood Billiards,** 5504 Hollywood Blvd., at the corner of Western Avenue, in Hollywood (☎ **213/465-0115**), has dozens of pool tables as well as backgammon, darts, and video games. The charge to play pool is $8 per hour.

GOLF   Most L.A. area golf courses are privately owned. Some of the prettiest ones, however, allow public access—for a fee.

At the **Industry Hills Golf Club,** 1 Industry Hills Pkwy., City of Industry (☎ 818/810-4455), two 18-hole courses planned by William Bell encompass eight lakes, 160 bunkers, and long fairways. An adjacent driving range is lighted for night use. Greens fees are $45 on Monday through Friday and $60 on Saturday and Sunday.

Located about an hour from Los Angeles, the **Monarch Bell Golf Course,** 33080 Niguel Rd., Laguna Niguel (☎ 714/240-8247), designed by Robert Trent Jones, Jr., is one of the most attractive in the area since it fronts the Pacific Ocean. Beautiful elevated greens and rolling fairways make this a popular course year-round. Greens fees are $75 Monday through Thursday and $100 Friday through Sunday, including the required cart rental.

HORSEBACK RIDING   The **Griffith Park Livery Stables,** 480 Riverside Dr., Burbank (☎ 818/840-8401), rents horses by the hour for western or English riding. There's a 200-pound weight limit, and children under 12 are not permitted to ride. Horse rental costs $13 per hour, and there's a two-hour rental maximum. The stables are open Monday through Friday from 8am to 7pm and Saturday and Sunday from 8am to 4pm.

JET-SKIING   At **Nature Tours,** 1759 9th St., Suite 201, Santa Monica (☎ 310/452-7508), intensive two-hour lessons teach all levels of riders how to get the most out of jet skis and wave runners. Beginners ski around Marina del Rey, while advanced jetters cruise up to Malibu. Midweek half-day trips to Pyramid Lake include jet-ski rental, lessons, and a lunch barbecue. The cost is about $150 per lesson or tour.

ROLLER SKATING   Who would even think of going to an indoor rink when the Venice Beach Walk is so near? Roller skating was practically invented here, and Los Angeles is certainly the world's center for in-line skating.

Renting both in-line Rollerblades and conventional skates, **Spokes 'n Stuff,** 4175 Admiralty Way, Marina del Rey (☎ 310/306-3332), is just one of many places to find wheels near the Venice Beach Walk. Kneepads and wrist guards come with every rental. Wheels cost $5 per hour.

SEA KAYAKING   Two area outfits offer possibilities for sea kayaking. **Island Packers,** 1867 Spinnaker Dr., Ventura (☎ 805/642-1393), arranges small groups who make the two-hour sail to Santa Cruz Island, then tour neighboring Anacapa Island by kayak. One-day excursions last about 10 hours, include continental breakfast and a picnic lunch, and cost $135. Longer adventures can also be arranged, including camping or lodging, for $215 to $445.

Southwind Sports Resource, 17855 Sky Park Circle, Suite A, in Irvine (☎ **714/261-0200**), combines sea kayaking with bird-watching on their tours of Upper Newport Bay. Trips cost $35 to $65. One-day Catalina Island kayaking trips are also arranged and cost about $110.

TENNIS   Public courts, administered by the City of Los Angeles Department of Recreation and Parks (☎ **213/485-5555**) are located all around the city. The Griffith Park tennis courts are some of the best in the country. All 12 outdoor courts are lighted for night play. Call the Department of Recreation and Parks for reservations.

WINDSURFING   Surfing meets sailing in this fun sport that is much more difficult than it looks. The **Long Beach Windsurfing Center,** 3850 E. Ocean Ave., Long Beach (☎ **310/433-1014**), rents boards by the hour. It's open daily from 10am to 6pm.

At **Malibu Ocean Sports,** on the beach in front of Marina del Rey's Cheesecake Factory (☎ **310/821-8960**), windsurfer rentals—including board, wet suit, and flotation devices—are $15 per hour. Lessons are offered on weekends; the three-hour course costs $45 and is guaranteed to teach you the basics.

8

Walking & Driving Around Los Angeles

ALL TOO OFTEN, IT SEEMS AS THOUGH THE SIGHTS IN LOS ANGELES ARE SO far apart from one another that you can spend an entire afternoon just traveling on the freeway. There are, however, some special areas in the city where many sights are grouped together, enabling you to leave your car and spend the day strolling. The following itineraries are ideal for such a venture.

Walking Tour 1
Downtown & Chinatown

Start   Los Angeles City Hall, 200 N. Spring St.
Finish   Chinatown.
Time   About two hours, not including food stops.
Best Times   During the day, and on weekends, when everything's open.
Worst Times   After dark.

This ever-expanding sprawl of a city did have an origination point: the downtown area, in and around the Old Plaza and Olvera Street. Due to concern about earthquakes, city-planning authorities originally prohibited the construction of buildings over 13 stories tall. This limitation led many companies to locate in outlying areas, leaving the original downtown to fall into relative disrepair. In 1957 new construction technology permitted tall buildings to be constructed safely; therefore, the downtown experienced a renaissance that included tall office buildings, fancy hotels, good restaurants, and a newfound tourist industry.

Los Angeles's downtown area is surprisingly accessible to walkers. In one easy stroll you can familiarize yourself with both the city's historic past and its bustling present. You can see a piece of city government, and immerse yourself in the cultural heritage that has become an integral part of Los Angeles life.

To reach the starting point of our downtown tour from U.S. 101 south, exit onto Los Angeles Street, turn right on 1st Street, and right again on Spring Street. Northbound 101 traffic should exit onto Alameda Street, turn right on 1st Street, and right again on Spring Street. Park near the:

1. **Los Angeles City Hall,** the only structure to surpass the 150-foot height limit prior to 1957. This much-photographed, beautifully angular building is famous for the roles it has played in "Superman," "Dragnet," and many other television shows. If you make an advance reservation, you can ascend to the observation tower on the top floor, where you'll be treated to great views of the city (depending on smog conditions). Tours are offered Monday through Friday at 10 and 11am only.

   Turn right onto Temple Street, and walk one block to the:

2. **Los Angeles Children's Museum,** 310 N. Main St.
   (☎ 213/687-8800). This delightful museum is great for
   travelers with kids in tow. It's a place where children learn
   by doing; they are encouraged to imagine, invent, create,
   pretend, and work together. See "Cool for Kids" in Chapter 7 for complete information.

   Continue north on Main Street, under U.S. 101, and
   enter the park. You are now in:

3. **El Pueblo de Los Angeles,** a historical complex of 27
   Mexican-style buildings ranging in date from 1818 to
   1927. Covering more than 44 acres, the site centers around
   bustling Olvera Street, an outdoor, cobblestoned marketplace that has the feel of old Mexico. During a stroll along
   Olvera Street, you'll encounter a variety of shops and
   eateries, and be entertained by street performers and ethnic
   bands.

   Olvera Street cuts straight through the park, and is the
   area's central attraction. The city's oldest structures line the
   street, which cuts through the:

4. **Old Plaza,** a pretty Spanish Mediterranean–style park that
   makes up the center of El Pueblo. The directory and map,
   located near the gazebo in the middle of the park, is a good
   place to get your bearings.

   The first place to stop in the Pueblo is:

5. **Sepulveda House,** 22 N. Main St. Built by Eliosa
   Martinez de Sepulveda in 1887, this was one of California's
   first hotels. Today the structure houses the Visitor
   Information Center (☎ 213/628-1274). It's open
   Monday through Friday from 10am to 3pm and on
   Saturday from 10am to 4:30pm. You can pick up a
   brochure and map here that includes a good self-guided
   tour. The best time to arrive at El Pueblo is between 10am
   and 1pm Tuesday through Saturday, when free guided
   tours of the historical site are offered. To take part, meet in
   front of Firehouse No. 1, next to the Information Center.

   Continue walking along Olvera Street where you will
   pass the:

6. **Old Plaza Church.** Completed in 1818, it's Los Angeles's
   oldest extant Catholic church. Today, its primarily
   Hispanic congregation is one of the largest in the United
   States.

   Farther along you'll see:

7. **Firehouse No. 1,** dating from 1884; it has not been a
   working firehouse for more than 100 years. The firehouse
   has served as a hotel, a store, and a saloon. Today it's a
   museum, where you can see some of the finest examples
   of American turn-of-the-century fire-extinguishing
   equipment.

Directly behind the firehouse is the:

8. **Victorian Garnier Building.** This is one of the few remaining structures from L.A.'s first Chinatown; most of the buildings were leveled in 1939 to make way for Union Station, the western terminus for the Union Pacific, Santa Fe, and Southern Pacific rail lines.

Back on Olvera, you'll encounter the:

9. **Avila Adobe,** 10 Olvera St. Recognized as the oldest private house in Los Angeles, this was the home of Don Francisco Avila, the Pueblo's first mayor. The simple interior is outfitted with period furnishings from the mid-19th century.

A few doors down you'll see the:

10. **Pelanconi House,** 17 W. Olvera St. Built in 1855, it's one of the city's oldest brick buildings.

Exit on the park's east side and visit:

11. **Union Station,** 800 N. Alameda St., one of America's last grand-scale train stations. Commuters and long-distance travelers continue to tread over the marble floors, beneath 50-foot cathedral ceilings. Built in 1939, the Spanish mission–style structure is still awesome and well worth a look.

Turn north, up Alameda Street, and step inside the:

12. **Main Post Office–Terminal Annex,** 900 Alameda St., to see the large Works Progress Administration (WPA) murals. These Depression-era paintings, commissioned by the Roosevelt administration in the 1930s, depict human communications throughout history.

Refueling Stop

Take a break from your tour and get a bite to eat at **Philippe the Original,** 1001 N. Alameda St. (☎ **213/628-3781**). It was founded in 1908 and claims to have created the French dip sandwich. While there's nothing stylish about the place, it's full of good old-fashioned value; great beef, pork, ham, turkey, or lamb French-dip sandwiches are served on the lightest, crunchiest French rolls.

Turn left onto Macy Street, walk three blocks, and turn right onto North Broadway. You are now looking toward:

13. **Chinatown.** Although this "little Asia" lacks the exotic excitement of its larger counterparts in San Francisco, New York, and Vancouver, L.A.'s Chinese section is a great place to shop, eat, and explore. Walk along:

14. **North Broadway,** Chinatown's primary thoroughfare. You are now heading into the heart of Chinatown, which flourishes primarily between College and Bernard Streets.

Walking Tour—Downtown & Chinatown

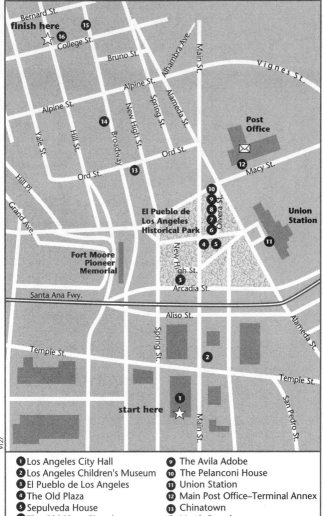

1. Los Angeles City Hall
2. Los Angeles Children's Museum
3. El Pueblo de Los Angeles
4. The Old Plaza
5. Sepulveda House
6. The Old Plaza Church
7. Firehouse No. 1
8. Victorian Garnier Building
9. The Avila Adobe
10. The Pelanconi House
11. Union Station
12. Main Post Office–Terminal Annex
13. Chinatown
14. North Broadway
15. Chinatown Arches and Pagoda Buildings
16. Bamboo Plaza

Refueling Stop

Turn left onto Sun Mun Way and visit **Grand Star,** 943 Sun Mun Way (☎ 213/626-2285)—an excellent Chinese eatery. Owned and operated by the Quon family since 1967, Grand Star offers an unusual selection of top-notch

Chinese dishes, including spicy chicken wings, Mongolian beef with mushrooms, and lobster Cantonese.

Just north of College Street, at Gin Ling Way, you'll see the:

15. **Chinatown Arches and Pagoda Buildings.** As the word "Chinatown," inscribed on the arches will attest, this is the area's formal entrance.

One block ahead, between North Hill and Bernard Streets is:

16. **Bamboo Plaza,** a small shopping mall filled with both Oriental and Occidental shops and restaurants. In the plaza, and on nearby streets you'll find many shops and restaurants that may interest you.

Final Refueling Stop

One of the last holdouts from the days when this used to be primarily an Italian neighborhood, **Little Joe's,** 900 N. Broadway (☎ 213/489-4900), opened as a grocery in 1927. Joe's has grown steadily over the years and now encompasses several bars and six dining rooms. You can get a full pasta dinner, eggplant parmigiana, sausage and peppers, and a variety of other excellent foods. Without doubt, Little Joe's is the best Occidental restaurant in Chinatown.

Walking Tour 2
Hollywood

Start   Mann's Chinese Theatre, 6925 Hollywood Blvd.
Finish   Capitol Records Building, 1756 N. Vine St.
Time   About 1¹/₂ hours, not including shopping.
Best Times   During the day, when shops are open and you can see the buildings.
Worst Times   At night, when the area becomes even more seedy.

The legend of Hollywood as the movie capital of the world still persists, though many of its former studios have moved to less-expensive and more spacious venues. The famous city where actresses once posed with leashed leopards is certainly on everyone's must-see list. And although the glamour is badly tarnished, and Hollywood Boulevard has been accurately labeled the "Times Square of the West" (the city itself seems to be unaware of its decline), there is still plenty to see. Shopping is good here, too. Between the T-shirt shops and frenzied pizza places, you'll find some excellent poster shops, film and souvenir stores, and assorted Hollywood memorabilia outfits. See Chapter 9 for specifics.

From U.S. 101, exit onto Highland Boulevard and turn right onto Hollywood Boulevard. Park as soon as you can and go three blocks ahead on your right to:

1. **Mann's Chinese Theatre,** one of Hollywood's greatest landmarks. Opened in 1927 as Grauman's Chinese Theatre, the imposing structure was the brainchild of impresario Sid Grauman. Opulent both inside and out, the theater combines authentic and simulated Chinese decor. Original Chinese heaven doves top the facade, and two of the theater's columns actually come from a Ming Dynasty temple. Despite its architectural flamboyance, the theater is most famous for its entry court, in which movie stars' signatures and hand- and footprints are set in concrete. Sid Grauman, who was credited with originating the idea of the spectacular movie "première," was an excellent promoter. To this day countless visitors continue to match their hands and feet with those of Elizabeth Taylor, Paul Newman, Ginger Rogers, Humphrey Bogart, Frank Sinatra, and others. It's not always hands and feet, though; Betty Grable made an impression with her shapely leg; Gene Autry with the hoofprints of Champion, his horse; and Jimmy Durante and Bob Hope used (what else?) their noses. The theater's name was changed to Mann's in the 1970s.

   Walk east on Hollywood Boulevard. You are now trodding along the famous:

2. **Walk of Fame,** where nearly 2,000 stars are honored in the world's most famous sidewalk. Bronze medallions set into the center of each star pay tribute to famous television, film, radio, and record personalities, from nickelodeon days to the present. Some of the most popular include Marilyn Monroe, 6744 Hollywood Blvd.; James Dean, 1719 Vine St.; John Lennon, 1750 Vine St.; and Elvis Presley, 6777 Hollywood Blvd. Each month another celebrity is awarded a star on the Walk of Fame, and the public is invited to attend. For dates and times, contact the Hollywood Chamber of Commerce, 6255 Sunset Blvd., Suite 911, Hollywood, CA 90028 (☎ **213/469-8311**).

   As soon as you cross Highland Avenue you'll encounter the:

3. **Hollywood Wax Museum,** 6767 Hollywood Blvd. (☎ **213/462-8860**). Cast in the Madame Tussaud mold, this museum features dozens of life-like figures of famous movie stars and events. One of the most talked-about images pairs John F. Kennedy with Marilyn Monroe— dress blowing up and all. A tableau of Leonardo da Vinci's *Last Supper,* as well as scenes depicting Queen Victoria and Martin Luther King, Jr., are on display. A "Chamber of Horrors" exhibit includes the coffin used in *The Raven,* as well as a scene from Vincent Price's old hit, *The House of Wax.* It's open Sunday through Thursday from 10am to midnight and on Friday and Saturday from 10am to 2am.

Farther along the block you'll see the:

4. Hollywood Egyptian Theater, 6712 Hollywood Blvd., one of the area's top theaters and the site of Hollywood's first première in 1923: *Robin Hood,* starring Douglas Fairbanks.

Refueling Stop

Established in 1919, **Musso & Frank Grill,** 6667 Hollywood Blvd. (☎ **213/467-7788**), may be Hollywood's oldest extant eatery. The restaurant was a hangout for Faulkner and Hemingway during their screenwriting days. The setting is richly traditional, and the extensive continental menu features everything from salads to seafood.

Just down the block is the beautiful art deco building that's the headquarters of:

5. Frederick's of Hollywood, 6608 Hollywood Blvd. (☎ **213/466-8506**). Easily one of the most famous panty shops in the world, Frederick's is also one of Hollywood's top tourist attractions. Everything from overtly tight spandex suits to skimpy bikini bras to sophisticated nighties are sold here. A small "museum" displays the undergarments of the stars. Even if you're not buying, stop in and pick up one of their informative catalogs.

Continue straight ahead, along several more tourist-oriented schlock-shop blocks, and you'll be standing at the intersection of:

6. Hollywood and Vine. Once considered the heart of Hollywood, this corner is legendary, not for its uneventful architecture, but for the big-name stars who crossed the intersection. When Greta Garbo walked down the street in trousers and was widely photographed, the pictures shocked women all over America. After recovering from their horror and the headlines—"Garbo Wears Pants"—women rushed to their astonished dressmakers (or, in some cases, their husbands' tailors) to have the slacks duplicated.

Just east of Vine Street is:

7. Pantages Theatre, 6233 Hollywood Blvd. (☎ **213/468-1700**). Built in 1930, this luxurious theater was opened at the very height of Hollywood's heyday. For 10 years this art deco beauty was the setting for the presentation of the Academy Awards, including the first televised Oscar ceremony. Since that time, the theater has been through several incarnations, and is now one of the city's leading legitimate theaters. Recent productions have included *Me and My Girl* and *Starlight Express,* as well as the Julie Andrews/Carol Burnett TV special, the Grammy

Walking Tour—Hollywood

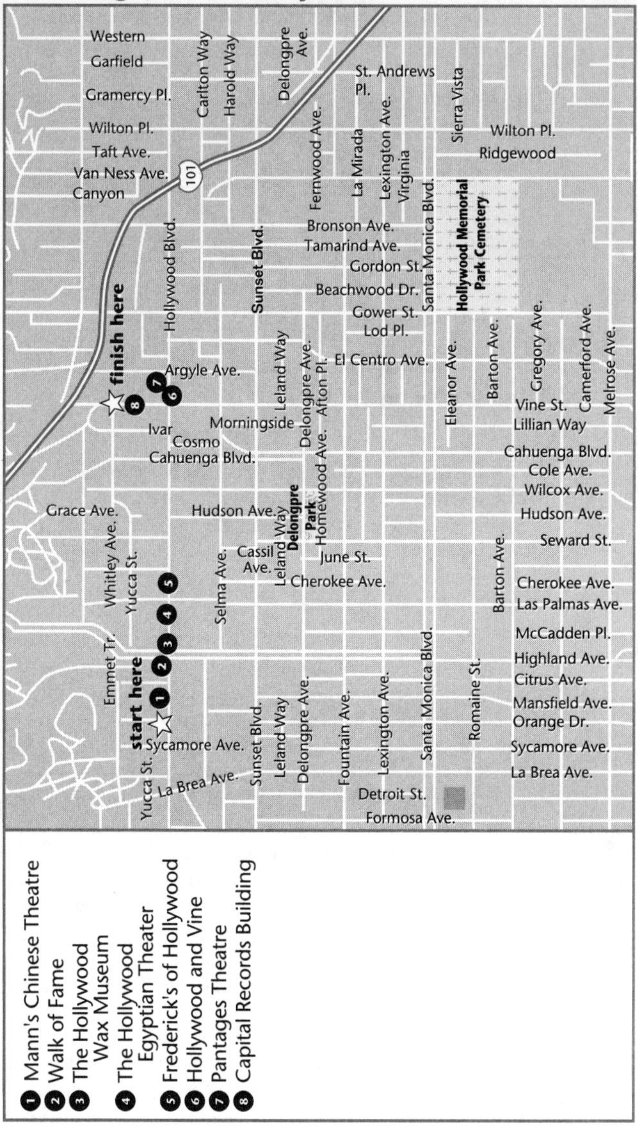

Map labels (streets and locations):

Western, Garfield, Gramercy Pl., Wilton Pl., Taft Ave., Van Ness Ave., Canyon, Carlton Way, Harold Way, Delongpre Ave., St. Andrews Pl., Fernwood Ave., La Mirada, Lexington Ave., Virginia, Sierra Vista, Wilton Pl., Ridgewood

101

Hollywood Blvd., Sunset Blvd., Bronson Ave., Tamarind Ave., Gordon St., Beachwood Dr., Gower St., Lod Pl., El Centro Ave., Santa Monica Blvd., Hollywood Memorial Park Cemetery

finish here, Argyle Ave., Leland Way, Delongpre Ave., Afton Pl., Eleanor Ave., Barton Ave., Gregory Ave., Camerford Ave., Melrose Ave.

Ivar, Cosmo, Cahuenga Blvd., Morningside, Homewood Ave., Vine St., Lillian Way, Cahuenga Blvd., Cole Ave., Wilcox Ave., Hudson Ave., Seward St.

Grace Ave., Whitley Ave., Yucca St., Hudson Ave., Delongpre Park, Leland Way

Selma Ave., Cassil Ave., June St., Cherokee Ave., Cherokee Ave., Las Palmas Ave.

Emmet Tr., start here, Fountain Ave., Lexington Ave., Santa Monica Blvd., Barton Ave., Romaine St., McCadden Pl., Highland Ave., Citrus Ave., Mansfield Ave., Orange Dr., Sycamore Ave., La Brea Ave.

Yucca St., Sycamore Ave., La Brea Ave., Sunset Blvd., Leland Way, Delongpre Ave., Fountain Ave., Detroit St., Formosa Ave.

9128

1. Mann's Chinese Theatre
2. Walk of Fame
3. The Hollywood Wax Museum
4. The Hollywood Egyptian Theater
5. Frederick's of Hollywood
6. Hollywood and Vine
7. Pantages Theatre
8. Capital Records Building

"Living Legend" Awards, and the televised Country/
Western Music Awards.

Turn north on Vine Street and walk half a block to the:

8. **Capitol Records Building,** 1756 N. Vine St. The tower's
design, shaped like a stack of records and topped by a
stylus, is said to have been conceived by songwriter Johnny

Mercer and singer Nat "King" Cole. The round structure has been a Hollywood landmark since its opening in 1956.

Final Refueling Stop

It's really just a dive, but the devotees of **Roscoe's House of Chicken 'n' Waffles,** 1514 N. Gower St. (☎ 213/466-7453), have included Jane Fonda, Stevie Wonder, the Eagles, and many other stars. It seems like a joke, but only chicken and waffle dishes are served. To reach the restaurant, continue east on Hollywood Boulevard for about five blocks and turn right onto Gower Street. Roscoe's will be about five blocks ahead.

Walking & Driving Tour 3
Beverly Hills

Start   Regent Beverly Wilshire Hotel, 9500 Wilshire Blvd.
Finish   Beverly Hills Hotel & Bungalows, 9641 Sunset Blvd.
Time   About two hours, if you don't stop to follow stars.
Best Times   Monday through Saturday from 10am to 6pm, when the stores are open.
Worst Times   At night, when shops are closed and you can't see the view.

The aura of Beverly Hills is unique. Beneath its veneer of wealth, it's a curious blend of small-town neighborliness and cosmopolitan worldliness. Many of southern California's most prestigious hotels, restaurants, high-fashion boutiques, and department stores are located here. Don't miss that remarkable assemblage of European-based super-upscale stores along Rodeo Drive. A shopping guide is available from the Beverly Hills Chamber of Commerce and Visitors Bureau (see "Tourist Information" in Chapter 4). Beverly Hills is also the adopted hometown of such motion-picture and TV stars as George Burns, Warren Beatty, James Stewart, Kirk Douglas, Linda Evans, Harrison Ford, Jacqueline Bisset, Frank Sinatra, and Jack Nicholson. Its first mayor was the homespun philosopher/comedian/star Will Rogers. Douglas Fairbanks and Mary Pickford led the migration of stars to the area when they built their famous home, Pickfair, atop the ridge at 1143 Summit Dr.; today a drive through the glens, canyons, and hillsides of Beverly Hills will reveal one palatial home after another. Nowhere else in the world are you likely to find such an assemblage of luxury homes—each one a virtual candidate for inclusion in *House Beautiful.* Beware of hawkers selling "Maps of Stars' Homes," though. Many of the occupants pinpointed have moved elsewhere (and some even to Forest Lawn—a cemetery).

From Santa Monica Boulevard, exit onto Wilshire Boulevard and continue east for eight blocks until you reach the:

Walking & Driving Tour—Beverly Hills

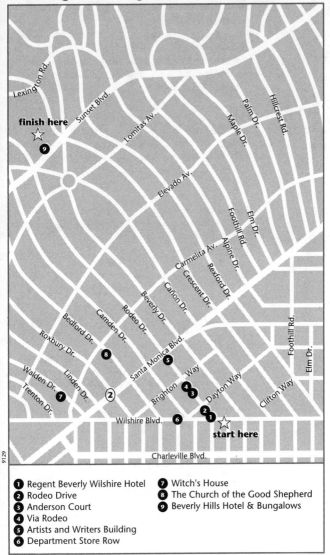

finish here

9

start here

1. Regent Beverly Wilshire Hotel
2. Rodeo Drive
3. Anderson Court
4. Via Rodeo
5. Artists and Writers Building
6. Department Store Row
7. Witch's House
8. The Church of the Good Shepherd
9. Beverly Hills Hotel & Bungalows

1. **Regent Beverly Wilshire Hotel,** 9500 Wilshire Blvd., one
   of the priciest hotels in the city. This grand Beverly Hills
   hotel has long attracted international royalty, media
   celebrities, stage personalities, presidents, and the usual
   smattering of rich and famous. Parts of the movie *Pretty
   Woman*, with Richard Gere and Julia Roberts, were filmed

here. The spacious lobby contains French Empire furnishings, French and Italian marble flooring, restored
bronze and crystal chandeliers, hand-wrought sconces, and
two paintings by Verhoven. If you're lucky enough to stay
here, you'll be greeted by a guest-relations officer who will
personally escort you to your room, and have the service of
a steward, stationed on every floor.

Refueling Stop

Inside the Regent Beverly Wilshire, the **Lobby Lounge** is
an elegant European-style salon serving light meals and
cocktails. It's best at teatime, daily from 3 to 5pm, and is
surely a place to see and be seen.

The hotel is located at the bottom of:

2. **Rodeo Drive,** Beverly Hills's most famous street, known
   for its haute couture boutiques, expensive jewelry shops,
   top restaurants, and major department stores. World-class
   names on the drive include Tiffany & Co. (210 N. Rodeo
   Dr.), Van Cleef & Arpels (300 N. Rodeo Dr.), Chanel
   (301 N. Rodeo Dr.), Bally of Switzerland (340 N. Rodeo
   Dr.), Gucci (347 N. Rodeo Dr.), and Cartier (370 N.
   Rodeo Dr.).
   Stroll along Rodeo Drive and poke into interesting
   shops while rubbing shoulders with T-shirted tourists and
   snazzy jet-setters.
   Halfway between Dayton Way and Brighton Way is:

3. **Anderson Court,** 332 N. Rodeo Dr., a Frank Lloyd
   Wright–designed art deco–style shopping complex. Built in
   1953, it's located right next to:

4. **Via Rodeo,** a pretty cobblestone shopping street that feels
   like a little bit of Europe in the sun.
   On the next block, at the corner of Little Santa Monica
   Boulevard, you'll find the:

5. **Artists and Writers Building,** 9507 Little Santa Monica
   Blvd., a squat Spanish-style structure that once housed the
   offices of Will Rogers, Billy Wilder, Ray Bradbury, and
   Jack Nicholson, among others.

Refueling Stop

The best-known Jewish deli around is **Nate & Al's,** 414 N.
Beverly Dr. (☎ 310/274-0101). Try a pastrami on
fresh-baked rye, chopped liver, a kosher frank, or hot
corned beef. It's not fancy; food can be ordered to go.

After a long stroll on Rodeo Drive, get into your car
and drive west from the Regent Beverly Wilshire Hotel
along Wilshire Boulevard. Here you'll pass:

6. **Department Store Row,** a fancy cluster of blocks that
   house some of the country's top names, including Neiman

Marcus (9700 Wilshire Blvd.), I. Magnin (9634 Wilshire Blvd.), and Saks Fifth Avenue (9600 Wilshire Blvd.).

After about eight blocks, cross Santa Monica Boulevard and turn right onto Carmelita Avenue. On your left, at the corner of Walden Drive, you'll see the:

7. **Witch's House,** 516 N. Walden Dr., a gingerbread-style cottage famous for its storybook look. Since it's a private residence, you won't be able to go inside.

After three blocks, turn right on Bedford Drive, and take a look at the:

8. **Church of the Good Shepherd,** 505 N. Bedford Dr., the oldest house of worship in Beverly Hills. Built in 1924, the church has seen its share of the rich and famous. In 1950, Elizabeth Taylor and her first husband, Nicholas Hilton, were married here. Good Shepherd funerals included those of Alfred Hitchcock, Gary Cooper, and Jimmy Durante.

Return to Carmelita Avenue and turn left onto Beverly Drive. Turn left onto Sunset Boulevard, and on your left you'll see the Will Rogers Park (not to be confused with the Will Rogers State Historic Park in Pacific Palisades). Just opposite the park is the:

9. **Beverly Hills Hotel & Bungalows,** 9641 Sunset Blvd. (☎ **310/276-2251**), one of the most famous stomping grounds of millionaires and maharajahs, jet-setters and movie stars. There are hundreds of anecdotes about this famous place, most of which took place in the hotel's Polo Lounge, one of the world's most glamorous bars. For years Howard Hughes maintained a complex of bungalows, suites, and rooms here, using some of the facilities for an elaborate electronic-communications security system, and a separate room for his personal food-taster. Years ago Katharine Hepburn did a flawless dive into the pool—fully clad in her tennis outfit, shoes and all. Dean Martin and Frank Sinatra once got into a big fistfight with other Polo Lounge habitués. And in 1969 John Lennon and Yoko Ono checked into the most secluded bungalow under assumed names, then stationed so many armed guards around their little hideaway that discovery was inevitable. So it goes. The stories are endless and concern everyone from Charlie Chaplin to Madame Chiang Kai-shek.

What attracts them all? For one thing, one another. And of course, you can't beat the service—not just the catering to such eccentricities as a preference for bear steak, but little things like being greeted by your name every time you pick up the phone. It doesn't hurt that the Beverly Hills Hotel is a beauty; its green-and-pink stucco buildings are set on 12 carefully landscaped and lushly planted acres. There are winding paths lined with giant palm trees throughout, and the privacy of each veranda is protected by flowering and leafy foliage.

9

Savvy Shopping in Los Angeles

Oₙₑ ᴏꜰ ᴛʜᴇ ʙɪɢɢᴇꜱᴛ ᴄɪᴛɪᴇꜱ ɪɴ ᴛʜᴇ Uɴɪᴛᴇᴅ Sᴛᴀᴛᴇꜱ, Lᴏꜱ Aɴɢᴇʟᴇꜱ ɪꜱ ᴡᴇʟʟ known for its plethora of top shops, trendy boutiques, and gaggle of shopping malls. Although the city is quite spread out, the shopping areas are distinct; each is oriented to a particular market.

1 The Shopping Scene

Shopping Areas

Hollywood Boulevard   One of Los Angeles's most famous streets is, for the most part, a sleazy strip. But between the T-shirt shops and frenzied pizza places you'll find some excellent poster shops, film and souvenir stores, and assorted Hollywood memorabilia outfits.

Melrose Avenue   The area between Fairfax and La Brea Avenues is one of the best shopping streets in the country for young, trendy fashions. Hundreds of stores sell the latest in clothes, gifts, jewelry, and accessories.

Venice Beach Walk   Stalls and shops sell youth-oriented street fashions to beachgoers and tourists who come here to see and be seen. Even if you're not shopping, come here for the carnival of people showing off their unique talents and fashions.

Rodeo Drive   Beverly Hills's most famous street is known for its haute couture boutiques, expensive jewelry shops, top restaurants, and major department stores.

Third Street Promenade   Packed with chain stores and boutiques, as well as dozens of restaurants and a large movie theater, Santa Monica's 3rd Street, between Broadway and Wilshire Boulevard, has recently become one of the most popular shopping areas in the city. The Promenade is closed to vehicular traffic.

Downtown Garment District   The blocks close to 9th Street are known for the many shops that sell clothes, luggage, and assorted goods at significantly discounted prices.

Hours, Taxes & Shipping

Store hours are generally Monday through Saturday from 10am to 6pm and on Sunday from noon to 5pm. Most department stores and malls stay open later—usually Monday through Friday from 10am to 9pm, on Saturday from 10am to 6pm, and on Sunday from 11am to 6pm.

The sales tax in Los Angeles is 8.25%; it is added on at the register for all goods and services purchased.

Most of the city's shops can wrap your purchase and ship it anywhere in the world via United Parcel Service (UPS). If they can't, you can send it yourself, either through UPS, at 10690 Santa Monica Blvd. (☎ toll free **800/222-8333**), and other locations; or through the U.S. Mail (see "Fast Facts: Los Angeles" in Chapter 4).

2   Shopping A to Z

Antiques

The Antique Guild, 8800 Venice Blvd., near Culver City.
☎ **310/838-3131.**

Billing itself as "the world's largest antique outlet," the Guild is a veritable warehouse of history, with more than two acres of antiques under one roof. Their buyers are constantly checking out, and purchasing, the entire contents of European castles, beer halls, estates, and mansions. New shipments arrive weekly, so the merchandise is constantly changing. Look for everything from old armoires to chandeliers to stained glass, crystal, china, clocks, washstands, tables, and mirrors, and much more. Open Monday through Saturday from 10am to 6pm and Sunday from 11am to 6pm.

Arte de Mexico, 5356 Riverton Ave., North Hollywood.
☎ **818/769-5090.**

Seven warehouses full of carved furniture and wrought iron reportedly once sold only to moviemakers and restaurants. One of the most fascinating places in North Hollywood. Open Monday through Saturday from 8:30am to 5:30pm and Sunday from 10am to 5:30pm.

Art Galleries

Brendan Walter Gallery, 1001 Colorado Ave., Santa Monica.
☎ **310/395-1155.**

This contemporary arts gallery specializes in furniture, vessels, paintings, and glass and metal sculpture. Open Tuesday through Saturday from 10:30am to 5:30pm.

The Broadway Gallery Complex, 2022–2114 Broadway, Santa Monica. ☎ **310/829-3300.**

Ten galleries showing a wide range of work are housed in this single Santa Monica complex. Featured contemporary artists include Barbara Ackerman, Ruth Bloom, Mark Moore, and Sylvia White. Open on Wednesday, Friday, and Saturday from 11am to 6pm; Thursday from 11am to 8pm; and Sunday from noon–4pm.

Christopher Grimes Gallery, 916 Colorado Ave., Santa Monica.
☎ **310/587-3373.**

The emphasis here is contemporary American art in a wide range of media, including painting, sculpture, photography, and video. Open Tuesday through Saturday from 10am to 5:30pm.

Gallery of Functional Art, 2429 Main St., Santa Monica.
☎ **213/450-2827.**

Tables, chairs, beds, sofas, lighting, screens, dressers, and bathroom fixtures are some of the functional art and art furniture pieces that are sold here. Smaller items such as jewelry, watches, flatware, candlesticks, ceramics, and glass are also shown. Open Tuesday through Friday from 11am to 7pm and Saturday and Sunday from 11am to 6pm.

Books

There are hundreds of bookshops in Los Angeles; below are some of the more specialized shops.

Audubon Society Bookstore, 7377 Santa Monica Blvd., West Hollywood. ☎ **213/876-0202.**

A terrific selection of books on nature, adventure travel, and ecology is augmented by birdwatching paraphernalia and regular L.A. nature walks. Phone for information. Open Tuesday through Saturday from 10am to 3pm.

Heritage Book Shop, Inc., 8340 Melrose Ave., Los Angeles. ☎ **310/659-3674.**

Specializing in rare books and manuscripts, Heritage is packed with first editions and special illustrations. Open Tuesday through Friday from 9:30am to 5:30pm and Saturday from 10am to 4:30pm.

C. G. Jung Bookstore & Library, 10349 W. Pico Blvd., Los Angeles. ☎ **310/556-1196.**

Specializes in analytical psychology, folklore, fairy tales, alchemy, dream studies, myths, symbolism, and other related books. Tapes and videocassettes are also sold. Open Monday through Saturday from noon to 5pm.

Mandala Bookstore, 616 Santa Monica Blvd., Santa Monica. ☎ **310/393-1953.**

In addition to crystals and Southeast Asian music, this store stocks many hard-to-find books on Buddhism and religion from Nepal, Tibet, and India. Open Monday through Saturday from 10am to 10pm and Sunday from 11am to 8pm.

Midnight Special Bookstore, 1318 3rd St., Santa Monica. ☎ **310/393-2923.**

Located on Santa Monica's Third Street Promenade, this medium-size general bookshop is known for its good small-press selection and regular poetry readings. Open Monday through Wednesday from 10:30am to 10pm, Thursday through Saturday from 10:30am to 11:30pm, and Sunday from 11am to 10pm.

Mysterious Bookshop, 8763 Beverly Blvd., West Hollywood. ☎ **310/659-2959.**

Over 20,000 used, rare, and out-of-print titles make this the area's best mystery, espionage, detective, and thriller bookshop. There are regular author appearances and other special events. Open Monday through Saturday from 10am to 6pm and Sunday from noon to 5pm.

Department Stores

Most L.A. department stores have their flagship store or a large branch either downtown or in Beverly Hills. Many stores also serve as anchors in L.A.'s largest shopping malls; here are some of the best known.

The Broadway, Beverly Center, 8500 Beverly Blvd., West Hollywood. ☎ **310/854-7200.**

Based in southern California, The Broadway sells moderately priced designer clothes, sportswear, and casual clothing; it also has excellent cosmetics and cookware departments. Open Monday through Friday from 10am to 9:30pm, Saturday from 10am to 8pm, and Sunday from 11am to 7pm.

Bullock's, 10861 Weyburn Ave., near Westwood Blvd., Westwood. ☎ **310/208-4211.**

Upper-middle-class fashion-conscious customers shop here for imported designer fashions and good-quality private label merchandise in all departments. Open Monday through Friday from 10am to 9pm, Saturday from 10am to 7pm, and Sunday from noon to 6pm.

Neiman Marcus, 9700 Wilshire Blvd., Beverly Hills. ☎ **310/550-5900.**

Distinctive men's and women's fashions, world-famous furs, precious jewels, unique gifts, and legendary personal service have made this one of California's most successful department stores. Open Monday through Saturday from 10am to 6pm.

Nordstrom, Westside Pavilion, 10830 W. Pico Blvd., West Los Angeles. ☎ **310/470-6155.**

Emphasis on customer service has won this Seattle-based store a loyal following. Equally devoted to women's and men's fashions, the store has one of the best shoe selections in the city, and thousands of suits in stock. The Nordstrom Cafe, on the top floor, is a great place for an inexpensive lunch or light snack. Open Monday through Friday from 10am to 9:30pm, Saturday from 10am to 8pm, and Sunday from 11am to 6pm.

Robinson's–May, 920 7th St., downtown. ☎ **213/683-1144.**

Home accessories, furniture, and household supplies are featured here, along with sportswear for women and large selections of costume jewelry. Open Monday through Saturday from 10am to 6pm and Sunday from noon to 5pm.

Saks Fifth Avenue, 9600 Wilshire Blvd., Beverly Hills. ☎ **310/275-4211.**

Los Angeles's oldest branch of this famous New York–based shop is as opulent as any. Saks sells fashions and gifts for men, women, and children, and has a well-respected restaurant on the top floor. Open Monday, Thursday, and Friday from 10am to 8:30pm; Tuesday, Wednesday, and Saturday from 10am to 6pm; and Sunday from noon to 5pm.

Eyewear

L.A. Eyeworks, 7407 Melrose Ave., Los Angeles. ☎ **213/653-8255.**

This hometown design shop has become world famous for its innovative Hollywood styles. This is its first storefront location. Open Monday through Friday from 10am to 7pm, Saturday from 10am to 6pm, and Sunday from noon to 5pm.

Strictly Sunglasses, in the Westside Pavilion, 10800 Pico Blvd.
☎ **310/446-1668.**
More than 600 designer and house brands—including Revo,
Serengeti, Ray-Ban, Vuarnet, Oakley, and Armani—range from $20
to $400 a pair. It's often the first to get new models, making this
shop tops on trendsetters' hit lists. Open Monday through Friday
from 10am to 9pm, Saturday from 10am to 7pm, and Sunday from
11am to 6pm.

Fashions

Battle Dress, 7318C Melrose Ave., Los Angeles. ☎ **213/935-7350.**
This store sells some of the most unusual leather frocks, tops, pants,
and boots; many of the handmade styles here were inspired by
authentic Cherokee designs. Bring your checkbook. Open Tuesday
through Saturday from noon to 7:30pm and Sunday from noon to
6pm.

Betsey Johnson Boutique, 7311 Melrose Ave., Hollywood.
☎ **213/931-4490.**
The New York–based designer came to L.A. with this trendy, cutesy
women's shop known for colorful prints and faddy fabrics. Open
Monday through Saturday from 11am to 7pm and Sunday from
noon to 6pm.

Bijan, 420 N. Rodeo Dr., Beverly Hills. ☎ **310/273-6544.**
This top-quality menswear shop features exquisitely tailored clothing
and accessories along with Bijan's fragrance collections. Open
Monday through Saturday from 10am to 6pm.

Boy London, 7519 Melrose Ave., Los Angeles. ☎ **213/655-0302.**
Once on the cutting edge of London's King's Road, Boy has toned
down a bit, now selling shirts and other clothes emblazoned with its
own logo. It's still cool, though. Open Monday through Friday from
11am to 8pm, Saturday from 11am to 9pm, and Sunday from noon
to 8pm.

Brooks Brothers, 604 S. Figueroa St., downtown. ☎ **213/629-4200.**
Brooks Brothers introduced the button-down collar, and
single-handedly changed the standard of the well-dressed
businessman. The multilevel shop also sells traditional casual wear,
including sportswear, sweaters, and shirts. Open Monday through
Saturday from 9:30am to 6pm.

Chanel, 400 N. Rodeo Dr., Beverly Hills. ☎ **310/278-5500.**
The entire elegant Chanel women's line is under one roof and
includes clothing, accessories, scents, cosmetics, and jewelry. Open
Monday through Saturday from 10am to 6pm and Sunday from
noon to 5pm.

Giorgio Beverly Hills, 327 N. Rodeo Dr., Beverly Hills.
☎ **310/274-0200.**
Giorgio's signature yellow-and-white-striped awnings mark the home
of the designer's apparel, gift, and fragrance collections. Open

Monday through Friday from 10am to 7pm, Saturday from 10am to 6pm, and Sunday from noon to 5pm.

Gucci, 347 N. Rodeo Dr., Beverly Hills. ☎ **310/278-3451.**

An elegant selection of apparel for men and women is offered by one of the best-known and most prestigious names in international fashion. In addition to shoes, leather goods, and scarves beautiful enough for framing, the shop offers pricey accessories like a $7,000 handmade crocodile bag. Open Monday through Saturday from 10am to 6pm.

Hermès, 343 N. Rodeo Dr., Beverly Hills. ☎ **310/278-6440.**

This Beverly Hills branch of Paris's 155-year-old House of Hermès is known for its superlative handmade leather goods, hand-screened silk ties and scarves, perfumes, and other gift items. Open Monday through Saturday from 10am to 6pm.

Hobie Sports, 1409 3rd St., Santa Monica. ☎ **310/393-9995.**

In addition to swimwear, Hobie Sports specializes in colorful surfer dude–style shorts and T-shirts. Open Monday through Thursday from 10am to 10pm, Friday and Saturday from 10am to 11pm, and Sunday from 11am to 8pm.

L.A. Equestrian Center's Dominion Saddlery, 480 Riverside Dr., Burbank. ☎ **818/842-4300.**

One of L.A.'s largest assortments of riding wear includes stretch Equijeans, leather lace-up boots, Lycra breeches, fox-hunting jackets, and riding crops. Nothing's cheap. Open Monday and Saturday from 9am to 5pm, Tuesday from 9am to 8pm, Wednesday through Friday from 9am to 6pm, and Sunday from 9am to 4pm.

Louis Vuitton, 307 N. Rodeo Dr., Beverly Hills. ☎ **310/859-0457.**

Carrying the largest selection of Vuitton items in the United States, this tony shop stocks luggage, business cards, handbags, wallets, and a seemingly endless variety of accessories. Open Monday through Saturday from 10am to 6pm and Sunday from noon to 5pm.

Na Na, 1228 3rd St., Santa Monica. ☎ **310/394-9690.**

This is what punk looks like in the 1990s: clunky shoes, knit hats, narrow-striped shirts, and baggy streetwear. Open Monday through Thursday and Sunday from 10am to 9pm and Friday and Saturday from 10am to 11pm.

Polo/Ralph Lauren, 444 N. Rodeo Dr., Beverly Hills. ☎ **310/281-7200.**

This Beverly Hills shop is the exclusive Los Angeles outlet for Polo/Ralph Lauren's apparel collections for men, women, and children. Selected home furnishings are also sold. Open Monday through Wednesday and Friday and Saturday from 10am to 6pm, Thursday from 10am to 8pm, and Sunday from noon to 5pm.

Ragtime, 7952 3rd St., Santa Monica. ☎ **213/655-1742.**

Vintage rags are given contemporary lives when dressed up by Ragtime owner Helen Levy. Old designer labels are sewn on T-shirts, and assorted fasteners decorate vintage vests. Open Monday through Saturday from 11am to 6pm.

Red Balls on Fire, 7708 Melrose Ave., Los Angeles.
☎ **213/655-3409.**

Outrageous stagewear and head-turning streetwear here include funky jackets and the wildest stretch pants. Try them on in dressing rooms made of purple velvet–lined upright coffins. Open Monday through Saturday from 11am to 8pm and Sunday from 11am to 7pm.

Retail Slut, 7264 Melrose Ave., Los Angeles. ☎ **213/934-1339.**

New clothing and accessories for hip guys and girls are offered at this famous rock 'n' roll shop. Unique designs are sold to a select crowd. Open daily from noon to 7pm.

Studio Wardrobe Services, 3953 Laurel Grove, Studio City.
☎ **818/508-7762.**

Although you may recognize some of the clothes here from Dennis Quaid, Kathleen Turner, or Sylvester Stallone movies, most were worn by extras before being turned over for public sale. Prices range from $25 to $1,500, and new shipments arrive weekly. Open Monday through Saturday from 10am to 6pm and Sunday from noon to 5pm.

Texas Soul, 7515 Melrose Ave., West Hollywood. ☎ **213/658-5571.**

Men's and women's boots, jackets, jewelry, and belts are peddled at this western leather shop. Plenty of working and walking boots are sold along with traditional cowboy styles. Open Monday through Saturday from 11am to 8pm and Sunday from noon to 7pm.

SECONDHAND

Aardvark's Odd Ark, 1516 Pacific Ave., Venice. ☎ **310/392-2996.**

This large storefront near the Venice Beach Walk is crammed with racks of antique and used clothes from the 1960s, '70s, and '80s. They stock everything from suits and dresses to neckties, hats, handbags, and jewelry. Aardvark's anticipates some of the hottest new street fashions. Open daily from 10:30am to 6:30pm.

Place and Company, 8820 S. Sepulveda Blvd., Westchester.
☎ **310/645-1539.**

Secondhand, mint-condition men's and women's designer duds include labels from Chanel, Armani, Blass, Ferré, Klein, Versace, and Valentino. $1,000-plus dresses and suits are sometimes priced as low as $350. Sportcoats, shirts, and designer sweaters are also sold. Open Monday through Saturday from 10am to 6pm.

Wasteland, 7428 Melrose Ave., Los Angeles. ☎ **213/653-3028.**

An enormous art-filled exterior fronts a large collection of vintage and contemporary clothes for men and women. Leathers, natural fibers, and dark colors predominate. Grandma's furniture is also for sale. Open Monday through Saturday from 11:30am to 8:30pm and Sunday from noon to 8pm.

Film Memorabilia

Book City Collectables, 6631 Hollywood Blvd., Hollywood.
☎ **213/466-0120.**

More than 70,000 color prints of stars past and present are available, together with a good selection of autographs, including those of Lucille Ball ($175), Anthony Hopkins ($35), and Grace Kelly ($750). Open Monday through Saturday from 10am to 9pm and Sunday from 10am to 6pm.

Cinema Collectors, 1507 Wilcox Ave., at Sunset Blvd., Hollywood.
☎ **213/461-6516.**

Original movie posters, magazines, stills, head shots, and associated memorabilia are cross-referenced on computer. Helpful, uniformed employees can answer your questions and help you find your way around. Open daily from 10am to 5:30pm.

Hollywood Book and Poster Company, 6349 Hollywood Blvd.,
Hollywood. ☎ **213/465-8764.**

Owner Eric Caidin's excellent collection of movie posters is particularly strong in horror and exploitation flicks (about $20). Photocopies of about 5,000 movie and television scripts are also sold for $10 to $15 each. Open Monday through Saturday from 11am to 7pm and Sunday from noon to 5pm.

The Last Moving Picture Show, 6307 Hollywood Blvd.,
Hollywood. ☎ **213/467-0838.**

Movie-related merchandise of all kinds is sold here, including stills from the 1950s and authentic production notes from a variety of films. Open Monday through Saturday from 10am to 6pm.

Star Wares on Main, 2817 Main St., Santa Monica.
☎ **310/399-0224.**

Owner Marcia Tysseling was governess to Joan Rivers's daughter. Now she's the proprietor of a unique resale boutique carrying celebrity clothes, props, movies, wardrobes, and autographed items. Threads include a gown from Madonna's *Blonde Ambition* tour, a tie clasp from Rudolph Valentino, a handbag and cigarette case from Bette Davis, original artwork from *Star Trek,* a miniature batwing from *Batman Returns,* and various other items. Ten percent of every sale of celebrity-owned merchandise goes to charity. Open daily from noon to 6pm.

Gifts

Alamo Flags, 1349A 3rd St., Santa Monica. ☎ **310/917-3344.**

In addition to country flags of all sizes, Alamo sells banners, ensigns, pennants, and standards emblazoned with all manner of signs and sayings. Nautical and special-occasion flags are some of its best-sellers. Open Monday through Friday from 9am to 9pm and Saturday and Sunday from 9am to 10pm.

Beverly Hills Baseball Card Shop, 1137 S. Robertson Blvd., Beverly Hills. ☎ **310/278-4263.**

From Ty Cobbs to Lou Gehrigs to Tom Seaversers and Mookie Wilsons, this warehouse of baseball history houses literally millions of cards, including rare rookie editions and other hard-to-find collectibles. Open Tuesday through Friday from 11am to 6pm and Saturday from 11am to 5pm.

Brian Jeffrey's Design Greenhouse, 7556 Melrose Ave., Los Angeles. ☎ **213/651-2539.**

One of the most beautiful stores on Melrose, Brian Jeffrey's is a professional decorator's dream store for interior plants, baskets and containers, candleholders, and wind chimes. A festival for the senses, the shop is cluttered with terrific visuals, smells great, and resounds with ethereal music. Open daily from 11am to 6pm.

Card de A, 1570 E. Rosecrans Ave., Manhattan Beach. ☎ **310/536-0040.**

No Hallmark Greetings here, just highly stylized designer greetings and occasion cards from small presses and individual producers. Handmade artcards are their specialty. Open Monday through Friday from 10am to 7pm, Saturday from 10am to 6pm, and Sunday from 11am to 5pm.

Condomania, 7306 Melrose Ave., Los Angeles. ☎ **213/933-7865.**

A vast selection of condoms, lubricants, and kits creatively encourage safe sex. Glow-in-the-dark condoms, anyone? Open Sunday through Thursday from 11am to 8pm and Friday and Saturday from 11:30am to 10:30pm.

Details, 8625 Melrose Ave., Los Angeles. ☎ **310/659-1550.**

Appropriately located near West Hollywood's Pacific Design Center, in a monstrous building known to locals as the "Blue Whale," Details offers huge selections of hard-to-find home-decorating items including imaginative cabinet and door pulls, hooks, knobs, towel bars, and kitchen and bath accessories from Europe and Japan. Open Monday through Friday from 10am to 7pm, Saturday from 10am to 6pm, and Sunday from 11am to 5pm.

Mayhem, 1411 3rd St., Santa Monica. ☎ **310/451-7600.**

Genuine autographed guitars and other entertainment-biz memorabilia from U2, Nirvana, Springsteen, Bon Jovi, Pearl Jam, and other rockers are sold to collectors who include the owners of the Hard Rock Cafes. It's as much a museum as a store. Open Sunday through Thursday from 11am to midnight and Friday and Saturday from 11am to 2am.

Off the Wall, 7325 Melrose Ave., Los Angeles. ☎ **213/930-1185.**

Oversize antiques include kitschy statues, deco furnishings, carved wall reliefs, Wurlitzer jukeboxes, giant restaurant and gas station signs, pinball machines, and lots and lots of neon. Open Monday through Saturday from 11am to 6pm.

Warner Brothers Studio Store, in the Beverly Center, 8500 Beverly Blvd., Los Angeles. ☎ **310/289-7954.**

Warner Brothers has taken merchandising to the next level with its string of shops selling T-shirts, watches, baseball caps, and other items emblazoned with images from its film, TV, and cartoon catalogs. Open Monday through Friday from 10am to 10pm, Saturday from 10am to 8pm, and Sunday from 11am to 6pm.

Z Gallerie, 2728 Main St., Santa Monica. ☎ **310/392-5879.**

This California-based chain offers a good selection of poster art, together with unusual gifts, matte black furnishings, and kitchenware. Open Monday through Saturday from 10am to 6:30pm and Sunday from 10am to 6pm.

Haircare

Melrose Beauty Center, 7419 Melrose Ave., Los Angeles. ☎ **213/651-4709.**

Aveda, Paul Mitchell, JoiCo, and other top haircare products that are labeled for "exclusive sale in salons" are sold here in economical larger sizes. Open daily from 11am to 8pm.

Jewelry

Cartier, 370 N. Rodeo Dr., Beverly Hills. ☎ **310/275-4272.**

One of the most respected names in jewelry and luxury goods has its Los Angeles shop near Brighton Way. The boutique's setting is as elegant as the beautifully designed jewelry, watches, crystal, and accessories on sale. Open Monday through Friday from 10am to 5:30pm and Saturday from 10am to 5pm.

King's Cross, 13045 Ventura Blvd., Studio City. ☎ **818/905-3382.**

King's Cross specializes in crosses, crucifixes, and rosaries made of gold, ivory, and pearl. Most are vintage models dating from the 1820s to the 1930s, with an emphasis on Victoriana. Prices range from $200 to $2,000. Open Monday through Saturday from 10am to 5pm and Sunday from noon to 5pm.

Maya, 7452 Melrose Ave., Los Angeles. ☎ **213/655-2708.**

This rather plain-looking store offers a huge variety of silver and turquoise rings and earrings from South America, Nepal, Bali, and central Asia. The shop's walls are cluttered with wooden Asian and South American ceremonial and ornamental masks. Open Monday through Saturday from 11am to 9pm and Sunday from 11am to 7pm.

Tiffany & Co., 210 N. Rodeo Dr., Beverly Hills. ☎ **310/273-8880.**

Amid sporadic pieces of crystal and china, shoppers will find an exquisite collection of fine jewelry known the world over for classic styles. Top designers include Elsa Peretti and Paloma Picasso. Open daily from 10am to 6pm.

Van Cleef & Arpels, 300 N. Rodeo Dr., Beverly Hills. ☎ **310/276-1161.**

There are three rooms of breathtakingly beautiful gems and jewelry at this shop. Pieces are expensive, but of the highest quality. Some creative fashions highlight an otherwise conservative collection. Open Monday through Friday from 10am to 5pm.

Leather

Leathers & Treasures, 7511 Melrose Ave., Hollywood.
☎ 213/655-7541.

Amid rows of cowboy boots, skin lovers will find an abundance of bomber jackets, pants, vests, accessories, and hats. It's a crowded little shop with a good, unusual selection of goods. Open Monday through Saturday from noon to 8pm and Sunday from 1 to 7pm.

North Beach Leather, 8500 W. Sunset Blvd., West Hollywood.
☎ 310/652-3224.

Primarily selling leather jackets and dresses, this San Francisco–based shop has up-to-the-minute fashions at high prices. Other leather items from casual to elegant are also available. Open Monday through Saturday from 10am to 7pm and Sunday from noon to 5pm.

Lingerie

Frederick's of Hollywood, 6606 Hollywood Blvd., Hollywood.
☎ 213/466-8506.

Behind the purple facade lies one of the most famous panty shops in the world. Everything from overtly tight spandex suits to skimpy bikini bras and sophisticated nighties are sold here. Even if you're not buying, stop in and pick up one of their famous catalogs. Open Monday through Thursday and Saturday from 10am to 6pm, Friday from 10am to 9pm, and Sunday from noon to 5pm.

Trashy Lingerie, 402 N. La Cienega Blvd., Hollywood.
☎ 310/652-4543.

Everything here is house-designed. They tailor-fit clothes ranging from tacky patent leather bondage wear to elegant bridal underthings. There's a $2 "membership" fee to enter the store, but even for browsers, it's worth it. Open Monday through Saturday from 10am to 7pm.

Malls & Shopping Centers

Like any city, Los Angeles's malls are filled with carbon-copy chain stores, but they also have a good selection of local specialty shops, and a taste of the avant garde.

ARCO Plaza, 505 S. Flower St., downtown.

ARCO Plaza offers convenient shopping and elegant dining in a unique subterranean mall. Located beneath the Atlantic Richfield/Bank of America's Twin Towers is a labyrinth of corridors leading to shops and restaurants. Stores and boutiques can be found on the second and third underground levels. The Greater Los Angeles Visitors and Convention Bureau is within ARCO Plaza's precincts.

And, of course, there are the shops—selling everything from needle-point patterns to insurance. Most shops are open Monday through Friday from 8am to 6pm and Saturday from 10am to 7pm.

Beverly Center, 8500 Beverly Blvd., at La Cienega Blvd., Los Angeles.
☎ **310/854-0070.**

One of the city's best-known malls also has one of the best locations. The 1991 film *Scenes from a Mall,* starring Woody Allen and Bette Midler, was shot here. About 170 shops occupy the huge, eight-story building, constructed with interesting exterior glass-covered escalators. Both the Broadway and Bullock's department stores are anchored here, sandwiching dozens of shops, restaurants, and movie theaters. The Warner Brothers Studio Store and Aveda Esthetique are two of the mall's newest additions. Despite the mall's immense size, it's actually quite a pleasant place to shop. Most shops are open Monday through Friday from 10am to 9pm, Saturday from 10am to 8pm, and Sunday from 11am to 6pm. Most restaurants stay open later.

The Broadway Plaza, 7th and Flower Sts., downtown.
☎ **213/624-2891.**

Anchored by the Hyatt Regency Los Angeles Hotel and the Broadway department store, the one-square-block Plaza encompasses more than 25 shops and 17 restaurants. Most of the shops are middle-class-oriented clothing chain stores.

Farmer's Market, 6333 W. 3rd St., near Fairfax, Los Angeles.
☎ **213/933-9211.**

Since 1934, this city market has been attracting locals and tourists with more than 100 restaurants, shops, and grocers. It has since become one of the area's top tourist draws, and is one of L.A.'s best places to spot celebrities. More than 110 retailers sell souvenirs, pet supplies, clothes, books, art, and anything else you can imagine. The best part of the market is the food stands—at least 25 in all—which sell fast foods from almost every international cuisine. Open Monday through Saturday from 9am to 6:30pm and Sunday from 10am to 5pm.

Fisherman's Village, 13763 Fiji Way, Marina del Rey.
☎ **310/823-5411.**

Containing about 30 specialty shops built in the style of an Old English whaling village, Marina del Rey's waterfront village is one of the city's most pleasant strolling malls. International imports are available in shops that line cobblestoned walks. The stores and restaurants surround an authentic 60-foot lighthouse. Open Sunday through Thursday from 9am to 9pm and Friday and Saturday from 9am to 10pm.

Glendale Galleria, Central Ave., at Hawthorne Ave., Glendale.
☎ **818/240-9481.**

Located in the eastern San Fernando Valley, the Glendale Galleria is one of the largest malls in the nation, occupying two levels in two wings and housing about 250 retailers. Five department stores compete for business here, along with well-known name-brand shops like Benetton, Ann Taylor, and ACA Joe. Open Monday through Friday from 10am to 9pm, Saturday from 10am to 8pm, and Sunday from 11am to 7pm.

Ports o' Call Village, Berth 77, Samson Way, between 6th and 22nd Sts., San Pedro. ☎ **310/831-0287.**

This collection of shops sells crafts and clothing from around the world. More than 80 international specialty shops offer such goods as hand-blown glass, Philippine jewelry, and Japanese gun-powder tea; while several restaurants provide myriad cuisines. You can watch a steady stream of yachts, luxury liners, tankers, freighters, schooners, and sailboats cruise by as you browse along the village's winding cobblestone streets. To reach Ports o' Call, take the Harbor Freeway to the Harbor Boulevard off-ramp and turn right. Open daily from 10am to 9pm.

Santa Monica Place, Colorado Ave., at 2nd St., Santa Monica. ☎ **310/394-5451.**

About 100 shops occupy three bright stories anchored by Robinson's–May and the Broadway department stores. The usual mall shops are augmented by more unusual finds like Frederick's of Hollywood, which sells lingerie, and the KCET Public Television's Store of Knowledge, selling T-shirts, mugs, gifts, educational software, and documentary video tapes. EATZ, the mall's ground-floor food pavilion, sells a world's array of fast foods, including several health-oriented eateries (see Chapter 6 for more information). Open Monday through Saturday from 10am to 9pm and Sunday from 11am to 6pm.

Sherman Oaks Galleria, 15301 Ventura Blvd., at Sepulveda Blvd., Sherman Oaks. ☎ **818/783-7100.**

This famous western San Fernando Valley mall is the hangout for dedicated valley girls, popularized by the movie *Fast Times at Ridgemont High.* Trendy, mainstream clothes are in abundance, sold from about 60 storefronts. Open Monday through Friday from 10am to 9pm, Saturday from 10am to 6pm, and Sunday from 11am to 6pm.

Universal CityWalk, at Universal Studios, Universal Center Drive, Universal City. ☎ **213/251-4638.**

Los Angeles's newest shopping-and-entertainment promenade is an ultrastylized urban street that looks just slightly saner than Toontown. More than three dozen shops and specialty restaurants include the Museum of Neon Art, a Panasonic electronics pavilion, and Wolfgang Puck Cafe. Both visually amazing and one of the few places in L.A. where you can stroll without a car, CityWalk is definitely worth a look. From U.S. 101, take the Universal City exit and follow the signs to CityWalk. Open daily from 11am to 11pm, with some restaurants staying open later.

Music

Pyramid Music, 1340 3rd St., Santa Monica. ☎ **310/393-5877.**

Seemingly endless bins of used cassette tapes and compact discs line the walls of this long, narrow shop on Santa Monica's Third Street Promenade. LPs, posters, cards, buttons, and accessories are also sold. Open Monday through Thursday from 11am to 11pm, Friday and Saturday from 11am to 1am, and Sunday from noon to 11pm.

Tower Records, 8811 W. Sunset Blvd., Hollywood.
☎ **310/657-7300.**

Tower insists that it has L.A.'s largest selection of compact discs—over 125,000 titles. The shop's blues, jazz, and classical selections are definitely greater than the competition's. Open Sunday through Thursday from 9am to midnight and Friday and Saturday from 9am to 1am.

Virgin Megastore, 8000 Sunset Blvd., Hollywood.
☎ **213/650-8666.**

Some 100 CD "listening posts" and an in-store "radio station" make this megastore a music browser's paradise. They claim to stock 150,000 titles, including an extensive collection of hard-to-find artists. Open Sunday through Thursday from 9am to midnight and Friday and Saturday from 9am to 1am.

Sports Equipment

Golf Exchange, 830 S. Olive St., Los Angeles. ☎ **213/622-0403.**

L.A.'s golf megastore sprawls across 10 rooms filled with clubs and accessories. An entire room is devoted to golf shoes, another to bags, and another to used clubs. There's also an indoor driving range so you can try before you buy. Open Monday through Friday from 9am to 5:30pm and Saturday from 9am to 4:30pm.

Horizons West, 2011 Main St., Santa Monica. ☎ **310/392-1122.**

Brand-name surfboards, wet suits, leashes, magazines, waxes, lotions, and everything else you need to catch the perfect wave are found here. Stop in and say "hi" to Randy, and pick up a free tide table. Open Monday through Saturday from 11am to 7pm.

Rip City Sports, 2709 Santa Monica Blvd., Santa Monica.
☎ **310/828-0388.**

Jim McDowell's top-rated designer skateboards are some of the world's most wanted. Many are handcrafted with the highest-quality wheels and bearings. Open Monday through Saturday from 10:30am to 6pm and Sunday from noon to 4pm.

Toys

F.A.O. Schwarz, in the Beverly Center, 8500 Beverly Blvd., Los Angeles. ☎ **310/659-4547.**

One of the world's greatest toy stores for both children and adults is filled with every imaginable plaything—from hand-carved, custom-painted carousel rocking horses, dolls, and stuffed animals to gas-powered cars, train sets, and hobby supplies. The new Barbie collection includes hundreds of models—from a three-foot-tall fiber-optically lighted Barbie to a $200 doll dressed by designer Bob Mackie. Open Monday through Friday from 10am to 9pm and Saturday and Sunday from 10am to 7pm.

Travel Goods

California Map and Travel Center, 3211 Pico Blvd., Santa Monica. ☎ **310/829-6277.**

Like the name says, this center carries a good selection of domestic and international maps and travel accessories, including guides for hiking, biking, and touring. Globes and atlases are also sold. Open Monday through Friday from 8:30am to 6pm, Saturday from 9am to 5pm, and Sunday from noon to 5pm.

10

Evening Entertainment in Los Angeles

Once criticized as a cultural wasteland, Los Angeles has increasingly attracted serious arts houses worthy of its size. The city has more than 150 active theaters, large and small, offering plays, revues, and concerts. There are more than 100 rock and jazz clubs, plus a number of major concert halls that regularly feature top-name performers. Without a doubt, the entertainment business—film, television, records, theater—is still the most important industry in Los Angeles. Check the "Calendar" section of the Sunday *Los Angeles Times* for good, if not comprehensive, listings of the upcoming week's events. *L.A. Weekly,* a free alternative weekly tabloid available at sidewalk stands, shops, and restaurants, should also be consulted.

1 The Performing Arts

There are two major charge-by-phone ticket agencies in the city: **Ticketmaster** (☎ 213/480-3232) and **Ticketron** (☎ 213/642-4242). Both sell computer-generated tickets to concerts, sporting events, plays, and special events.

Theatre L.A. (☎ 213/688-ARTS) sells discounted performing arts tickets for same-day seats at such venues as the Mark Taper, Doolittle, Pantages, Pasadena Playhouse, and other under-100-seat houses. Tickets are usually about half price. Callers are either referred to theater box offices or can order by phone. Theatre L.A. is open Tuesday through Saturday from noon to 5pm.

Major Performing Arts Companies

Los Angeles's most prestigious performing arts companies all call the Music Center of Los Angeles County "home."

CLASSICAL MUSIC & OPERA

Los Angeles Philharmonic, Dorothy Chandler Pavilion, the Music Center, 135 N. Grand Ave., downtown. ☎ 213/850-2000.

The city's top symphony is the only really major "serious music" name in Los Angeles. Many symphony watchers believe the Philharmonic's music director, Esa-Pekka Salonen, will continue to concentrate on contemporary compositions in order to attract a younger concert audience. In addition to regular performances at the Music Center, it offers a popular summer season at the Hollywood Bowl. The season runs from October to May.

Admission: Tickets, $6–$50.

Los Angeles Master Chorale, the Music Center, 135 N. Grand Ave., downtown. ☎ 213/972-7211.

The 120-voice chorale sings a varied repertoire, including classical and lighter contemporary compositions, under the direction of its music director, Paul Salamunovich. World premières and guest choirs sometimes perform. The season runs from October to June.

Admission: Tickets, $7–$44.

Los Angeles Music Center Opera, the Music Center, 135 N. Grand Ave., downtown. ☎ **213/972-7211.**

Internationally renowned, the Los Angeles Opera stages classic operas with a variety of guest stars.

Admission: Tickets, $21–$115.

DANCE

Although the best dance companies in the world are not located here, most—including the American Ballet Theatre, the Joffrey Ballet, Martha Graham, and Paul Taylor—perform on an annual basis at one of the major concert halls listed below. Check the Sunday "Calendar" section of the *Los Angeles Times.*

Major Concert Halls & All-Purpose Auditoriums ———

Dorothy Chandler Pavilion, the Music Center, 135 N. Grand Ave., downtown. ☎ **213/972-7211.**

Home of the Los Angeles Philharmonic, Master Chorale, Music Center Opera, and the Joffrey Ballet, this 3,197-seat multipurpose theater hosts regular concerts, recitals, opera, and dance performances. The American première of the London hit musical *Me and My Girl* was presented here, as are regular televised ceremonies like the Academy Awards. Ticket prices vary, depending on the performance.

Greek Theatre, 2700 N. Vermont Ave., Griffith Park. ☎ **213/665-1927.**

The Greek Theatre is a place where the entertainment ranges from performances by the Dance Theatre of Harlem to rock artists like Elvis Costello and the B-52's. The theater was designed in the style of the classical outdoor theaters of ancient Greece. Dance groups and national theater societies also perform here. Tickets run $25 to $60, depending on the performance.

Hollywood Bowl, 2301 N. Highland Ave., at Odin St., Hollywood. ☎ **213/850-2000.**

According to legend, the Bowl was created in the early 1920s when a musician—hiking in the hills—was startled to discover its perfect natural acoustics. Launching into song, he heard his voice carried virtually to the ridges of the mountains. Music lovers banded together, financing tiers of seats to be dug, Greek fashion, out of the mountainside. Box seats were installed in the front, and since many were reserved for film stars, intermission time at the Bowl became an extra added attraction.

Now one of America's most famous outdoor amphitheaters, the Bowl is known for its outstanding natural acoustics. This is the summer home of the Los Angeles Philharmonic Orchestra, as well as the resident Hollywood Bowl Orchestra. Their seasons begin July 1 and end around mid-September.

Internationally known conductors and soloists often join the L.A. Philharmonic in classical programs on Tuesday and Thursday nights. Friday and Saturday concerts are often "pops" shows that feature orchestrated contemporary music.

The Major Concert/Performance Halls

Ahmanson Theatre, the Music Center, 135 N. Grand Ave., at 1st Street, downtown (☎ **213/972-7211**).

Dorothy Chandler Pavilion, the Music Center, 135 N. Grand Ave., downtown (☎ **213/972-7211**).

Greek Theatre, 2700 N. Vermont Ave., Griffith Park (☎ **213/665-1927**).

Hollywood Bowl, 2301 N. Highland Ave., at Odin Street, Hollywood (☎ **213/850-2000**).

James A. Doolittle Theatre, 1615 N. Vine St., Hollywood (☎ **213/972-7372**).

L.A. Sports Arena, 3939 S. Figueroa St., Los Angeles (☎ **213/748-6136**).

Mark Taper Forum, the Music Center, 135 N. Grand Ave., at 1st Street, downtown (☎ **213/972-7373**).

Pantages Theatre, 6233 Hollywood Blvd., Hollywood (☎ **213/468-1700**).

The Shrine Auditorium, 665 W. Jefferson Blvd., Los Angeles (☎ **213/748-5116**).

Shubert Theatre, 2020 Ave. of the Stars, ABC Entertainment Center, Century City (☎ toll free **800/233-3123**).

Universal Amphitheatre, 100 Universal City Plaza, Universal City (☎ **818/622-3931**).

Wilshire Theatre, 8440 Wilshire Blvd., Beverly Hills (☎ **213/653-4490**).

Something is happening almost every night during the summer. The season also includes a jazz series, a Virtuoso series, and a Sunday Sunset series. Several weekend concerts throughout the season feature fireworks, including the traditional July 4th Weekend Family Fireworks picnic concerts.

Picnicking at the Bowl is an established part of the classical concert ritual. You can order a picnic basket with a choice of hot and cold entrees, and a selection of wines and desserts from the Hollywood Bowl (call **213/851-3588** the day before), which you can pick up on Pepper Tree Lane on your way in and enjoy on the picnic grounds before the concert. If you're sitting in a box, you can have your picnic delivered to you there! It's cheaper, of course, to bring your own. For evening performances, be sure to bring a sweater or jacket—it gets chilly in those hills.

The box office is open in May and June, Monday through Saturday from 10am to 6pm; and July to September, Monday through Saturday from 10am to 9pm and on Sunday from noon to 6pm. The Bowl is closed from October to April.

Admission: Classical and Virtuoso concerts, $1 on the lawn, $22.50 for bench seats, $25–$88 for box seats; other events vary in price. Parking costs $7 to $20, subject to availability and advance reservations; it's free in off-site lots, but there's a $2-per-person charge for the parking shuttle.

The Music Center of Los Angeles County, 135 N. Grand Ave., downtown. ☎ 213/972-7211.

Los Angeles's largest and most prestigious performing arts facility encompasses three distinct theaters: the Dorothy Chandler Pavilion (see above), the Ahmanson Theatre, and the Mark Taper Forum (see "Theaters," below). Free tours are scheduled on a regular basis. Call **213/972-7483** for information and reservations. All theaters are handicapped-accessible. Ticket discounts are available for students and senior citizens for most performances in each theater.

The Shrine Auditorium, 665 W. Jefferson Blvd., Los Angeles. ☎ 213/748-5116.

Once the Al Malaikah Temple, the 1920s-era Shrine stands out for its unusual Middle Eastern decor. The auditorium's 6,300 seats offer good sightlines for both local and international acts.

Admission: Ticket prices vary, depending on the performance.

Universal Amphitheatre, 100 Universal City Plaza, Universal City. ☎ 818/622-3931.

This 6,251-seat enclosed theater is adjacent to the Visitors Entertainment Center at Universal Studios. It's well designed—no seat is more than 140 feet from the stage—and only top names perform here, usually for three to five days. Tickets are often sold out well before the concert dates, so check the box office as soon as possible.

Admission: Tickets, $25–$75.

Wilshire Theatre, 8440 Wilshire Blvd., Beverly Hills. ☎ 213/468-1716.

The Wilshire opened in 1980 with *The Oldest Living Graduate,* starring Henry Fonda. More recent productions have included blockbuster musicals like *A Chorus Line.* Rock and jazz concerts are held here, too. Call to see what's on.

Admission: Tickets, $25–$60.

Theaters

MAJOR PLAYHOUSES

Ahmanson Theatre, the Music Center, 135 N. Grand Ave., at 1st St., downtown. ☎ 213/972-7211.

L.A.'s top legitimate playhouse has 2,071 seats, and is the home base of the Center Theater Group, which stages a full season of plays each year—usually from mid-October to early May. Offerings have included Christopher Reeve and Christine Lahti in *Summer and Smoke,* Daniel J. Travanti in *I Never Sang for My Father,* and the West Coast première of Neil Simon's *Broadway Bound.* Visiting productions are also offered here, including a special long run of *Phantom of the Opera.*

A variety of international dance companies and concert attractions round out the season.

Admission: Tickets, $20–$50; reductions for specified performances available for students and seniors.

James A. Doolittle Theatre, 1615 N. Vine St., Hollywood. ☎ **213/462-6666** or **972-0700.**

The Doolittle Theatre offers a wide spectrum of live theater productions, such as Amy Irving in the Pulitzer Prize– and Tony Award–winning *Heidi Chronicles,* Neil Simon's Pulitzer Prize–winning *Lost in Yonkers,* and August Wilson's *Two Trains Running.*

Admission: Tickets, $20–$42.

Mark Taper Forum, the Music Center, 135 N. Grand Ave., at 1st St., downtown. ☎ **213/972-0700.**

Adjacent to the Ahmanson Theatre, this 747-seat circular theater is the Music Center's intimate playhouse. The emphasis here is on new and contemporary works, since the theater specializes in world and West Coast premières. Recent offerings have included the nationally acclaimed productions of *The Kentucky Cycle,* parts one and two of *Angels in America,* and *Twilight: Los Angeles, 1992.*

Admission: Tickets, $22–$35; reductions available on the day of performance.

Pantages Theatre, 6233 Hollywood Blvd., Hollywood. ☎ **213/468-1770.**

This luxurious Hollywood landmark dates from 1930. For 10 years it was the setting for the presentation of the Academy Awards, including the first televised Oscar ceremony. It's been through several incarnations, including one as a fine movie house. In 1977 the Pantages returned as a leading legitimate theater with a production of *Bubbling Brown Sugar.* Recent productions have included *Joseph and the Amazing Technicolor Dreamcoat* and concerts by Bob Dylan and the Gypsy Kings.

Admission: Tickets, $25–$60.

Shubert Theatre, 2020 Ave. of the Stars, ABC Entertainment Center, Century City. ☎ toll free **800/447-7400.**

This opulent theater presents big-time musicals—like *Cats, Sunset Boulevard,* and *Les Misérables.* It's located directly across from the Century Plaza Hotel.

Admission: Tickets, $25–$65.

SMALLER THEATERS

Akin to New York's Off-Broadway or London's "Fringe," Los Angeles's small-scale theaters often outdo the slick, high-budget shows. Here, talented performers entertain for the love of their craft. Tickets usually cost $10 to $20. Call the theaters and check newspaper listings for current performances.

Actors Circle Theatre, 7313 Santa Monica Blvd., West Hollywood. ☎ **213/882-8043.**

Winner of six "Dramalogue" awards in 1993, this 47-seat theater presents contemporary and original works throughout the year.

Actors Forum, 3365¹/₂ Cahuenga Blvd., Hollywood.
☎ **213/850-9016.**

Opened in 1975, this intimate, 49-seat theater often presents world premières by local playwrights. They also offer Tuesday-night workshops.

Attic Theatre, 6562¹/₂ Santa Monica Blvd., Hollywood.
☎ **213/469-3786.**

Everything from Shakespeare to modern musicals is performed in this intimate 50-seat theater. The Attic is located in a former World War II parachute factory.

Cast Theatre, 804 N. El Centro, Hollywood. ☎ **213/462-0265.**

The oldest small theater in Hollywood is also widely recognized as one of the best. The Cast Theatre is a recipient of the Hollywood Arts Council's Theatre Arts Award.

The Coast Playhouse, 8325 Santa Monica Blvd., West Hollywood.
☎ **213/650-8507.**

The 99-seat Coast presents contemporary and classical plays and musicals, staged Wednesday through Sunday.

Colony Studio Theatre, 1944 Riverside Dr., Silver Lake.
☎ **213/665-3011.**

The theater's resident company has played in this air-conditioned, 100-seat, converted silent movie house for almost 20 years. Recent productions include the musical *Candide* and the classic American comedy *The Front Page.*

The Complex, 6476 Santa Monica Blvd., Hollywood.
☎ **213/465-0383** or **464-2124.**

There's always something happening on at least one of the Complex's five stages. Call for the latest information.

Henry Fonda Theatre, 6126 Hollywood Blvd., Hollywood.
☎ **213/480-3232** or **468-1700.**

Formerly called the Music Box, this is one of Hollywood's oldest theaters. For a while it was a movie house, but has now been restored as a legitimate theater.

Globe Playhouse, 1107 N. Kings Rd., West Hollywood.
☎ **213/654-5623.**

Headquarters of Thad Taylor's Shakespeare Society of America, the Globe features plays by and about the Bard. The playhouse also houses a Shakespeare exhibit, with more than 1,000 collector's items and memorabilia.

Il Vittoriale, 2035 N. Highland Ave., Hollywood. ☎ **213/480-3232.**
Once a historic American Legion Post, the space has been transformed into an elaborate three-story, 10-room Italian country "villa." This

is the setting for *Tamara*, a unique environmental theater show, where audience members follow the character of their choice from room to room. Intermission buffet is included with admission.

The Lee Strasberg Theatre Institute, 7936 Santa Monica Blvd., West Hollywood. ☎ **213/650-7777.**

A well-known acting school, the Strasberg Institute sometimes presents productions for the public, including young people's programs. There are four theaters here, ranging from 25 to 99 seats.

Melrose Theater, 733 N. Seward St., Los Angeles.
☎ **213/465-1885.**

The theater's award-winning company performs dramas and musicals in this beautifully restored art deco building.

Odyssey Theatre Ensemble, 2055 Sepulveda Blvd., West Los Angeles. ☎ **310/477-2055.** Fax 310/444-0455.

For over 25 years the Odyssey Theatre has been performing exploration-oriented pieces from contemporary, classical, and original sources, with a strong leaning toward international and multicultural works. They perform 10 to 20 productions per year.

Stella Adler Theater, 6773 Hollywood Blvd., Hollywood.
☎ **213/465-4446.**

One-acts and other small plays are featured here.

2   The Club & Music Scene

Los Angeles's jaded music consumers are forever looking for something new and different. Always a pioneer when it comes to pop culture, the city's club and music scene offers every kind of entertainment available—from classic to cutting edge. Los Angeles just might be the best place on earth to hear up-and-coming bands, as the world's wannabes gravitate here in hopes of landing a coveted recording contract.

Comedy Clubs

Each of the following venues claims to have launched the careers of the same well-known comics—and it's probably true. Emerging funny men and women strive to get as many "gigs" as possible, playing all the clubs; so choose your club by location.

Comedy Store, 8433 Sunset Blvd., West Hollywood.
☎ **213/656-6225.**

Owner Mitzi Shore (Pauly's mother) has created a setting in which new comics can develop and established performers can work out the kinks in new material. It's always vastly entertaining. There are three showrooms.

The Best of the Comedy Store Room, which seats 400, features professional stand-ups continuously through the night on Monday, and during two separate shows on the weekends. Several comedians are always featured, each doing about a 15-minute stint. The talent here is always first-rate, and includes regulars on the "Tonight Show" and other television programs.

The Original Room features a dozen or so comedians back-to-back nightly. Monday night is amateur night, when anyone with enough guts can take the stage for three to five minutes.

The Belly Room alternates between comedy stage and piano bar, with Sunday nights reserved as a singer showcase.

The "Best" room is open on Monday from 8pm to 1am and Friday and Saturday with shows at 8 and 10:30pm. The Original and Belly Rooms are open nightly from 8pm to 1am. Drinks cost $3.75 to $7.

Admission: "Best" room, $6 Mon, $12–$14 Fri–Sat; Original Room, Mon free with a two-drink minimum, $6 Tues–Fri and Sun, $8 Sat; Belly Room, free–$3 plus a two-drink minimum.

Groundling Theatre, 7307 Melrose Ave., Los Angeles.
☎ **213/934-9700** or **934-4747.**

Los Angeles's most celebrated improvisational theater group is a must-see for anyone who likes to laugh and be entertained by a top acting troupe. Call for showtimes.

Improvisation, 8162 Melrose Ave., West Hollywood.
☎ **213/651-2583.**

Improvisation offers something different each night. The club's own television show, "Evening at the Improv," is now filmed at the Santa Monica location for national distribution. Although there used to be a fairly active music schedule, the Improv is now mostly doing what it does best—showcasing comedy. Major stars often appear here, for example, Jay Leno, Billy Crystal, and Robin Williams. Shows are on Sunday and Thursday at 8pm and Friday and Saturday at 8:30 and 10:30pm.

Admission: $8 plus a two-drink minimum Sun and Thurs, $10–$11 plus a two-drink minimum Fri–Sat.

Rock & Blues Clubs

Canter's Kibitz Room, 419 N. Fairfax Ave., Los Angeles.
☎ **213/651-2030.**

Canter's, one of the city's most established 24-hour Jewish restaurants, features Tuesday-night jams just after 9pm in the Kibitz Room. Members of Guns 'n' Roses, the Black Crowes, Pearl Jam, and other bands have been known to play here, along with other rockers who play till 2am.

Admission: Free.

Club Lingerie, 6507 W. Sunset Blvd., Hollywood. ☎ **213/466-8557.**

Emerging rock 'n' roll bands and other contemporary styles play every night at Hollywood's oldest continuously operating club. When the bands stop, DJs start, and feet keep moving to the beat. Open daily from 9pm to 2am.

Admission: $6–$15.

Doug Weston's Troubador, 9081 Santa Monica Blvd., West Hollywood. ☎ **310/276-6168.**

Located at the edge of Beverly Hills, the Troubador usually serves up local rock bands back-to-back by the half dozen. An adventurous booking policy ensures a good mix, and so many bands each night usually means that there'll be at least one you'll like. Usually open daily from 8pm to 2am.

Admission: $5–$15.

8121 Club, 8121 Sunset Blvd., Hollywood. ☎ **213/654-4887.**

An underground all-acoustic club for locals who are in-the-know, the 8121 features three to five acts per night. Open daily from 8pm to 2am.

Admission: Free–$7.

Gazzarri's on the Strip, 9039 Sunset Blvd., near Doheny Dr., Hollywood. ☎ **310/273-6606.**

Once self-described as "Hollywood's oldest disco," Gazzarri's has now changed to a live-music format, offering rock 'n' roll bands almost nightly. Sometimes it's hip hop and other nights it's rap. The age group is early 20s; dress is casual. Credit cards are not accepted and you must be at least 18 to get in. It's usually open Wednesday through Saturday from 8pm to 2am.

Admission: $10–$14.

House of Blues, 8430 Sunset Blvd., West Hollywood. ☎ **213/650-0247.**

Looking very much like a Disney-inspired shanty shack, this new blues joint—owned in part by Harvard University, actors Dan Aykroyd and Jim Belushi, and members of the rock band Aerosmith—features live blues performances and southern-style cooking daily from 11am to 2am; bands usually start around 9pm. The club is the third in a series of successful blues houses—founder Isaac Tigrett also helped originate the Hard Rock Cafe chain.

Admission: Free–$30, depending on who's playing.

McCabe's Guitar Shop, 3101 Pico Blvd., Santa Monica. ☎ **310/828-4497,** or **310/828-4403** for recorded information.

One of the most unusual music venues in the city, McCabe's is an actual guitar store that features regular live weekend performances in its small, 150-seat theater. Top-level performers include both new and established artists. No alcohol is sold, but coffee, tea, juices, and cookies are available. Phone to see what's on.

Admission: $12.50–$20, depending on who's playing.

The Roxy, 9009 Sunset Blvd., West Hollywood. ☎ **310/276-2229,** or **316/276-2222** for a recording.

Probably the top venue in L.A., the medium-sized Roxy specializes in showcasing the music industry's new signings, as well as smaller established bands, and occasionally even superstars such as David Bowie and Bon Jovi. The roster is usually packed with Los Angeles bands you've never heard of, often three or four per night. There's no age limit for entry, but only those over 21 may legally purchase alcohol. It's usually open daily from 8pm to 2am.

Admission: $5–$20.

Whiskey A-Go-Go, 8901 Sunset Blvd., West Hollywood.
☎ **310/652-4202.**

One of Hollywood's legendary clubs, the Whiskey packs 'em in with hard rock and alternative rock double and triple bills. All ages are welcome. It's open daily from 8pm to 2am.

Admission: $5–15.

Jazz & Latin Clubs

Like the bands that play in them, jazz clubs come and go. Check the ads in L.A.'s newspapers, and contact the **L.A. Jazz Society** (☎ **213/469-6800**)—a nonprofit organization formed to promote jazz and its artists—to see what's on.

Candilejas, 5060 Sunset Blvd., Hollywood. ☎ **213/665-8822.**

This medium-sized club is one of the premier places to hear hot salsa. Puerto Rican and African-Cuban bands perform almost every night. Open Sunday through Thursday from 9pm to 2am and Friday and Saturday from 9pm to 4am.

Admission: $5–$10.

Catalina's Bar & Grill, 1640 N. Cahuenga Blvd., Hollywood.
☎ **213/466-2210.**

International and local jazz musicians perform here most nights, and food is always available. Open daily from 7pm to 2am.

Admission: $15–$20 plus a two-drink minimum.

Vine Street Bar & Grill, 1610 Vine St., Hollywood.
☎ **213/463-4375.**

Famous-name jazz celebrities perform almost nightly in this intimate, art deco restaurant. Call for the latest information. Open daily from 5pm to 2am.

Admission: $7–$15.

Dance Clubs

Hollywood in general, and the down-and-dirty Sunset Strip in particular, continues to be at the center of Los Angeles's nightlife scene.

The very nature of the club scene demands frequent fresh faces, thus making recommendations outdated before the ink can even dry on the page. Most of the venues below are promoted as different clubs on various nights of the week, each with its own look, sound, and style. Many of the rock clubs listed above are also dedicated to dance disks on different nights of the week. The weekly listings magazine *L.A. Weekly* contains the latest, but it's not comprehensive. Discount passes and club announcements are often available at trendy clothing stores along Melrose Avenue.

Palladium Hollywood, 6215 Sunset Blvd., Hollywood.
☎ **213/962-7600.**

Lawrence Welk used to do his famous New Year's Eve show from here. Today the huge club is one of the best venues in town, featuring everything from rock to salsa. Call to see what's on. It's open Wednesday through Saturday from 7pm to 2am.
Admission: $15–$25.

Roxbury, 8225 Sunset Blvd., Hollywood. ☎ **213/656-1750.**

A labyrinthine dance club, the Roxbury attracts a trendy crowd that dresses to impress. There are four full bars and DJ dancing Tuesday through Saturday from 6pm to 2am.
Admission: $10.

3   The Bar Scene

Bars

Lava Lounge, 1533 La Brea Ave., Hollywood. ☎ **213/876-6612.**

Located at Sunset Boulevard, this retro dive bar with a very mixed crowd is slightly seedy, grungy, artsy, and fringy. Great jazz, often trios, plays in a room with a sordid tiki-hut decor. Weekdays can be hit or miss, while weekends are always crowded. It's open daily from 9pm to 2am.

Tatou, 233 N. Beverly Dr., Beverly Hills. ☎ **310/274-9955.**

Very L.A., Tatou is a trendy meeting place with three distinct atmospheres. A loud restaurant is fronted by a 1930s-style stage where great jazz and rock bands perform. The back bar enjoys a view of the table and stage action but is both quieter and more interactive. The upstairs dance floor fills up on weekends, when great-looking trendies bop to the latest beats. Open Monday through Friday from 6pm to 2am and Saturday from 6:30pm to 2am.
Admission: $15–$20.

Hotel Bars

Bel Air Hotel Bar, 701 Stone Canyon Rd., Bel Air.
☎ **213/472-1211.**

One of the mellower places for a quiet, romantic evening, the ritzy Bel Air bar offers good piano music in an upscale setting. It's open Sunday through Thursday from 11am to 1am and Friday and Saturday from 11am to 2am.

The Brasserie Bar, in the Bel Age Hotel de Grande Classe, 1020 N. San Vicente Blvd., West Hollywood. ☎ **310/854-1111.**

One of the classiest and prettiest bars in the city, this place regularly features top-notch jazz performers. Open Sunday and Monday from 10:30am to 9:30pm and Tuesday through Saturday from 10:30am to 1am.

The Grand Avenue Bar, in the Biltmore Hotel, 506 S. Grand Ave., Los Angeles. ☎ 213/624-1011.

During the day, the bar offers a cold lunch buffet. At night the drinkery becomes popular for its showcases of top-name jazz performers. Open Monday through Saturday from 5pm to midnight.

The Lobby Club Bar, in the Peninsula Beverly Hills, 9882 Santa Monica Blvd., Beverly Hills. ☎ 310/551-2888.

Beverly Hills's best-looking crowd comes here nightly to see, be seen, drink expensive drinks, and hear pianist George Bugatti tickle the ivories of his Kimball baby grand. Sinatra's even stopped in and stayed after hours to croon. Open daily from 11:30am to 2am.

Whiskey, at the Sunset Marquis Hotel and Villas, 1200 N. Alta Loma Rd., West Hollywood. ☎ 310/657-1333.

The Whiskey is one of the most exclusive rooms in Hollywood. Rock 'n' rollers like Mick Jagger, Axel Rose, and Robert Plant cavort with model/actresses, Eurotrash, bimbo chicks, and guys who wear tank tops under sports jackets. Make sure you're either staying at the hotel or you know somebody—or you probably won't get in. Open daily from 9pm to 2am.

Pool Halls

Gotham Hall, 1431 3rd St., Santa Monica. ☎ 310/394-8865.

Grape- and mustard-colored walls, contemporary cut-steel railings and light coverings, and ultramodern furniture make this futuristic pool hall one of the most interesting in L.A. Seventeen regulation-size tables are overlooked by a balcony bar. Pool prices are $7 to $14 per hour. Open Monday through Friday from 4pm to 2am and Saturday and Sunday from noon to 2am.

Yankee Doodles, 1410 3rd St., Santa Monica. ☎ 310/394-4632.

Grimier if not noisier than Gotham Hall (see above), this sports bar–cum–pool hall features 32 pool tables on two levels, battling satellite TVs, and lousy food. Pool costs $6 to $12 per hour. Open daily from 11am to 2am.

Gay & Lesbian Bars & Clubs

Catch One, 4067 W. Pico Blvd., Hollywood. ☎ 213/734-8849.

This is one of the best dance clubs in the city for both gays and lesbians. Big crowds are attracted by a good sound system. There are four bars on two floors. Theme nights vary, so you have to call to see what's on. Open on Tuesday and Wednesday from 3pm to 2am and Thursday through Saturday from 3pm to 4am.

Circus Disco, 6655 Santa Monica Blvd., Hollywood.
☎ 213/462-1291.

It's not always gay night, but when it is, the club is packed with a predominantly young, Latino crowd. Hip hop and house music are the preferred sounds. Open Friday through Wednesday from 9pm to 2am.

Admission: $8–$12 cover.

Micky's, 8857 Santa Monica Blvd., West Hollywood.
☎ **310/657-1176.**

Both a dance club and a restaurant, Micky's creates a high-energy atmosphere popular with a youngish crowd. The good-looking club occupies two levels and serves full meals. Open daily from noon to 2am.

Admission: Free–$7.

The Mother Lode, 8944 Santa Monica Blvd., West Hollywood.
☎ **310/659-9700.**

Frequented by a young, upwardly mobile crowd, this collegiate-looking bar is made for drinking, and there's often a line to get in. Open daily from noon to 2am.

The Palms, 8527 Santa Monica Blvd., West Hollywood.
☎ **310/652-6188.**

Reputedly the oldest lesbian bar in the city, this busy hangout is becoming more popular with gay men as well. Open daily from noon to 2am.

Spike, 7746 Santa Monica Blvd., West Hollywood. ☎ **213/656-9343.**

The pool- and pinball-playing Levi's and leather crowd here likes the bar's techno, house, and rock selections. Open Sunday through Thursday from noon to 2am and Friday and Saturday from noon to 4am.

Admission: Free–$7.

11

Easy Excursions from Los Angeles

Los Angeles is situated within the most fascinating and diverse area of southern California. And the contrasts of the region are even more spellbinding than its beauties. There are arid deserts and smartly sophisticated seaside resorts. Humming industrial cities and serene, sun-drenched Spanish missions contrast with rolling hillsides, wildly rugged mountain ranges, a plethora of theme parks, and an off-shore island that has been transformed into the ultimate close getaway.

Using Los Angeles as either your travel base or your springboard, you can reach any of these points within a few hours or less by car or public transport. The purpose of this chapter is to give you a glimpse of some of the attractions beckoning beyond Coit Tower . . . how to get there and what to expect.

---

1 Santa Catalina Island

22 miles W of mainland Los Angeles

GETTING THERE • By Plane   Valley Executive Charter (☎ 310/982-1575) flies from the Long Beach Municipal Airport, 4100 Donald Douglas Dr., Long Beach (☎ 310/421-8293), to Catalina's Airport in the Sky (☎ 310/510-0143), 1,600 feet above the sea-level town of Avalon. Tickets are $300 per person. Taxis and buses meet each flight in Catalina.

• By Boat   The *Catalina Express* (☎ 310/519-1212, or toll free 800/995-4386) operates up to 20 daily departures year-round to Catalina from San Pedro and Long Beach. The trip takes about an hour. One-way fares from San Pedro and Long Beach are $17.75 for adults, $16 for seniors, $13.25 for children 2 to 11, and $1 for infants. Long Beach fares are about $2 higher for all except infants, who are still charged $1. The *Catalina Express* departs from the Sea/Air Terminal at Berth 95, Port of L.A. in San Pedro; the *Catalina Express* port at the *Queen Mary* in Long Beach; and from the *Catalina Express* port at 161 N. Harbor Dr. in Redondo. Call for information and reservations.

Note: There are specific baggage restrictions on the *Catalina Express*. Luggage is limited to 50 pounds per person; reservations are necessary for bicycles, surfboards, and dive tanks; and there are restrictions on transporting domestic pets—call for information.

ESSENTIALS • Orientation   The picturesque town of Avalon is the island's only city. Named for a passage in Tennyson's *Idylls of the King,* Avalon is also the port of entry for the island. From the ferry dock you can wander along Crescent Avenue, the main road along the beachfront, and easily explore adjacent side streets.

Visitors are not allowed to drive cars on the island. Walk around Avalon and take tours to points inland (see "What to See and Do," below). About 86% of the island remains undeveloped. It's owned by the Santa Catalina Island Conservancy, which endeavors to preserve the island's natural resources.

• **Information**   The **Catalina Island Chamber of Commerce and Visitor's Bureau,** Dept. FLA, P.O. Box 217, Avalon, CA 90704 (☎ 310/510-1520), located on the Green Pleasure Pier, distributes brochures and information on island activities. It also offers information on local airlines, hotels, boat transport, and sightseeing tours, as well as brochures on camping, hiking, fishing, and boating. Write ahead for an extremely useful free 88-page visitor's guide.

The Santa Catalina Island Company–run **Visitor's Information Center,** which is just a minute away from the chamber of commerce on Crescent Avenue, across from the Green Pleasure Pier (☎ 310/510-2000), handles hotel reservations, sightseeing tours, and other island activities.

———————————————————————————

Located 22 miles west of Long Beach, Catalina is a small, cove-fringed island famous for its laid-back resorts, largely unspoiled landscape, and crystal-clear waters. Because of its relative isolation, tourists don't crowd Catalina as they do the mainland. Visitors who do show up have plenty of elbow room to boat, fish, swim, scuba dive, and snorkel. There are miles of hiking and biking trails, and golf, tennis, and horseback-riding facilities abound.

Catalina is so different from the mainland that it almost seems like a different country—remote and unspoiled. The island separated from the mainland more than 500,000 years ago and evolved to meet environmental challenges. Even today there is unique plant life here, and archeology has revealed traces of a stone-age culture. From the time of its discovery by Western explorers in the 1600s until the turn of the 20th century, Catalina was primarily a place for pirates and smugglers. The island was purchased by William Wrigley, Jr., the chewing gum manufacturer, in 1915 in order to develop a fashionable pleasure resort. To publicize the new vacationland, Wrigley brought big-name bands to the Avalon Casino Ballroom, and he moved the Chicago Cubs baseball team, which he owned, to the island for spring training. His marketing efforts succeeded, and Catalina became a favorite vacation resort spot for wealthy mainlanders. It no longer takes spectacular marketing to entice visitors to Catalina; the island's hotels are often fully booked months in advance. But Catalina is still far from overrun with tourists; it's still a genuinely tranquil and charming retreat.

What to See & Do

Avalon Casino and Catalina Island Museum, at the end of Crescent Ave. ☎ 310/510-2414.

The Avalon Casino is the most famous and one of the oldest structures on the island. Built in 1929 as a resort for vacationers from the mainland, its massive circular rotunda, topped with a red-tile roof, is the building's most famous feature—it appears on posters and postcards in shops all around town. The Avalon Casino is widely known for its beautiful art deco ballroom that once hosted such top bands as the Tommy Dorsey and Glen Miller orchestras. You can see the inside of the building by attending a ballroom event or a film (the Casino is Avalon's primary movie theater). Otherwise, admission is by guided tour only, operated daily by the Santa Catalina Island Company (see "Organized Tours," below).

The **Catalina Island Museum,** located on the ground floor of the Casino, features exhibits on island history, archeology, and natural history. The small museum also has an excellent relief map that details the island's interior.

Admission: $1 adults, free for children under 12.

Open: Daily 10:30am–4pm.

Avalon Pleasure Pier, Crescent Ave. and Catalina St., Avalon.

Jutting out into Crescent Cove, the wood-plank pier offers excellent views of the town and surrounding mountains. Food stands and bait-and-tackle shops line the pier, selling fish to eat and cast.

Lover's Cove, at the end of Crescent Ave., Avalon.

One of Catalina's top draws is its crystal-clear waters and abundant sea life. Lover's Cove is filled with colorful fish and rich kelp beds. Several Avalon companies rent scuba and snorkeling equipment. Santa Catalina Island Company, Avalon Harbor Pier (☎ toll free **800/626-7489**), offers glass-bottom-boat tours of the area leaving every hour daily from 11am to 4pm. The trip takes about 40 minutes and costs $7.50 for adults and $3.75 for children. The company also offers tours of the underworld in their new semisubmersible submarine. This 60-foot, 50-ton vessel allows visitors to see panoramic underwater views. The trip costs $18 for adults and $12 for children. Call for times.

ORGANIZED TOURS

Since visitors are not allowed to drive cars around the island, it may be difficult to tour Catalina on your own; therefore, organized tours are recommended. The Santa Catalina Island Company's Discovery Tours, Avalon Harbor Pier (☎ toll free **800/626-7489**), operates several motorcoach excursions that depart from the tour plaza in the center of town on Sumner Avenue.

The Skyline Drive tour basically follows the perimeter of the island and takes about 1³/₄ hours. Trips leave several times a day from 11am to 3pm and cost $14 for adults, $10.50 for seniors, and $8 for children 3 to 11.

The Inland Motor Tour is more comprehensive; it includes some of the 66 square miles of preserve owned by the Santa Catalina Island Conservancy. You'll see El Rancho Escondido—for refreshments—and probably have a chance to view buffalo, deer, goats, and boars. Tours, which take about 3³/₄ hours, leave at 9am. From June to October there are additional schedules. Tours cost $24.50 for adults, $19 for seniors, and $13 for children 3 to 11; free for children under 3.

Other excursions offered by the company include a 40-minute Casino Tour, which explores Catalina's most famous landmark; a 50-minute Avalon Scenic Tour, a nine-mile introductory tour of the town; and a one-hour Flying Fish Boat Trip, during which an occasional flying fish lands right on the boat.

Check with the Catalina Island Company for other tour offerings, as well as various dining cruises.

Where to Stay

Catalina's 30 or so hotels (none of which belongs to a chain) are beautifully situated and maintain an almost affected unpretentiousness. Somehow they seem to go out of their way not to be quaint or charming. Don't worry about your hotel's decor (or lack of it), since there's nary an eyesore on the entire island. If you do plan to stay overnight on Catalina, be sure to reserve a room in advance, since the hotels regularly reach 100% occupancy, especially on weekends.

Catalina Canyon Hotel, 888 Country Club Dr., Avalon, CA 90704. ☎ **310/510-0325,** or toll free **800/253-9361.** Fax 310/510-0900. 80 rms. A/C TV TEL **Directions:** From Avalon Pleasure Pier, go up Catalina Avenue, turn right onto Tremont Street and then left onto Country Club Drive to the hotel.

Rates: $75–$135 single or double. Additional person $20 extra. AE, MC, V.

The Catalina Canyon Hotel is set on beautifully landscaped grounds in the foothills of Avalon. The guest rooms are tastefully decorated and comfortably furnished (no-smoking rooms are available); all have AM/FM radios and balconies overlooking the outdoor pool and Jacuzzi. The Canyon Restaurant serves breakfast, lunch, and a continental dinner. Room service is available. Cocktails may be enjoyed in the lounge or on the outdoor terrace overlooking the pool. The hotel is adjacent to a golf course and tennis courts. A courtesy van meets guests at the air and sea terminals.

Catalina Island Inn, 125 Metropole (P.O. Box 467), Avalon, CA 90704. ☎ **310/510-1623.** Fax 310/510-7218. 35 rms, 1 suite. TV **Directions:** From the Avalon Pleasure Pier, go right on Crescent Avenue two blocks to Metropole, then turn left to the hotel.

Rates (including continental breakfast): May–Sept, holidays, and weekends year-round, $75–$160 single or double; $185 minisuite. Oct–May except holidays and weekends, $45–$130 single or double; $155 minisuite. AE, DISC, MC, V.

Innkeepers Martin and Bernadine Curtin have created some of the most attractive accommodations in town. Pale blue-gray rooms are accented in peach and set off by blue carpeting and green bedspreads. Shuttered windows and stained-glass lighting fixtures add further charm. All rooms have color TVs. There are no telephones in the rooms, but the front desk will take phone messages. There are ice and soda machines in the hall.

Hotel Macrae, 409 Crescent Ave. (P.O. Box 1517), Avalon, CA 90704. ☎ **310/510-0246,** or toll free **800/698-2266.** 23 rms. TEL **Directions:** From the Avalon Pleasure Pier, walk north on Crescent Avenue.

Rates (including continental breakfast): Summer, $90–$170 single or double. Winter, $50–$110 single or double. MC, V.

This pleasant two-story hostelry is right across from the beach. It's decorated in bright, cheerful colors—parrot green, orange, yellow, red, and white. Rooms are individually equipped with heaters for chilly nights. In the center of the hotel is a large, open courtyard, perfect for lounging or sunning.

Zane Grey Pueblo Hotel, off Chimes Tower Rd. (P.O. Box 216), Avalon, CA 90704. ☎ 310/510-0966, or toll free 800/378-3256. 17 rms. **Directions:** From the Avalon Pleasure Pier, go north on Crescent Avenue, turn left onto Hill Street and right onto Chimes Tower Road.

> **Rates** (including continental breakfast): June–Sept, $75–$125 single or double. Nov–Mar, $55 single or double. Rest of the year, $65–$85 single or double. Slightly higher on weekends and holidays. Additional person $35 extra AE, MC, V.

The most superb views on the island are from the lofty Zane Grey Pueblo Hotel. This Shangri-la mountain retreat is the former home of novelist Zane Grey, who spent his last 20 years in Avalon enjoying isolation with an ocean view. He wrote many books here, including *Tales of Swordfish and Tuna,* which tells of his fishing adventures off Catalina Island.

The hotel has teak beams that the novelist brought from Tahiti on one of his fishing trips. Most of the rooms also have large windows and ocean or mountain views. They have all been renovated with new furniture, carpeting, and ceiling fans. An outdoor patio has an excellent view, while the original living room has a grand piano, a fireplace, and a TV. The hotel also offers pool/sun deck, with chairs overlooking Avalon and the ocean. Coffee is served all day, and there's a courtesy bus to town.

Where to Dine

MODERATE

The Busy Bee, 306 Crescent Ave. ☎ 310/510-1983.

> **Cuisine:** AMERICAN. **Reservations:** Not accepted. **Directions:** From the Avalon Pleasure Pier, walk two blocks north on Crescent Avenue to the end of Metropole.
>
> **Prices:** Appetizers $3–$6; main courses $7–$15. AE, CB, DC, DISC, MC, V.
>
> **Open:** Summer, daily 8am–10pm. Winter, daily 8am–8pm.

The Busy Bee has been an Avalon institution since 1923. The restaurant is located on the beach directly over the water. You can eat in any one of several locations, including a lovely wraparound outdoor patio.

The fare is light—deli style. Breakfast, lunch, and dinner are served at all times; the extensive menu includes omelets, various sandwiches and salads, and Buffalo burgers. The restaurant grinds its own beef and cuts its own potatoes for french fries. Salad dressings are also made on the premises. Even if you're not hungry, come here for a drink; it's Avalon's only bar on the water.

El Galleon, 411 Crescent Ave. ☎ 310/510-1188.

Cuisine: AMERICAN. **Reservations:** Not required.

Prices: Appetizers $5–$12; main courses $7–$18 at lunch, $11–$37 at dinner. AE, DISC, MC, V.

Open: Lunch daily 11am–2:30pm; dinner daily 5–10pm. (Bar, daily 10am–1:30am.)

El Galleon is large, warm, and woody, complete with portholes, rigging, anchors, big wrought-iron chandeliers, oversize tufted-leather booths, and tables with red-leather captain's chairs. There's additional balcony seating, plus outdoor café tables overlooking the ocean harbor. Lunch choices include fresh seafood, burgers, steak, stews, salads, and sandwiches. The dinner menu features many seafood items too, like cioppino, fresh swordfish steak, and broiled Catalina lobster tails in drawn butter. "Turf" main dishes range from country-fried chicken and beef Stroganoff to broiled rack of lamb with mint jelly.

INEXPENSIVE

Sand Trap, Avalon Canyon Rd. ☎ 310/510-1349.

Cuisine: CALIFORNIA/MEXICAN. **Reservations:** Not accepted. **Directions:** From the Avalon Pleasure Pier, go up Catalina Avenue and turn right onto Tremont; take the next left onto Falls Canyon Road, which soon turns into Avalon Canyon Road.

Prices: Appetizers $2–$5; main courses $4–$12. No credit cards.

Open: Daily 7:30am–3:30pm.

Long a local favorite, the Sand Trap is a great place to escape from the bayfront crowds. Enjoy breakfast, lunch, or snacks while looking out over the golf course. Specialties of the house include delectable omelets served till noon and soft tacos served all day. Either can be made with any number of fillings, including Cheddar cheese, mushrooms, turkey, homemade chorizo, spicy shredded beef, sour cream, and salsa. Burgers, sandwiches, salads, and chili are also served. Beer and wine are available.

2   Orange County: Disneyland, Knott's Berry Farm & Environs

27 miles SE of downtown Los Angeles

GETTING THERE • By Plane   Most visitors who fly in to see Orange County theme parks arrive via Los Angeles International Airport (LAX), located about 30 miles west of Disneyland and Knott's Berry Farm.

John Wayne International Airport, in Irvine, is Orange County's largest airport. Located about 15 miles from Disneyland and 20 miles from Knott's Berry Farm, the airport is served by Alaska Airlines, American Airlines, Continental, Delta, Northwest, TWA, and United.

• By Train   The nearest Amtrak (☎ toll free **800/USA-RAIL**) stations are located in San Clemente and San Juan Capistrano, near the coast in the southern part of the county. Trains travel both north and south between Los Angeles and San Diego. Call for fare and schedule information.

• **By Bus** Greyhound/Trailways (☎ toll free **800/231-2222**) can get you here from anywhere.

• **By Car** From Los Angeles, take I-5 south. Exit south onto Beach Boulevard for Knott's Berry Farm. Continue for another five miles to the Harbor Boulevard exit for Disneyland. The theme parks are about an hour's drive from downtown Los Angeles.

ESSENTIALS • Orientation Located just blocks south of the Santa Ana Freeway (I-5), about five miles from each other, both Disneyland and Knott's Berry Farm are relatively compact theme parks completely surrounded by hotels, fast-food restaurants, and other tourist-oriented facilities.

The surrounding communities of Anaheim and Buena Park, respectively, are primarily residential and not too exciting from a tourist's perspective.

• **Information** For information relating specifically to Disneyland, call the park (☎ 714/999-4565). The **Anaheim Area Visitor and Convention Bureau,** 800 W. Katella Ave. (P.O. Box 4270), Anaheim, CA 92803 (☎ **714/999-8999**), can fill you in on other area attractions, beaches, and activities.

For information relating specifically to Knott's Berry Farm, call the park (☎ 714/220-5200). The **Buena Park Convention and Visitors Office,** 6280 Manchester Blvd., Suite 103 (☎ 714/562-3560, or toll free **800/541-3953**), has other area information.

Some people might say that the Orange County cities of Anaheim, Fullerton, Buena Park, and Irvine are among the most physically unprepossessing towns in California, but nevertheless they attract the most visitors.

The natural surroundings may not be as inspiring as other parts of the state, but the specially created attractions are enchanting—transformed by the magic wand of Walt Disney into a wonderful world of make-believe. And Disneyland is just one of the spectacular sights in the area. There are also Knott's Berry Farm, the Movieland Wax Museum, and more. So take the kids—and if you don't have any kids, be a kid yourself for a while.

Tourist board protests to the contrary, Anaheim *is* Disneyland. Once a sleepy little town in the Valencia orange-grove belt, Anaheim has now become a playground of hotels, restaurants, and various other tourist-oriented attractions.

Knott's Berry Farm's Buena Park is just five miles west of Disneyland's Anaheim, but don't even think about conquering them both in the same day. Several hotel options are listed below so that you can stay a few days and do what appeals to you the most.

What to See & Do

⭐ **Disneyland**, 1313 Harbor Blvd., Anaheim. ☎ **714/999-4565.**
Even the most jaded nose can hardly turn up at Disneyland. It's that special—a world of charm and magic, an "open sesame" to one's lost childhood, an extravagant doorway to yesterday and tomorrow. Opened in 1955 and constantly expanding, Disneyland has steadily grown to become the top tourist attraction in California.

The entertainment complex is divided into several theme "lands," each containing tailored rides and attractions. Many visitors tackle the park systematically, beginning at the entrance and working their way clockwise around the park. But a better plan of attack may be to arrive early and run to the most popular rides first—Space Mountain, Big Thunder Mountain Railroad, Splash Mountain, and Pirates of the Caribbean. Lines for these rides can last an hour or more in the middle of the day.

The main drag of a small turn-of-the-century American town, **Main Street U.S.A.** is at the entrance to the park. This is a good area to save for the end of the day—particularly the "Great Moments with Mr. Lincoln," a patriotic look at America's 16th president, where you can rest your weary feet. You can start by touring the entire park by train—a 19th-century steam train departs from the Main Street Depot and completely encircles the park. After sunset during summer, there's a Main Street Electrical Parade spectacular—with fabulous whirling lights followed by Fantasy in the Sky fireworks.

In **Adventureland,** inspired by exotic regions of Asia, Africa, and the South Pacific, electronically animated tropical birds, flowers, and "tiki gods" present a musical comedy in the Enchanted Tiki Room. On the Jungle Cruise, which is within a spear's throw, passengers are threatened by wild animals and hostile natives. New Orleans square offers the ghost-packed Haunted Mansion; Pirates of the Caribbean is a hydroflume ride down a plunging waterfall and through pirate caves; and Splash Mountain is one of the largest towering log-flume attractions in the world.

Getting its inspiration from 19th-century America, **Frontierland** is full of dense forests and broad rivers inhabited by hearty pioneers. You can take a raft to Tom Sawyer's Island and board the Big Thunder Mountain Railroad, a roller coaster that races through a deserted 1870s mine.

The storybook theme of **Fantasyland** is illustrated with several rides based on famous children's books, including *Through the Looking Glass* and *Peter Pan.* The seemingly unrelated Matterhorn Bobsleds, a roller-coaster ride through chilling caverns and drifting fog banks, is here, too; it's one of the park's most popular rides.

Exploring the world of the future, **Tomorrowland** offers some of the park's best attractions. Space Mountain, a pitch-black indoor roller coaster, is one of the best-known rides at Disneyland. Captain Eo, a 3-D motion picture musical, is a space adventure starring Michael Jackson. One of the newest attractions is Star Tours, a 40-passenger StarSpeeder that encounters a spaceload of misadventures on the way to the Moon of Endor.

Disneyland

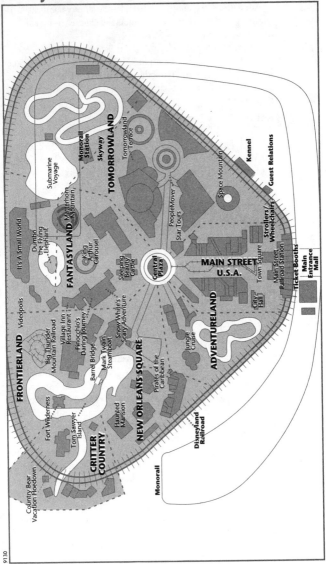

The "lands" themselves are only half the adventure. Other attractions include roaming Disney characters, penny arcades, restaurants and snack bars galore, fireworks (during summer only), mariachi bands, ragtime pianists, parades, shops, marching bands, and much more.

Admission (including unlimited rides and all entertainment): $31 adults and children over 12, $25 seniors and children 3–11; children under 3 free. Parking costs $5.

Open: Mid-Sept to May, Mon–Fri 9am–6pm, Sat–Sun 9am–midnight; June to mid-Sept plus Thanksgiving, Christmas, and Easter, daily 8am–1am. **Directions:** From I-95 or Fwy. 91 south, pass the Beach Boulevard exit and travel for five miles to the Harbor Boulevard exit.

★ **Knott's Berry Farm,** 8039 Beach Blvd., Buena Park. ☎ **714/827-1776,** or **714/220-5200** for a recording.

In 1920, Walter and Cordelia Knott arrived in Buena Park in their old Model T Ford and leased a small farm on 10 acres of land. Things got tough during the Great Depression, so Cordelia set up a roadside stand selling pies, preserves, and home-cooked chicken dinners. Within a year sales were up to about 90 meals a day. Lines became so long that Walter decided to create an Old West Ghost Town as a diversion for waiting customers, and that's how it all began. The Knott family now owns the farm that surrounds the world-famous Chicken Dinner Restaurant, an eatery that now serves over a million meals a year! And Knott's Berry Farm has emerged as the nation's third-best-attended family entertainment complex (after the two Disney facilities). The park still maintains its original Old West motif and is divided into four Old Time Adventures areas.

Old West Ghost Town, the original attraction, is a collection of authentic buildings that have been relocated from actual deserted western towns and refurbished. Visitors can pan for gold, climb aboard the stagecoach, ride rickety train cars through the Calico Mine, get held up aboard the Denver and Rio Grande Calico Railroad, and hiss at the villain during a melodrama in the Birdcage Theater.

Fiesta Village's south-of-the-border theme means festive markets, strolling mariachis, and wild rides like Montezooma's Revenge—a loop roller coaster that turns you upside down and goes backward.

The Roaring '20s Amusement Area contains the thrilling Sky Tower, a parachute jump that drops riders into a 20-story free fall. Other white-knuckle rides include XK-1, the ultimate flight simulator "piloted" by the riders; the $7-million Kingdom of the Dinosaurs ride; and Boomerang, a state-of-the-art roller coaster that turns riders upside down six times in less than one minute.

Wild Water Wilderness is a $10-million, 3 1/2-acre attraction styled like a turn-of-the-century California wilderness park. The top ride here is a white-water adventure called Bigfoot Rapids.

Camp Snoopy is meant to re-create the picturesque California High Sierra. Its six rustic acres are the playing grounds of Charles Schulz's beloved beagle, Snoopy, and his pals, Charlie Brown and Lucy, who greet guests and pose for pictures.

Admission (including unlimited access to all rides, shows, and attractions): $27 adults, $18 seniors over 60, $16 children 3–11, free for children under 3.

Open: Summer, Mon–Thurs 9am–11pm, Fri–Sun 9am–midnight; the rest of the year, Mon–Thurs 10am–6pm, Fri–Sun 10am–10pm. Closing times vary, so call for the latest information. **Directions:** From I-5 or Calif. 91, exit south onto Beach Boulevard. The park is located about half a mile south.

Medieval Times, 7662 Beach Blvd., Buena Park. ☎ **714/521-4740,** or toll free **800/899-6600.**

Basically, Medieval Times is a dinner show for those of us who were unlucky enough not to have been born into a royal family somewhere in 11th-century Europe. Guests crowd around long wooden tables and enjoy a four-course "banquet" of roast chicken, spareribs, herbed potatoes, and pastries. More than 1,100 people can fit into the castle, where sword fights, jousting tournaments, and various feats of skill are performed by colorfully costumed actors, including knights on horseback.

It's kind of ridiculous, but kids love it, and Medieval Times is extremely popular year-round.

Admission: Sun–Fri $32 adults, $20 children 12 and under; Sat $35 adults, $20 children.

Open: Shows Mon–Fri at 7pm, Sat at 6:30 and 8:45pm, Sun at 2 and 5pm. Times can vary, so call for the latest information. **Directions:** From I-5 or Calif. 91, exit south onto Beach Boulevard. The attraction is located about a quarter of a mile south.

Movieland Wax Museum, 7711 Beach Blvd. (Calif. 39), Buena Park. ☎ **714/522-1155.**

At the Movieland Wax Museum, located one block north of Knott's Berry Farm in Buena Park, you can see wax-molded reviews of past cinematic attractions—everything from Bela Lugosi as *Dracula* to Marilyn Monroe in *Gentlemen Prefer Blondes.*

Mary Pickford, "America's Sweetheart," dedicated the museum on May 4, 1962. It has risen steadily in popularity ever since, with new stars added yearly, taking their place next to the time-tested favorites. The museum was created by a film addict, Allen Parkinson, who saw to it that some of the most memorable scenes in motion pictures were re-created in exacting detail in wax, with such authentic touches as the ripped dress of Sophia Loren in *Two Women.*

Some of the most popular teams are featured in tableaux: Humphrey Bogart and Katharine Hepburn in *The African Queen,* Myrna Loy and William Powell in *The Thin Man,* Greta Garbo and John Gilbert in *Queen Christina,* Clark Gable and Vivien Leigh in *Gone with the Wind,* and Stan Laurel and Oliver Hardy in *The Perfect Day.* Later sets include *Star Trek* and *Superman.*

Admission: $12.95 adults, $10.55 seniors, $6.95 children 4–11, free for children under 4.

Open: Sun–Thurs 9am–7pm, Fri–Sat 9am–8pm. **Directions:** From either the Santa Ana Freeway (I-5) or the Riverside Freeway (Calif. 91), take the Beach Boulevard exit south straight to the museum. Parking is free.

Richard Nixon Library and Birthplace, 18001 Yorba Linda Blvd., Yorba Linda. ☎ **714/993-5075.** Fax 714/528-0544.

There has always been a warm place in the hearts of Orange County locals for Richard Nixon, the most vilified U.S. president in modern history. This presidential library, located in Nixon's boyhood town, celebrates the roots, life, and legacy of America's 37th president. The nine-acre site contains the actual modest farmhouse where Nixon was born, manicured flower gardens, and a modern museum containing presidential archives.

Displays include videos of the famous Nixon-Kennedy TV debates, a statuary summit of world leaders, gifts of state, and exhibits on China, Russia, and Vietnam. There's also an exhibit of the late Pat Nixon's sparkling First Lady gowns. There's a 12-foot-high chunk of the Berlin Wall symbolizing the defeat of Communism yet hardly a mention of Nixon's leading role in the anti-Communist McCarthy "witch hunts." There are exhibits on Vietnam yet no mention of Nixon's illegal expansion of that war into neighboring Cambodia. Only the Watergate Gallery is relatively forthright, where visitors can listen to actual White House tapes and view a montage of the president's last day in the White House. Rotating exhibits include never-before-displayed photographs and Nixonalia that illuminate this controversial president's private and public life.

On April 27, 1994, former President Nixon was buried here beside his wife, Pat, who died in 1993.

Admission: $4.95 adults, $2.95 seniors, $1 children 8–11; children under 8 free.

Open: Mon–Sat 10am–5pm, Sun 11am–5pm. **Directions:** From Los Angeles, take I-5 south to Calif. 91 east; exit north onto Calif. 57, then turn east onto Yorba Linda Boulevard to the museum.

Where to Stay

EXPENSIVE

Disneyland Hotel, 1150 W. Cerritos Ave., Anaheim, CA 92802. ☎ **714/778-6600.** Fax 714/965-6597. 1,131 rms, 62 suites. A/C MINIBAR TV TEL **Directions:** From I-5, exit south onto Harbor Boulevard, turn right onto Katella Avenue, pass the Disneyland parking lot, and turn right onto West Street; the hotel is ahead on your left, at Cerritos Avenue.

Rates: $140–$220 single; $150–$240 double; from $425 suite. AE, MC, V. **Parking:** $10.

The "Official Hotel of the Magic Kingdom" offers its guests the most convenient transportation to the park via a monorail system that runs right through the hotel. Located on 60 attractively landscaped acres, the hotel offers six restaurants, five cocktail lounges, 20 shops and boutiques, every kind of service desk imaginable, a "wharfside" bazaar, a walk-under waterfall, three pools, and 10 night-lit tennis courts. An artificial white-sand beach is also adjacent to the hotel.

The rooms are not fancy, but they are comfortable and attractively furnished with king-size beds, table, and chairs. Many rooms feature framed reproductions of rare Disneyland conceptual art; no-smoking rooms are available.

MODERATE

Howard Johnson Motor Lodge, 1380 S. Harbor Blvd., Anaheim, CA 92802. ☎ **714/776-6120,** or toll free **800/654-2000.** Fax 714/533-3578. 313 rms, 6 suites. A/C TV TEL

Directions: From I-5, exit onto Harbor Boulevard south.

Rates: $60–$80 single or doubles; $95 minisuite; $145 two-room suite. Children under 18 stay free in parents' room. AE, CB, DC, DISC, MC, V. **Parking:** Free.

In a six-acre parklike setting, this relatively elegant building was designed in a contemporary style by award-winning architect W. L. Pereira. Almost like a resort, it's located just opposite Disneyland. Roofed balconies open onto a central garden with two heated pools for adults and one for children. Garden paths lead under eucalyptus and olive trees to a splashing circular fountain. During the summer, you can watch the nightly fireworks display at Disneyland from the upper balconies.

Rooms, some offering Disney views, are equipped with large color TVs showing in-room movies and coffee/tea-making facilities. Services and facilities include a game room, a car-rental desk, room service, self-service laundry facilities, and babysitting for $8 per hour (four-hour minimum).

There's a Howard Johnson's restaurant on the premises, open around the clock and serving all the famous flavors. A bar/lounge adjoins.

Sheraton-Anaheim Hotel, 1015 W. Ball Rd., Anaheim, CA 92802. ☎ **714/778-1700,** or toll free **800/325-3535.** Fax 714/535-3889. 500 rms, 31 suites. A/C MINIBAR TV TEL

Directions: From I-5 north, exit onto Ball Road west; the hotel is on your right as you reach the top of the ramp.

Rates: $95–$135 single; $100–$145 double; from $150 suite. Children 17 and under stay free in parents' room. AE, CB, DC, MC, V. **Parking:** Free.

Looking very much like an English Tudor castle, the Sheraton-Anaheim rises to the festive theme-park occasion with an unusual architectural design and unique public facilities that include a 24-hour restaurant, lobby lounge/bar, California-style delicatessen, and free shuttle service to and from Disneyland and the airport.

Rooms are completely modern and outfitted with separate dressing rooms, color TVs, and radios; some also have refrigerators. No-smoking rooms are available. The hotel is adequate, but it's clear that guests are really paying for the location—just blocks from Disneyland.

INEXPENSIVE

Farm de Ville, 7800 and 7878 Crescent Ave., Buena Park, CA 90620. ☎ **714/527-2201.** Fax 714/826-3826. 130 rms. A/C TV TEL

Directions: From I-5, exit onto Beach Boulevard south; after about two miles, turn right onto Crescent Avenue to the hotel.

Rates: $35 single; $40 double (additional person $4 extra); units for four to six $80. AE, MC, V. **Parking:** Free.

Although it's just a motel, the Farm de Ville has a lot to offer. It's located close to Knott's Berry Farm's south entrance and is convenient to all the nearby attractions, including Disneyland (just 10 minutes away).

Although they're not immaculately clean, the rooms are spacious and well furnished; each has a radio, dressing area, and individually controlled heat and air-conditioning. Facilities include two pools, two wading pools for kids, two saunas, and a coin-op laundry.

Fullerton Hacienda AYH Hostel, 1700 N. Harbor Blvd., Fullerton, CA 92635. ☎ **714/738-3721.** Fax 714/738-0925. 24 beds. **Directions:** From I-5 south, take Calif. 91 east and exit onto Harbor Boulevard north (the second Harbor Boulevard exit); continue for half a mile past Brea Avenue; the hostel is located in the park on your right; look for the park entrance.

Rates: $14 for AYH/IYHF members, $17 for nonmembers. MC, V. **Parking:** Free.

Just outside Anaheim is this ultimate in economy near Disneyland and Knott's Berry Farm. It's located on the site of an old dairy farm, surrounded by greenery (including lemon trees), rabbits, squirrels—and other country life. The sparse accommodations are comfortable, and the manager is congenial and helpful. The hostel provides complete kitchen and bathroom facilities. It operates under a cooperative arrangement: You're expected to clean up after yourself, and leave the hostel tidy. The maximum stay is three consecutive days in the summer, five days the rest of the year. Smoking is not allowed, and the hostel closes at 11pm; guests are given keys for late returns.

Motel 6, 921 S. Beach Blvd., Anaheim, CA 92804. ☎ **714/220-2866.** 55 rms. A/C TV TEL **Directions:** From I-5 south, exit at Beach Boulevard and turn right; the motel is located about five miles ahead on your right, just before Ball Road.

Rates: $35 per room (up to four adults). AE, MC, V. **Parking:** Free.

Happily, this well-placed and priced Motel 6 is close to both Disneyland and Knott's Berry Farm, between Ball Road and Calif. 91. It's easy on the budget, clean, efficient, and comfortable. There are a pool and satellite TV.

Where to Dine

Neither Anaheim nor Buena Park is famous for its restaurants. If you're visiting the area just for the day, you'll probably eat inside the theme parks; there are plenty of restaurants—in all price ranges—to choose from at both Disneyland and Knott's Berry Farm. For the most unusual dinner you've ever had with the kids, see Medieval Times (see "What to See and Do," above).

Mr. Stox, 1105 E. Katella Ave., Anaheim. ☎ 714/634-2994.
  Cuisine: AMERICAN. **Reservations:** Not required. **Directions:** From I-5, exit onto Harbor Boulevard south and turn left onto Katella Avenue to the restaurant.
  Prices: Appetizers $5–$10; main courses $10–$25. AE, DC, MC, V.
  Open: Lunch Mon–Fri 11am–2:30pm; dinner Mon–Sat 5:30–10pm, Sun 5–9pm.

Hearty steaks and fresh seafood are served in an early California setting. Hot main-dish specialties include roast prime rib of beef au jus and mesquite-broiled fish, veal, and lamb; sandwiches and salads are also available. Homemade desserts such as chocolate-mousse cake are unexpectedly good. Mr. Stox has an enormous wine cellar, and there's live entertainment every night.

Peppers Restaurant, 12361 Chapman Ave., Garden Grove.
  ☎ 714/740-1333.
  Cuisine: CALIFORNIA/MEXICAN. **Reservations:** Not required. **Directions:** From I-5, exit south onto Harbor Boulevard and turn left onto Chapman Avenue to the restaurant.
  Prices: Appetizers $3–$7; main courses $9–$14. AE, CB, DC, DISC, MC, V.
  Open: Lunch Mon–Fri 11am–3pm; dinner daily 5:30–10pm; brunch Sun 10am–3pm.

Located just south of Disneyland, this colorful California/Mexican-themed restaurant features mesquite-broiled "Norteno" cuisine and fresh seafood daily. Mexican specialties include all types of tacos and burritos, but the grilled meats and fish are best. Dancing is available nightly to Top 40 hits, starting at 8pm, and there's a free shuttle to and from the area hotels.

---

3   Newport Beach & Laguna Beach

30 miles SE of downtown Los Angeles

GETTING THERE • By Plane   Los Angeles International Airport (LAX) is located approximately 35 miles northwest of Newport, along the Pacific Coast Highway (Calif. 1). John Wayne International Airport, in Irvine, is only about a mile from Newport Beach on the Newport Freeway (Calif. 55).

• By Train   The nearest Amtrak (☎ toll free **800/USA-RAIL**) station is located at 26701 Verdugo St. in San Juan Capistrano, about 15 miles from Newport Beach. Trains travel both north and south between Los Angeles and San Diego. Call for fare and schedule information.

• By Bus   Greyhound/Trailways (☎ toll free **800/231-2222**) can get you here from anywhere.

• By Car   From Los Angeles, take I-5 or I-405 south. Exit south onto the Newport Freeway (Calif. 55), and continue to the end in Newport Beach. It's about a one-hour drive from downtown Los Angeles.

ESSENTIALS • Orientation　Newport Beach encompasses several islands and peninsulas, as well as a good-sized swath of mainland. Balboa Island and Lido Isle are the two largest, though each is only 10 to 20 blocks long and only 3 or 4 blocks wide. The islands are situated in a gentle harbor, protected by the giant Lido Peninsula that reaches out from the mainland like a gnarled finger.

• Information　The **Newport Beach Conference and Visitors Bureau,** 366 San Miguel, Suite 200, Newport Beach, CA 92660 (☎ **714/644-1190,** or toll free **800/94-COAST**), distributes the requisite maps, brochures, and information. Write for a free visitor's package.

Like a jigsaw puzzle of islands and peninsulas, Newport Beach is a major southern California recreational resort. Once a cattle ranch above an uncharted estuary, Newport is now a busy harbor that embraces the delightful peninsula/island town. The phenomenal growth of hotel and restaurant facilities in the last few years indicates that Newport Beach is fast becoming one of southern California's most popular coastal towns. It's an excellent vacation base from which to explore other coastal beaches, as well as sights in Anaheim and Buena Park.

Laguna Beach, just south of Newport, is smaller, more charming, and somewhat quieter than its neighbor. Especially on weekends, the town is packed with tourists attracted by beautiful beaches, terrific shops, top-of-the-line accommodations, and great restaurants. July and August are Laguna's brightest months, when a world-famous **Festival of the Arts** (☎ 714/494-1145) takes over the town. The **Pageant of the Masters** (☎ **714/497-6582,** or toll free **800/487-3378**), in which live actors reenact famous artworks, such as Steuben's *Orpheus,* shouldn't be missed.

What to See & Do

Balboa Pavilion, 400 Main St., Balboa. ☎ **714/675-9444.**

Designated as a California Historical Landmark, Balboa Pavilion was built in 1905 and originally served as a bathhouse. Today, the cupola-topped structure is a major focus of activity. Restored to its original "waterfront Victorian" splendor, the pavilion serves as the Newport terminal for Catalina Island Passenger Service boats, harbor cruises, and whale-watching trips. It's also home to several restaurants and shops. For cruise and charter information, call **714/673-5245**; for sport-fishing information, call **714/673-1434.**

You can also ferry from here to Balboa Island, across the small bay. Rides cost 90¢ for cars and 40¢ for each adult passenger. Ferry service is daily from 7am to 6:30pm.

Directions: From Calif. 1, turn south onto Newport Boulevard, which becomes Balboa Boulevard on the peninsula, and continue straight to the pavilion.

Fashion Island, Newport Beach. ☎ 714/721-2000.

One of the most successful malls in America, Fashion Island encompasses over 75 good-quality shops, including Mondi, Victoria's Secret, Benetton, Boxer Bay, Nautica, and Cole Haan. The sprawling complex—anchored by Neiman Marcus, I. Magnin, the Broadway, and Robinson's–May—includes a dozen restaurants and is surrounded by several luxury hotels.

Harbor Cruises, Catalina Passenger Service, Balboa Pavilion, 400 Main St., Balboa. ☎ 714/673-5245.

The best way to see Newport is from the bay. Several 45-minute narrated harbor cruises are offered daily. The boats pass the fancy homes that have made the area famous and the cruise guides provide passengers with good historical information on the area. Cruise times vary, so call for information.

Admission: Tickets, $6–$8 adults, $4 seniors, $1 children 5–11, free for children under 5.

Mission San Juan Capistrano, Ortega Hwy. (Calif. 74), San Juan Capistrano. ☎ 714/248-2049.

The "miracle" of the swallows of Capistrano takes place each year on March 19, St. Joseph's Day. According to legend, the little birds wing their way back to this mission annually, arriving here at dawn.

The 7th in California's chain of 21 missions, San Juan Capistrano is the state's most tourist-oriented. Full of small museums and various stone rooms that are as quaint as they are interesting, the mission is a mix of old ruins and working buildings. Outdoor excavations reveal original 18th-century floorings, while the intimate mission chapel is still regularly used for religious services.

The swallows are said to take flight again on October 23, after bidding the mission "farewell." In reality, however, you can probably see the well-fed birds here any day of the week, winter or summer.

Admission: $4.

Open: Daily 8:30am–5pm. **Closed:** Thanksgiving, Christmas.

Newport Harbor Art Museum, 850 San Clemente Dr. ☎ 714/759-1122.

The museum presents varying exhibitions of 20th-century works of art. The emphasis here is on California paintings, sculpture, installations, and photographs. Note that the galleries are closed between exhibitions; call for the current schedule before heading out.

Admission: $4 adults, $2 students 12–17 and seniors (aged 65 and over), free for children under 12.

Open: Tues–Sun 10am–5pm. **Directions:** From Calif. 1, turn left onto Newport Center Drive and bear left around the oval to Santa Barbara Drive; take the next right onto San Clemente Drive to the museum.

Where to Stay

EXPENSIVE

Doryman's Inn Bed & Breakfast, 2102 W. Ocean Front, Newport Beach, CA 92663. ☎ **714/675-7300.** 8 rms, 2 suites. A/C TV TEL
Rates (including breakfast): $135–$230 single or double; from $185 suite. AE, MC, V.

Doryman's opulent rooms combine luxury with romance, making it one of the nicest bed-and-breakfasts to be found anywhere. Rooms are outfitted with French and American antiques, floral draperies and spreads, beveled mirrors, and cozy furnishings. In every room are working fireplaces and sunken marble tubs, some fitted with Jacuzzi jets. King- or queen-size beds, lots of plants, and good ocean views round out the decor.

Doryman's location, directly on the Newport Beach Pier Promenade, is also enviable, though some may find it a bit too close to the action. Breakfast, served in a charming dining room, includes fresh pastries and fruit, brown eggs, yogurt, cheeses, and international coffees and teas.

Four Seasons Hotel Newport Beach, 690 Newport Center Dr., Newport Beach, CA 92660. ☎ **714/759-0808,** or toll free **800/332-3442.** Fax 714/760-8073. 221 rms, 64 suites. A/C MINIBAR TV TEL
Rates: $195–$235 single; $225–$265 double; from $295 suite. Children under 18 stay free in parents' room. Additional person $30 extra. AE, DC, MC, V.

Polished and professional, this member of the world-class Four Seasons group gets high marks for its comprehensive facilities. Rooms, conservatively designed in unoffensive beiges, contain firm beds, terry-cloth bathrobes, oversize closets, and marble baths. Most rooms have small balconies, though the Newport skyline is nothing special to look at. The impeccable service means intense attention to details, butlers on 24-hour call, and high-quality furnishings and food.

The hotel is expensive and attractive to both the old-money crowd and the nouveau riche. Because of their larger size, rooms with two double beds are the hotel's best value. Guests are encouraged to bring their pets, and doggie biscuits and dog food are always available.

Dining/Entertainment: The Pavilion Restaurant, serving French/California cuisine, is popular with locals at lunch. The poolside Cabana Cafe enjoys a nice garden setting, and afternoon tea and evening cocktails are served in the lobby-level Conservatory Lounge.

Services: 24-hour room service, concierge, evening turndown, complimentary transportation from Orange County Airport, overnight laundry and shoeshine.

Facilities: Pool, whirlpool, fitness club, two lighted tennis courts, business center, gift shop.

★ **Hyatt Newporter,** 1107 Jamboree Rd., Newport Beach, CA 92660. ☎ **714/729-1234,** or toll free **800/233-1234.** Fax 714/644-1552. 386 rms, 20 suites, 4 villas. A/C TV TEL

Directions: From Calif. 1, exit north onto Jamboree Road; the hotel is just ahead on your right, near Backbay Drive.

Rates: $139–$170 single; $164–$195 double; from $300 suite. AE, CB, DC, DISC, MC, V. **Parking:** Free.

Located on 26 landscaped acres, the Hyatt Newporter is a resort complex par excellence, an important hub of activity in this beach town. The John Wayne Tennis Club is on the premises—a top facility that includes 16 championship courts (all lit for night play), spa equipment, a steam/sauna, and a clubhouse. In addition, the hotel boasts a nine-hole, par-three golf course, three heated Olympic-size pools, three whirlpools, and a children's pool, as well as a fitness room and volleyball court; also available are shuffleboard, Ping-Pong, jogging trails, and much more.

The rooms, decorated in pastel tones, have contemporary furnishings, marble baths, and deluxe amenities. All have balconies or terraces with a view of the back bay, gardens, or golf course.

In addition to offering an attractive view of the back bay, the three-bedroom villas have a separate living and dining area, fireplace, and access to a private swimming pool.

Dining/Entertainment: Three meals a day are offered in the Jamboree Cafe, a casual California-style eatery. Dinner is served in both Ristorante Cantori, a northern Italian dining room, and in the award-winning gourmet room—The Wine Cellar—the hotel's flagship restaurant.

Services: Room service, concierge, evening turndown.

Facilities: 16 lighted tennis courts nine-hole golf course, three heated pools, three whirlpools, health spa, tour desk, car rental, gift shop, beauty salon.

Newport Beach Marriott Hotel and Tennis Club, 900

Newport Center Dr., Newport Beach, CA 92660.
☎ **714/640-4000,** or toll free **800/228-9290.** Fax 714/640-5055.
586 rms. A/C TV TEL **Directions:** From Calif. 1, turn left onto Newport Center Drive and continue straight to the hotel.

Rates: $139–$149 single; $139–$169 double. AE, CB, DC, DISC, MC, V. **Parking:** $6.

This 15-story hotel was built around a 9-story atrium and a large 19th-century Italian Renaissance-style fountain; it's a clever design. Most of the guest rooms, all strikingly decorated with cheerful drapes and spreads, offer ocean views. In addition to the usual amenities, each room is equipped with a radio, individual climate controls, and an iron and ironing board.

Two swimming and hydrotherapy pools are surrounded by a palm-lined sun deck. Eight tennis courts (all lit at night) are complemented by a well-stocked pro shop and snack bar. There's also a good health club, and golfing is available next door at the Newport Beach Country Club's 18-hole course.

Dining/Entertainment: J.W.'s California Grill is a pleasant and cheerful indoor/outdoor restaurant serving fresh seafood and American favorites.

Services: Room service, concierge, evening turndown.

Facilities: Two pools, eight lighted tennis courts, health club, pro shop, off-premises golf course, tour desk, car rental.

Surf & Sand Hotel, 1555 S. Coast Hwy., Laguna Beach, CA 92651. ☎ **714/497-4477,** or toll free **800/524-8621.** 155 rms, 2 penthouses. MINIBAR TV TEL **Directions:** From Los Angeles, take I-5 to the Laguna Canyon off-ramp and head west to the ocean; turn south on South Coast Highway and the hotel will be on your right.

Rates: Oct–Apr, $160–$245 single or double; from $375 penthouse. May–Sept, $200–$295 single or double; from $475 penthouse. Additional person $10 extra. AE, CB, DC, DISC, MC.

What is today the best hotel in Laguna Beach started in 1937 as a modest little hotel with just 13 units. The Surf and Sand has come a long way. Still occupying the same fantastic oceanside location, the hotel now features dozens of top-of-the-line luxurious rooms that, despite their standard size, feel enormously decadent. Decorated in white—from walls to linens to furnishings—the rooms are very bright and beachy. Purposeful architecture ensures that every room gets an oceanfront view. All have private balconies, marble baths, robes, in-room safes, and radio alarm clocks; some have whirlpool tubs. Try to get a deluxe corner room.

Dining/Entertainment: Splashes Restaurant (see "Where to Dine," below) serves three meals daily in a beautiful oceanfront setting. The green-and-black Towers Restaurant, located on the hotel's ninth floor, offers contemporary northern Italian cuisine. Because the windows don't open, a sound system was installed to pipe in the sounds of the surf below. It's open for dinner nightly from 5:30pm.

Services: Room service, concierge, overnight laundry/dry cleaning, complimentary morning newspaper, evening turndown.

Facilities: Heated pool, gift shop, hair salon, boutique.

MODERATE

Laguna Riviera on the Beach, 825 S. Coast Hwy., Laguna Beach, CA 92651. ☎ 714/494-1196. Fax 714/494-8421. 41 rms. TV TEL **Directions:** From Los Angeles, take I-5 to the Laguna Canyon off-ramp, head west to the ocean, and turn south on South Coast Highway; the hotel will be on your right, at the corner of St. Ann's Drive.

Rates (including continental breakfast): Sept 12–June 12, $63–$93 single or double, $90–$149 oceanfront single or double. June 13–Sept 11, $72–$123 single or double, $115–$170 oceanfront single or double. MC, V.

What makes Laguna so special are the cliffs that drop straight down to the beach. This two-story pink-and-green motel takes full advantage of its clifftop site, offering terrific views from each of its unobstructed oceanfront rooms. Large decks gulp in the views, and an onshore breeze always seems to blow. The Riviera is a truly magical place to fall asleep listening to ocean waves that are literally a skipping-stone's throw away.

Don't be misled: The hotel's guest rooms are rather plain. Certainly they're no match for the views, as evidenced by the hotel's own motto: "You cannot be both grand and comfortable." But if you're looking for well-priced, down-to-earth accommodations within walking distance of downtown Laguna Beach, the oceanfront rooms at the Riviera are my highest recommendation; rooms without a view are another matter entirely.

Vacation Village, 647 S. Coast Hwy., Laguna Beach, CA 92651. ☎ **714/494-8566,** or toll free **800/843-6895.** Fax 714/494-1386. 100 rms, 38 suites. TV

Rates: $80–$195 single or double; from $205 suite. AE, CB, DC, DISC, MC, V.

Vacation Village has something for everyone. A cluster of seven oceanfront and near-the-ocean three- to five-story motels includes rooms, studios, suites, and apartments. Most of the accommodations are standard motel fare: bed, TV, table, basic bath. The best rooms are oceanfront in a four-story structure overlooking the Village's private beach. Umbrellas and back rests for beachgoers are available in summer. The Vacation Village Restaurant serves meals, cocktails, and refreshments all day. Facilities include a private beach, two pools, and a whirlpool.

Where to Dine

EXPENSIVE

Chanteclair, 18912 MacArthur Blvd., Irvine. ☎ **714/752-8001.**

Cuisine: CONTINENTAL. **Reservations:** Recommended. **Directions:** From Newport Beach, take the Newport Freeway (Calif. 55) north one mile to San Diego Freeway (I-405) east and go just one exit to MacArthur Boulevard south; the restaurant is straight ahead opposite the Airport Terminal, between Campus and Douglas Drives.

Prices: Appetizers $5–$13; main courses $14–$25. AE, CB, DC, MC, V. **Open:** Lunch Mon–Fri 11:30am–2:30pm; dinner Mon–Sat 5:30–11pm; brunch Sun 10:30am–2:30pm.

Chanteclair is expensive and a little difficult to reach, but it's included here because of its excellence. The restaurant is designed in the style of a provincial French inn. The rambling stucco structure, built around a central garden court, houses several dining and drinking areas: a grand and petit salon, a boudoir, a bibliothèque, a garden area with a skylight roof, and a hunting lodge–like lounge. Furnished in antiques, it has five fireplaces.

At lunch you might order grilled lamb chops with herb-and-garlic sauce, chicken-and-mushroom crêpes, or Cajun chard ahi. Dinner is a worthwhile splurge that might begin with a lobster bisque with brandy or Beluga caviar with blinis. For a main dish I recommend the rack of lamb with thyme sauce and roasted garlic. The captain will be happy to help you choose from the considerable selection of domestic and imported wines.

Five Feet Restaurant, 328 Glenneyre, Laguna Beach.
☎ 714/497-4955.

Cuisine: CALIFORNIAN/ASIAN. **Reservations:** Recommended.
Prices: Appetizers $5–$10; main courses $14–$24. AE, MC.
Open: Lunch Fri only, 11:30am–2:30pm; dinner Sun–Thurs 5–10pm,
Fri–Sat 5–11pm.

If the atmosphere were as good as the food, Five Feet would be one
of the best restaurants in California. Chef/proprietor Michael Kang
has created one of the country's most innovative and interesting restaurants, combining the best in California cuisine with Asian tech-
nique and ingredients. Outstanding appetizers include spicy Chinese
shrimp ravioli, goat-cheese wontons with raspberry coulis, and salad
of foie gras and pear with truffle vinaigrette. Main courses run the
gamut from tea-smoked filet mignon topped with Roquefort cheese
and candied walnuts to a hot Thai-style mixed grill of veal, beef, lamb,
and chicken stir-fried with sweet peppers, onions, and mushrooms
in curry-mint sauce.

Unfortunately, the dining room's gray-concrete walls are not much
to look at, and the exposed vents on an airplane hanger–size wooden
ceiling just look unfinished, not trendy industrial. Aging metal chairs,
and unspectacular faux-marble tables complete the decor, which is
only brightened by an exceedingly friendly staff and truly unparalleled food.

Marrakesh, 1100 W. Coast Hwy., Newport Beach. ☎ 714/645-8384.
Cuisine: MOROCCAN. **Reservations:** Recommended. **Directions:**
From Newport Boulevard, turn east onto the Pacific Coast Highway (Calif.
1); the restaurant is directly ahead, near Dover Drive.
Prices: Appetizers $6–$8; main courses $16–$22. AE, CB, DC, MC, V.
Open: Dinner only, Sun–Thurs 5–10pm, Fri–Sat 5–11pm.

The decor is exotic, with dining areas divided into intimate tents
furnished with Persian carpets, low cushioned sofas, and authentic
Moroccan works of art.

Dinners here are something of a ritual feast that begins when a
server comes around to wash your hands. Everyone in your party
shares the same meal—an eight- or nine-course feast that's eaten with
your hands. Meals start with Moroccan soup and a tangy salad that's
scooped up with hunks of fresh bread. Next comes b'stila, a
chicken-filled pastry topped with cinnamon; or kotban, a lamb shish
kebab marinated in olive oil, coriander, cumin, and garlic. Main-dish
choices are squab with rice and almonds, chicken with lemon and
olives, fish in a piquant sauce, and rabbit in garlic sauce. Leave room
for the next course of lamb and vegetables with couscous, followed
by fresh fruits, tea, and Moroccan pastries.

Splashes Restaurant and Bar, in the Surf and Sand Hotel,
1555 S. Coast Hwy., Laguna Beach. ☎ 714/497-4477.
Cuisine: MEDITERRANEAN. **Reservations:** Accepted only for dinner.
Prices: Appetizers $5–$9; main courses $16–$22; lunch $8–$12. DC,
DISC, MC, V.
Open: Daily 7am–10pm.

Almost directly on the surf, this light and bright southwestern-style restaurant basks in sunlight and the calming crash of the waves. Floor-to-ceiling windows maximize this view, and good food completes the stimulation of the senses. Splashes is truly stunning.

In addition to the usual eggs and pastries, breakfasts include huevos rancheros and homemade duck hash. Lunch might offer crab cakes, eggplant cannelloni, and pizzas topped with shrimp, spinach, roasted peppers, and Fontina cheese. At dinner, a basket of fresh-baked crusty bread prefaces a long list of appetizers that might include wild-mushroom ravioli with lobster sauce or sautéed Louisiana shrimp with red chiles and lemon. Gourmet pizzas also make great starters and are topped with interesting combinations like grilled lamb, roasted fennel, artichokes, mushrooms, and feta cheese. Main courses change daily and might offer baked striped bass, roasted and braised duck with red wine, or risotto with vegetable-and-cheese ratatouille.

21 Oceanfront, at McFadden's Landing, 2100 W. Oceanfront, Newport Beach. ☎ 714/675-2566.

Cuisine: SEAFOOD. **Reservations:** Recommended.
Prices: Appetizers $5–$6; main courses $16–$24. MC, V.
Open: Dinner only, daily 4–11pm.

If it weren't for the windows overlooking Newport Pier, you'd hardly know that you're at the beach at this dark, clubby restaurant with turn-of-the-century decor. Occupying the second floor of a historic building, the dining room has an upscale New Orleans feel, with a mirrored black-and-purple decor that includes a cloth-covered ceiling, candlelit tables, and semicircular leatherette booths.

A truly terrific wine list compliments thoroughly American dishes like Maryland softshell crab, rack of lamb, grilled abalone, Porterhouse steaks, bouillabaisse, and swordfish. Meals are well prepared and attractively presented. Get dessert elsewhere, then walk it all off on the promenade and pier.

MODERATE

The Cannery, 3010 Lafayette Ave., Newport Beach.
☎ 714/675-5777.

Cuisine: SEAFOOD. **Reservations:** Recommended. **Directions:** From Calif. 1, turn south onto Newport Boulevard and, after you cross the bridge, turn left onto 31st Street; the restaurant is directly ahead, at Lafayette Avenue.
Prices: Appetizers $5–$7; main courses $12–$20; Sun brunch $9–$14. AE, CB, DC, MC, V.
Open: Lunch Mon–Sat 11:30am–3pm; dinner Mon–Sat 5–10pm, Sun 4:30–9pm; brunch Sun 10am–2:30pm.

The Cannery is housed in a remodeled 1934 fish cannery that used to turn out 5,000 cases of swordfish and mackerel a day. Now a historical landmark, the two-story restaurant is a favorite among locals and tourists alike—for good food, a colorful atmosphere, and friendly service. In the upper lounge, tables surround a corner platform where there's live entertainment every Thursday evening and Sunday afternoon.

Fresh fish and local abalone are specialties here. At dinner there's always a super-fresh chef's catch of the day. Other good choices are prime rib, chicken, and pasta dishes. At lunch you might ask for shrimp and fries, or sandwiches and salads.

The restaurant also serves a champagne buffet brunch while you cruise Newport Harbor aboard the Cannery's *Isla Mujeres;* the cost is $30. Call for information and reservations.

Rockin' Baja Lobster, at the Newport Beach pier, 2104 W. Ocean-front, Newport Beach. ☎ 714/723-0606.

> **Cuisine:** MEXICAN/SEAFOOD. **Reservations:** Not accepted.
> **Prices:** Appetizers $4–$10; main courses $9–$13; lunch $6–$11. AE, DISC, MC, V.
> **Open:** Sun–Thurs 10am–11pm, Fri–Sat 10am–1am.

A "margarita Mexican" joint, Baja Lobster is a fun, touristy restaurant that's especially popular during lunch and afternoon happy hours. Most of the dishes are deep-fried, including the signature Baja Bucket, a mountain of seasoned lobster tails served with Caesar salad, beans, rice, and tortillas. Pastas and burgers are also offered, as well as tacos, fajitas, and seafood-stuffed chiles rellenos.

4   Palm Springs

103 miles E of Los Angeles, 135 miles NE of San Diego

GETTING THERE • By Plane   Several airlines service the Palm Springs Municipal Airport, 3400 E. Tahquitz-McCallum Way (☎ 619/323-8161), including Alaska Airlines, America West, American, Delta, Skywest, TWA, United, and USAir. Flights from Los Angeles International Airport take about 40 minutes.

• By Bus   Greyhound/Trailways (☎ toll free 800/231-2222) can get you here from anywhere. The central terminal is located at 311 N. Indian Ave. (☎ 619/325-2053).

• By Car   From I-10, take the Calif. 111 turnoff to Palm Springs. You drive into town on East Palm Canyon Drive, the main thoroughfare. The trip from downtown Los Angeles takes about 2¹/₂ hours.

ESSENTIALS • Orientation   The downtown area of Palm Springs stretches about half a mile along Palm Canyon Drive, a wide storefront-lined boulevard of restaurants, clothing stores, and hotels. The mountains lie directly west, while the rest of Palm Springs is laid out in a grid to the east. Tahquitz-McCallum Way, a street as wide as Palm Canyon Drive, creates the town's primary intersection and runs through the heart of downtown.

• Information   The **Palm Springs Desert Resorts Convention and Visitors Bureau,** in the Atrium Design Centre, 69-930 Calif. 111, Suite 201, Rancho Mirage, CA 92270 (☎ 619/770-9000, or toll free 800/417-3529), offers maps, brochures, and advice. It's open Monday through Friday from 8:30am to 5pm.

Palm Springs

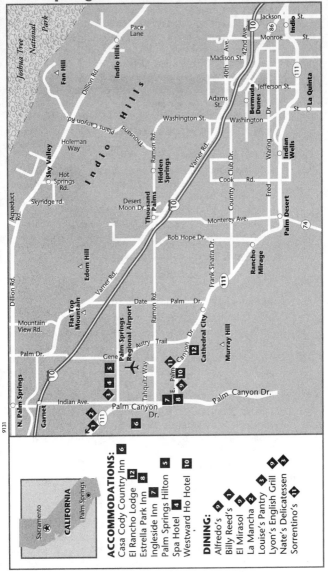

ACCOMMODATIONS:
Casa Cody Country Inn 6
El Rancho Lodge 12
Estrella Park Inn 8
Ingleside Inn 7
Palm Springs Hilton 5
Spa Hotel 4
Westward Ho Hotel 10

DINING:
Alfredo's 9
Billy Reed's 1
El Mirasol 9
La Mancha 2
Louise's Pantry 3
Lyon's English Grill 9
Nate's Delicatessen 9
Sorrentino's 11

The **Palm Springs Chamber of Commerce,** 190 W. Amado Rd.,
at the corner of Belardo Road (☎ **619/325-1577**), offers similar
information as well as hotel reservations. The office, near the heart
of town, is open Monday through Friday from 8:30am to 4:30pm.

The self-proclaimed golf, tennis, and swimming pool capital of the world, Palm Springs is the traditional playground of the tasteless rich whose primary residences are often in Los Angeles. Famous residents include the Gabor sisters, Kirk Douglas, and Dean Martin. The honorary mayor is Bob Hope, and, until recently, the elected one was Sonny Bono (of Sonny and Cher fame).

The sun shines almost every day of the year here, which can make it extremely uncomfortable during summer, when temperatures regularly reach into the 100s. Palm Springs, designed with the rich in mind, was intended as a respite from L.A. winters. Hotel prices and availability are closely related to the seasons; in the middle of summer even the best accommodations can be had for a song.

A large number of golf tournaments are regularly held here, including the Bob Hope Desert Classic and the Nabisco Dinah Shore Invitational. The town has more than 300 tennis courts, 42 golf courses (although only seven 18-hole courses are public; the average greens fees are $50), and more than 7,000 swimming pools—one for every five residents!

What to See & Do

Palm Springs is a resort community, so there isn't much to do aside from sunning, swimming, dining, playing, and relaxing.

Indian Canyons, S. Palm Canyon Dr., Palm Springs.
☎ **619/325-5673.**

Located on Native American–owned lands, the canyons are full of hiking trails through Palm, Andreas, and Murray Canyons. If you're able to do some light hiking, the canyons offer visitors some of the best natural sights in the area. You'll walk through palm groves, see desert plants and animals, encounter a trading post, and even visit a waterfall with picnic tables nearby. When writing for information, address your letters to A.C.B.C.I., 110 N. Indian Ave., Palm Springs, CA 92262. The canyons are closed from June to September.

Admission: $5 adults, $3.50 students, $2.50 seniors (62 and over) $1 children.

Open: Daily 8am–5pm.

Palm Springs Aerial Tramway, Tramway Rd.–Chino Canyon, Palm Springs. ☎ **619/325-1391.**

To gain a bird's-eye perspective on the town, take a ride on the Aerial Tramway, which ascends $2^{1}/_{2}$ miles up the slopes of Mount San Jacinto. You'll travel from the desert floor to cool alpine heights in less than 20 minutes; in winter the change is dramatic, from warm desert to deep snowdrifts. There's a cafeteria at the top, as well as a cocktail lounge, gift shop, and picnic area. It's also the starting point for 54 miles of hiking trails dotted with campgrounds. A special ride 'n' dine combination includes a sunset dinner at the Alpine Restaurant and costs only $3 more than the ride alone—a great bargain.

Admission: $16 adults, $10 children 5–12, children under 5 free; ride 'n' dine $19 adults, $12.95 children.

Open: Mon–Fri 10am–8pm, Sat–Sun 8am–8pm; 1 hour later during daylight saving time.

ORGANIZED TOURS

Palm Springs Celebrity Tours, 333 N. Palm Canyon Dr., Suite 113A, Palm Springs (☎ **619/325-2682**), has been around since 1963. Their professional guides know all the ins and outs of Palm Springs and specialize in personal tours and small groups; their air-conditioned deluxe coaches seat up to only 14.

The 1- and 2¹/₂-hour tours provide a comprehensive look at Palm Springs, including the homes of certain movie stars and celebrities. The longer excursion includes everything you'd see during the shorter tour plus the estates of Frank Sinatra and businessman Walter Annenberg, who has his own golf course. You'll also see the Tamarisk, Canyon, and Thunderbird country clubs, where the international elite meet to play. Then it's on to the Eisenhower Medical Center and beautiful date groves, with a brief stop for refreshments.

The 1-hour tour meets at the office at the above address. For the 2¹/₂-hour excursion, Celebrity Tours will pick you up at any hotel in Palm Springs. Reservations are required and should be made at least a day or two in advance. Tours are conducted daily; call for departure times. The 1-hour tour costs $11 for adults, $10 for seniors, and $6 for children under 12; the 2¹/₂-hour tour is $16 for adults, $14 for seniors, and $8 for children under 12.

Where to Stay

EXPENSIVE

Ingleside Inn, 200 W. Ramon Rd., Palm Springs, CA 92264. ☎ **619/325-0046**, or toll free **800/772-6655.** Fax 619/325-0710. 29 rms, 16 suites. A/C TV TEL

Rates (including continental breakfast): Oct–May, $95–$265 single or double; from $295 suite. June–Sept, $75–$235 single or double; from $225 suite. AE, DISC, MC, V. **Parking:** Free.

Some of the most charming rooms in town can be found at this 65-year-old hideaway estate. Each room and suite is uniquely decorated with antiques—perhaps a canopied bed or a 15th-century vestment chest. Many rooms have wood-burning fireplaces; all have in-room whirlpools, steambaths, and refrigerators stocked with complimentary light snacks and beverages. Once you pass the imposing wrought-iron gates, you leave the bustling world of the 20th century behind and enter an old-world era of luxurious relaxation and fine, unstuffy, remarkably friendly service.

If you decide to stay here, you'll join the ranks of Elizabeth Taylor, Howard Hughes, John Wayne, Bette Davis, Salvador Dalí, and Gary Cooper, all of whom have enjoyed these luxurious facilities at one time or another.

A major renovation was completed in the summer of 1990. The redecorated accommodations include new drapes, spreads, and upholstery. Three rooms were gutted and rebuilt to include totally secluded patios blessed with a magnificent view of the mountains, and with wood-burning fireplaces.

Dining/Entertainment: Melvyn's, one of Palm Springs's most prestigious "in" spots, is located downstairs, and definitely worth a visit even if you're not staying here. Frank and Barbara Sinatra hosted a dinner here on the eve of their wedding. The food is excellent, the celebrity-watching first-rate, and the decor lovely.

Services: Room service, concierge, massage, complimentary limousine service.

Facilities: Pool, Jacuzzi, croquet, shuffleboard, sundry boutiques, business center, tour desk, car rental.

Palm Springs Hilton, 400 E. Tahquitz Canyon Way, Palm Springs, CA 92262. ☎ 619/320-6868, or toll free 800/522-6900. Fax 619/320-2126. 260 rms, 71 suites. A/C MINIBAR TV TEL

Rates: Dec–May, $195–$225 single or double; from $265 suite. June–July 4 and Sept–Nov, $145–$175 single or double; from $205 suite. July 5–Aug, $90–$110 single or double; from $125 suite. Children under 17 stay free in parents' room. AE, CB, DC, DISC, MC, V. **Parking:** Free self-parking, $4 valet.

One of the town's most glittering resorts has the atmosphere of a busy country club. A large group-oriented hotel, the three-story Hilton blends into the natural environment and reflects the sand colors of the desert. The lobby, rooms, and restaurants are all contemporary and filled with original art, mostly contemporary serigraphs by David Weidman and sculptures by local artists.

Guest rooms—built around a central garden and swimming pool and decorated in soft earth tones—are large and residential in feel, with sitting areas and large window shutters. All rooms have patios or balconies, large baths with thermostatically regulated showers, brass fixtures, and individual temperature controls.

Dining/Entertainment: The Terrace Restaurant, overlooking the pool area, offers a continental cuisine at breakfast, lunch, and dinner daily. There's also a poolside dining facility for snacks, and Harvey's bar/lounge.

Services: Room service, concierge, complimentary airport transportation.

Facilities: Pool, two Jacuzzis, six tennis courts, pro shop, exercise room, tour desk, car rental, beauty salon, video game room.

Spa Hotel & Mineral Springs, 100 N. Indian Canyon Dr., Palm Springs, CA 92263. ☎ 619/325-1461, or toll free 800/854-1279. Fax 619/325-3344. 230 rms, 20 suites. A/C MINIBAR TV TEL

Rates (including continental breakfast): Jan–May, $105–$185, single or double. June–Sept, $55–$95 single or double. Oct–Dec, $95–$135 single or double. Year-round, from $125 suite. Additional person $20 extra. Various pampering packages are available. AE, CB, DC, MC, V. **Parking:** Free.

One of the unique choices in town is the only full-service "spa" resort. The site was formerly a shrine for Native American Cahuillas who claimed the springs had magical powers to cure illness. Modern Americans still make this claim and come here to pamper the body and soul by "taking the waters." There are three pools on the premises. One is a conventional outdoor swimming pool; the other two are filled from underground natural springs brimming with revitalizing minerals. There are an additional 30 indoor sunken Roman swirlpools, which are also fed from the springs.

The price of a guest room includes hot springs immersion, eucalyptus inhalation, sauna, cooling room, outdoor mineral pools, solarium, and gym. A variety of additional treatments are also available, including exercise classes, herbal wraps, herbal baths, loofah scrubs, salt glows, massages, and computerized body stretches.

Services: Evening turndown, massage, facials, manicures, pedicures, and other beauty treatments.

Facilities: Complete gym and spa, three lighted tennis courts.

MODERATE

Casa Cody Country Inn, 175 S. Cahuilla Rd., Palm Springs, CA 92262. ☎ **619/320-9346**, or toll free **800/231-2639.** Fax 619/325-8610. 17 rms, 7 suites. A/C TV TEL **Directions:** From Palm Canyon Drive, turn west on Tahquitz Canyon Way and take the second left onto Cahuilla Road to the inn.

Rates (including breakfast): Mid-Dec to Apr, $65–$175 single or double. May–June, $60–$160 single or double. July–Sept, $45–$105 single or double. Oct to mid-Dec, $60–$160 single or double. Oct–Apr, from $105 suite. May–Sept, from $75 suite. Additional person $10 extra. AE, MC, V. **Parking:** Free.

Originally built by Harriet Cody, a relative of Buffalo Bill Cody, the Casa Cody is a recently restored, very attractive inn peacefully nestled in the heart of Palm Springs at the base of the mountain. The hotel offers lovely, spacious, ground-level accommodations, most with wood-burning fireplaces and private patios. Elegant touches include saltillo tile floors, dhurri rugs, and original artwork; furnishings are in a comfortable Santa Fe style.

There are two swimming pools and a tree-shaded whirlpool spa. Services include complimentary poolside breakfast. Arrangements can be made for nearby tennis and golf, and access to a private health spa. Complimentary bicycles are available, and the Carl Lyken mountain trailhead is located within walking distance.

Estrella Park Inn, 415 S. Belardo Rd., Palm Springs, CA 92262. ☎ **619/320-4117.** Fax 619/323-3303. 37 rms, 27 cottages. A/C TV TEL **Directions:** From Palm Canyon Drive, turn west on Tahquitz Way, then left onto Belardo Road to the hotel.

Rates (including continental breakfast): Jan to mid-Apr, $110–$130 single or double; $160–$200 one-bedroom cottage; $185–$235 two-bedroom cottage. Mid-Apr to May and Oct–Dec, $95–$105 single or double; $135–$160 one-bedroom cottage; $160–$185 two-bedroom cottage. June–Sept, $79–$89 single or double; $119–$129 one-bedroom cottage; $129–$139 two-bedroom cottage. Monthly rates available. AE, DC, DISC, MC, V. **Parking:** Free.

One of the best moderately priced establishments, the Estrella Inn is located on a quiet, secluded street that seems to be miles from everywhere, even though it's just a block from the center of town. The rooms vary widely in size—from very small quarters to cottages with decks, wet bars, full kitchens, and fireplaces.

There are two swimming pools and a children's pool, two Jacuzzis, and a lawn and court games area. There's no restaurant, but the inn serves a complimentary continental breakfast every morning in the lobby lounge.

INEXPENSIVE

El Rancho Lodge, 1330 E. Palm Canyon Dr., Palm Springs, CA 92264. ☎ **619/327-1339.** 19 rms. A/C TV TEL

Rates (including continental breakfast): June–Sept, $40–$60 single or double. Oct–May, $56–$80 single or double. Monthly discounts available. AE, DISC, MC, V. **Parking:** Free.

Relatively small in size, El Rancho is most popular with guests over 50, which gives it a congenial community feeling. The rooms are simple but pleasantly furnished, spacious, and nicely maintained. They're all situated around a large heated pool and spa.

Most of the rooms have one king-size bed or two twin beds. Some of the larger rooms also have full kitchens and some have two full baths—a luxury rarely found even in pricey hotels.

Ironside Hotel, 310 E. Palm Canyon Dr., Palm Springs, CA 92262. ☎ **619/325-1995.** 6 rms. A/C TV TEL

Rates: $40–$70 single or double. AE, MC, V. **Parking:** Free.

Excellent rates and a good Palm Springs location are the main draws of this otherwise basic hotel. Each room here is very clean, with white furniture and contemporary floral prints. Rooms have either two double beds or one queen-size bed. Look for the small peach-colored hotel flying bright flags out front.

Westward Ho Hotel, 701 E. Palm Canyon Dr., Palm Springs, CA 92264. ☎ **619/320-2700,** or toll free **800/854-4345, 800/472-4313** in California. Fax 619/322-5354. 208 rms. A/C TV TEL

Rates: $42 single; $52 double. AE, MC, V. **Parking:** Free.

Rooms at this pleasant, comfortable, and well-priced motel have a modified western look. Most accommodations also have attractive Indian-print spreads, hanging cylinder lamps, upholstered chairs with casters, and dark-wood furnishings. A heated "therapy" pool for guests at the center of the complex is surrounded by comfortable lounges. There's also a small wading pool for children. During holiday periods and special events there is a two-night minimum stay, and rates are slightly higher.

One of the conveniences of the motel is that it adjoins Denny's, a coffee shop–style restaurant that's open 24 hours.

Where to Dine

There are many attractive restaurants in Palm Springs and more in the offing, but frequently the food is not as smart as the surroundings. Some of the best restaurants in town are in hotels—notably **Melvyn's** at the Ingleside Inn, and the **Terrace Restaurant** at the Hilton (see "Where to Stay," above). Other good choices are listed below.

EXPENSIVE

Alfredo's, 292 E. Palm Canyon Dr. ☎ 619/325-4060.
  Cuisine: ITALIAN. **Reservations:** Not required.
  Prices: Appetizers $4–$7; main courses $15–$20; lunch $7–$12. AE, DISC, MC, V.
  Open: Daily 11:30am–11pm.

The exterior of Alfredo's has always attracted me. It's simple, uncluttered, and inviting, with a forthright ALFREDO'S sign in neon script. The restaurant is just as handsome inside—dusty-rose and cream walls, with complementary maroon-and-cream furnishings, scenic lithographs, smoked mirrors, and frosted-glass art deco lamps overhead.

Appetizers include Mama's fava beans, a Sicilian-style artichoke, and mozzarella marinara—deep-fried cheese cooked with the chef's special sauce. Interesting salads range from the house's dandelion salad (yes, dandelion) to a cold seafood-and-linguine combination.

Main courses range from veal marsala or filet mignon "Alfredo style" to pizza. And the spicy chicken wings must be the best this side of Buffalo, N.Y. (Alfredo's hometown). They come in hot, medium, or mild, and are served authentically—with celery sticks and bleu-cheese dip. If you thought that spaghetti and meatballs was not exactly an inspired choice for dinner, try this. Not to be ignored either is veal Alfredo—veal cutlets and eggplant in light batter, sautéed, separated with prosciutto, topped with mozzarella, then baked and finished with Alfredo's special sauce.

MODERATE

Las Casuelas Terraza, 222 S. Palm Canyon Dr. ☎ 619/325-2794.
  Cuisine: MEXICAN. **Reservations:** Not required.
  Prices: Appetizers $4–$7; main courses $7–$13; lunch $4–$9. AE, DISC, MC, V.
  Open: Daily 11am–10pm.

The upscale Mexican style that typifies much of Palm Springs is epitomized in this festive restaurant, outfitted with stone archways, terra-cotta floors, and white plaster walls. In addition to a busy bar—where live entertainment is featured on weekends—the piazzalike eatery encompasses several indoor dining rooms as well as a popular terrace, spiced with small tables, a stone fountain, and hanging ferns.

While Las Casuelas Terraza's food is not outstanding, it never takes a back seat to the bar—a situation that's typical of most California/ Mexican "margarita" restaurants. All the "hits" are here: nachos, burritos, tacos, quesadillas, and the recommendable fajitas with chicken, steak, or shrimp. Huevos rancheros and a variety of Mexican-style omelets are also available for brunch.

Lyon's English Grill, 233 E. Palm Canyon Dr. ☎ 619/327-1551.

Cuisine: ENGLISH/JEWISH. **Reservations:** Not required.
Prices: Appetizers $3–$10; main courses $14–$20. AE, CB, DC, MC, V.
Open: Dinner only, daily 4–11pm. **Closed:** July.

Lyon's English Grill has an almost theatrical woody English-pub ambience composed of stained-glass windows, old pub signs and maps, Tudor beamed walls, and heraldic banners suspended from the ceilings. Even the menus were made in England, originally for a restaurant in Hampton Court.

One of the grill's most unusual menus combines English and Jewish specialties like steak-and-kidney pie, matzoh-ball soup, prime rib, and chicken in the pot. Starters include shrimp scampi, sautéed mushrooms, and potato skins. Main courses run the gamut from filet mignon and barbecued ribs to roast chicken and steak-and-kidney pie. Of course, since you're in California, Cobb salad and fresh fish are also available.

Sorrentino's, 1032 N. Palm Canyon Dr. ☎ 619/325-2944.

Cuisine: SEAFOOD. **Reservations:** Recommended.
Prices: Appetizers $3–$9; main courses $12–$30. AE, CB, DC, MC, V.
Open: Dinner only, Sun–Thurs 5–9:30pm, Fri–Sat 5–10:30pm.

When you're in the mood for a truly fresh seafood dinner, visit Sorrentino's, undoubtedly the best seafood restaurant in town. Its Italian-American origins are reflected by the decor: green banquettes against orange walls decked with oil paintings and wrought-iron-encased fixtures.

Virtually all the fish is fresh, and when it's "fresh frozen"—more often than not the case in Palm Springs—Sorrentino's tells you so. Some of the great choices on the extensive menu include a hearty cioppino with lobster, shrimp, clams, crab, squid, and fish, served with rice; king crab legs; abalone steak; and fresh fish broiled, poached, baked, and grilled. Several Italian-style meat choices are also available, as is a special children's dinner that offers a choice of four main courses. The wine list, both domestic and imported, is limited but good. Sorrentino's has a huge bar adjacent to the main dining room, so you won't mind the inevitable wait for a table.

Billy Reed's, 1800 N. Palm Canyon Dr. ☎ 619/325-1946.

Cuisine: AMERICAN. **Reservations:** Accepted only for large parties.
Prices: Appetizers $2–$4; main courses $8–$20. AE, CB, DC, DISC, MC, V.
Open: Daily 7am–11pm.

For hearty home-cooking, a great selection, huge portions, and small-town ambience, you can't beat Billy Reed's. The entrance sports the characteristic Palm Springs hacienda look—small fountain, foliage, and a cool patio—but the Spanish resemblance ends there.

Wicker furniture graces the outer lobby, and the interior is American/Victorian, with lace curtains and Tiffany stained-glass lamp shades. Somehow it all works. And though the place is huge, the low ceilings and overhead pot-and-mug collections make it seem warm and friendly.

You can start your day here with a breakfast such as sausage and eggs served with hash browns, toast, and butter. At lunch you might order the shrimp Louis, served with garlic toast or cornbread; a delicious chicken pot pie; or a bowl of chili with cubed sirloin and beans. Among the main-course options are jumbo prawns, top sirloin, fried chicken, prime rib, or broiled scallops and shrimp en brochette with bacon, mushroom caps, and onions.

INEXPENSIVE

El Mirasol, 140 E. Palm Canyon Dr. ☎ 619/323-0721.

> **Cuisine:** MEXICAN REGIONAL. **Reservations:** Not required.
> **Prices:** Appetizers $4–$7; main courses $6–$11; lunch $5–$9. MC, V.
> **Open:** Lunch daily 11am–3pm; dinner daily 5–10pm.

A fine alternative to the better-known Mexican eateries in Palm Springs, El Mirasol is a well-priced family restaurant, simply decorated with dark-wood furniture, a beautiful desert mural on one wall, and potted plants. Classic Mexican combinations include tacos, enchiladas, chiles rellenos, tostadas, and burritos; for the benefit of brunchers, egg dishes, including huevos rancheros or chorizo and eggs, are also served. But the excellence of the menu is in the many "especialidades de la casa"—whether you choose the pork chile verde cooked with green chiles and tomatillos, or opt for the well-seasoned shrimp rancheros, a special treat prepared with bell peppers, onions, olives, and tomatoes.

The chefs use only pure corn and olive oil, and prepare their guacamole without salt or mayonnaise.

Louise's Pantry, 124 S. Palm Canyon Dr. ☎ 619/325-5124.

> **Cuisine:** AMERICAN. **Reservations:** Not accepted.
> **Prices:** Appetizers $3–$6; main courses $8–$10; lunch $5–$7. No credit cards.
> **Open:** Daily 7am–9pm. **Closed:** Mid-June to mid-Sept.

Louise's Pantry is a real fixture on the Palm Springs eating scene. It's a small place—just 47 seats—but it packs 'em in every day and night, and with good reason. It's hard to match Louise's quality and even harder to beat the price.

This is like a real American diner; it offers burgers, sandwiches, triple-deckers, and salads. The restaurant squeezes fresh orange juice daily, grinds its own beef, and bakes the sweet rolls, cornbread, pies, and cakes on the premises. There are three to six specials each evening, plus choices from a regular list of eight entrees, such as roast beef, homemade meatloaf, grilled pork chops, New York steak, and fish and chips. Specials of the day may include lamb shanks, roast turkey, and pork tenderloin.

Louise's Pantry also serves breakfast, with all sorts of accompaniments. You can even create your own omelet from a lengthy mix-and-match list of goodies. No alcohol is served.

Nate's Delicatessen and Restaurant, 100 S. Indian Ave.
☎ **619/325-3506.**
Cuisine: JEWISH. **Reservations:** Not required.
Prices: Appetizers $3–$7; main courses $6–$9. AE, CB, DC, DISC, MC, V.
Open: Daily 8am–8pm.

One of the really enjoyable eating experiences in Palm Springs is Nate's Delicatessen and Restaurant, also known as Mister Corned Beef of Palm Springs. Unlike its New York, Los Angeles, or San Francisco deli counterparts, Nate's looks like a well-bred restaurant, but not to worry—it has all the great aromas of a super deli.

For breakfast, there are omelets in every conceivable combination—with salami, pastrami, corned beef, chopped liver, and the like—as well as eggs with onions, lox, whitefish, and even grilled knockwurst. French toast and pancakes are also available.

At lunch, sandwich fillings are piled high onto homemade warm rye bread (or whatever bread or roll you prefer). Everything comes with a relish tray of kosher pickles and old-world sauerkraut. They have eight varieties of salad, blintzes, gefilte fish, potato pancakes, and knishes, too.

The restaurant's $11 nine-course dinner includes juice or homemade chopped liver, soup or salad, main dishes ranging from baked or fried chicken to corned beef brisket or seafood catch of the day. An extensive à la carte menu is also available.

A Side Trip to Joshua Tree National Monument

Located 140 miles east of Los Angeles and 45 miles northeast of Palm Springs is the 558,000-acre Joshua Tree National Monument, connecting the Mojave and Colorado Deserts. It is named after the large yucca belonging to the agave family that thrives in this region at elevations above 3,000 feet. These 20- to 30-foot-tall cactus "trees," with spindly green knobs at the end of each branch, were named by early Mormon settlers who thought their unusual forms looked like Joshua beckoning them farther west.

The monument is comprised of two distinct halves; both deserts average summer temperatures of 100° to 110°F. The eastern half is lower than the west's 3,000-plus-foot elevation and receives even less than its neighbor's average annual eight inches of rain. Scattered about this arid region are five oases where water can be found at or near the surface. Golden eagles, tarantulas, stinkbugs, sidewinders, and other desert animals are attracted to these watering holes, as are jackrabbits, coyotes, and rattlesnakes.

GETTING THERE   There are two main entrances to Joshua Tree. The more popular is the northwest entrance, near Twentynine Palms. From Palm Springs, take Indian Avenue north and turn right onto

Calif. 62 north. Once in Twentynine Palms, pass the traffic light and then turn right onto National Monument Drive. At this entrance the Oasis Visitors Center offers information and advice on visiting the park, along with trail maps and safety information. It's open daily from 8am to 4:30pm.

To reach the southeast entrance, take Interstate 10 east for 55 miles from Palm Springs. This entrance is served by the Cottonwood Visitors Center, which is open daily from 8am to 4pm.

SEEING THE MONUMENT   Over 3,500 rock climes make Joshua Tree one of the world's most popular climbing areas. Most visitors, however, come to hike and camp and to experience Joshua's distinctive magnificence. Most of the western part of the park is relatively flat, so the trails there are not particularly strenuous. Still, be sure to carry an ample supply of water since desert hiking leads to fast dehydration. There are dozens of marked trails, and park rangers can suggest paths that are best suited for you.

If your visit here is short and you want to get an overall feel of the park's incredible diversity, enter via the Oasis Visitors Center (see "Getting There," above) and take the picturesque Barker Dam Trail, which wends its way through flatlands and large rock formations, past Native American petroglyphs, to a little private reservoir. Alternatively, hike the short Hidden Valley Loop, an archetypal Western walk dotted with tall red rock formations that will seem familiar if you're a fan of old cowboy films.

Be aware that the desert is a very fragile ecosystem that's vigilantly protected by the federal government. Half a dozen plant species found here are currently threatened or endangered. The desert tortoise is one of the most imperiled animals; visitors are asked not to touch these or any other animals (or plants) in the park.

Admission is $5 per car or $3 per person if you walk in. All queries regarding Joshua Tree National Monument should be addressed to 74485 National Monument Dr., Twentynine Palms, CA 92277 (☎ 619/367-7511). If you plan to camp in the park, phone ahead because reservations are required at some sites.

5 Palm Desert

118 miles E of Los Angeles, 15 miles SE of Palm Springs

GETTING THERE • By Plane   Palm Springs Municipal Airport, 3400 E. Tahquitz-McCallum Way (☎ 619/323-8161), serves the entire Palm Springs Desert Resorts community. Flights from Los Angeles International Airport take about 40 minutes.

• By Bus   Greyhound/Trailways (☎ toll free **800/231-2222**) can get you here from anywhere. The closest stop is located at 311 N. Indian Ave., Palm Springs (☎ **619/325-2053**).

• By Car   From Los Angeles, Palm Springs is an easy two-hour drive via the San Bernardino Freeway (Interstate 10). When approaching Palm Springs, exit onto Calif. 111 (Palm Canyon Drive), which runs through all the resort towns before reconnecting with I-10 just past Indio.

ESSENTIALS • **Orientation**   Palm Desert is small. El Paseo, the town's primary commercial thoroughfare, is shaped like a giant horseshoe that connects with East Palm Canyon Drive at both ends. In between are gridlike residential streets that are easy to negotiate.

• **Information**   Visitor information is provided by the **Palm Springs Desert Resorts Convention and Visitors Bureau,** in the Atrium Design Centre, 69-930 Calif. 111, Suite 201, Rancho Mirage, CA 92270 (☎ **619/770-9000,** or toll free **800/417-3529**). Its staff can help with maps, brochures, and advice Monday through Friday from 8:30am to 5pm.

Located in the center of the Coachella Valley, Palm Desert is home to more golf courses than any other desert city. There's not that much to see and do here; shopping and sunning rank among the town's top activities.

What to See & Do

El Paseo, Palm Desert's main commercial thoroughfare, is located one block from Calif. 111. Dozens of specialty shops, selling everything from handcrafted jewelry and knickknacks to designer fashions, make this a fun place to walk and shop. Many of the town's restaurants are also located on this strip (some are listed below). Hats are highly recommended for daytime strollers.

The Living Desert, 47-900 Portola Ave. ☎ **619/346-5694.**

This largely outdoor museum is cleverly designed to acquaint visitors with the unique habitats that make up the southern California desert. Various components of this distinctive ecosystem are represented, including live tarantulas, scorpions, and snakes, as well as less harmless squirrels, bats, and lizards. Desert flora are also exhibited, along with informative displays about the effects of temperature, wind, and moisture on the desert community.

Although you'll rarely see them in the wild, native coyotes, foxes, bobcats, and other larger animals also make their home here. Fifty-minute guided tours are conducted daily, via motorized tram. Don't forget a hat and sunscreen. The museum is closed during most of the unbearably hot summer season.

Admission: $7 adults, $6 seniors (62 and over), $3.50 children 6–15; children under 6 free.

Open: Daily 9am–5pm (last admission at 4:30pm). **Closed:** June 16–Aug, Dec 25.

Where to Stay

VERY EXPENSIVE

Marriott'S Desert Springs Resort and Spa, 74885 Country Club Dr., Palm Desert, CA 92260. ☎ **619/341-2211,** or toll free **800/228-9290.** 844 rms, 51 suites. A/C MINIBAR TV TEL

Rates: Dec–May, $205–$335 single or double; from $575 suite. June–July, $120–$195 single or double; from $375 suite. Aug–Nov, $105–$180 single or double; from $375 suite. AE, CB, DC, DISC, MC, V.

A tourist attraction in its own right, Marriott's Desert Springs Resort is worth a peek even if you're not lucky enough to stay here. Visitors enter this artificial desert oasis via a long palm tree–lined road wending its way past a small pond that's home to a gaggle of pink flamingos. Once inside, guests are greeted by a shaded marble lobby "rain forest" replete with running water and the squawk of tropical birds. Canopied water taxis congregate here, ready to float guests to their rooms.

While the rooms here are not as fancy as the lobby would lead you to believe, they are exceedingly comfortable, decorated with muted pastels and contemporary furnishings. There is a large variety of accommodations, differing in size and location. Most have large baths, outfitted with hairdryers, full-length mirrors, and separate tubs. Suites have large sitting/dining areas furnished with Murphy beds.

Most of the resort's guests are attracted by excellent golf and tennis facilities. The spa is an added perk, offering massages, facials, aerobics classes, and supervised weight training. There are also the requisite Jacuzzis and swimming pools.

Dining/Entertainment: The Club Room is open for breakfast and lunch, serving eggs, sandwiches, and salads. Lunches are also served in the Lake View restaurant. Dinner choices include the Sea Grill and Oyster Bar, which features mesquite-grilled meat and fish; Tuscay's Ristorante, an Italian eatery; and Mikado, the resort's Japanese restaurant. Costa's lounge features dancing nightly.

Services: Room service, concierge, babysitting, overnight laundry, special children's programs.

Facilities: Car-rental desk, two 18-hole golf courses, putting course, driving range, full-service spa, 20 tennis courts (7 lighted), two outdoor pools, indoor lap pool, three outdoor Jacuzzis, jogging trail, games room.

MODERATE

Deep Canyon Inn, 74-470 Abronia Trail, Palm Desert, CA 92260. ☎ **619/346-8061,** or toll free **800/253-0004.** Fax 619/341-9120. 31 rms, 1 apartment. A/C TV TEL

Rates (including continental breakfast): Jan–May, $65–$150 single or double; $185 apartment. June–Dec, $45–$110 single or double; $145 apartment. AE, DC, DISC, MC, V.

The earth-toned Deep Canyon Inn, a block from Calif. 111, is a homey alternative to the many large chain hotels in the area. Behind a bevy of brightly colored flags are the nicely remodeled rooms, outfitted with dark rattan furnishings and natural-tone prints. Except for their exceptionally large size, the guest rooms are in no way outstanding. Still, accommodations are quite adequate and include modern furnishings and clean tiled baths. Higher-priced rooms include separate kitchens stocked with cookware and dishes. French doors on second-story rooms open onto small balconies overlooking the hotel's central courtyard and pool.

Shadow Mountain Resort and Racquet Club, 45-750 San Luis Rey, Palm Desert, CA 92260. ☎ 619/346-6123. 60 rms, 100 suites. A/C TV TEL

Rates: May 28–Sept 24, $81–$100 single or double; from $150 suite. Jan 3–Feb 11, Apr 18–May 27, Sept 25–Nov 24, and Nov 29–Dec 23, $110–$135 single or double; from $167 suite. Rest of the year, $134–$170 single or double; from $200 suite. AE, MC, V.

Shadow Mountain is a collection of individually owned condominiums that are rented when their owners are away. There's a wide range of accommodations, from one-room studios with kitchenettes to large two-bedroom units, and all are uniquely decorated according to their owner's tastes. Don't worry, though: Each fully equipped apartment has to conform to the resort's good standards. Although the resort lacks many services usually identified with good hotels (room service, a concierge), it delivers the main ones, including a helpful staff and daily maid service. Particularly recommendable for families, homey Shadow Mountain happily dispenses with the pretensions and stuffiness sometimes associated with large resorts. In addition to 16 tennis courts, the resort encompasses four heated pools, and five whirlpools dotted across the property.

A small restaurant is open seasonally for light lunches and refreshments, and a bar is open on weekend nights only.

INEXPENSIVE

Gala Villa Inn, 73-721 Shadow Mountain Dr., Palm Desert, CA 92260. ☎ 619/346-6121. 21 rms. A/C TV TEL

Rates: June–Oct, $35–$42 single or double. Nov–Jan, $55–$65 single or double. Feb–May, $64–$72 single or double. AE, MC, V.

So what if the decor hasn't changed since the 1950s? Basic and totally serviceable, the Gala Villa Inn represents one of the best-priced picks in the area. Most of the inn's rooms contain two double beds, and many also have kitchens. Most important, there's a pool for quick desert relief.

Where to Dine

EXPENSIVE

La Quinta Cliffhouse, 78-250 Calif. 111, La Quinta.
☎ 619/360-5991.

Cuisine: CALIFORNIAN. **Reservations:** Recommended.
Prices: Appetizers $2–$7; main courses $14–$27; brunch $8–$13. AE, DISC, MC, V.
Open: Dinner Sun–Thurs 5–9:30pm, Fri–Sat 5–10pm; brunch Sun (in fall only) 10am–2pm.

King of its own little hill on the east side of Calif. 111, La Quinta Cliffhouse successfully combines respectable food with a spirited site.

The stairs leading to the restaurant's entrance wind through a rocky waterfall. The best seats are at the thatched-wood tables on the restaurant's outdoor terrace. Inside is not shabby either, with oak tables atop a bright ethnic-print carpet. Residential-quality southwestern artwork, shaded chandeliers, and beamed ceilings round out the decor.

The entirely à la carte menu ensures that you'll pay handsomely for your dinner, but plenty of regulars attest to its worth. A large steamed artichoke served with drawn butter is my appetizer pick, followed by fresh mahi-mahi prepared with soy and ginger and topped with razor-thin stir-fried vegetables. Filet mignon, pork ribs, and several chicken selections keep the grill busy. Without exception, every dish is expertly handled and artfully presented.

Some of the more unusual Sunday brunch selections include crab cakes Benedict and seafood quiche filled with bay shrimp, Dungeness crabmeat, artichoke hearts, and Gruyère cheese.

MODERATE

Cedar Creek Inn, 73-445 El Paseo. ☎ 619/340-1236.

Cuisine: AMERICAN. **Reservations:** Recommended.
Prices: Appetizers $2–$5; main courses $7–$22; lunch $5–$9. AE, MC, V.
Open: Daily 11am–9pm.

The appropriately named Cedar Creek Inn sounds just like the quiet country hideaway it is. Choose to sit either inside, beside well-dressed windows and under wood-beamed ceilings, or on one of two trellis-covered patios.

Straightforward soups and sandwiches are served throughout the day, along with a well-stocked salad bar. Reservations are encouraged at dinner, which is both more popular and more formal. Rack of lamb is the house specialty, but a good selection of fresh fish and chicken is also available.

Dakota Bar and Grill, 73-260 El Paseo. ☎ 619/346-0744.

Cuisine: AMERICAN. **Reservations:** Not required.
Prices: Appetizers $5–$8; main courses $9–$24; lunch $6–$13. DC, MC, V.
Open: Daily 11:30am–10pm.

Smoky meats, burgers, chicken, and fish, served in a Wild West interior, combine to make the Dakota the desert's best barbecue. The country-and-western interior of buffalo horns, fake rocks, and fictitious wooden signs reminds diners of gold-rush days. Of the three strengths of chili, "suicide" is hottest and requires plenty of ice water. Most items here are reasonably priced, as surely the Cattle Baron's Special—two double cheeseburgers and a bottle of Dom Pérignon champagne—is just a menu joke; there are few takers at $125 a pop.

Tsing Tao, 74-040 Calif. 111, Suite E. ☎ 619/779-9593.

Cuisine: CHINESE. **Reservations:** Not required.
Prices: Appetizers $5–$10; main courses $8–$18; fixed-price lunch $5–$7. AE, MC, V.
Open: Lunch Mon–Fri 11:30am–2:30pm; dinner Sun–Thurs 5–9:30pm, Fri–Sat 5–10:30pm.

In a strip mall on Calif. 111, this small Chinese restaurant offers a welcome alternative to the usual Cal-Mex fare so popular in this desert community. No red-and-white pagoda here! Contrasty black-lacquer chairs and white-clothed tables are clean, elegant, and tastefully modern.

The restaurant's good-value fixed-price lunches include main courses like almond chicken, shrimp mixed with Chinese greens, and curry chicken, all served with egg-flower soup, fried wantons, rice, fortune cookies, and tea. All the other Mandarin trademarks are also available for both lunch and dinner, including sweet-and-sour shrimp, moo shu pork, lobster Cantonese, and tangerine beef.

INEXPENSIVE

Mickey's Sandwich Shop, 73-655 El Paseo, Unit G.
☎ **619/346-1072.**

Cuisine: SANDWICHES. **Reservations:** Not accepted.
Prices: Sandwiches and salads $3–$5. No credit cards.
Open: Lunch only, Mon–Fri 10am–3pm.

For a good lunch at a reasonable price, it's hard to top Mickey's, where an arm's-long list of sandwiches and salads offers plenty of choices for under $5. It's just a simple "to go" place, where all the usual meats and cheeses are augmented by seafood and vegetarian selections. Homemade salads include tuna, fruit, pasta, vegetable, and chicken. Brownies, cookies, and cheesecakes are available for dessert.

---

6 Santa Barbara

336 miles S of San Francisco, 96 miles N of Los Angeles

GETTING THERE • By Plane   The Santa Barbara Municipal Airport (☎ **805/967-7111**) is located in Goleta, about 10 minutes north of downtown Santa Barbara. Major airlines servicing Santa Barbara include American Eagle (☎ toll free **800/433-7300**), Skywest/Delta (☎ toll free **800/453-9417**), United (☎ toll free **800/241-6522**), and USAir Express (☎ toll free **800/428-4322**). Yellow Cab (☎ **805/965-5111**) and other metered taxis line up outside the terminal and cost about $20 to a downtown hotel.

• By Train   Amtrak (☎ toll free **800/USA-RAIL**) offers daily service from both San Francisco and Los Angeles. Trains arrive and depart from the Santa Barbara Rail Station, 209 State St. (☎ **805/963-1015**); fares can be as low as $20 to Los Angeles.

• By Bus   Greyhound/Trailways (☎ toll free **800/231-2222**) maintains a daily schedule into Santa Barbara from both the north and south. The central bus station is located right downtown at Carillo and Chapala Streets.

• By Car   U.S. 101, one of the state's primary north-south roadways, which runs right through Santa Barbara, represents the fastest land route to here from anywhere. From the north, you can take Calif. 154, which meets U.S. 101 at Los Olivos and cuts across the San Marcos Pass, a scenic route into Santa Barbara.

ESSENTIALS • Orientation State Street, the city's primary commercial thoroughfare, is in the geographic center of town. It ends at Stearns Wharf and Cabrillo Street; the latter runs along the ocean and separates the city's beaches from touristy hotels and restaurants.

• Information The **Santa Barbara Visitor Information Center,** 1 Santa Barbara St., Santa Barbara, CA 93101 (☎ **805/965-3021**) is on the ocean, at the corner of Cabrillo Street. This small but busy office distributes maps, literature, an events calendar, and excellent advice. Be sure to ask for their handy guide to places of interest and public parking. The office is open Monday through Saturday from 9am to 5pm and on Sunday from 10am to 5pm; it closes one hour earlier in winter and one hour later in July and August. A second **Visitor Information Center,** open Monday through Friday from 9am to 5pm, is located in a storefront at 504 State St. in the heart of downtown.

Be sure to pick up a free copy of *The Independent,* a weekly listing of events, from one of the sidewalk racks around town.

Santa Barbara's geographical position has everything to do with its charm. Nature has smiled on this small notch of land between the Santa Ynez Mountains and the Pacific Ocean; the sun-blessed southern Californian town is one of the world's most perfect places. Spoiled Santa Barbara is coddled by wooded mountains, caressed by baby breakers, and sheltered from tempestuous seas by rocky offshore islands. Located 90 miles north of Los Angeles—just far enough to make the Big City seem at once remote and accessible—the town feels small, and growth is generally frowned upon. Because there are few employment opportunities and real estate is expensive, demographics have favored college-age students and rich retirees, whom the locals refer to as "almost wed and almost dead."

Visually, downtown Santa Barbara is distinctive for its homogeneous Spanish-Mediterranean buildings, all of which sport matching red-tile roofs. But it wasn't always this way. Named in 1602 by a Carmelite friar sailing with Spanish explorer Sebastián Vizcaíno, Santa Barbara had a thriving Native American Chumash population for hundreds, if not thousands, of years. The town's European era began in the late 18th century, around a presidio, or fort, that still stands reconstructed today in its original town-center spot. The earliest architectural hodgepodge was destroyed in 1925 by a powerful earthquake that leveled Santa Barbara's business district. Out of the rubble rose Spanish-Mediterranean Santa Barbara, a stylish planned town that continues to rigidly enforce its strict building codes.

What to See & Do

⭐ **County Courthouse,** 1100 Anacapa St. ☎ **805/962-6464.**
Occupying a full city block and set in a lush tropical garden, this courthouse is a supreme example of Santa Barbara nouveau-Spanish architecture—a tribute to bygone days when style and elegance outweighed more practical considerations. Few would guess that it was

built as late as 1929. The architect, William Mooser, was assisted by his son who had lived in Spain for 17 years and was well versed in Spanish-Moorish design. Among its most impressive features are the towers and a turret, graceful arches, unexpected windows, brilliant Tunisian tilework, a winding staircase, intricately stenciled ceilings, palatial tile floors, lacy iron grillwork, heavy wood doors, and Spanish lanterns resembling hammered iron. The magnificent historic murals by Dan Sayre Groesbeck depicting memorable episodes in Santa Barbara history are worth a visit in themselves. A compact elevator takes visitors up to the 85-foot-high observation deck roof of the clock tower. From here visitors are treated to fine views of the ocean, mountains, and the red terra-cotta-tile roofs that cover the city.

A free guided tour is offered on Wednesday and Friday at 10:30am and Monday through Saturday at 2pm.

Admission: Free.

Open: Mon–Fri 8am–5pm, Sat–Sun and holidays 9am–5pm.

Moreton Bay Fig Tree, Chapala and Montecito Sts.

Famous for its massive size, Santa Barbara's best-known tree has a branch spread that would cover half a football field. It has been estimated that well over 10,000 people could stand in the tree's shade, while its roots run under more than an acre of ground. Planted in 1877, the *Figus macrophylla* is a native of Moreton Bay in eastern Australia. It is related to both the fig and rubber tree but produces neither figs nor rubber. The tree is hands down the largest of its kind in the world. Once in danger of being leveled (for a proposed gas station) and later threatened by excavation for nearby U.S. 101, the revered tree is now the unofficial home of Santa Barbara's homeless community.

★ **Santa Barbara Mission,** Laguna and Mission Sts.
☎ **805/682-4173** or **682-4175.**

Called the "Queen of the Missions" for its twin bell towers and graceful beauty, Santa Barbara's hilltop mission overlooks the town and the Channel Islands beyond. The structure's gleaming-white buildings are surrounded by green lawns with flowering trees and shrubs. The Santa Barbara Mission was established in 1786 and is still used by a local parish. Displayed inside are a typical missionary bedroom, 18th- and 19th-century furnishings, paintings and statues from Mexico, and period kitchen utensils, including grinding stones, baskets, and copper kettles. The museum also displays Native American tools, crafts, and artifacts.

Admission: $2 adults, free for children under 16.

Open: Daily 9am–5pm.

Santa Barbara Museum of Natural History, 2559 Puesta del Sol Rd. ☎ **805/682-4711.**

Located just beyond the mission, this museum focuses on the display, study, and interpretation of Pacific Coast natural history: flora, fauna, and prehistoric life. The museum's architecture—typical Santa

Barbara style—reflects early Spanish and Mexican influence, with ivory-colored stucco walls, graceful arches, arcades, and a central patio. Exhibits range from diagrams to dioramas. Native American history is emphasized, including basketry, textiles, and a full-size replica of a Chumash canoe. Other displays encompass everything from fossil ferns to the complete skeleton of a blue whale. An adjacent planetarium projects sky shows every Saturday and Sunday.

The museum store has a nice selection of books, jewelry, textiles, and handcrafted gifts.

Admission: $4 adults, $3 seniors and teens, $2 children.

Open: Mon–Sat 9am–5pm, Sun and holidays 10am–5pm.

Santa Barbara Museum of Art, 1130 State St.
☎ 805/963-4364.

Considering the relatively small size of the community served by this museum, the Santa Barbara Museum of Art is extraordinary. From Egyptian reliefs to kinetic sculptures, there's something of interest for everyone. Top draws include Greek and Roman sculpture, representative works from the Italian Renaissance and Flemish schools, European impressionist paintings (including some by Monet and Degas), and works by such early-20th-century European modernists as Chagall, Hoffmann, and Kandinsky. If all that isn't enough, you'll also find a selection of American art by O'Keeffe, Eakins, Sargent, Hopper, and Grosz; as well as Asian sculpture, prints, ceramic ware, scrolls, screens, and paintings. The museum's photography collection boasts more than 1,500 items.

Most of the museum's 15,000-plus works are exhibited on a rotating basis in climate- and light-controlled galleries. Temporary shows include traveling exhibitions and local features. Free docent-led tours are scheduled Tuesday through Sunday at 1pm. Focus tours are held on Wednesday and Saturday at noon.

Admission: $3 adults, $2.50 seniors (over 65), $1.50 children 6–16; children under 6 free. Free for everyone Thurs and the first Sun of each month.

Open: Tues–Wed and Fri–Sat 11am–5pm, Thurs 11am–9pm, Sun noon–5pm.

Santa Barbara Historical Museum, 136 E. de la Guerra St.
☎ 805/966-1601.

Local-lore exhibits include late-19th-century paintings of California missions by Edwin Deakin; a 16th-century carved Spanish coffer from Majorca, home of Padre Serra; and objects from the Chinese community that once flourished here, including a magnificent carved shrine from the turn of the century.

History buffs will appreciate some of the other displays, including early pieces of correspondence, antique dolls, period clothing, and assorted memorabilia. A knowledgeable docent leads a most interesting free tour every Wednesday, Saturday, and Sunday at 1:30pm.

Admission: Free, but donation requested.

Open: Tues–Sat 10am–5pm, Sun noon–5pm.

Santa Barbara Botanic Garden, 1212 Mission Canyon Rd.
☎ **805/682-4726.**

About 1½ miles north of the mission, the garden encompasses 65 acres of native trees, shrubs, cacti, and wildflowers, and more than five miles of trails. Docent tours are offered daily at 2pm, with additional tours on Thursday, Saturday, and Sunday at 10:30am.

Admission: $3 adults, $2 children 13–19 and seniors (over 64), $1 children 5–12, free for children under 5.

Open: Nov–Feb, Mon–Fri 9am–4pm, Sat–Sun 9am–5pm; Mar–Oct, Mon–Fri 9am–5pm, Sat–Sun 9am–6pm.

Stearns Wharf, at the end of State St. ☎ **805/963-2633.**

In addition to a small collection of second-rate shops, attractions, and restaurants, the city's 1872-vintage pier offers terrific views of the city and good drop-line fishing. The Dolphin Fountain at the foot of the wharf was created by Bud Bottoms for the city's 1982 bicentennial (copies are located in Puerto Vallarta, Mexico; Toba, Japan; and Yalta, Ukraine).

Santa Barbara Zoological Gardens, 500 Ninos Dr.
☎ **805/962-5339,** or **962-6310** for a recording.

Sometimes when you're driving around the bend on Cabrillo Beach Boulevard, you can spot the head of a giraffe poking up through the palm trees. This is not your imagination—it's the intimate Santa Barbara Zoo, where all 700 animals can be seen in about 30 minutes. Most of the animals are displayed in naturalistic open settings. The zoo encompasses a children's Discovery Area, miniature train ride, small carousel, and gift shop. The picnic areas (complete with barbecue pits) are underutilized and especially recommendable. Beautiful botanic displays augment the animal exhibits.

Admission: $5 adults, $3 seniors and children 2–12, free for children under 2.

Open: June–Aug, daily 9am–6pm; Sept–May, daily 10am–5pm; last admission is one hour prior to closing.

Where to Stay ———————————————————————————

VERY EXPENSIVE

★ **Four Seasons Biltmore,** 1260 Channel Dr., Santa Barbara, CA 93108. ☎ **805/969-2261,** or toll free **800/332-3442.**
Fax 805/969-4682. 234 rms, 24 suites. A/C MINIBAR TV TEL
Directions: From U.S. 101, exit onto Olive Mill Road, which turns into Channel Drive, to the hotel.

Rates: $295–$350 single or double; from $595 suite. Special midweek and package rates available. AE, DC, MC, V. **Parking:** $10.

The most elegant hotel in town is also one of the most prestigious in California. Its beautiful 21 acres of gardens front a private ocean beach. When the Biltmore opened in 1927, a concert orchestra performed twice daily in the dining room, and separate quarters were provided for personal servants who accompanied guests. Although few people travel with servants these days, the hotel still emphasizes service.

Santa Barbara

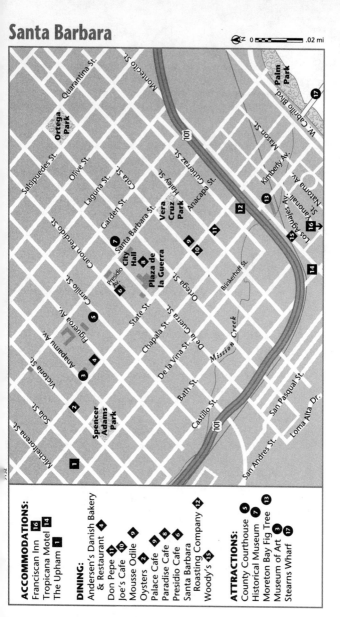

Designed by Reginald Johnson, the hotel's award-winning Spanish architecture combines Portuguese, Basque, Iberian, and Moorish elements in a graceful blend of arcades, winding staircases, patios, and artistic walkways, with lovely hand-painted Mexican tiles and grillwork throughout. The beauty of the estate is further enhanced by imposing views of the Pacific Ocean, the Santa Ynez Mountains, and the hotel's own palm-studded formal gardens. This refined resort hotel features deluxe accommodations with plush Iberian-style furnishings. Many of the rooms have romantic Spanish balconies and/or fireplaces, and some have private patios. All have ceiling fans and individual climate controls, as well as terry-cloth robes and hairdryers. Cottage suites, which are set back on the property, are as private as they are elegant.

Dining/Entertainment: La Marina restaurant offers elegant dining and a select list of California-inspired specialties such as smoked white fish with whipped potatoes, and roast venison with port-wine sauce. The Patio, a glass-enclosed atrium, is more casual, serving breakfast, lunch, dinner, and Santa Barbara's best Sunday brunch. La Sala lounge is a terrifically comfortable room serving afternoon tea and evening cocktails. There's live piano music nightly.

Services: Concierge, 24-hour room service, evening turndown, overnight shoeshine, exercise classes, complimentary bicycle rental, video library, special programs for children.

Facilities: Three lighted tennis courts, two pools, putting green, shuffleboard and croquet courts, beachfront cabañas, sun deck, beauty salon, and gift shop.

★ **San Ysidro Ranch,** 900 San Ysidro Lane (off U.S. 101), Montecito, CA 93108. ☎ **805/969-5046,** or toll free **800/368-6788.** Fax 805/565-1995. 45 cottages, 26 suites. MINIBAR TV TEL **Directions:** From U.S. 101, take the San Ysidro Lane exit and turn toward the mountains; follow the road for about two miles to the ranch.

Rates: $225–$375 double; $475–$550 cottage room; from $650 suite. AE, MC, V.

Since 1940, when Vivien Leigh and Laurence Olivier were married here, San Ysidro Ranch has won raves as one of southern California's most distinguished hotels. Its coveted private location, at the top of a deceptively modest foothill road, surrounded by tall oaks and gracious willows, is the Ranch's primary charm. Over the years, Winston Churchill, Sinclair Lewis, Rex Harrison, Groucho Marx, and Sidney Poitier have all signed the register at this quiet, beautifully landscaped 540-acre retreat. In 1953, John and Jacqueline Kennedy chose to honeymoon here for a week.

The Ranch, as it's known locally, is Santa Barbara's top-rated hideaway. Opened in 1893, the Ranch is comprised of about a dozen free-standing cottages nestled near the base of their own private mountain. Rooms are decorated with charming country-inn antique furnishings. All have working fireplaces, most have private decks or patios, and some have outdoor hot tubs. Weddings, commonplace here, are held most weekends amid truly magnificent jasmine- and honeysuckle-edged gardens that explode with year-round color.

Dining/Entertainment: The Stonehouse restaurant, in the old citrus-packing house, is a charming candlelit dining room with a beamed ceiling, shuttered windows, antique furnishings, and paintings of local landmarks adorning the white sandstone walls. A delightful and airy glass-enclosed café area adjoins, its view of the grounds enhanced by many hanging plants inside. The Plow and Angel bar is a good place for drinks. It draws a local crowd and features live music on the weekends.

Services: Room service, concierge.

Facilities: Two tennis courts, pool, riding stables, badminton, croquet, hiking and riding trails.

EXPENSIVE

⭐ **The Upham,** 1404 De La Vina St., Santa Barbara, CA 93101.
☎ **805/962-0058,** or toll free **800/727-0876.** Fax 805/963-2825.
49 rms, 3 suites. TV TEL **Directions:** From U.S. 101, exit at Mission Street and turn right onto De La Vina Street; the hotel is six blocks ahead at Sola Street.

Rates (including continental breakfast): $100–$185 single or double; from $200 suite. Additional person $10 extra. AE, CB, DC, DISC, MC, V.

Established in 1871, the Upham, located right in the heart of town just two blocks from State Street, is one of the oldest and most charming hotels in Santa Barbara. Built by Amasa Lyman Lincoln, a Boston banker, the Upham's bed-and-breakfast design is reminiscent of an old-fashioned New England boarding house. A two-story clapboard structure, it has wide eaves and is topped by a glassed-in cupola and a widow's walk that faces the sea.

Fronted by a pair of immense ivy-entwined palms, the entrance is through a large colonnaded porch surrounded by a well-tended garden with neat flowerbeds. Refurbished in 1983, guest rooms are outfitted with antique armoires, brass or four-poster beds, and pretty pillow shams. Many rooms have private porches and fireplaces. The Master Suite features a fireplace, Jacuzzi, private yard, and king-size bed.

Complimentary wine, cheese, and crackers are served in the lobby and garden each afternoon. Louie's at the Upham, a cozy restaurant, is open for lunch and dinner.

MODERATE

Bath Street Inn, 1720 Bath St., Santa Barbara, CA 93101.
☎ **805/682-9680,** or toll free **800/788-BATH, 800/549-BATH** in California. 10 rms. **Directions:** From U.S. 101, exit at Mission Street and turn right on De La Vina, then right on Valerio, and right again onto Bath Street.

Rates (including breakfast): $90–$150 single or double. AE, MC, V.

This handsome Victorian inn was built more than 100 years ago. The historic residence has two unusual features—a semicircular "eyelid" balcony and a hipped roof, unique even for Santa Barbara. The century-old trees, the flower-filled patio with white wicker furniture, the brick courtyard, and the graciousness of the innkeepers are all part of the inn's charm.

The living room is the hearth of this home, comfortable and inviting, with a fireplace, Oriental rug, period prints, and fresh flowers. The dining area has a traditional blue-and-white floral-print wallpaper that complements the finely crafted woodwork and furnishings.

Each individually decorated room has its own special charm. One features a king-size canopied bed, and from another under the eaves you can enjoy superb sunsets from a private balcony. Guests enjoy complimentary evening refreshments, and access to the inn's bicycles. Pets are not accepted, and no smoking is allowed in the house. Two new guest rooms are located in the inn's Summer House, both with fireplaces, TVs, and phones.

Best Western Encina Lodge, 2220 Bath St., Santa Barbara, CA 93105. ☎ **805/682-7277,** or toll free **800/526-2262.** Fax 805/563-9319. 121 rms, 38 suites. A/C TV TEL **Directions:** From U.S. 101, exit at Mission Street and turn left onto Bath Street; the hotel is two blocks ahead at Los Olivos Street.

Rates: $102–$112 single; $106–$118 double; from $116 suite. AE, CB, DC, DISC, MC, V.

Set in a quiet residential area, this hotel is a short walk from the mission and a mere five-minute drive from the beach. All rooms are immaculate and tastefully decorated. Soft goods—furnishings, bedspreads, rugs—all look spanking new. Second-floor accommodations in the old building, outfitted with beamed raw-pine ceilings, are best. All rooms come with coffeemakers, hairdryers, fresh fruit, candies, and cookies. Old-wing rooms have showers only; the rest have tub/shower combinations and dressing rooms.

Facilities include a pool, whirlpool, sauna, lobby shop, beauty parlor, and barbershop. There is also complimentary airport and Amtrak pickup. The ever-changing menu in the hotel restaurant might feature sweet-and-sour chicken, barbecued ribs, and crab Mornay.

Miramar Hotel-Resort, 1555 S. Jameson Lane (P.O. Box 429), Montecito, CA 93102. ☎ **805/969-2203.** Fax 805/969-3163. 160 rms, 40 suites. A/C TV TEL **Directions:** From U.S. 101, take the San Ysidro exit and turn toward the ocean; Jameson Lane parallels the freeway right near the overpass.

Rates: $75–$145 single or double; from $130 cottage suite. AE, MC, V.

The Miramar's blue-roofed cottages, which can be seen from U.S. 101, have long been a famous Santa Barbara landmark. Actually located in Montecito, a ritzy area just south of Santa Barbara, the hotel dates from 1887, when the Doulton family began to augment their meager farm income by taking in paying guests. When a railroad was built, the property was split in two. The Miramar became an important rail station when affluent guests began arriving in their own private railroad cars. As the popularity of beach and ocean vacations grew, the hotel became a very chic place to stay.

The modern Miramar is set on 14 garden acres overlooking the Pacific Ocean. Guest-room furnishings are indifferent at best, but accommodations are quite comfortable. The best rooms are oceanfront on the second floor. Some of the attractive, homey cottages have fully equipped kitchens.

Facilities include two pools, four tennis courts, a paddle-tennis court, 500 feet of private sandy beach, saunas, exercise rooms, bike rental, and table tennis. Golf and horseback riding are nearby. The dated Terrace Dining Room, filled with potted palms, is open for breakfast, lunch, and dinner. Sandwiches, salads, steaks, and seafood are featured. The Railroad coffee shop serves late breakfast and lunch. There's live music Thursday through Saturday nights in the adjoining Santa Fe–Amtrak Railcar Diner.

INEXPENSIVE

Franciscan Inn, 109 Bath St., Santa Barbara, CA 93101.
☎ **805/963-8845.** Fax 805/564-3295. 53 rms, 25 suites. TV TEL
Directions: From U.S. 101, take the Castillo Street exit and turn toward the water; turn left onto Mason Street and drive one block to the hotel.

Rates (including continental breakfast): $65–$95 single or double; from $100 suite. Additional person $8 extra. AE, CB, DC, MC, V.

This excellent choice is just off Cabrillo Boulevard, one short block from the marina and beach. Each individually decorated room is airy, comfortable, and spacious; most have ceiling fans. Bathrooms come stocked with thick, fluffy towels. Several rooms have fully equipped kitchenettes. Suites are split-level, complete with a living room, a separate kitchen, and sleeping quarters that can accommodate up to four adults. One suite also has a fireplace.

Breakfast is served in the comfortable lobby. The inn is just steps away from several restaurants for other meals. There are also a heated pool, Jacuzzi, and coin-operated laundry; complimentary newspapers are distributed every morning. Reservations should be made well in advance, especially for May through September.

Motel 6, 443 Corona del Mar, Santa Barbara, CA 93103.
☎ **805/564-1392.** 52 rms. TV TEL **Directions:** From U.S. 101, exit at Milpas Street and head toward the ocean; turn left, drive one short block, then turn left again onto Corona del Mar.

Rates: $43 single; $47 double. Additional adult $7 extra. AE, DISC, MC, V.

Inexpensive, clean accommodations near the beach are not easy to find, but this basic motel fits the bill. There's a small heated pool and cable color TVs; local phone calls are free. Be sure to reserve far in advance since this motel books up quickly.

Motel 6, 3505 State St., Santa Barbara, CA 93105. ☎ **805/687-5400.**
60 rms. TV TEL **Directions:** From U.S. 101, exit at Mission Street and turn left onto State Street; the motel is about one mile ahead, between Las Positas and Hitchcock Way.

Rates: $41 single; $46 double. Additional adult $6 extra. AE, CB, DC, DISC, MC, V.

On "upper" State Street, this motel's location is not as desirable as those by the beach. But it is nice, featuring a large pool, and there's plentiful shopping nearby.

Mountain View Inn, 3055 De La Vina St., Santa Barbara, CA 93105. ☎ **805/687-6636.** 34 rms. TV TEL **Directions:** From U.S. 101, exit at Mission Street, turn toward the hills, and left onto State Street; the hotel is located about 10 blocks ahead, at the corner of State and De La Vina Streets.

Rates (including continental breakfast): Late Sept–May, $60–$75 single or double. June–early Sept, $75–$87 single or double. Two-night stays required on weekends. AE, DISC, MC, V.

Although it occupies a busy street corner, close to shops, sights, and restaurants, this well-priced inn maintains a hometown bed-and-breakfast atmosphere. Each room is individually decorated—some with lace tablecloths and ruffled pillow shams and matching comforters. Accommodations are bright and cheery and outfitted with both niceties (fresh flowers) and necessities (small refrigerators). The inn surrounds a large heated pool, and is adjacent to a small park, complete with a children's playground.

Coffee, tea, fresh juice, and croissants are served each morning in the lobby.

Sandpiper Lodge, 3525 State St., Santa Barbara, CA 93105. ☎ **805/687-5326.** Fax 805/687-2271. 75 rms. TV TEL **Directions:** From U.S. 101, take the Las Positas exit and turn toward the moun-tains; turn left onto State Street and look for the motel on your left.

Rates: Late Sept–June, $48–$58 single or double; $53–$63 triple; July–early Sept, $58–$68 single or double; $63–$73 triple. Weekly and monthly rates available. AE, CB, DC, MC, V.

Modest accommodations at low rates make this small hotel one of Santa Barbara's best buys. Nothing's fancy here, but the rooms are clean and tastefully (if sparsely) decorated. The lodge's "upper" State Street location means that you'll have to drive to the beach and down-town shopping areas, but both are just 10 minutes away.

Coffee and tea are available all day, and some rooms include small refrigerators. There's also a pool on the premises.

★ **Tropicana Inn and Suites,** 223 Castillo St., Santa Barbara, CA 93101. ☎ **805/966-2219,** or toll free **800/468-1988.** Fax 805/962-9428. 31 rms, 16 suites. TV TEL **Directions:** From U.S. 101, exit at Castillo Street and turn toward the water; the hotel is two blocks ahead between Montecito and Yanonali Streets.

Rates (including continental breakfast): $82–$122 single or double; $112–$199 suite. Additional person $5 extra. AE, DISC, MC, V.

This recently renovated pink-stucco structure is just a short walk from the beach. The rooms are homey, attractive, and equipped with AM/FM radios and refrigerators. The suites, which have a large bedroom and living room, accommodate up to eight adults. They also have large eat-in kitchens that are fully equipped with ovens, full-size refrigerators, toasters, and even eggbeaters and potholders. Suites can be economical if you use them to do your own cooking. Facilities include a heated pool and Jacuzzi, both of which are away from the street and very private, with lots of room for sunning. No smoking is allowed in any of the rooms.

Where to Dine

MODERATE

★ **Brophy Bros. Clam Bar & Restaurant,** yacht basin and marina. ☎ 805/966-4418.

> **Cuisine:** SEAFOOD. **Reservations:** Not accepted. **Directions:** From Stearns Wharf, drive west on Cabrillo Boulevard past the Castillo Street traffic light and turn left at the first light, which is Harbor Way; Brophy Bros. is a short walk along the yacht basin, on the second floor of the small light-gray building ahead on your right.
> **Prices:** Appetizers $5.50–$9.50; main courses $7–$16. AE, MC, V.
> **Open:** Sun–Thurs 11am–10pm, Fri–Sat 11am–11pm.

I am reluctant to tell even more people about one of my favorite restaurants in Santa Barbara. First-class seafood is served in beautiful surroundings that overlook the city's lovely marina from a second-floor location. The restaurant is a fun, friendly, noisy, convivial mix of locals and tourists almost every night of the week. Dress is casual, service is excellent, and it's hard to beat the view of fishing boats, sailboats, and power launches. There are fewer than 24 tables, and about 10 seats at an open oyster bar. Most of the chairs are usually occupied, and the wait on a weekend night can be up to two hours.

Portions are huge, and everything on the menu is good. Favorites include New England clam chowder, cioppino (California fish stew), and any one of an assortment of seafood salads. The scampi is consistently good, as are the tuna, shark, swordfish, salmon, and all fresh fish. A nice assortment of beers and wines is available.

Joe's Cafe, 536 State St. ☎ 805/966-4638.

> **Cuisine:** AMERICAN. **Reservations:** Recommended; but not accepted Sat. **Directions:** From Stearns Wharf, drive up State Street; the restaurant is on your right at Cota Street.
> **Prices:** Appetizers $2–$5; main courses $7–$19. AE, MC, V.
> **Open:** Mon–Sat 11am–11:30pm, Sun 4–11:30pm.

Joe's food is not great, but there's something about this straightforward American eatery that's very alluring. Maybe it's the mixed drinks, some of the city's strongest. One of downtown's longest-lived institutions, Joe's has been offering good home-cooking since 1928. Southern-style fried chicken, hefty 12-ounce charcoal-broiled steaks, and pan-fried rainbow trout are menu staples. The ravioli is lacking but addicting. And every Wednesday seems like Thanksgiving as the kitchen turns out plate after plate of turkey, mashed potatoes, cranberry sauce, and stuffing.

The decor is as down-home as the food: red-and-white-checked tablecloths, captain's chairs, mounted hunting trophies, and photos of old Santa Barbara on the walls. There are no desserts on the menu. "We give them enough starch without it," explains the owner.

Mousse Odile, 18 E. Cota St. ☎ 805/962-5393.

Cuisine: FRENCH. **Reservations:** Not required. **Directions:** From Stearns Wharf, drive up State Street and turn right onto Cota Street three blocks past the U.S. 101 underpass.

Prices: Appetizers $4–$7; main courses $13.25–$17; breakfast $4–$7; lunch $4.25–$10. AE, MC, V.

Open: Breakfast Mon–Sat 8–11:30am; lunch Mon–Sat 11:30am–2:30pm; dinner Mon–Thurs 5:30–9pm, Fri–Sat 5–9:30pm.

The restaurant's brasserie side, nicely outfitted with oak flooring, red-and-blue-checkered tablecloths, and fresh flowers, is the setting for breakfast and lunch. It's not fancy, though it does have a pleasant, simple French provincial air. There's a bar along one wall, and a refrigerated case and counter to the rear.

Breakfast choices include various quiches, waffles with crème anglaise (a delicious light custard sauce), and a variety of omelets served with French bread, applesauce, and potatoes au gratin. Most *specialités de la maison* are also served with fresh fruit—slices of banana, orange, and strawberries. The lunch menu includes cold pasta salad with smoked salmon and peas, and foot-long Parisian sandwiches of roast lamb or chicken and white veal sausage.

The simple, somewhat formal adjoining dining room opens in the evening for dinner. The wood-and-window interior is illuminated by art deco lamps and brightened with green plants, fresh flowers, and candles on every table. Leg of lamb, roasted with garlic and herbs, is especially recommended. Other offerings might include Norwegian salmon poached in champagne and port wine, or filet mignon with pepper sauce and cognac. Appetizers include julienned celery root in mustard sauce, and marinated mussels or warm smoked salmon with pasta, caviar, and chives. There is no bar, but a nice selection of California and French wines is available. By the way, save room for dessert—mousse is the restaurant's specialty.

★ **Oysters,** Victoria Court, 9 W. Victoria St. ☎ 805/962-9888.

Cuisine: CALIFORNIAN. **Reservations:** Recommended. **Directions:** From Stearns Wharf, drive up State Street and turn left onto Victoria Street, 10 blocks past the U.S. 101 underpass; the restaurant is immediately on your left.

Prices: Appetizers $4–$14; main courses $6–$11 at lunch, $9–$17 at dinner. AE, DC, DISC, MC, V.

Open: Lunch Mon–Sat 11:30am–2:30pm; dinner Tues–Sun 5–10pm; brunch Sun 10am–2:30pm.

Hidden behind lush bushes near the corner of State Street, Oysters' small, oddly shaped, window-wrapped dining room provides some of the best food in the city. Despite its name, the restaurant is not a shellfish bar; it's a select sampling of California cuisine offered by Jerry and Laurie Wilson, a brother-and-sister team. Still, oyster appetizers are on the menu: grilled with cilantro butter, chopped into corn fritters, and stewed with spinach and shallots. Pasta, chicken, and veal main courses are also available, but the best ones are usually the daily fresh market specials like poached trout with salmon mousse, or saffron rice with Cajun sausage, lobster, and scallops. Desserts here are predictably decadent, but even the richest-looking chocolate torte should be passed up for the restaurant's home-churned ice cream.

Palace Cafe, 8 E. Cota St. ☎ 805/966-3133.

Cuisine: CAJUN/CREOLE/CARIBBEAN. **Reservations:** Recommended.
Directions: From Stearns Wharf, drive up State Street and turn right onto Cota Street, three blocks past the U.S. 101 underpass.
Prices: Appetizers $3.50–$8.50; main courses $12–$22. AE, MC, V.
Open: Dinner only Sun–Thurs 5:30–10pm, Fri–Sat 5:30–11pm.

The Cajun-style Palace Cafe enlarged its reputation when it became a regular stop for the press corps that followed Ronald Reagan to his nearby ranch during his presidency. It's terminally busy, and both the food and the atmosphere are far more casual than the prices, The restaurant is divided into two similar rooms, both of which include high ceilings, overhead fans, simple wood tables, bentwood chairs, and various posters and paintings.

Each table is topped with a huge bottle of Tabasco sauce, followed by a basket of hot muffins, including Cheddar-corn jalapeño. Favorite starters are Cajun popcorn (Louisiana crayfish tails dipped in a cornmeal-buttermilk batter and flash-fried) and Cuban black-bean soup. Main courses emphasize seafood. Louisiana barbecue shrimp are sautéed with three-pepper butter and served with white rice. An assortment of blackened fish and filet mignon is served with a side of browned garlic butter. Rabbit is sometimes available, as is veal flambéed with sherry and finished with an oyster-sherry cream sauce. Although it's not on the menu, vegetarians should ask for the vegetable platter; it's terrific. For dessert, the tart, tasty key lime pie is unusually good. Although the restaurant apparently has a liquor license, they ridiculously offer only a single, nasty drink: the spicy hot "Cajun" martini. Stick to beer and wine.

★ Pan e Vino, 1482 E. Valley Rd., Montecito. ☎ 805/969-9274.
Cuisine: ITALIAN. **Reservations:** Recommended.
Prices: Appetizers $4–$9; pastas $8–$10; meat and fish dishes $10–$18. No credit cards.
Open: Mon–Sat 11:30am–9:30pm, Sun 5–9:30pm.

Allow me to wax philosophical about my favorite restaurant in Santa Barbara. It's the perfect Italian trattoria, with food as good as you'd find in Rome and surroundings that are far better. The simplest dish—spaghetti topped with basil-tomato sauce—is so delicious it's hard to understand why diners would want to distract their tastebuds with more complicated concoctions. Yet numerous tastings have proved this kitchen capable of most anything. A whole-artichoke appetizer—steamed, chilled, and filled with breading and marinated tomatoes—is absolutely fantastic. Pasta puttenesca, with tomatoes, anchovies, black olives, and capers, is always tops, as are the nightly risotto, meat, and fish selections. Pan e Vino gets high marks for its terrific food, attentive service, and authentic and casual atmosphere. Although many diners prefer to eat outside, beneath heat lamps and a tarp on the restaurant's intimate patio, my favorite tables are inside, where seemingly just-off-the-boat waiters scurry between tables with obvious professional experience. The only drawback to this restaurant of superlatives is that it doesn't accept credit cards—but there's an ATM around the corner.

Paradise Cafe, 702 Anacapa St. ☎ 805/962-4416.

Cuisine: AMERICAN. **Reservations:** Accepted only for large parties.
Directions: From Stearns Wharf, drive up State Street and turn right onto Ortega Street, five blocks past the U.S. 101 underpass; the restaurant is located one block from State Street on the corner of Ortega and Anacapa Streets.
Prices: Appetizers $4–$7; main courses $6–$17; breakfast $4–$7; lunch $6–$9. AE, MC, V.
Open: Mon–Sat 11am–11pm, Sun 8:30am–11pm.

White linen tablecloths and blond-wood floors give this converted home a relaxed elegance that seems like quintessential Santa Barbara. The most coveted seats, however, are outside, on the open brick patio behind tall hedges and colorful wildflowers.

Excellent salmon, swordfish, half-pound burgers, and 22-ounce T-bone steaks are prepared on an open oak grill. Devoid of heavy sauces, meals here are consistently fresh and simple. Paradise Pie, an extremely decadent chocolate dessert, is an absolute must.

The downstairs bar, well known for strong drinks, is especially popular with the local 30-something crowd.

Piatti's Ristorante, 516 San Ysidro Rd., Montecito.
☎ 805/969-7520.

Cuisine: ITALIAN. **Reservations:** Recommended. **Directions:** From Stearns Wharf, take Cabrillo Boulevard east to U.S. 101; exit at San Ysidro Road and follow it toward the mountains about half a mile to the restaurant.
Prices: Appetizers $4–$8; main courses $8–$18. AE, MC, V.
Open: Sun–Thurs 11:30am–10pm, Fri–Sat 11:30am–11pm.

Piatti's is 10 minutes south of downtown Santa Barbara in the exclusive residential hideaway of Montecito. During warm weather, the best seats are at the faux marble–topped tables set under handsome cream-colored umbrellas on the outdoor patio.

The spacious interior is airy, comfortable, and relaxed. Everything is attractive here, from the small bar to the exhibition kitchen, to the upscale good-looking clientele. The dining room has a polished country look, complete with pine sideboards, wall murals, and terra-cotta tile floors.

Exceptional appetizers include fried calamari with spicy aioli sauce, fresh sweetbreads with porcini mushrooms, and Parma prosciutto served with fresh fruit and Parmesan cheese. Featured main dishes include homemade ravioli filled with spinach and ricotta cheese and served with creamy lemon sauce; and lasagne al pesto—with layers of pasta, pesto, grilled zucchini, sun-dried tomatoes, pinenuts, and cheeses. Both are rich and delicious. A specialty of the house is oak wood–roasted chicken with roasted rosemary potatoes and vegetables.

There's an excellent selection of California and Italian wines, many available by the glass. There's also a full bar.

Your Place, 22A N. Milpas St. ☎ 805/966-5151.
Cuisine: THAI. **Reservations:** Recommended. **Directions:** From Stearns Wharf, take Cabrillo Boulevard east and turn left onto Milpas Street; the restaurant is about a mile ahead on your right at Mason Street.
Prices: Appetizers $3–$7, main courses $5–$13. AE, DC, MC, V.
Open: Tues–Thurs and Sun 11am–10pm, Fri–Sat 11am–11pm.

There are an unusually large number of Thai restaurants in Santa Barbara, but when locals argue about which one is best, Your Place invariably ranks high on the list. In addition to a tank of exotic fish, carved screens, and a serene Buddha, the restaurant's decor includes an impressive array of framed blowups of restaurant reviews.

Traditional dishes are prepared with absolutely fresh ingredients and represent a veritable cross section of Thai cuisine. There are more than 100 menu listings, including lemongrass soups, spicy salads, coconut curries, meat and seafood main dishes, and a variety of noodles. It's best to begin with soup, ladled out of a hotpot tableside, and enough for two or more. Tom kah kai, a hot-and-sour chicken soup with coconut milk and mushrooms, is excellent. Siamese duckling, a top main dish, is prepared with sautéed vegetables, mushrooms, and ginger sauce. Like other dishes, it can be made mild, medium, hot, or very hot, according to your preference. The restaurant serves wine, sake, beer, and a variety of nonalcoholic drinks, including hot ginger tea.

INEXPENSIVE

Andersen's Danish Bakery and Restaurant, 1106 State St.
☎ 805/962-5085.
Cuisine: DANISH. **Reservations:** Not required. **Directions:** From Stearns Wharf, drive up State Street; the restaurant is on your right, near Figueroa Street.
Prices: Breakfast $4–$9; lunch $5–$10. No credit cards.
Open: Wed–Mon 8am–6pm.

Only tourists eat here, but this small place is eminently suited to people-watching or reading the day's paper. You'll spot it by the red-and-white Amstel umbrellas protecting the outside diners seated on wrought-iron garden chairs. Even mid-November can be warm enough to eat outdoors at 9am.

The food is both good and well presented. Portions are substantial and the coffee is outstanding. A set breakfast includes eggs, bacon, cheese, fruit, homemade jam, and fresh-baked bread. Fresh fruit is also available.

For lunch, try soup and a sandwich, or liver pâté and quiche. Vegetarians can opt for an omelet with Danish Havarti cheese, a vegetable sandwich, or a cheese plate with fruit. Fresh fish and smoked Scottish salmon are also usually available. A daily changing selection of European dishes may include Hungarian goulash, frikadeller (Danish meatballs), schnitzel, duckling, chicken with caper sauce, Danish meatloaf, and roast turkey with caramel sautéed potatoes. But if you yearn for smörgåsbord, Andersen's is a first-rate choice. Wine is available by the bottle or glass; beer is also served.

Cuca's, 315 Meigs Rd. ☎ **805/966-5951.**
Cuisine: MEXICAN. **Reservations:** Not accepted.
Prices: Tacos $2–$3; burritos $3–$4. No credit cards.
Open: Daily 10am–10pm.

Around lunchtime, when Cuca's becomes the de facto "anchor" store of a particularly dull strip mall, it's hard to find a single seat at any of the restaurant's half-dozen outdoor tables. Though they're uncommon only in size, Cuca's extra-large, brick-weight burritos are packed solid with chicken or beef, rice, beans, and avocado. The truly excellent vegetarian variation, made with stir-fried vegetables, suggests a giant Chinese eggroll and would be heralded as "genius" if it appeared on one of Spago owner Wolfgang Puck's menus.

Cuca's is located atop an elevated area of the city known as "The Mesa." There's a second Cuca's at 626 W. Micheltorena (☎ **805/962-4028**).

Don Pepe, 617 State St. ☎ **805/962-4495.**
Cuisine: MEXICAN. **Reservations:** Not accepted.
Prices: Appetizers $2–$5; main courses $5–$8; tacos and burritos $2–$4; breakfast $3–$5. MC, V.
Open: Sun–Thurs 8am–11pm, Fri–Sat 8am–2am.

Don Pepe isn't just another burrito joint. In fact, it's not a burrito joint at all. With the exception of taking customers' orders at the front counter, Don Pepe is a full-service restaurant serving traditional Mexican dishes to Mexican and American workers and a few adventurous tourists.

Appetizers include nachos, guacamole, and chicken or pork soup. Main dishes include whole fish cooked in garlic butter, chicken with mole sauce, and grilled shrimp with wine and olives. Every meal starts with complimentary freshly made tortilla chips, and most come with rice, beans, and salad. Of course, Don Pepe's can also make meat or fish burritos. My favorite—chicken mole—isn't on the menu but is always available.

La Super-Rica Taqueria, 622 N. Milpas St. ☎ **805/963-4940.**
Cuisine: MEXICAN. **Reservations:** Not accepted. **Directions:** From Stearns Wharf, take Cabrillo Boulevard east and turn left onto Milpas Street; the restaurant is about two miles ahead on your right between Cota and Ortega Streets.
Prices: Main courses $3–$6. No credit cards.
Open: Sun–Thurs 11am–9:30pm, Fri–Sat 11am–10pm.

Following celebrity chef Julia Child's lead, several south-coast aficionados have deemed this place the best Mexican restaurant in California. Excellent soft tacos are the restaurant's real forte; filled with any combination of chicken, beef, cheese, cilantro, and spices, they make a good meal. My primary complaint about this restaurant is that the portions are quite small; you have to order two or even three items in order to satisfy average hunger.

There's nothing grand about La Super-Rica except the food. The plates are paper, the cups Styrofoam, and the forks plastic. Unadorned wooden tables and plastic chairs are arranged under an unappealing tent; you might want to order your food "to go" and then have your meal on a pretty beachside bench.

Woody's Beach Club and Cantina, 229 W. Montecito St. ☎ 805/963-9326.

Cuisine: AMERICAN BARBECUE. **Reservations:** Not accepted. **Directions:** From Stearns Wharf, go one block west on Cabrillo Boulevard, turn right onto Chapala Street, then left onto Montecito Street.
Prices: Appetizers $2–$5; main courses $4–$18. MC, V.
Open: Mon–Sat 11am–11pm, Sun 11am–10pm.

This place is woody, all right—sort of "early cowpoke," with real wood paneling, post-and-beam construction, wood booths, and wood-plank floors. Order at the counter just inside the door, have a seat, and wait for your number to be called. Barbecued chicken and ribs head the menu. A variety of burgers, tacos, pizza, chili by the bowl, and French fries round out the offerings. Woody's home-smoked meats smothered in sauce might not be the best barbecue in the world, but they're easily the best in town. Children's portions are also available. Popular with fraternity types, Woody's sells beer by the glass, jug, bucket, or bottle.

A second Woody's is located in nearby Goleta, at 5112 Hollister Ave. (☎ **805/967-3775**).

A CAFE

Santa Barbara Roasting Company, 321 Motor Way. ☎ 805/962-0320.

Cuisine: CAFE. **Reservations:** Not accepted.
Prices: Coffee $1; pastries $1–$2. AE, DISC, MC, V.
Open: Daily 7am–midnight.

The RoCo is a morning ritual for what seems like half of Santa Barbara—and for good reason. The strongly brewed beans are freshly roasted on the premises, and your choice of regular or unleaded is served bottomless. This is the coffee I dream of when I'm away; unfortunately, I can't say the same for their cakey baked goods, which used to be better.

Sports & Recreation ─────────────────

One of the best things about Santa Barbara is the accessibility of almost every sport known to humankind, from mountain hiking to ocean kayaking. This is the southern California of the movies, where windsurfing and bunjee jumping are everyday activities. Pick up a free copy of "Things to See and Do" at the Santa Barbara Visitor Information Center, 1 Santa Barbara St., Santa Barbara, CA 93101 (☎ 805/965-3021).

BICYCLING A relatively flat, two-mile palm-lined coastal pathway runs along the beach and is perfect for biking. More adventurous riders can peddle through town, up to the mission, or to Montecito, the next town over. **Beach Rentals,** 8 W. Cabrillo Blvd. (☎ 805/963-2524), at State Street, rents well-maintained 1- and 10-speeds. They also have tandem bikes and surrey cycles that can hold as many as four adults and two children. Rates vary depending on equipment. Bring an I.D. (driver's license or passport) to expedite your rental. They're open daily from 8am to dusk.

GOLF At the **Santa Barbara Golf Club,** 3500 McCaw Ave., at Las Positas Road (☎ 805/687-7087), the 18-hole course is 6,009 yards and encompasses a driving range. The golf shop and other nonplaying facilities were reconstructed and refurbished early in 1989. Unlike many municipal courses, the Santa Barbara Golf Course is well maintained and was designed to present a moderate challenge for the average golfer. Greens fees are $18 Monday through Friday ($13 for seniors) and $20 on Saturday and Sunday ($17 for seniors). Optional carts cost $20.

An 18-hole, 7,000-yard course, the **Sandpiper,** 7925 Hollister Ave. (☎ 805/968-1541), a pretty oceanside course, has a pro shop and driving range, plus a coffee shop. Greens fees are $50 Monday through Friday and $70 on Saturday and Sunday. Carts cost $22.

HIKING The hills and mountains surrounding Santa Barbara have excellent hiking trails. One of my favorites begins at the end of Mission Canyon Drive. Take Mission Canyon Road past the mission, turn right onto Foothill Road, and take the first left onto Mission Canyon Drive. Park at the end (where all the other cars are) and hike up. You can buy a trail map at the Santa Barbara Visitor Information Center.

HORSEBACK RIDING Several area stables rent horses, including **San Ysidro Ranch Stables,** 900 San Ysidro Lane (☎ 805/969-5046, ext. 252). They charge $35 for a one-hour guided trail ride; reservations are essential.

POWER BOATING & SAILING The **Sailing Center of Santa Barbara,** at the Santa Barbara Breakwater (☎ 805/962-2826, or toll free 800/350-9090), rents 40-horsepower boats and sailboats ranging from 13 to 50 feet. Both crewed and bare-boat charters are available by the day or hour. The center also offers sailing instruction for all levels of experience.

ROLLER SKATING **Beach Rentals,** 8 W. Cabrillo Blvd. (☎ 805/963-2524), rents conventional roller skates as well as in-line skates. The charge of $5 per hour includes wrist and knee pads.

SPORT FISHING, DIVING & WHALE-WATCHING   Sea Landing, at the foot of Bath Street and Cabrillo Boulevard (☎ 805/963-3564), makes regular sport fishing runs from specialized boats. They also offer a wide variety of other fishing and diving cruises. All boats are equipped with a stocked galley (food and drink served on board), and rental rods and tackle are available. Rates vary according to excursion, and reservations are recommended.

Whale-watching cruises are offered from February to the end of April, when the California gray whale makes its migratory journey from Baja, Mexico, to Alaska. Whale tours cost $22 for adults, $12 for children, and sightings of large marine mammals are guaranteed.

Shopping

State Street from the beach to Victoria Street is the city's chief commercial thoroughfare, and has the largest concentration of shops. Although many of the stores here specialize in T-shirts and postcards, there are a number of boutiques as well. The best way to become familiar with the area is to walk; the entire stretch is less than a mile. If you get tired, hop on one of the city's free electric shuttle buses that run up and down State Street at regular intervals.

Brinkerhoff Avenue, off Cota St., between Chapala and De La Vina Sts.

Santa Barbara's "antique alley" is packed with Victorian antiques shops selling quilts, antique china, Early American furnishings, jewelry, Orientalia, unusual memorabilia, bric-a-brac, and interesting junk. Most shops are open Tuesday through Sunday from 11am to 5pm.

El Paseo, 814 State St.

A picturesque shopping arcade, El Paseo is lined with stone walkways reminiscent of an old street in Spain. Built around the 1827 original adobe home of Spanish-born Presidio Commandante José de la Guerra, the mall is lined with charming shops and art galleries, each of which is worth a look.

Paseo Nuevo, State and Canon Perdido Sts.

Opened in mid-1990, this Spanish-style shopping mall in the heart of downtown is anchored by Nordstrom and the Broadway, two West Coast–based department stores. Between these giant stores are smaller chain shops like Victoria's Secret, Brentano's bookshop, and Express clothing store.

Evening Entertainment

THEATERS

Center Stage Theater, Chapala and De La Guerra Sts., upstairs at Paseo Nuevo. ☎ 805/963-0408.

The city's newest stage is a "black box" theater that can transform seating and sets into innumerable configurations. It's an intimate space that's often booked by local talent for plays, musical performances, and comedy. Call to see what's scheduled while you're in town. The box office is open Tuesday through Sunday from noon to 5:30pm and one hour before showtime.

Admission: Tickets, $6–$12.

Lobero Theater, 33 E. Canon Perdido St. ☎ 805/963-0761.

Built by Italian immigrant Giuseppi Lobero in 1872, Santa Barbara's largest playhouse bankrupted its owner and quickly fell into disrepair. Rebuilt in 1924, the beautiful Lobero has struggled from season to season, boasting a spotty career at best. Many famous actors have performed here, including Lionel Barrymore, Edward G. Robinson, Clark Gable, Robert Young, Boris Karloff, and Betty Grable, as well as such concert luminaries as Andrés Segovia, Arthur Rubinstein, Igor Stravinsky, and Leopold Stokowski. More recent productions have included the Martha Graham Dance Company.

The theater is home to the Santa Barbara Civic Light Opera, an excellent musical theater troupe that usually stages a repertoire of four plays from September to June. A wide variety of other productions are also offered throughout the year. Call the theater to find out what's on during your stay. The box office is open during the summer, Monday through Saturday from noon to 5pm; during the winter, Monday through Friday from 10am to 5:30pm and on Saturday from 10am to 5pm.

Admission: Tickets, usually about $25.

Arlington Theater, 1317 State St. ☎ 805/963-4408.

Now primarily a movie theater, the Arlington regularly augments its film schedule with big-name theater and musical performances. The theater's interior is designed to look like an outdoor Spanish plaza, complete with trompe l'oeil artwork and a shimmering ceiling that winks like thousands of stars. The ornate theater, opened in 1931 at the birth of the talking-picture era, quickly became Hollywood's testing ground for unreleased movies; big stars flocked to Santa Barbara to monitor audience reaction at sneak previews. The box office is open Monday through Saturday from 9am to 6pm and on Sunday from 9am to 4pm.

Admission: Tickets, $7–$40.

Earl Warren Showgrounds, Las Positas Rd. and U.S. 101. ☎ 805/687-0766.

Whether it be a rodeo, circus, or factory outlet sale, something's always happening at this indoor/outdoor convention center. Banquets, antiques shows, barbecues, rummage sales, flower shows, music festivals, horse shows, dances, and cat shows are just some of the regular annual offerings. Call to find out what's planned while you're in town. Entry fees range from free to $20, and opening times vary for each event.

BARS & CLUBS

Beach Shack, 500 Anacapa St. ☎ **805/966-1634.**

Live local bands almost every night attract a good-looking college crowd. Tiki hut–themed bars are located both inside and out, away from the busy dance floor. Open Tuesday through Sunday from 7pm to 2am.

Admission: Free–$5.

Joe's, 536 State St. ☎ **805/966-4638.**

Packed on weekend nights with college-age locals, Joe's is known for its particularly powerful drinks and good-looking beachy crowd. Food is served at tables and booths until 11pm, but mingling at the adjacent bar is best. Open Monday through Saturday from 11am to 11pm and Sunday from 4 to 11pm.

Admission: Free.

Mel's, in the Paseo Neuvo Mall, 6 W. De La Guerra St.
☎ **805/963-2211.**

There seems to be no stigma against alcoholism at this divey old drinking room located in the heart of downtown. The compact bar attracts a good cross section of regulars. Open daily from 7am to 2am.

Admission: Free.

Revival, 18 E. Ortega. ☎ **805/730-7383.**

Santa Barbara's most alternative nightclub enjoys a Los Angeles–style warehouse setting, with a mixed gay/straight crowd. Under high ceilings are two bars, a pool table, an indoor fountain, and the largest dance floor in town. Regular theme nights are interspersed with occasional live local bands. Open Sunday, Monday, and Wednesday through Friday from 9pm to 2am and Saturday from 7:30pm to 2am.

Admission: Free–$5.

⭐ **The Wildcat Lounge,** 15 W. Ortega. ☎ **805/962-7970.**

Duncan Wesley's Wildcat Lounge is easily the "happeningest" place in town. The excellent CD jukebox and intentional-kitsch decor attract local 20- and 30-somethings to a nightspot that otherwise amounts to little more than a good bar with interesting lighting and a pool table. Open daily from 4pm to 2am.

Admission: Free

Index

288

Accommodations

EXCURSION AREAS

Newport Beach & Laguna Beach

Restaurants